ONE INFANTRYMAN'S JOURNEY

Second Edition March 2011
First Edition December 2010

ISBN-10: 0615403956
ISBN-13: 978-0-615-40395-3
Library of Congress Control Number: 2010910145

Published by Aperture Press
Reading, PA
www.AperturePress.net

To order additional copies:
Call toll-free 1-888-926-4591
Email rivermeadows@juno.com
Amazon.com
BarnesAndNoble.com

ONE INFANTRYMAN'S JOURNEY

Pennsylvania Farm Boy in Korea

Walter Mahlon Zweizig
Shirley Zweizig Nestler

Dear friend,

Thank you for your sacrifice on behalf of my freedom. Enjoy the book & May God Bless!

Shirley Z-N 5/9/13

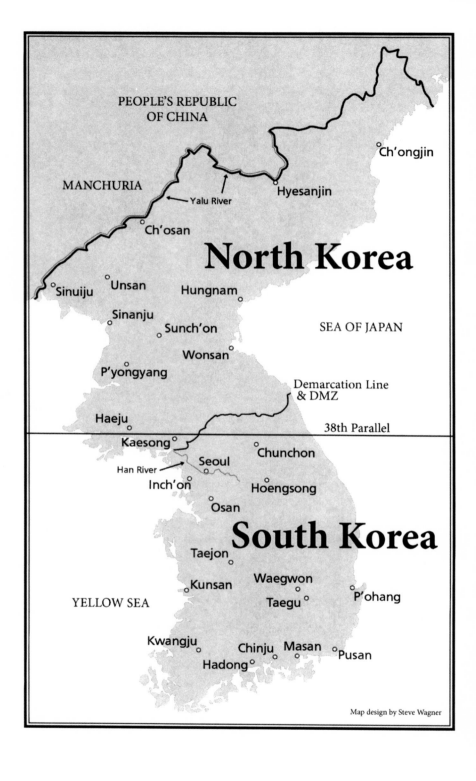

PEOPLE'S REPUBLIC
OF CHINA

Ch'ongjin

MANCHURIA

Yalu River

Hyesanjin

Ch'osan

North Korea

Sinuiju   Unsan   Hungnam

Sinanju

Sunch'on   SEA OF JAPAN

Wonsan

P'yongyang

Demarcation Line
& DMZ

Haeju

38th Parallel

Kaesong   Chunchon

Han River   Seoul

Inch'on   Hoengsong

Osan

South Korea

Taejon

Kunsan   Waegwon

YELLOW SEA   Taegu   P'ohang

Kwangju   Chinju   Masan

Hadong   Pusan

Map design by Steve Wagner

Japan

Abashiri

HOKKAIDO

Sapporo

Tsugaru Strait

Aomori

Akita

Sendai

Nagano

SEA OF JAPAN

Tokyo

HONSHU

Yokohama

Mt. Fuji

Itami Air Base

Kyoto

Nagoya

Nara

Kobe

Osaka

Hiroshima

SHIKOKU

Osaka Bay

Kochi

Sasebo

KYUSHU

PACIFIC OCEAN

Nagasaki

Kagoshima

Map design by Steve Wagner

CONTENTS

ACKNOWLEDGMENTS

One Infantryman's Journey - *Pennsylvania Farm Boy in Korea* is written in a creative nonfiction genre. Through dozens of interviews, tapings, and notes, plus endless hours of research, the book expands and expounds upon the experiences expressed in the memoir Act Now, Think Later by SGM Walter M. Zweizig, U.S. Army Retired. Sergeant Zweizig, having no children of his own, had recorded his first Korean tour in print so that his nieces and nephews would know he did more than "cut grass" which he did in his retirement years following employment at Dana Corporation. Act Now, Think Later is on file at the U.S. Army War College in Carlisle, Pennsylvania.

The co-authored version, One Infantryman's Journey, includes childhood memories, adult attitudes, and spiritual approaches of both authors that come together in one voice. The writing was completed in 2006, during Walt's lifetime, with a few footnotes added following his death on November 5, 2009 and prior to publishing in 2010.

I wish to acknowledge the following people for their editorial prowess of the finished product: Shirley Aldenderfer, Erin Caretti, Nancy Harbach, Christopher Klim, Gloria Ruth, John Smither, Mark Yanes, and Roslyn Yocum.

Mark, what a privilege to have your professional edits when I consider you've been a "critiquer" for one of the best-known and best-selling writers of all time, James Patterson. Awesome! And Erin, Nancy, and Gloria, thanks for your invaluable input with respect to your experience of living and working within the Korean and/or Japanese cultures. John, I thank you for your service to the Allied cause in WWII and for sharing your military expertise on behalf of this book. Shirley, whom I drove nuts with my lack of pronouns, articles, and "that's"—(sorry, chalk it up to my journalistic writing in a previous life where brevity counted), your edits had the additional benefit of re-educating me on grammatical rules. I'd long forgotten what antecedents, progressive verbs, gerunds, and dangling participles were. And my dear cousin Roslyn, how can I give you enough thanks for lending your understanding, support, and critical eye to the narrative.

My mentor Christopher Klim—author of several books and candidate for movie rights on <u>Jesus Lives in Trenton</u>, without your professional assistance in shaping the story, <u>One Infantryman's Journey</u> would not have been possible. My sincerest thanks.

A very special thanks to graphic designer and publicist Steve Wagner of Aperture Press. My gratitude can't stretch far enough for taking care of all of those myriad details involved in publishing <u>One Infantryman's Journey</u> and preparing the book for print.

Last yet foremost, my humble thanks to Jesus Christ the Creator God of the universe who whispered, *Do it for Me, Do it for Me, Do it for Me*, who lifted me up when I was down, who cared, who loved. To Him be given the credit, the honor, and the glory!

Shirley Zweizig Nestler

Dedicated to all American men and women in uniform,
in particular, the wounded and suffering who risked their lives
to preserve the freedom of this wonderful country of ours,
the United States of America.

PROLOGUE

I WANT YOU FOR U.S. ARMY - Nearest Recruiting Station.
- Army Recruitment Poster

Ever since my early teens, I longed to join the Army. My soldier brother Robert wrote home how much he enjoyed Germany in general and good-looking girls in particular. Girls were not necessarily my motivation, for I was much too bashful. But because I had a good understanding of a German dialect, "Pennsylvania Dutch" as locals call it, Germany was where I'd feel at home and still have a chance to see the world.

Additional prodding came during lunch breaks at Glen Gery Brick in Shoemakerville where I was gainfully employed while still at home on the farm. There, scores of World War II veterans worked. Their constant talk of Germany and military life fueled my passion and stirred such excitement I was hooked like a fish on baited line. In retrospect, many of their stories were glorified. Yet at the time, any reason to defer enlistment until spring as planned was totally out of the question.

The man in the recruiting office on South Sixth Street in downtown Reading convinced me a hitch in Germany following basic training should not be a problem. Therefore, on January 12, 1948, three days after my eighteenth birthday, I bit the bullet and enlisted in the United States Army.

The following story is the journey through my first tour of duty as closely as I remember it. My cousin and I created several character descriptions and dialogue to better fill in memory gaps, reflecting the era, community, and personalities involved while still remaining true to the storyline. Names are changed to protect the innocent and, in some cases, the not so innocent. Childhood memories, adult attitudes, and spiritual approaches are a blend of joint authorship, coming together in one voice.

Oh, one more thing. The book is a gift to veterans at military hospitals who are convalescing from wounds sustained during their service to this country in preserving its freedom. Net profit from other book distributions goes to Disabled American Veterans or Paralyzed Veterans of America. To help support these worthy causes and for a good read in general, please recommend <u>One Infantryman's Journey</u> to family, friends, and neighbors. Enjoy and May God Bless!

Walter M. Zweizig

INTRODUCTION

*War is people getting caught up
in events they don't understand.*
- Daniel Webster

Fort Dix, one of the Army's training grounds on the eastern seaboard, was named for Major General John Adams Dix, a veteran of
the War of 1812, another war people don't talk about, much less understand. But it was the start of everything for us and for me, too.
It meant the beginning of a long succession of battles using bullets
and threats and spies and blockades—anything you could think of
to tweak or kill the other guy. I didn't know a thing about that. I had
signed up for adventure before we were even into another war and
perhaps for a way to prove myself in a rapidly realigning world. I
guess I was changing, too. Before this thing was over, I'd change my
mind about a lot of things.

PART I

Getting It Right

We cannot build the future for our youth,
But we can build our youth for the future.
- Franklin Delano Roosevelt

My name is Walter Zweizig. I am seated in front of the bar-racks furnace meant to keep a bunch of new recruits like my-self barely warm. You wouldn't imagine it'd get much colder in here at night. Up until the furnace went cold, which was what it did. I let the dang thing go out on my watch, fell asleep against the side of the dang thing, and let the fire die out. Everyone wanted to kill me in the morning, including the sergeant in charge.

The thing about the Army is that, if you get something wrong, they tell you to do it over and over until you either follow instructions as they intend, or figure it out on your own. You know, the right way, the wrong way, or the Army way. I am doing the latter, because the furnace job is mine for three weekends straight until I figure out how to stay awake long enough to feed it through the night.

I already nodded off twice…

Saturday came on miserably damp and bleak. Dark clouds filled the cold January sky with a threat of rain while we rode due east in what soon became a raw and wintry downpour. It even snowed some by the time our unheated trucks arrived at Fort Dix. Our poorly clad feet for such inclement weather had barely hit the soggy ground when orientation began. A mean sergeant in charge made us line up by the largest pothole he could possibly have found.

"Tetch Hut!" he bellowed.

Touch what? Could that be short for attention? I straightened.

When he dressed the line, he cast a critical glance my way and said,

"What's the matter, sonny? Don't you like to get your feet wet? Fall in! Come on, move it up! Dress it up! " Not once did he compromise his own posture that looked as if a steel rod had been shoved up his four-foot spine.

Battling an urge to punch him in the mouth, I yielded, stepping into the pothole that by this time loomed as large as an ocean might appear to a puddle. Icy wintry slosh soaked my ankles and oozed down inside my low tie dress shoes. The sergeant displayed a short smile of approval and moved on.

Before I continue, there is something you need to understand. To become a drill instructor, one requires a particular kind of pettiness. A second requisite: voice lessons to deepen and widen the vocal chords. Else, how could trainees be reached who might otherwise escape the DI's vociferous outbursts? And forget all that diaphragm nonsense of proper breathing in and out. Not important. Only volume and hatefulness count. In the final analysis, the candidate must achieve a perfect score in the military's Employee Relations Incompetence test. I jest, but surely you get the drift.

We knew not right from left, but with travel bag in hand, marched in ragged columns to our new living quarters—a dimly lit hall with tired gray walls yellowed by smoke and an air that reeked of stale tobacco. A dreary dusk peeked through small curtainless windows on the south side. Two rows of double bunks stretched before us.

"Just what I always wanted, a prison cell with personality," said one recruit. He was chubby—fat actually—and built somewhat like a cotter pin, a kid who probably was the butt of his peers' jokes in school and was pushed around and bullied. Over-sized ears supporting coke bottle lenses quickly earned him the nickname "Four

Eyes." Four Eyes pitched his small suitcase on the first cot.

Another recruit tested the buoyancy of a stripped, striped mattress by dropping his husky bulk on top, lit up a cigarette, and admired a circular puff of carbon.

"Well, it sure ain't much," he said. "They had better than this at cub scouts when I were a kid." A second smoke ring spiraled through the first.

Okay, you guys, knock it off, I thought, but didn't have the guts to say. *It's home for the next eight weeks whether we like it or not.* Dix was not home. No place compared to home. Still, one wouldn't say I was accustomed to private or frilly sleeping quarters. Growing up, I shared a bed with one of five siblings who ranged in various stair step sizes penciled on the kitchen wall. At least now I needn't deal with covers pulled off my hindey during the long, chilly night.

After dark, they gifted us with two blankets and a pillow, no sheets, and told us to get some sleep.

"Do these things come with instruction?" mumbled one of the guys after we returned to our bunks with our bundles.

"Oh, I'm sure we'll get all the instructions we want by tomorrow," someone offered.

"My mother forced me to make my bed," said another, "so I outsmarted her and slept on top of the covers. My father said I was displaying a spirit of independence and an ability to solve problems."

"Is that what you're going to tell the sarge if he catches you, that you are demonstrating your independence?"

As if he heard, the mean sergeant popped in and warned that by tomorrow we'd be able to bounce a quarter off our beds. For now, we best hit the hay since,

"...morning comes mighty early around here!"

"Hey, what about chow?" called out Four Eyes, but the sergeant had disappeared.

"Boy, I'm hungrier than a bear in spring time," said Mark Wolfen, rubbing his flat belly. "Wonder when they plan on feeding us."

My belly growled, too, for recognition. We heard no mention of supper, not even a hint of enticing kitchen smells. The only odor in our barracks came from foul-smelling, wet woolen socks. All manner of dull and vivid argyles hung overhead to dry on the hissing, clanging heat ducts.

*The furnace fire showed red through the grate. Darn, if it wasn't hyp-
notizing, just glowing like that. I clutched the shovel and counted the
coals it held, giving my mind something to ponder. What was wrong
with me? Plenty of nights, like before, going to the Reading Fair or to
Hershey Park, or if I was going to meet some new girl, I couldn't sleep
at all. I tried to picture them now, especially the girls. I needed to keep
my foggy brain running instead of counting coal, which is what it really
wanted to do.*

That first night, before the whole furnace debacle, I crawled
between those scratchy woolen GI blankets, plopping my head
down on a pillow nearly as hard as stone. As I lay on the thin
mattress, arms locked behind my head, I stared wide-eyed at the
dim outline of bed boards above. Could it be I was in the Army?
Off to wonderful, far-away places? I just turned eighteen and was
never farther than Hershey's Zoo and Amusement Park, a mere
hour's drive west of our dairy farm in southeast Pennsylvania.
How exciting to think what lay ahead. Places like Washington,
D.C. perhaps. Overseas. Germany, I mused. Unlike my soldier
brother Robert, more than good-looking German women came
to mind. I'd research my cultural heritage and later impress the
heck out of Uncle Raymond. He was the keeper of lineage updates
on Zweizig beginnings. (See Addendum.)

Thoughts shifted to second gear and considered higher priorities. Touring the German countryside, for example. According to books from the school library, farmers lived in villages and
rode out to fields in carts or on tractors to till the land and harvest crops. And imagine this, dairy cows were kept inside barns
all year long—right in town, for goodness sake. "Well, guys. I
need to go back to town now and help with the milking and barn
chores. See you tomorrow," I say to my Glen Gery co-workers
when punching out.

Did they build barns into dirt banks like ours at home, I wondered? We drove from the rear directly on to the threshing floor.
Most likely they did, too, since Uncle Raymond said Pennsylvania
Dutch barns are of Swiss German style. Hex signs, were they painted on barn fronts in colorful distelfinks? Or, maybe with black
and white Holstein cows in a field of green? Horses pulling plows?

I no sooner fell asleep then someone turned the lights on and shouted:

"Let's go! Everyone out in the company street at next whistle blow! You have ten minutes!"

Troops marched and counted cadence while moving through snow and slush toward the mess hall two blocks away.

"Hup, two, three, four! Hup, two, three …."

It was the dead of winter, 1948.

Legs drooping over the side of the bunk, I checked the Bulova wristwatch my parents had given me at Confirmation.

"Good grief!" I said, or something more appropriate. "It's only four in the morning! Even the roosters don't wake up this early back home."

A shrouded figure in the next bunk stirred. Size fourteen feet stuck over the end of the cot, and an arm hung limply down the side.

"They don't where I live neither," said the shrouded figure. Mark Wolfen struggled out of his cover, exposing a thin but well- muscled chest. A farmer's tan still covered his long gangly arms. This sandy-haired, tall, lean drink of water was obviously from the rural south. I went to a cattle auction once with Pop where I heard someone talk just like that. The man was from Tennessee. Maybe that's where this guy came from. All I knew was he talked kind of funny and appeared backward. Before I had a chance to ask where he lived, he beat me to it.

"Where y'all from?" he said.

My reply wasn't exactly the King's English either. Pennsylvania Dutch people, most in my generation anyway, birthed into households where English was a second language. An accent was something to be ashamed of. Outside the confines of the rural countryside, such as we were labeled dutchified. Often, parents refrained from speaking dialect at home to homogenize offspring into the "English" culture. If not Pennsylvania Dutch—a corruption of German anglicized from Deutsch, you were automatically considered an *Anglisher*, whether your ancestral roots traced back to the great little isle or not. Even town kids looked down on farm kids as hicks from the sticks and too dutchified for their alleged worldly way of speaking.

Annual trips to the county seat at Reading replaced hand-me-downs seeing much use or abuse. On one of these shopping excursions, a smart-alec stuck out her city-bred tongue at me. Even though I hadn't opened my mouth and, talk about an inferiority complex, I just knew her rudeness stemmed from my being a dutchie.

Today, in my twilight years, v's and w's still get *ferhuddled* on occasion. So for shame on my thoughts poking fun back then at the tainted way Wolfie spoke. It spawned a good laugh when Larry Viscardi interrupted us that morning in a strange and sophisticated voice all his own.

"Well, I can tell neither of you guys are from Joisey, that's for sure!" he said. Larry was a city type. It showed by the fine store-bought plaid shirt he wore tucked inside belted corduroys and his smooth, non-calloused hands when we shook the night before. Larry reminded me somewhat of the railroad workers back home. Names were so unusual and complicated we simply grouped these people as The Italians. Short in stature, the foreigners bore deep-rooted, thick dark wavy crops of hair and had oily skin bronzed by both sun and cold. Twisted English words always ended in the vowel "a" when they spoke, restless hands decoding a string of verbal messages as they rushed along. If I happened to be in Kliney's General Store at the same time The Italians shopped, I couldn't for the life of me determine what they said. But never mind. They didn't talk to me, a youngster hiding well behind Pop's baggy bib overalls. But Larry Viscardi, second generation, was understandable, even for me.

A two-minute conversation during reveille that first morning, when country met city in three distinct accents, created a tight bond amongst us that would continue throughout our eight weeks of basic training.

My head snapped up from my chest. Where am I? The fire. I leaned toward the furnace. Still going. Thank God! I pitched in another shovel of coal and stoked the ashes for a while. It wasn't just humiliating if I'd let it burn out again, the whole barracks would pay for my stupidity, and not just for being cold. They might be made to run the length of the concourse several times or any other of a half dozen things they'd use to whip us into shape. I took a deep breath and twisted my neck. I can do this. I can do this. I can do this.

The mess hall could seat a thousand men. It was half-filled when we entered that first morning. Everyone talked at once.

"This place is noisy as a hog pen at slop time," remarked Wolfie. He stretched every word to form twice as many syllables as Webster intended. And twice as flat. Why couldn't he just spit out what he wanted to say so we could hurry on with what we were doing which was moving in line to pick up much delayed nourishment. Even his movements for selecting food came slow and indecisive while I followed impatiently behind.

"You'd think Uncle Sam could afford to give us more than one tiny slab of butter for two pieces of toast," he drawled when the kitchen help plopped bread and butter on his plate. After we sat down, he brought up the deficiency once more. "I'm trying to make it reach," he said, scraping his knife across four corners of crusted surface. All the while, his elbows bent outward like chicken wings into my limited space.

"If you ask me, this excuse for toast is so hard and cold," bellyached Four-Eyes, "that more butter would just curl up in a ball and roll off the side. It makes me sick!" He picked up his toast, took a bite out of it, chewed, swallowed and made a dissatisfied face. His face pinched up like a reject from a pickle factory. A total downer. Pessimist. I wasn't familiar with the word at the time, but I knew enough he was the type of person who feels good when he feels bad knowing he feels bad when he should feel good.

"I must be a god or something, what with these burnt offerings they're giving me," added Larry. He laughed at his own feeble joke and licked grape jelly off his nicotine-stained fingers before ducking his head up and down for each bite of bread as though bobbing for apples.

I didn't think it was as bad as all that. I kind of liked my toast on the dark side, with lots of warm butter, of course. But I was not one to complain. I wasn't brought up that way.

"So, chum," said my new city friend from New Jersey around a gigantic mouthful. "Today they'll teach us how to shoot a rifle, I'll bet. What do you think?"

"Maybe," I said. No johnny-come-lately in that department, I already knew how to shoot though didn't think it right to brag. I did most of my catching on to things in this new way of life by observing others and listening. Little did either of us know that before getting into the mechanics of soldiering, we'd first learn how to fix a proper bed, shine shoes, and say "Sir, Yes, Sir!" and "Sir, No, Sir!" without any tremor in the voice.

A sergeant stood up. Sergeants, in the thirties as a rule, were World War II vets who continued on in the military.

"AT EASE!" he screamed at the top of his lungs. He most likely was a drill instructor at one time or another and now exercised experienced authority to hear his tablemate. Forks and spoons dropped to the table. A few feet shuffled here and there until the hall became so quiet you could've heard a flea sneeze. Seconds later, a ripple of snickers at the table to our right broke the silence. "Okay, you two! Dump your chow and OUT!" The stern-faced sergeant pointed to the mess hall's exit.

God gave us two ears and one mouth because we're expected to listen twice as hard when someone speaks instead of making ourselves heard at the same time. I saw through the window the violators pondered this concept while they stood at attention in the cold rain that continued in earnest since our arrival at camp.

Famished, I quickly lost interest in my peers' misfortune. I'd had this ongoing hand-to-mouth relationship with food for the past seventeen years and was so hungry even fish would have tasted good. Well, on second thought, maybe not fish. I returned to my undercooked bacon, overcooked eggs, and cold toast blackened around the edges.

We moved outdoors after breakfast and marched in orderly formation to an old movie theater. Inside, sergeants ready to pounce on you for any unsatisfactory behavior lined three walls. Soon, from behind a plush red curtain, a colonel—a tall man in dress uniform with a brisk command about him—strutted center stage. Commotion from the floor stopped. Following a brief introduction, the officer cleared his throat as a sign he had something important to say. We listened. Then he quoted the Articles of War from an open notebook in his hand. Following each article, he took a moment to let what he had just said sink in. Most of his statements closed with, "...and the penalty shall be death or as the courts martial shall direct!"

My folks drove a message home by the seat of my pants. Here, the Army was sure to shoot me if I made an error, now or forever more. Judging by stiff necks and rigid profiles, others feared the same. I was not this scared since I rode the Jack Rabbit by mistake at Hershey Park and couldn't peel my white knuckles from the safety bar. More than once the thought occurred that maybe, just maybe, enlistment was a grave mistake. Discussing this with my buddies sometime later, I quipped,

"Why couldn't I have flat feet!"

"Ha!" laughed Larry. "That probably wouldn't have worked either. On the truck here from Philly, one of the guys said he suddenly got the jitters when he was being tested so he answered every question with a no. Y'know what the sarge said?"

"I don't."

"The Army wants smart guys like you. If you had been dumb, you would've tried on purpose to answer the questions incorrectly so you wouldn't pass." That was an old technique unwilling draftees had tried back in the war.

I woke up on the floor, curled up like a bundle of rope. I checked the furnace. My hands and feet tingled as if a thousand little pins jabbed me. The furnace wasn't red anymore, and I jammed in three more shovels full of coal. The ashes were gray, barely breathing.

I rushed back to my bunk, crumbled up a note a cousin had written before I left. I liked her and that note an awful lot, but now I leaned over the open furnace hatch, blowing wind into it so it'd catch fire and save me. The little paper lit and then caught the splintery edges of wood kindling I had also thrown in. Whew! That was close.

Leaning back, I grabbed my thigh really hard and pinched it, but I was starting to feel numb. Tired numb. That's a weird feeling, for sure. Down the road, dug in a foxhole that I could never imagine for a minute I'd be lodged inside, if I pulled this little dozing off routine, I'd likely be killed for real and not by some angry CO. Yeah, or falling asleep on guard duty when you know they're out there counting your hide. That's worse than waking up cold in the

*morning. You'd wake up real cold, dead cold. Little did I know, I'd
see plenty of that, so I suppose this was all good practice for keeping
my own hide on my bones.*

After the theater, after making us feel like kid idiots that I guess
was their job when addressing recruits, we were shuttled to another hall where we exchanged street clothes for ill-fitting olive drabs
and clunky boots. The first time I wore the boots, I looked over my
shoulder to see what made that awful noise. Good grief, it was me!
Getting dog tags came next on the agenda. These were two little
metal plates on a chain that hung from your neck, one so that when
you died they could rip if off for their records and the other would
remain with my body. Comforting thought. Stamped on mine was:

    Walter M. Zweizig
    Service No. RA13265210B
    Blood Type: A Positive
    "P" for Protestant

Following the identification process, they herded us into a barber-
shop where the all-American, clean shave crew cut gave us the mark
of distinction from civilians. Six skillful barbers sheared the flock.
Heads that looked like inverted bowling pins emerged one by one
from a long room floored wall to wall with hair. Black, brown, red,
blonde, sandy, long, short, thick, thin, curly, wavy, straight. Back in
the barracks, we had a kick teasing each other.

    "Ha! You look like a bald mannequin I saw in Macy's store
window!"

    "Buddy, you're not too bright considering you have a head shaped
like a light bulb!"

    One guy inserted an index and little finger between his lips and
whistled, then said,

    "Oh, sweetheart. Aren't you cute! Can I take you out tonight?"

    When my squinty sometimes hazel sometimes gray sometimes
blue eyes stared back at me from the wall mirror in the washroom, I
realized this was no cosmetic improvement. Yet, though I can't speak
for anyone else's fate, my buzz-cut brown mane became a definite
convenience in the shower. Soon other benefits surfaced as well.

Like banishing brush and comb. Like eliminating greasy Vaseline, a goopy pomade to keep in place wayward strays and cowlicks that defied all other restraint. Like no more *schtrubbley* bad hair days!

Our company had four frame barracks, each two stories high, seventy or eighty feet long. Each floor had two rows of double bunks on either side of a center aisle. In front of the bunks were footlockers in which we kept our underwear, socks and personal effects. Our uniforms hung from a rod behind the bunks.

On the first floor in a separate compartment were several toilets in two rows facing each other. An adjacent room had a row of washstands on one wall and urinals on the opposite. Next to this was a room with four showerheads. In design, modesty and privacy were low priority.

Each barrack had a boiler room on the side. The CQ (charge of quarters) clerk from the orderly room kept the fires during the day. For night, they assigned someone from each building. Piece of cake! You cranked this big old coal furnace a few times, coaxed down the ashes, and opened the door. A shovel or two of fresh coal over the healthy orange flame caused delightful sparks to dance around a burning mass. With a clunk, the metal door of the furnace silenced the roar. That's all there was to it. Then you relaxed in this cozy warm environment and an hour later repeated the function. Anyway, that was the idea. At some unfortunate point between the fourth or fifth hour of my first duty, I disgraced myself by falling into a hopeless coma. The barracks transformed into a meat locker by morning, and icy stalactites hung with abandon from all four washroom showerheads.

"You will be fireman until you get it right!" scolded the squatty sergeant in charge.

Each night, I installed a bumper jack in one of my eyes and jump-started my heart with a large thermos of thick black coffee. As wise old Ben Franklin once said, "Those things that hurt, instruct." Aside from going on strike the morning after my gross negligence, the guys loved it. A lot of them never got to be fireman because I stole the duty for three weekends straight.

We spent most daylight hours in rigorous physical activity that stringently tested our endurance skills. We marched for miles through rain, snow, raw sleet, or whatever wintry mix nature presented. We trained in weaponry and marksmanship and infantry combat tactics and performed close order drills; … "Fall in!" …"Left turn!"… "Right turn!"… "About face!" … "Forward march"… plus lots of pushups, situps, running, and …

Before continuing, let me ask you a question. What gets bigger and bigger the more you take away from it? You needn't scroll to the end of the chapter. I'll give you the answer here. It's a hole. I mention this because none of us understood why we required so much practice at digging a hole in the ground and with a shovel no larger than a tablespoon and always, always under the eagle eye of a sergeant threatening all sorts of dire consequence if you didn't get it right. To top it off, after size and neatness were accomplished to his satisfaction, we shoveled it closed, only to begin again. Our bodies obeyed, but our minds had time for critical digression and evaluation. There was little use for such senseless discipline. But we'd be proven wrong, something we would come to think of many times in months to come.

Evenings were spent in classroom work, rifle sighting, compass and map reading, etcetera.

One of the sweetest sunrises I've ever seen, and I have seen some good ones, like the sun over the green rolling pastures of our farm, was the one that came up over the flat ugly horizon of Dix the Monday morning after my third weekend on furnace duty. That big orange ball never looked so good. I leaned back against my bunk, tired as all get-out, fixed at half strength for the day ahead, but proud as all get-out that I finally got it right. It seemed like a big deal to me at the moment, but it was only a little trail for me in the days ahead. You can count on that being a fact. Events were happening all over the world, which as far as I was concerned had nothing to do with me or us, events that would make my stay in the Army a lot different from what I expected and a whole lot tougher than worrying about some silly old furnace burning out.

During the eighth and final week of basic training, orders included a map-reading expedition. Four men comprised a team. They gave each team a map, compass, and flashlight. The objective was to find our way back through the dark using these three aids and our God-given noodles. Fort Dix, New Jersey is several hundred square miles in size, so, mind, this task was akin to finding a needle in a haystack. One incentive: first team to return to the company area was guaranteed no KP for an entire weekend.

Other than not being awakened by the company clerk at three thirty in the morning, escaping duty in the garrison was not a big deal, not for me at least. The job entailed nothing more than being a glorified bus boy, setting and clearing tables, scrubbing pots and pans, or, assisting the mess sergeant in peeling fifty sacks of spuds, then slicing, hashing, chopping, carving, frying, boiling, or smashing afterward. Or, waiting tables in the officers' mess hall. You see, officers had special dining privileges. We peons stood in long lines outside, rain or shine, inching our way forward tortoise-slow to the greasy spoon. Commissioned and non-commissioned officers walked right on by, went inside, sat down and were served five-star restaurant style. But, I speak only for myself. The rest of the recruits, next to scrubbing the barracks floor with your own toothbrush, KP duty got thumbs down if given a choice. Hence, the incentive.

Blindfolded, we were transported by truck to the field, each team going to a separate, unknown location. Ours reached its drop point twenty-five minutes later in the middle of nowhere. Larry switched on the flashlight, then fumbled in his pocket and retrieved a small compass. He unsnapped its canvas case.

"Well, that's north," my Italian buddy said, shooting light into a moonless night filled with forest pine. He kicked a crooked groove in the sandy soil with his combat boot.

"So what's that supposed to tell us?" said the freckle-faced, red-headed Kelly from Albany. "We need to know which way is back to camp!" In reality, Kelly verbalized more than I wish to state. Whenever he opened his mouth, the names of at least two members of the Holy Trinity along with a few favored verbs, some of which I'd never heard before, rolled off his crude Irish tongue.

"Beats me!" I said.

Puzzled, we stared at the quivering arrow on the compass pointing true north.

Private Wegley, fourth member of our party, was a laughing, good-natured sort from the town of Skippack located on the outskirts of Philadelphia. He was a big, broad-shouldered fellow built like a massive bulldog. Muscles in places I didn't even have places turned my eyes green with envy. We roomed in the same barracks hall.

"Okay," Wegley said, "where's the map, you bozos!"

The map. Of course. We spread the map on the ground and, using the compass as the instructor taught, oriented ourselves to what appeared the proper direction, then traipsed a good half hour through woods and along dirt trails before stopping for a recheck and cigarette break.

I acquired the habit at Glen Gery. Smoking was the only excuse one had for breaks. Though I must say had I not come into the Army with a veteran addiction, I'd have started soon enough. Cigarettes were the norm, you could even say promoted by the military. Everyone smoked. Our faces lit up like each day was the Fourth of July. No fear of the Grim Reaper's harvest, like today, when 350,000 lives go up in fumes each year through tobacco-related illnesses. (See Addendum.)

"Shhhh...," Larry cautioned after extinguishing his butt. "I hear something."

I heard it, too. Traffic hummed. We walked toward the sound for two hundred yards to our left and came to a two-lane, hard-surfaced road. According to the map, this road headed back toward camp. We rounded a bend and spotted lights a short distance away. It was an Esso gas station. Kelly asked directions.

"It's straight ahead," the attendant said. "But if you wait fifteen minutes 'til I close up, I'll give you a lift."

We traveled approximately three miles on the back of this good old soul's old pickup before stopping at a crossroad where he headed in the opposite direction. Putting leather to the road once more, we walked ten to fifteen minutes when a two and a half ton Army truck passed and pulled over.

"Want a lift?" the driver called back.

"Sure, if you're headed for the base," I said, running up to him. I'd grown bolder in talking with strangers as the weeks wore on.

"Hop in."

It was downhill from there on. Maybe like me, you'll find such terminology puzzling, a contradiction, much as "pretty ugly" or "jumbo shrimp." Southern New Jersey is flat as a pancake, so "downhill" rules out any physical sense. I've discovered that downhill can mean the pits to one person, while sliding with ease opposed to an uphill battle for another. Not to worry; I'll clarify. We were almost there, and surely no more barriers would keep us from meeting time or destination.

The kind gent dropped us off a block from the PX, the Army's post exchange. Not to arrive back at the company area before a reasonable time elapsed, we chose to play pool.

"Okay, who's going to check it out?" Larry asked, reaching for a cigarette. He lit and exhaled a cloud of smoke into the New Jersey night.

"You brought it up," said Wegley. "You're on, Bud." Not a good thing if we ran into someone we knew at the PX, in particular, NCOs who might possibly recognize us.

Minutes later, Viscardi signed a thumb's up.

Inside was dark, noisy, smoky, and the place, as usual, smelled of stale beer. From the jukebox came, "...I'm looking over a four-leaf clover...." There was a shuffleboard on one side and in the center were two billiard tables. All were occupied. A young buck, who by all appearances was three sheets to the wind, had just sunk the eight ball on the break and bumped Wegley with the cue stick, the epitome of someone itching for a fight. Wegley shook his head.

"No, that's all right, Buddy," he said, raising both hands in front of him, palms out. "You just stay put. We're grabbing seats at the snack bar."

There were four vacant stools together. We sat. Wegley laid a silver half on the counter and ordered coffee, indicating the four of us with a sweep of his hand. Alcohol breath was a no-no this particular evening. Kelly mashed the stub of his latest cigarette in the aluminum foil ashtray and leaned over the counter.

"Hey, you really fill that thing out!" he said to the cute waitress.

She ignored his remark, and her small yet in some details overabundant body turned back toward the stove and poured coffee.

"Will there be anything else?" she said as she placed the steaming mugs in front of us.

"Yeah, now that you ask. What time do you get off?" Kelly lit up another weed, further contributing to the silvery haze in the room.

"Quitting time," she teased. Her cheeks broke into the biggest dimples I'd ever seen.

"Do you have a sister?" cut in Wegley. "We could make it a foursome." He slapped Kelly on the back.

Everyone laughed.

"If I did, why would we want to go out with either of you?"

I wondered the same.

"Try us and find out!" said Wegley.

"Why can't you be like him?" She flashed a bright smile in my direction.

"Hey, Walt, how are you? We're supposed to be like you, she says."

He laughed and so did I. Everyone laughed.

It was usually like this. While guys made out with anything that wore a skirt, the gals turned their attention toward me. But don't get me wrong. I never quite made it to the top of the most wanted list. I was much too shy.

Shyness was inherent in our household. Cousin BJ teases me to this day how she and her sister Jeannette from the city visited us on the farm, and they'd see a head pop out here and there behind the kitchen coal stove. Why, we even had a wooden bench behind the stove so we could hide in comfort while company was present.

I wished in a way I was outgoing like others, but could never think of the right thing to say when it came right down to it. In fact, I didn't talk much at all if I didn't have something to talk about. I just sat back, not knowing half the time what to do with my hands in the presence of a lady. Stick them in my pockets? Scratch my head?

It was easy to see showing off and wisecracking wouldn't get my buddies past first base with this gal. I doubt if anyone impressed her for that matter. She saw men in uniform every day. After her comment, I smiled and blushed, embracing the theory that heat rises to the top, then lifted the hot cup of coffee to my lips and proceeded in pain as if swallowing a mouthful of crushed glass.

Deciding earlier not to return to our meeting point before one, we hung out at the PX until it closed at eleven. It's a curious thing.

When running late, time waits for no one. Every hour flies by like a clock with wings, each minute a second, each second a nanosecond. But when you're in a delay mode, well, it's amazing how time stands still. Anxious to put an end to this waiting game, fifteen minutes in front of the hour, we sprinted to our rendezvous point as fast as a buck flees a hunter to give the impression we did a lot of hoofing.

The place was deserted. We hid behind a nearby building and alternated turns peeking around the corner. Soon, a jeep pulled up with our company's commanding officer, Lieutenant Mackley, and a sergeant. We repeated our fake marathon. "And the winner is..." We never bragged too much about this lest someone ask questions we couldn't or didn't want to answer. Of course, it really was swell skipping KP.

No pass or fail at completion of basic training. Like it or not, suffer or endure, laugh or cry, you measured up to whatever was asked during those two months, and that was the end of it. And to think most, not knowing a gun from a slingshot when we began, now brimmed with potential. We had toughened mentally, emotionally, and physically, and emerged steely as nails. Officers not only drilled and grilled to make us sound and savvy, but also taught duty, honor, and pride. I remember the first time we outfitted in full dress, it seemed we stood much taller and straighter than before. We represented the greatest Army in the world—the Army of the United States of America, willing and able to defend our country if, God forbid, the need occurred.

To celebrate our achievement, they scheduled a large parade.

A special order posted on our barrack's bulletin board the Friday night before promoted each recruit to private first class. Puffed up, everyone, using a sewing kit nicknamed "housewife," sewed a single stripe on the uniform for the next day's event.

But mischief is bound to happen when you have a bunch of young whippersnappers feeling their oats with a bag of unused childhood pranks. It began when Wegley returned from the washroom.

"Here, catch this!" he said as he pitched a water-filled balloon to Wolfie who was admiring his shirt, freshly pressed and ready for wear with the new stripe in place.

"Whoa! You almost got my shirt," he said, catching the flying missile, then relaying it to me like it was a hot potato.

"Bernie, look out! Here it comes!" I yelled, sailing the balloon across the barracks to the other end.

Soon, excessive trips were made to the rec hall to snatch more balloons laying ready to blow up for the parade.

Our CO, discovering the mess on his nightly check around ten, reported his findings to the officer of the day. By eleven, we found ourselves outside the barracks and, as the roster was read, demoted back to private.

"...and get those stripes torn off before parade time Saturday!"

The problem wasn't the three dollars a month difference the promotion made in our paychecks. Nor was it the challenging and frustrating half-hour we wasted sewing stripes on in the first place when it took seconds to rip them off. No, it was the hollow, empty egos, deflated like stuck balloons before the party began. We learned the name of the game is discipline.

Discipline is getting up at four in the morning whether you like it or not, running ten miles in the rain even if you hurt. Running ten miles rain or shine with blistering feet inside boots you can't cut holes in like Granny Zweizig did to relieve pressure on her bunions. Or, stoking the coal furnace in the boiler room every hour every night for three weekends straight. Discipline! Discipline! Discipline! Without discipline an alternate consequence could be severe. Like now, getting busted. Maybe busted big time after the grueling and taxing climb to the top is achieved. Or thrown into the brig, or wounded in combat. Or countless troops losing their lives in battle. Or losing a war due to lack of discipline. Who was it that said:

"If it weren't for the nail, the shoe would be lost. If it weren't for the shoe, the horse would be lost. If it weren't for the horse, the battle would be lost. If it weren't for the battle, the war would be lost."

Yes, discipline is the stuff soldiers are made of. Discipline is a nail.

The parade ended at eleven thirty. Release for a three-day leave followed with instructions to report back on base no later than midnight the coming Wednesday.

Making the Best of It

History isn't just people doing bad things,
Sometimes it's people trying to do good things,
But something goes wrong.
                                        - *C. S. Lewis*

A three-day leave is about as speedy as a passing wind. I no sooner arrived home and told everyone I was going to Germany when I found myself back on the train again headed for Trenton. But not on to Germany I soon discovered.

At Dix, they handed me a large manila envelope. It contained my records, meal tickets, and marching orders. I tore open the brief. In large bold letters, my assignment read:

Far East Area Command in Japan (FEACOM)

Japan? I was shell-shocked! How could this be? The recruiting office in Reading all but promised an assignment in the European theater. Germany, they said. Had they lied? Grown men don't cry, certainly not tough-as-leather ones coming from the farm. Now, I knew the resistance Peter endured when he plugged the hole in the dyke. In a blur, I read on:

"...Seven Days Travel Authorized, to arrive NAT April 12, 1948 at Fort Lawton, Seattle, Washington."

By degrees, I became aware one cannot fight city hall. Nor, the United States Army.

Some time after April Fool's Day, I left Trenton late afternoon on the "Pennsie," the Pennsylvania Railroad, the nation's largest. In New York City, I'd switch for Chicago. Never in all my life had I been in a building so huge and with ceilings so high as in the concourse of the Pennsylvania Station in New York. It seemed the whole world intersected at this railroad center, trains coming from every direction and going everywhere else there was to go (except Germany). To Florida and Canada, Washington, D.C. Timbuktu. Confusing schedules for departure and arrival around the clock were posted everywhere or called out over a loud public address system.

"Train Number 44 on Track 8 for Piscatawny...."

After some length, I found my connection to Chicago where I'd make another change.

Trains fascinated me, especially freights. I often paused in the field and waved to the proud engineer in his steamy, glistening black locomotive as it pounded north or south along the Schuylkill River by our farm, pulling an endless string of clickety-clacking cars behind. I wondered about names of far-away places like Chesapeake and Ohio, C&E, Northern Pacific, Topeka, Boston and Maine.... Names were subtle give-aways from where these trains originated or where they might return. It was a curiosity how cars from diverse places hitched together into one single train going in one single direction.

Back when coal was king, open cars on our Reading Company line were either loaded with anthracite from Schuylkill County to the north or empty ones returning to the mines. (Just prior to the Civil War, the Reading Railroad Company had become the largest corporation in the world.) But what was inside those multi-colored boxcars? What stories did they have to tell? These were questions to contemplate as one waited at a railroad crossing when a train rumbled by. Then, it was like watching an exciting travel adventure on film. Now, it's just an interruption in our rush to be someplace else.

"All a-b-o-a-r-d!" I heard from somewhere. A whistle blew three long blasts, air hoses hissed, wheels squealed, and we were on our way. An old conductor in black uniform appeared.

"Your ticket, young man," he mumbled through a tobacco-swollen cheek.

I showed him my pass, sat back, and watched the tall city stream by on the other side of the window. From the Big Apple, we pushed on to Chicago during the long night hours. Since the government hadn't shelled out Pullman for this particular leg of the trip, I slept upright in my seat, bookended by an overweight passenger and the window and about as comfortable as a horse might be in a doghouse.

At dawn, the state-of-the art diesel-fueled train rolled through a small town in Indiana. I stared out the window and listened to the rat-a-tat-tat of the wheels while we passed old brick buildings with smoking stacks belching black soot, then shabby houses with wash hanging on backyard lines. The engineer sounded his whistle at a main street crossing where life stirred, and people were on the move. Soon, we were in open country where I hoped to see farmers working the fields. April was damp and rainy and apparently the soil too wet to deal with. There was no field activity throughout the entire Midwest, (nor on the flat, windswept plains beyond).

"Next stop, Chicago!" announced the conductor, strolling through the car. Chicago's railroad yard was the largest in the world. Most trains crossing the United States stopped and started there— freights carrying things and passenger trains carrying people. After arriving in the Windy City early evening, I transferred to another passenger train due west.

I was sitting alone in the dining car for dinner, the leftovers meal we called supper at home. A woman came by my table and surprised the heck out of me.

"Hi! Mind if I join you?" she said, flashing a beautiful smile that increased a dimple in her left cheek. I always noticed dimples.

She was older, maybe thirty-five, a good-looker and quite shapely in a dark-colored coat suit. Long slim fingers with a diamond in place clutched a pair of short black gloves even though it was warm inside our car. A pocketbook was tucked under an arm.

Blood rushed upwards, and my response got stuck somewhere

north of my Adam's apple. Lowering myself in the seat, I nodded tentatively while she slipped in across from me. Except for answering
questions with yes, no, or maybe, I participated very little in that first
conversation with this beautiful red-haired woman with the upswept
pompadour. I was too bashful. But she was friendly and outgoing.

"...I'm on my way back to Oregon after visiting my in-laws in
Cleveland," she said. "They lost two sons in the war, my husband
Wayne being one of them. They were both killed in Normandy during the invasion." There was no mistaking the moisture in her eyes
as she stared at her plate, pushing around under-cooked peas with
her fork before scooping them up with the help of a dinner roll. She
chewed the peas thoughtfully, swallowed, and went on.

"Wayne's parents never really got over it, and now the father just
had a heart attack."

I didn't know what to say about such devastating news. I said
nothing.

"He's doing okay, though. It was a mild one, fortunately." She
blinked remotely for a moment and faced me again. "Will you be
going overseas?"

I nodded, said,

"They're sending me to Japan." I was kind of glad now I wasn't
going to Europe where all those terrible things happened to this nice
lady and her family just a few short years ago.

Her laughter broke the somber mood. Serving two tables behind me, the waiter had tipped his tray and almost spilled hot coffee on a big fat lady diner. My friend thought this was funny. She
laughed easily. I liked that.

After a few meals together, I loosened up some and became more
comfortable in her presence. She always insisted on paying the tab
in spite of my government meal tickets. I recall being late for one of
the sittings, and she came searching. A couple of other servicemen
noticed this and teased me to high heaven.

"Hey! Mama's waiting for you in the next car!"

"Is your mother escorting you to Seattle?"

"Aw, mommy's little boy is going away."

Robert O'Malley wore dark horn-rimmed glasses and was dressed in
a gray business suit and white dress shirt, open three buttons from

the neck. A yellow and black striped tie was stuffed inside the magazine rack in front of his seat. He sat next to me and was dozing behind the *Chicago Tribune* when I poked him lightly with my elbow.

"Excuse me," I said. The train had stopped in Havre, which was the name on a wooden plaque hanging above the station's platform. I had a hankering for a coke from the soft drink cooler on the platform.

Before stepping out into the aisle to let me pass, the journalist, writing for some magazine, a name beyond my recognition, folded the newspaper and exchanged it for a small black book he took in and out of a leather brief case throughout our journey.

"Kerplop!" said the machine after I sank a dime into the slot.

Next thing I knew, the train was moving, and I wasn't on it. Like a runaway kid riding the rails, I ran along side for several panicky paces and did something I always thought would be fun to do. I jumped onto the moving train or, to be more precise, fell into it like a mailbag tossed from a platform. Later, I learned it was not a scheduled stop, only for the engine to take on water. Since I hadn't time to pop the lid in the machine, I used a pocketknife with an opener to reach the longed-for beverage. Settled safely in my seat, enjoying what was left of the sticky liquid that fizzled away in a carbonated fizz, I considered the historical challenges of the great iron horse pulling me across the vast west.

The Central Pacific and Union Pacific railroaders battled forty-foot snowdrifts, mountains and mountainous canyons, rivers, sub-zero temperatures, desert heat, water shortage, and hostile Indians before linking up in the desolate Utah landscape in 1869 to complete the first transcontinental railroad. Within the next thirty years, four more transcontinental railroad lines clanged to completion, including the Great Northern with the buffalo logo, the one I traveled on.

It was difficult to cross this great country of ours and not only imagine the railroad, but also Wells Fargo, Indians and cavalry and wagon trains and mountain men and white-faced cattle and chuck wagons and six-guns and Winchester rifles. Men chasing other men and animals across the rugged landscape.

"Hard to imagine this country was running with outlaws, Indians, and buffalo when they built this railroad," I said to impress the middle-aged gentleman next to me.

"Hmmm. What was that?" He was busy penciling copious notes in the little black book, using his brief case for a prop.

"I said, the place was swarming with Indians and buffalo when they worked on this railroad track just a short time ago."

He sighed, closing the journal, and stuck the pencil behind his ear.

"Yes, sad, isn't it that both were decimated so we could travel to Seattle in ease."

Silence.

We both gazed at the passing landscape of scrubby grassland stretching in every direction. In the distance, cattle grazed around a windmill that penetrated the big blue western sky.

"We were a warring nation back then," I said. "There's always a winner and a loser in a war, and the Indians lost."

"So true!" he said with a bitter laugh. "But one must ask the question why we were at war to begin with. Was it to procure more land? Maybe."

I nodded thoughtfully. His eyes met mine. A deep frown collected on his forehead.

"You see, we white people are always busy discovering land where people already are," he said. "And then there's another unethical dark side to our conquest. The natives relied on the buffalo for survival, and the military realized that, by wiping out the buffalo, they'd rid the natives as well. The saying back then was, 'Every buffalo dead is an Indian gone!'"

Bile rose from my stomach.

"The soldiers acted under orders from Washington," I said, defending the uniform that wrapped my soul. My profound statement put a period to our conversation. I finished the coke and stuck the empty bottle in the magazine rack and prepared to put aside this nonsense by taking a snooze.

"Unfortunately, you are right," said Robert, breaking the short silence. He cocked his head to the side supported by a smooth finger below the chin, still focusing on the window scene.

"Yet that hardly justifies the cause," he continued. "The military just came through the grueling War Between the States to free people of color from slavery. And, before that, our forefathers fought the British in the name of freedom. Where did the government come off feeling justified in killing the Indian for the sake of acquiring more land? There was plenty here for all of us, including the buffalo and the ranchers' cattle, or sheep herds if you will. We Americans are supposed to be in the business of liberating people, not slaughtering them for our own greedy purposes."

Before I could offer a heated rebuttal, my lady friend (someone on my Christmas card list if I remembered her name) came by. She waved me to follow her to the observation car. There, lungs exchanged stale cigar and cigarette smoke for fresh, crisp Rocky Mountain air. In between steam vapors that drifted by our open car, we saw vast stretches of woodland evergreens against a bright azure horizon. What a beautiful contrast. I wondered what my sister Catherine would say. She wouldn't be caught dead in a dress that shared the two colors. Girls!

"You say you've never been out west before?" asked the lady friend.

I shook my head and said,

"No farther west than Hershey Park in Pennsylvania."

"I understand," she said, sympathizing for my sheltered beginnings. "Well, while you're here, you don't dare miss what's coming up."

By all means, I was in for a rare treat as we traveled through the Rockies, somewhere between the Yellowstone and Glacier National Parks. This had to be the most beautiful area in the whole wide world. Distant rugged peaks, some blotted from view by wisps of white, pierced a sky as blue as a robin's egg. Water bounded down gullies and gushed out of fissures in the rock face. Water ran with abandon like I'd never seen before, as if God had too much of it and had simply flung it at this part of the landscape. Forested foothills surrounded picture postcard-blue lakes. Rivers and streams shaped by snow and ice created magnificent miniature waterfalls for as far as the eye could see. Even in these daylight hours, deer grazed peacefully in the lower meadows where patches of green and wildflowers surfaced through the snow, oblivious to the smoking noisy monster rushing by. It was difficult at best to stay attached to Planet Earth and not float on to Heaven. The Rocky Mountains were as good as it could get!

Five days from the time I left Trenton, we steamed into Seattle. I had no idea how close or far away the base was from the city. A civilian in the railroad terminal suggested I check the busses in the parking lot. A brown Army bus with "Fort Lawton" painted on the side stood out. There was no way I could have missed this for its letters were as mammoth as the Chew Mail Pouch Tobacco ad painted on a neighboring farmer's barn back home. The door was open.

"This thing going to Fort Lawton?" I asked the sergeant in the driver's seat. Fort Lawton was the Army's overseas staging area. I was the only one from the 9th Infantry Training Division at Fort Dix who went to this particular camp.

"I sure as thunder ain't going to Fort Knox!" he returned in a snotty voice, leveling a look at me that would have felled a lesser man. He must have sensed I was green as goose grass in a summer meadow and wouldn't dare snap back. I wanted to, but didn't.

When the bus arrived at my destination, around nine that night, Sergeant Snotty Wise Butt dropped me off by what appeared to be an old shed with a coal bin on the side. The windowless, cave-like building covered with dark green tarpaper over a rounded roof stood approximately sixty feet long. Enhancement on the interior was not much better. The hall was dim and smoky. Two naked ceiling bulbs lit the rectangular room, and one small potbelly stove in the center was the only heat to ward off the chilly dampness, or tried to. These drab, drafty, anything but comfortable quarters would serve as home away from home for fifteen of us until shipping out a week or so later. I grabbed a bed and spilled the contents of my duffel bag on top. Before long, a staff sergeant came by.

"Since you have the first bunk, you'll be acting corporal in charge," he said to me. "It's your job to get the men up for breakfast, make sure everyone makes a neat bed and keeps the place spic and span."

The sergeant handed me an elastic arm sleeve displaying two stripes and left. Before I considered this awesome responsibility, one of the guys called from across the room.

"Hey, corporal, what time is breakfast?"

I squared shoulders and stretched to my full five-feet-ten and a half. I was not as confident as I would make myself sound.

"The mess hall is only several doors down. Good or bad, we'll smell it in the morning," I said, or something equally as brilliant.

Minutes later, I issued my first order.

"Okay, it's time to outen the lights!" I called with some authority to the guy nearest the switch.

"Do what?"

"Outen the lights," I repeated with slight annoyance. "You know, make them out. It's bedtime!"

"Hey, stucko," offered the guy in the bunk next to the switchman, "He means kill them!"

This would be one of many corrections to my Pennsylvania Dutch vernacular.

We spent the next two days receiving additional clothing and attending orientation sessions, coupled with Troop Information and Education (TI&E). At least four classes on venereal disease were presented. These VD films with extreme close-ups of advanced stages of disease evoked raised eyebrows to say the least. Mind you, we're talking here of kids barely out of knickers. And after all, we were still in an era preceding school sex education and rarely, if ever, any from home. (Of course the effect of all this greatly diminished down the road once recruits learned that the military had a backup system for moments when testosterone drove men to the red-light district. Our instructors hammered home that immediately after sexual contact, the lust-filled soldier should look for the little green light above a doorway that signaled a government-operated prophylactic station designed to halt the spread of VD. Right.)

In due respect, I'm not claiming innocence from those things that came naturally in life. Besides some limited personal experience, I knew about the birds and the bees, having witnessed many a calf in the making. But, for goodness sake, discovering how sleeping around can cause such horrible, debilitating diseases as gonorrhea and syphilis was another matter entirely! Sure, these awful training films were made in the comfort of Hollywood. Nevertheless, a teachable moment, making genuine impressions that would remain throughout my entire tour of duty regardless of random pro-stations in the wing.

Third day at Fort Lawton was shots day. We required two more shots before boarding ship and trudged through a long line at the hospital wing in a manner suggesting we were about to face a firing squad.

A civilian clerk emerged from nowhere and scrutinized the line with a certain amount of arrogance. She was a thickset woman, early fifties, not necessarily fat but had wide thighs and shoulders. She wore her graying hair drawn tight behind her head. A little beak-mouth perched itself between pendulous cheeks as if ready to pick at fallen prey.

"I'm looking for Private Zweizig," came out of the little beaked mouth.

Someone pointed in my direction.

"Are you Private Zweizig?" she said, a forefinger stabbing the air in front of me.

"Yes, Ma'am. I am."

"It seems there is no record here of any previous shots." The woman held a stack of papers two feet thick bound together with a humongous metal clip. She juggled her pile and held an opened legal-sized manila folder in my face. "Here, you can see for yourself."

They were my documents all right. The orders for Japan shouted at me in large bold letters.

"This doesn't make sense," I murmured thoughtfully, thumbing through the folder, then returned it to her pile. "I gave all my records to the personnel people when I arrived on base."

"Well, they're not here!" she said, tapping her size ten orthopedics on the wooden floor.

"If my shot records are not in that file, then they've got to be someplace else."

"Well, I need to inform you that you'll have to retake all your previous shots, including the four given to you at Fort Dix!"

Like a tick burrowing for blood, this woman was determined to literally and figuratively needle me. Her voice gained in both volume and authority, saying,

"We can't let you go overseas without all your shots, now can we?"

"I am not taking them over again!" I said this time. She just didn't get it.

"You have no choice, Sir!" she countered.

"If anything from my file is lost, the Army lost it, not me!" My own voice had raised uncontrollably, my stomach starting a fast dive downward. We had a further exchange of words that increased in intensity until our flare-up attracted the attention of a 1st lieutenant.

"What's all the ruckus about?" he wanted to know.

"This young fellow here refuses to take his shots," scolded Miss Tick. She fixed a contemptible look on me that bore two clean holes through my head where my eyes once were.

Before I had a chance to defend my case, the officer ushered me like a chastised schoolboy into another room where nurses fluttered around like moths at a porch light on a July evening. One presented me to a doctor who sat amidst multiple trays of syringes and hypodermic needles the size of hayfork tines. He stared up at me over half-glasses resting on the end of a long nose with a Himalaya on top and asked me to please take a seat across from him. The odor of tincture and antiseptic played havoc with my senses as I rolled up my sleeves upon his directive. I extended my left arm first, squeezed shut my eyes and let him have at it. The flesh on both arms looked as pink as the pincushion in Mom's sewing basket by the time they were through puncturing me ninety minutes later. (See Addendum.)

I swear they gave me quadruple the inoculations just to drive home their silly point that the Army is never wrong. Let's keep this off the record for now, but if I ever become president of these United States, my first executive order is to dispense with injections of any sort. It follows then that my second executive order would be the location of proper landfills to discard trashed piles of vaccines, needles, and syringes. And you can only guess what my third executive order would be. You got it: Expending Miss Tick and her kind from the government's payroll and reducing the national debt to zero.

I spent two days on guard duty and hated every blooming minute. Looking back on the incident with the perspective of experience, I assume make-work detail was necessary to keep us occupied and out of trouble while waiting to ship out. The Navy Supply Yard five miles from base stored everything from life rafts to cases of Spam. There, I sat in an inflated raft for the entire time doing nothing more than watching the stupid entrance to the stupid depot. B-o-o-r-r-r-ing! Compared to this, a still life painting of an empty milk pail is uncontrollably exciting. Hold that thought, for you see, there's something to be said about pails.

When I was a kid, I frequently overheard in our local Pennsylvania Dutch dialect that so and so had kicked the bucket. No one seems to know how such ridiculous superstitions evolved, but it was an understood expression someone in the neighborhood had died. Afraid of life squeezed out at a young and tender age, I avoided playing near buckets for fear of tripping against one with a clumsy foot. So when you think about it, milk buckets have lots of character and are hardly considered boring. But that's neither here nor there. This job had to be the most monotonous duty they could possibly have thought up. I mean, who would want to steal Spam! (See Addendum.)

During watch the second day, a towering Navy chief dressed in stiff blue dungarees and a naval shirt came by.

"Take a hike, kid," he said to me.

I thought this address disrespectful. Nonetheless, he wore more stripes than I. Being accustomed by now to taking orders without question, I walked to the end of the building and turned the corner. I spied around the edge and saw him lift the raft. He slid the structure to the side and scratched around like a chicken after grubs.

My mouth dropped open and seemed to be stuck in that position while he pulled a folded tote bag out of his pants' pocket, filled it with several cans of Spam, and replaced the half-empty case back into the cavity before covering it again with the raft. Errand complete, the anonymous officer, bag of Spam cradled under an armpit, strolled off into the opposite direction like this had been a perfectly normal thing to do on an April morning in a naval supply yard five miles from Fort Lawton.

After pushing eyes back into sockets and clamping unhinged jaws back to normal closure, I returned to my post and realized the extent of his pilferage. According to inventory, at least six or seven cases had disappeared from storage shelves. And how Spam ended up in the hole beneath the raft puzzles me to this day. How did it get there? Where was it going? Did he sell Spam on the black market? I imagine even pig meat has illicit value when you come right down to it. Or were his intentions philanthropic, like supporting an impoverished family with a Charles Dickens' Tiny Tim in its midst? An orphanage?

Theft was a reportable offense, of course. But how is a lowly private in the Army going to arrest a chief in the Navy? He would simply say, "That's the way we store Spam in the Navy, sonny boy." No, I wasn't touching that one. Not with a ten-foot oar!

Second last day at Fort Lawton was scheduled off time, an opportunity to peel a small portion of the large apple state, read, call home, or hang out at the PX. Maybe write letters. Before we left home for Fort Dix, high school chum Bob Gehman and I exchanged our girls' names for pen pals. I just finished a letter to his friend Barbara Lutz and started one to Mom when our 1st sergeant strode into the barracks.

He was a stocky, balding man, or so it appeared beneath his cap. A World War II vet probably in his mid-forties. It gave him great pleasure to exert authority by watch-dogging through our hall on meaningless occasions. This time, there seemed a mission.

"A truck will be by shortly to take you to supply where your good corporal will draw sickles for each of you." His voice was nasal, like maybe a clothespin pinched his nose.

There was silence in the room.

"This same truck," he said, "will take you to the officers' quarters off base to cut the unsightly weeds around those buildings and the coal bin."

This time there was an inaudible response, bordering on a collective sigh.

"Any questions?"

Silence.

"Anyone object?"

Silence.

He might as well have asked, is there air. This was just another hare-brained excuse for the Army to be in charge of our lives, defying Uncle Herbert's logic: "You can take a horse to water, but you can't make him drink." It was clear Uncle Herbert had never served in the United States Army.

"Will someone please remind me why I enlisted," complained one of the guys after the sergeant left.

"Yeah, anyway, what were you thinking?"

"That's just the problem, I wasn't."

Disappointed, we cast aside our well-made plans, in some cases some not-so-well-made, while the good corporal signed out sixteen sickles from supply. I played my temporary rank to the hilt and sat up front with the driver, while fifteen unhappy troopers piled into the rear of the closed truck. When we arrived at our designated location, both driver and I jumped off and opened the rear tailgate.

"Okay, you guys. Everybody out! On the double!" I commanded in my best John Wayne voice, half-joking.

The joke was on me. The back of the truck was empty except for a heap of short-handled circular blades. I could only speculate what had happened to my men in the meantime.

One must do what one must do. A gloomy corporal took fourteen sickles and hid them behind the coal bin. I was responsible for these and, with the day going badly enough as it were and these being five or six bucks a piece, I wasn't about to lose sight. The phrase, "I won't do it; it's not my job," is used in my personal code of ethics about as much as the old field shed full of cobwebs is used on our farm. Stupid order or no, there was a job to do. With two blades, one in each hand, I put my nose to the grindstone, all the while mumbling and grumbling about the art of dodging labor by those less inclined.

Afterward, I learned every time the truck stopped at a traffic light or stop sign a couple of guys jumped out, off to shooting pool and drinking beer at the PX. You were right after all, my dear, wise Uncle Herbert. My Army cap goes off to you!

Was it a breach in discipline, those guys taking off like that? After all, an order is an order. Depends on whom you talked to. Let's just say I was accountable. Reporting on them would have simply gotten me into trouble. Besides, were I not the corporal in charge, I probably would have done the same.

On April 18, 1948, a troop ship, measuring nine hundred and twenty feet in length and painted in wartime battleship gray with its name in white on the bow—USS Alexander, waited in the foggy half-light of early morning. As we prepared to board, I glanced upward and saw a line of sailors in dungarees leaning over the railing, watching the loading operation. An officer with a clipboard and pen in hand stood to the left of the gangplank. His roster contained all Army personnel headed overseas, numbering nine hundred sixty-six. We boarded in alphabetical order.

My cousin Shirley had the same surname. Her high school principal reversed the order at commencement, saying she was last throughout twelve years of school, so at this particular time she'd be first to receive a diploma. More than once, well-meaning people said to both of us not to fret about the consistent tail-end position, that The Good Book promises "...the last shall be first, and the first shall be last." Whatever that means neither of us is quite sure. Yet here for the first time ever, I was neither first nor last. I was Number 965. A fellow named Zynn brought up the rear. We wore these individual numbers chalked on our helmets and tagged to our shirts as personal identification for the entire time at sea.

Weighty duffle bags in hand, we filed up the gangplank one by one and on through a turnstile of posts and yellow hemp. There was much pushing and shoving, cussing, too, as heads banged into overhead pipes while we struggled through low hatchways to reach our stuffy compartments below deck. As soon as I deposited my gear in a rack, I fought my way back on top to catch the goings on and wound through heavy deck traffic wheeling trolleys of suitcases and trunks apparently going to the upper deck where several hundred ranking military dependents and their offspring would room. Other work crews were loading and unloading crates and boxes, jamming them into holds through hatches that were quarter the size of the cargo they were jamming in. Out on the dock, yellow tow motors busied themselves with the normal functions of shipping and receiving as they serviced our ship and others lined up in port.

[Here's a curious aside. Using a car, train, or truck as transport, movement of supplies is called "shipment." On a ship? You got it. "Cargo." Go figure!]

At 2:00 p.m., two pebble-sized tugboats straddled the Alexander and nudged this massive hulk of steel toward the Puget Sound and open sea.

My thirty-month tour of active duty had just begun.

The Tour Begins

The sun is like God. You can't look at it.
But without it, you can't look at anything else.
- Ravi Zacharias

L ife at sea was for the most part duller than Pop's old rusty scythe in the rear of the tool shed. To start things off, I suffered a good case of seasickness. I'd never been on an ocean-going vessel before and unused to heaving floors and a jostling horizon. "Pacific" means "calm," though you could've fooled me as nausea rolled over me in waves as large as those slapping against the ship's hull.

It began with my first meal. One look at the chow on my plate, and I didn't feel so good, my stomach churning like a paddle in a boat's wake. I was dumbfounded. Me, sick? Yet there I was, running for the closest head like the best of them. To my utter dismay, other losers occupied the stalls leaving no place to get sick in except the sink. That is where it happened. Being sick and tired of being sick and tired, my appetite and will to live returned after three days aboard.

Time dragged. What made the trip so dull? Little to do, except daily calisthenics, close order drills, and fast sweaty runs on deck. Same old, same old. Once in awhile you stood guard to assure no one fraternized with civilians. Some worked the laundry. Some peeled potatoes. Some played cards. Some watched swabbies swab the deck or paint (they were always painting). Or exchanged scuttlebutt, the Navy's term for unfounded rumor. Or just plain old hung out shooting the bull about home, women, sports, and cars while lingering over cups of potent Navy coffee. Plus, lots of eating.

We chose food cafeteria style and stood at counters to eat, a long line on each side. You held onto the tray for dear life lest the ship pull a sudden table-clearing roll. Else, your tray slid to the end of the counter and dumped its contents on the floor, creating one more horrific mess for sailors to clean up.

Middle class parents in every generation give counsel to offspring on taking food for granted. The saying in my day was: "*Ach*, take all you want, but eat all you take. We can't waste food, you know, not with all those starving children in China."

We were steeped in the Great Depression while I was growing up. But I never knew it. Our kitchen table was a virtual horn of plenty, making my attitude on such logic one of sheer puzzlement. If I didn't clean up the boiled cabbage or crock sauerkraut on my plate, a veggie I wasn't fond of in the first place, how should that impact kids straight down through the earth's axis, the other end of the world? I now stood, heading for the other end of the world, eating boiled cabbage.

On ship we, too, had plenty of grub, enough to feed an army, so-to-speak. I cared less how much I ate or left on my tray. While servings were nothing to write home about, I was no real fuss bud at the feed trough.

But many grumbled about lousy chow. Sometimes peas were hard as bullets. Other times so mushy they labeled it split pea soup. Spaghetti often crunched when you chewed or formed balls of paste that stuck to the roof of your mouth like putty to a stone wall. Yet I would not have known the difference in consistency were it not pointed out. Pasta was rarely found on our German dinner table in my boyhood home.

Eggs were stored two years too long or dehydrated, for goodness sake, and only scrambled—no over easy or sunny side up for dippy bread. Bacon, undercooked or burnt to a crisp, was seldom just right. Though some complained, fried potatoes thick with grease were not distasteful. On the farm, we butchered and dressed, and, of course, ate our own meats and meat byproducts. Though not by today's dietary standards, back then, lots of lard made home fries taste like home fries should.

If any of us were the least concerned, which I don't think we were, the government assured daily menus represented basic food groups to keep troops nourished and healthy. Beans and lentils of every variety filled pots for nutritional value. Often at night, an artillery of BB guns ripped with abandon in a traditional contest exclusive to males for the longest, loudest, or most creative. Bottom line, the Navy's galley compared similarly to the Army's mess hall. Food was food no matter where.

Stateside pranks and antics carried on.   More than once a latecomer to bed found his bunk short-sheeted. Or worse, an itch treatment saturated the bottom sheet. In those days, we used shaving brushes. Long before the word recycle was invented, we recycled worn brushes after new ones were issued. Bristles were cut into hundreds of tiny pieces and scattered on the sheet of an unsuspecting victim. Whenever such mischief occurred, suppressed laughter throughout the dark hall intermingled with cussing that could make even a sailor blush.

Switching combat boots comprised another favorite trick. From outward appearance, all boots were created equal. Every now and then, a surprise morning inspection (not aboard ship) caught two fall guys who discovered one size does not fit all. Stripes were either sewn or glued on shirts. Wearing a shirt where a jokester loosened the ends of the glued-on stripes earned an automatic demerit. Sometimes a guy laid everything out to perfection, went to the shower, came back, donned uniform, and stood ready for muster. The inspector gave a citation—the bad kind—because the "U.S." brass button on his coat lapel was upside down. Such a caper cost a weekend pass.

Mischief and mishap were often interchangeable. Army fatigues were issued in olive drab known as OD. But washed-out ones faded to an even more drab and much preferred shade of green. A bunch of us hung out at the stern one day, chewing the fat.

"Joe! Why don't you tie a rope around those ugly bloomers of yours and hang them off the fantail," teased one of the guys. Salty water and the propeller's turbulent action swished pants back and forth with the same effect of an old ringer washer. When they dried, they were wrinkled, white streaks of salt running through them, but the much desired color was achieved.

"Yeah, anyway. You look like an olive tree at harvest time. We'll even help you!" After a major scuffle, Joe's arms were locked behind while two others pulled down his pants, Joe responding in a language not suitable for readership. One of the guys took a rope from a lifeboat and tied a slipknot around a leg and threw the pants overboard. The rope, like a long thin snake, slithered across the deck and disappeared.

"Hey! At least someone coulda hung on to the dang rope!" said Joe as he watched his pants swish-swash away into the deep blue much to the snorting delight of we onlookers. But Joe was hardly amused. Especially after supply deducted nine bucks from his next pay to provide new issue. Not to mention they were in the original olive drab.

Of course, officers knew about practical jokes and how they occurred. But it comes back to discipline. It was your personal responsibility to be aware of all circumstances at all times of whatever went on around you. If you slipped up, it could cost someone's life. Perhaps your buddy's. Perhaps your own.

A few things were actually enjoyable at sea. One was watching dolphins as they ran the flanks of the ship. They raced side by side, skipped in and out amongst the plentiful waves, dove and leapt into the air, then splashed back into the sea. I was intrigued, too, by slender, long-winged birds that followed us across the Pacific, swooping down now and then to pluck garbage thrown from the ship.

The spectacular sky at dusk was another. On a clear evening, a crimson sun cast its final blessing on the long boring day amidst glowing shades of pink and deep purple before sinking into the west. Or was it east? I couldn't be sure. Like time itself, things became muddled. When we left Seattle, we headed west. Somewhere along the way we lost a day and now neared the Far East. Where that day went exactly, I couldn't tell you. Technically, I didn't exist for twenty-four hours. The good news was they promised we'd gain the day back on return to the States thirty months from then.

While I viewed the sunsets at sea, an expression came to mind:

"Red at night, sailor's delight; Red in morning, sailor takes warning."

Raised two states inland, we substituted "traveler" and used that little ditty for making hay.

I wanted to go top deck for a better ocean view. Officers and their families and dependents were quartered up there in fine staterooms with fine dining halls and facilities I imagined equivalent to those on a luxury cruise liner. But that deck was off limits to ordinary people like me. Guards were posted at the foot of each staircase.

"Get back down here where you belong! You know that deck is off limits," I said when I was on guard and another second-class soldier tried to go up.

"Who says?"

"Orders, man! They have their place, and you have yours. Now get your butt out of here!"

"Okay, you can stick that next floor up your rear end!" The disgruntled vagrant disappeared.

I was only doing my job. But to tell the truth, my attitude was similar and grossly resentful of the discrepancy. What rankled me most was that free-roaming officers moseyed up and down the steps without a smile in my direction, like I was just another imbecilic steel post along their imbecilic way. Now, in looking through a rear view mirror, I understand the Army's wisdom in protecting the many female dependents from such as we. But then, this type of treatment stank as far as I was concerned. We might just as well have been steerage. Thinking hard on it, we were!

On the thirteenth day at sea, the Japanese islands arose in the distance. Shipping and receiving hadn't sent forth a dove. But I guarantee we were just as happy as Noah to see land, remembering the Ark was built by amateurs and our ship, like the Titanic, designed by professionals.

On the afternoon of the following day, our long ocean voyage finally came to an end. Miniature tugboats escorted our massive piece of steel to Yokohama's dockside. Dockworkers rushed to tie her up. We had arrived.

Long before disembarking, all Army personnel assembled into lettered groups according to the section they were assigned. A higher-ranked person, most often a sergeant, managed each group.

"...Group M will form over on the starboard side!" came orders through the P.A. system.

I followed the other thirty-nine men in my group.

"Which is the starboard side?" someone asked me.

"How should I know?" I said. "I'm not in the Navy."

"I think it's the opposite of port side," said another wise guy.

Nothing short of divine intervention, a group of us congregated in one particular area. Letters and numbers were chalked on helmets, and it was doggone conspicuous when S-48 stood in our midst. Vertically challenged, he looked young enough to play dress-up with older shipmates.

"Hey, runt. You don't belong here!" Did he miss the memo?

The kid stared disbelieving at his towering accuser. He coughed impatiently, then removed his helmet, where an ID was scratched across the front, and settled it again.

"Uh, oh. I wonder where 'S' is?" the runt said. He didn't take up much space and stood tippy-toed, surveying the crowded deck through Army issue steel-framed glasses.

"They're probably on the other side of the ship," I said, feeling sorry for the kid. "Why don't you save yourself some time and jump off here and swim over."

Following this organized confusion, we disembarked. I experienced a strange sensation after I left the gangplank and was surprised to discover the relationship between my mind and legs, usually a good one, had broken down. Sea legs, they call it. I was suddenly transported back to Hershey Park's funhouse with its trick mirrors, curvatures, popup monsters, and moving floorboards. My out-of-control mobility, or immobility if you will, compared to stepping off those moving floorboards. At least then, my legs continued forward to stationary ground. Now, they just wanted to stick in the ground like fence posts. I gripped the railing and placed one foot deliberately before the other until I reached the dock. I held still for a moment, loathing to embarrass myself around the others before filling in the line.

After reassembling on dock, we marched four hundred yards to a waiting troop train.

Trains, like everything else I would discover in Japan, were small. In length and width, our car barely stretched to one-half the size of an American one. We laughed and joked about the tight fit for our large bodies and gear appendages. Some men copped out in the overhanging baggage racks for additional room and rest. Mind you, it took a great number of cars and minutes to load nine hundred some giants aboard.

Out on the platform and shoulder high to U.S. Military Police scurried Japanese railroad employees uniformed in black or green. And conductors and porters. All mixed into the throbbing tempo of the railway station. Finally, after huffing and puffing, hissing and chugging, our locomotive moved its tremendous burden forward.

At the railroad crossing, people stood in family groups, watching and waving as we passed by. One adorable little girl dressed in a colorful gown and wooden shoes turned away when I smiled at her. Twins in a backpack about toppled the poor little woman next to her when she had let go of the girl's hand to wave. Men on ricksha paused and looked on in wonderment, as did a few drivers of small cars. We scarcely built up momentum, when the train came to a screeching halt. A flock of Japanese children ran alongside. They huckstered everything from china dolls and trinkets to cheap "Made in Japan" junk abundant since the war in our local Miller's Five & Dime store. (See Addendum.)

"Hey, Joe," mouthed one cute kid, singling me out. He reminded me of a barn cat awaiting handouts when you milked a cow. "I give Japanese money for American," he said this time. "Okay?"

"Okay, then." I reached through the bottom half of the open window, and, after giving him a quarter, retrieved a small fist full of crumbled paper money. The boy examined the coin and broke into a smile as wide as my hometown state. Our smiles matched tooth for tooth. And it did the heart good.

"Do you know what that stuff in your hand is worth?" said a sergeant, observing the exchange.

I hadn't thought about it and, still smiling, shook my head.

He had served in Okinawa during the war and claimed familiarity with Japanese currency.

"Those yen notes are probably worth less than two cents a piece," he said.

I wasn't one to pinch pennies until they screamed, but a quarter was a quarter. Why, that was a whopping month's wage when I was a kid. It paid for a haircut, or a movie with two cups of popcorn, or six selections on the jukebox at Rip Trexler's after the movies. At eighteen, I had an even firmer grasp on finances and realized I'd been taken. I was in this country less than half a day, and I'll be darned if a skinny little pipsqueak didn't con me out of hard earned cash. This was not going to happen again. I closed the smoke-fogged window and sat back, dreaming of being anywhere else in the whole wide world. Another two and a half years to go!

The train, maybe shifting to another track earlier, gave several jerky fits and starts and thrust forward with decided gumption. I sat in silence and surrendered to a rhythm of clickety clack until we pulled into Camp Zama, twenty-five miles away. The camp was an 8th Army replacement depot servicing Army units throughout Japan. I spent two days there, after which twenty-one of us rode in the same car on a train headed for Osaka, home of the 25th Infantry "Lightning" Division.

Japan slid by on the other side of the glass. It was all so new, and I wasn't about to miss a thing. We rolled through the city, then small towns and villages and glimpsed busy little people in ricksha, on bicycles, and on foot. Pigs and chickens scratched around in dirt alleys next to wooden sheds only a wee bit smaller than the small, tidy people dwellings next to them. There were few children. Perhaps they were in school.

Pennsylvania is on the same latitude as this region of Japan. Back home, spring activity, besides milking and the normal care of livestock, included fence repair, preparing machinery for tillage, hauling manure, and spreading lime and fertilizer. Weather permitting, my brothers Leroy and John had already plowed, harrowed, and begun sowing oats and planting corn. (See Addendum.)

Planting went on here as well. Farmers lived in villages dotted throughout the valleys and walked out to rice-terraced hillsides to work the land. Again, as with everything else, fields were small, maybe the size of a house lot in today's suburban America. Barefoot peasants toiled in these little plots, usually women, a mother in loose fitting kimono and conical straw hat that looked like if you pushed down at the peak, it would spin around like a toy top. More often than not, a baby tied to a cloth cradle hung from her shoulders. I wondered what prevented the child from falling head first into shin deep water while the petite woman bent over to part and plant the rice seedlings she had pocketed in her apron.

This experience was like passing through a time warp. How labor intensive their farming methods! At home, we had already progressed from horses to tractors. One of the most exciting days of my life was December 31, 1943. Clarence Seaman from Dauberville delivered our first tractor, a beautiful deep red Farmall H. It cost $1,175.80, Pop complaining he didn't even knock off the eighty cents. It was during the war and had, amazingly so in these rationed times, rubber on the huge steel wheels. It started with a crank. For initiation, my brothers and I hooked up all the sleds we could find and pulled them behind the tractor up the snowy hill. The old man blew his stack when he saw the tire marks. But what was he to do? Take the tractor away from us? No, of course, not; we boys were the ones who did the work. From that day forward, things were easier on the farm. We still worked with horses, but the tractor took top priority. A new era had begun.

Perhaps it wasn't fair to contrast the Japanese to our industrialized agricultural nation. From outward appearance at least, these people seemed prosperous, healthy, and happy.

Later, I witnessed their rural lifestyle up close. While they grew numerous grains and vegetables, rice was the predominant crop in addition to fish. They worked the ground with crude rakes and flooded the land before planting the seedlings. I saw no irrigation pipes. Though down the road, some farmers channeled mountain runoff collected below the village and pumped water back up the mountain to circulate through irrigation streams. At this time, I saw no pumps. For the most part, they diverted water into narrow manmade streams by using a wooden wheel surrounded by cups. The white-clothed, barefoot farmer then worked on this water paddle, while resting his arms on a log frame as he pedaled. The wheel created a nice constant movement of water. The Japanese are petite. You put an American on one of these wheels who weighs forty or fifty pounds more than the average Japanese male, and it throws the wheel completely off balance. One of our guys tried it and made for a good laugh as the wheel spun out and dumped him into the mud.

Oh, yes, the mud. I'd be remiss not mentioning the mud. Even filtered through closed train windows, the stench from foul-smelling rotting goo in the paddies was enough to clean out blocked sinuses once and for all. A far more effective remedy than the aroma one breathed while spring-cleaning standing steer pens at home.

Although most people lived in villages, some lived outside. A house in the country, usually topped by a thatched roof, was often no bigger than a one room living space, maybe 24' x 24' for the entire family. For eating, they squatted on rice straw mats called *tatami* and at night unrolled pads called *futon* for sleeping. A "warm area" was heated by a hot pot placed in the middle of a table. Outside in a lean-to where the actual cooking took place stood a clay charcoal stove (fueled in earlier days by animal dung). It had a hard burnt ground surface and steel plate on top. After the fire reached the required temperature for preparing food, the steel plate was lifted and the cook pot placed over the open hole. The stove, while relatively crude, functioned quite well.

Their most popular dish I found gross and not to my liking, no matter to what sense it tried to appeal. They filled a four to six inch round tin with rice one and a half inches deep topped with a couple of eyeless fish heads and smacked away at this foul concoction with the same dry snappy noises our shep dog back home made munching field finds. I guess it comes back to foods you were raised on. These modest Japanese folk might have grossed out big time on a Pennsylvania Dutch *housefrau's* greasy home-fried potatoes.

Laundering was eco-friendly. Women carried dirty clothes to the closest stream, scrubbed them by hand, and lay them on flat rocks to dry. (I use the adjective "dirty" rather loose. Nothing in Japan was dirty; that is, other than their crude sanitation methods. More on that later.)

For such a small country, Japan exhibits an exceptional variety in surface features. We had gone from a vast coastline and monotonous seascape to an interior of disconnected regional landscapes. As the train snaked inland across the island of Honshu toward the Akaishi Range, we plunged through more rice paddies. Also strip farming. The mini fields were bordered by persimmon trees and looked like colorful squares in a Pennsylvania Dutch patchwork quilt. I couldn't help but compare to what I left behind.

At the start of the 18th century, a mild climate, fertile soil, and the Schuylkill River combined to attract European immigrants to present-day Berks County, my home sweet home in the southeast region of Penn's Woods. Pennsylvania German farms in my youth were moderately sized, numerous, and prosperous-looking. Out buildings were painted fresh white with decorative hex signs on barn fronts and kept in top condition. Fences were trimmed and crops given the utmost in loving care.

Farmers wore many caps. Not only were they tillers of the land and experts in animal husbandry, but also mechanics, meteorologists, carpenters, painters, masons, and the list goes on and on.

We grew a variety in wheat, oats, barley, corn, and hay to sustain dairy herds, poultry, and hogs; plus acres of potatoes and other "truck" vegetables for city huckstering and home cooking. If you starved on the farm, it was only because you were lazy.

Like passing through the American Rockies, I felt a privileged observer of the Creator's marvelous handiwork. I pressed my nose against the window like a child gazing hungrily at cookies and pastries on display in a bake shop. The landscape that filled the horizon was truly amazing, a spectacular vista changing around each bend in the track. One rugged mountain gorge after another appeared. Tumbling snow-fed streams tapered off into gentle lush vegetation. From far away, we spied volcanic peaks above narrow plains and rivers, then sped along shores of sparkling emerald green lakes. Trick photography could not begin to capture the intrinsic beauty I was seeing.

There it was! A panoramic view to top all others! Mr. Adams' geography lessons were not in vain. Though I must admit, the black and white photo of Mt. Fujiyama in my fifth grade textbook did little justice to this eighth world wonder that made me feel so small and insignificant. The volcano's been dormant since 1707 and rises to a head spinning, dizzying height of 12,388 feet to become the highest peak in Japan.

The sky was cloudless that day, a most unusual event I later realized. On top of the majestic snow-capped cone hovered in delicate balance an eye-blinding early afternoon sun. For a moment, it looked as if with a slight push from behind, the brilliant solar star might coast down the sloping side of the mountain, directly into Lake Kawaguchi below. Before I had time to imagine the consequence of such a supernatural phenomenon, Fuji disappeared from sight.

At dusk, our train dragged wearily into Osaka Railroad Station. An Army corporal met us, and we marched to a waiting troop truck for a short ride to the Gosho Building. This building served as the 25th Infantry Division's replacement depot. We had missed both our noon and evening meals, and by now the four-letter F word was foremost in everyone's mind. FOOD. Nine at night, they led us to a small mess hall where we eagerly crowded the serving tables like pigs at the trough, only to receive cold cuts on dry bread and warm bitter coffee. Disappointing as ants must feel at a picnic on a rainy day!

After our poor excuse for a meal, they issued new assignments. Many of the guys were hours from their final destination, some as far as Nagoya where they joined the 25th Division Artillery. I was trained and classified as an infantry rifleman. Now I found myself assigned to the pistol-toting 25th Military Police Company right there in Osaka, three blocks from the Gosho.

An MP came by in a jeep and escorted me to Military Police Headquarters. He filled his crisp, starched uniform snugly. The light khaki cloth accentuated polished brass insignia, service ribbons, unit badge, whistles and chains, and catchy shoulder patches. His side arms were secured with white braided lanyard and his hair was cut so short none of it showed beneath the rim of his hat that was secured by a white cellophane strap tucked neatly below his tight chin. This stuck-up young man made quite a pompous image that was soon to be me!

A New Life Begins

You cannot strengthen the weak by weakening the strong.
You cannot build character and courage by taking
away man's initiative and independence.
You cannot help men permanently by doing for them what
they could and should do for themselves.
                              - President Abraham Lincoln

I spent the next two weeks in class concerning respective duties and familiarization of weapons, vehicles, and radio equipment used by the military police. This was a real spit and polish outfit. During inspection, shoes sparkled and mirrored to such a high gloss I could've used them to comb my hair that, by the way, was now sprouting length to its roots. Trousers and shirts required sharp, distinct creases. Snow-white gloves and polished brass were mandatory. They issued two additional shirts and trousers because of constant inspection.

I pulled my first duty at the beginning of the third week. Guard posts rotated, meaning you didn't return to the same post for at least two weeks. One week was walk patrol. No stopping, no sitting, no loitering for three hour stretches. Boring, boring, boring! This duty was followed by one week of roving patrol in a jeep that fared a little better. Swing shifts consisted of six hours on, eighteen off. This routine continued six days, then off seventy-two hours. The same schedule repeated.

Animals roam in packs and herds, some in pairs. Few are loners. Man overwhelmingly belongs to the former group for there is something unnatural about being alone. Loneliness was a constant ache. I became so bored and lonely and frustrated after a month, I was ready to throw in the towel. I left a pretty girl behind, gave up the farm and a decent paying job as a bricktosser at the brickyard, for this? Obviously, the brain of a cauliflower. Yet one needs to keep on keeping on. No longer involvement on my part, it was total commitment.

My cousin taught me the difference. She told of the time the minister and his wife were coming for breakfast, and the animals decided to participate. The cow said she'd contribute rich creamy milk, and the hens promised their finest eggs. Dobbin offered to fetch the pair from town and bring them to the farm. The pig stood off to the side while the negotiating went on and said not a word, until Bossie suggested she provide the bacon or ham and sausage.

"Yeah, sure," Miss Piggy complained. "You guys are willing to be involved, but, with me, it's total commitment!"

Stick a fork in me; I'm done.

One day while on roving patrol, I spotted the 25th Division's recruiting office and decided the next off-shift I'd pay them a visit. After all, isn't it the squeaky wheel that gets the oil? Patience is not something I do particularly well. I dropped by the following day.

The office was crowded with gray file cabinets, each with folders piled high on top. They took up half the room. In the other half was a roll-away drop-leaf table housing two Royal typewriters—one opened with a black ribbon dangling down its side, a telephone and two or three other serious looking gadgets I couldn't readily identify. Opposite stood a moderately sized metal desk and an old wooden swivel chair in which sat a cigar-chomping sergeant who surely served in the Army decades before a gleam appeared in my parents' eyes. He was preoccupied with papers behind an over-flowing in-box.

I stood, waiting impatiently to be acknowledged. The day was warming up and the room was poorly ventilated. I was hot and suddenly felt a little foolish having come here impulsively. Without looking up, the sergeant mumbled something and waved me to a straight-back chair in the corner where soon all the cares of the Army left me.

First item on the agenda upon returning home was finishing high school. Then I'd learn a trade so that after the service I could accomplish more than milking cows twice a day or tossing bricks. Perhaps Joan and I would marry and raise a batch of kids. During the two hours, or was it six or seven, and four packs of cigarettes while waiting for the sergeant to acknowledge me, I had each one of the kids' futures etched in stone. Including shipping one off to ministry.

"Ministry? I don't want to become an old preacher," says my reluctant eighteen-year old.

"Why not?" I say. "That's a good life."

"Sure!" he says. "I can dunk people in the bathtub and marry silly people while their silly mothers watch and cry!"

"Now wait a minute!" says I. "There's a lot more to being a minister than that. Why it's a great honor. Out of all the cousins, Grempop Zweizig, whose first name I proudly carry in the middle, chose ME to become a minister!"

"Grempop Zweizig? He was old! What did he know!"

"Listen, young man! He may have been old and worn out and took his teeth out on occasion, but there was much wisdom from experience that could probably put you in your place when you talk that way about your elders."

"Sorry, Dad. It's just that I don't want to be a minister. Besides, you didn't want to either or you would have."

"You're right," I say. "But I often think I should've listened to him." *You know, coulda, woulda, shoulda.*

"That was you, not me," he argues. "I'm going to join the Army and become a brave soldier just like you were."

Brave? Little does he know I cut and ran to the States to escape the rigors of military life as it were.

"Well, what's YOUR problem?" the sergeant growled, interrupting my business forecast.

I rose from the hard seat and plowed through a thicket of gray smoke toward his crowded desk. I hadn't given forethought to role-play before entering and was unprepared for the long wait and now rude reception. Somehow I mustered the courage and pressed on, remembering the answer to any unasked question is always no.

"Sir I wish to extend my enlistment three years and return to the States if that is possible Sir," I said expectantly in one quick breath. My voice sounded natural enough, to my own ears at least. But my toes curled, and my feet pushed deep into their shoes like added weights on a scale.

The shriveled old pickle's left eyebrow shot upward. It was quite obvious he regarded me merely as an ink spill on his scattered papers. He tucked his chin deeper into the pillow of fat that was his neck and said,

"Return where? The States?" He leaned back and puffed on his cigar, adding more carbon to the already stinky smoke-pitted room.

"Yes, Sir. That's right, Sir, the States." *You know, the United States of America states—those states!*

The sergeant's scowl changed to a smile that bordered on a smug when he learned I was in Japan only six weeks. He chewed on his cigar, settled back in his squeaky chair, and laced chubby fingers over his chubby chest.

"Hey, captain," he yelled across the office. "I got a green one out here!"

I wanted to spit on the only spare spot of gray metal visible on the sergeant's desk.

"Is that so!" came a grating voice from the next room. His beefy gut arrived around the corner several moments before the chassis appeared.

The captain, whose name has long since evaporated from my memory, was built like Humpty Dumpty, and thinning black hair streaked in white topped his egg-shaped Humpty Dumpty face. He eyeballed me for five minutes and grimaced, exposing two chipped, tobacco-stained teeth holding a short wooden pipe in place. He snorted derisively and seemed to find all of this humorous as the two of them debated my future as if I weren't even present. I bristled at being shunted aside in so off-handed a manner while they both made a mockery of my situation. *Oh, how I hate it when people make a mockery of someone's personal problem!*

"Permission denied!" croaked the old sergeant finally, clearly pleased to inform me so. He rubbed his heavy jowls, then added,

"Get a girl and get laid, and I guarantee a month from now you'll be back in here to re-enlist for another three years." He ground out his cigar in an over-flowing ash tray on his desk and flipped his hand in a dismissive gesture, like brushing a crumb from the table. Then he picked up a few papers the way figures of higher authority learn to do to communicate the meeting is over.

You jerk, you...(I've applied the rubber end of the pencil to my extended thoughts.) Trained to respect those in authority no matter what, I snapped to attention, rendered a proper salute, and did an about face. There are knuckleheads and then there are knuckleheads, I concluded.

"It'll be for Japan again next time," threatened the sergeant's words that caught up with me from behind as I mentally slammed the front door.

So much for soaring hopes and crushing disappointments. I don't think God ever had a bad day. But if He did, I'd bet dollars to donuts Osaka recruitment office staff would be Exhibit A!

I discovered Yours Truly was not the only fly wanting to get off the sticky flypaper. Others suffered from the same disability—a need for coaxing to become a buddy. There were some who took introverts like myself and lifted with mild success the baggage we carried from sheltered childhoods. Like a southpaw living in a right-handed world, I adjusted and became more at ease outside my comfort zone. Loneliness gradually faded.

Getting more into my job helped, too, and I became more confident. I did everything by the book and observed all the rules. Well, more or less, sort of.

On one memorable occasion, a burly, brawny, strapping fella from Springfield, Ohio named Fastnacht and I were sent to Skimi Warehouse where we patrolled a half-dozen buildings from the outside.

"Next time you buy!" I said to Fastnacht when we ran into one another the third time. This was not supposed to happen according to routes mapped out.

"How 'bout we take a break from this drag and play a little shot putt," he suggested on one of these erroneous meetings.

"That's not a good idea," I said. "It's a great one!" I was not averse to breaking the rules if a more fun alternative presented itself.

We checked the immediate grounds and found a couple of stones the size of a steel ball. A dead tree limb with a knobby crook at one end functioned sufficiently to draw a starting line in the spotty grass.

Fasnacht looked down at me from his gigantic athletic frame that dwarfed me by two feet and a hundred and fifty pounds. He was as long as a side of beef with a sack of potatoes thrown in.

"You first," he said. A champion shot putter back in high school, he was giving me the advantage. I didn't do bad considering. Still, his stone far surpassed mine. And again, and again, until he complained his finger hurt. From squeezing and heaving the stone, the cheap Japanese ring he wore collapsed and pinched the circulation to the point where it even discolored his skin. Combining our might, we could not reshape or remove the damaged ring.

"You look like death warmed over, Buddy," said I.

"Gee, thanks for the compliment," said he, on the verge of passing out. "Maybe you better call a medic."

We were six miles away with only a field phone between us and civilization.

"Hello? Hello?" I called into the crackling headset.

No answer; only squawks of static. They were probably screwing off at the other end just like we were. I tried again,

"Hello...Hello...Hello!"

After my fifth attempt, our six-hour shift replacements came by and rushed my partner to the closest hospital where they sawed off the ring. It's my understanding Private First Class Fastnacht and his nicotine-stained finger survived this unpleasant ordeal. I've often been curious how he explained the incident. Truth be known, they would have incriminated me as well. But soldiers rarely ratted on one another. There were no repercussions.

Best MP duty was roving patrol. This was Occupied Japan, and everywhere were symbols of the occupation: separate restaurants, waiting rooms, drinking establishments, special occupation force trains, etcetera. Also, numerous houses of prostitution and lots of hookers on the streets. We checked VD cards when they frequented a cabaret where servicemen hung out. If these *pan pan* girls, as they were labeled, had checkups within the past thirty days and their cards so indicated, they were okay. If card times expired, we loaded the girls in the jeep and took them to the Tennojui Hospital for an exam and card update. (See Addendum.)

I recall many a time on the way to the hospital having a Japanese policeman in the rear of the jeep seated between young girls with hormones on fire. All things considered, some of our weaker cops back in the States might have, I suspect, yielded to the age-old temptation, much like a stallion in a corral of fillies in heat. But here things were different. No horse play. Japanese authorities were strict disciplinarians and doubtful a bad cop amongst them.

Jurisdiction issued new cards every three months, but some of the girls managed updates through unauthorized dealers. In any event, it was obvious the existing system wasn't working. The VD count escalated upwards by eight percent since U.S. military occupation.

(Today, patronizing a house of ill repute while in the military is a punishable offense. Perhaps it was back then as well, but never enforced. I don't know.)

Don't confuse these gals of the night with their high society counterpart, the geisha—those exotic playthings for the rich and famous. To do so compares a moth to a butterfly. Girls we contended with on the streets of Japan dressed in American-style clothes and spike heels and trimmed their lips and cheeks bright red to impress young GIs. Geisha wear special makeup, extravagant kimono, and hair-do's befitting a queen. She's a cultured Japanese hostess, a moving work of art, trained in entertaining rich and powerful men by dance, song, and clever conversation.

An apprenticed geisha is recruited at a tender age, maybe as early as six or seven, and often against her choice (at least at the time of this story) as in "kidnapped" or "sold." After abduction, the girl is raised and mentored in a geisha house, and, similar to a butterfly coming out of the cocoon, goes through a gradual evolution process until prepared for debut into appropriate society. Male connections are made through teahouses attended within her district. Revenue from this nightly entertainment is then split with the house where she resides.

A geisha's life becomes a total commitment to the profession. No one-night stands, no dates, no falling in love, no marriage, no children. What is permitted is sharing an apartment with a *danna* (keeper) while he's in town. His support becomes her largest source of income. Such suitors run the gamut from corporate executives and high-ranking military brass of whatever nation to officials of state like princes, kings, and presidents.

This lifestyle of the geisha is highly respected within Japanese society. The lowly American GI could never afford a geisha, and I'd venture to say the average has never and will never see one. But in the unlikely event a geisha is approached by a soldier, she ignores him and shuffles right on by.

Girls at the Kabuki cabaret fell somewhere in between the hookers on the street and the sophisticated Geisha. They were dance hall girls who were legitimately employed by the cabaret for legitimate entertainment. I remember one incident, however, when a few cocky MPs harassed a couple of these girls and made them undress, then forced them into sexual overtures. It's called rape in civilian society. I reported this to my captain. At first he didn't react, then I threatened to go to the inspector general. The cabaret was closed for four days but life went on as usual after that.

Worst duty was stockade patrol. This entailed walking six hours along a thirty-six inch planked footpath on top of a fence the height of the Great Wall of China. Here, you always carried a loaded carbine. You took lots of harassment from prisoners in the yard below, a place I would never have wanted to find myself. Bent figures drifted aimlessly in the open area. Others propped themselves up against the building, and a few sat in small clusters on benches, talking. No one moved fast in prison.

"Hey, what's the weather like up there?" said one particular dude, trekking along from the inside.

"Same as down there, hot," I returned. It was mid-August, and my starched long-sleeved shirt was stifling.

"Where're you from, boy?" The man appeared much older than I. And bored. I heard when the stockade door closes, there's nothing left but all the time in the world.

"Back home," I said, keeping my answer short and curt on purpose. Actually, we were not allowed to converse with inmates.

"Any ammo in that gun?" he asked.

"What do you think?"

"Prove it! Shoot up in the air and stir up a little excitement around this place. Things are getting pretty dull."

I ignored him, and, after a while, noticed he gave up on his little game and disappeared.

Offenses deserving incarceration ranged from black market activity, maybe GIs assaulting one another or Japanese nationals, or typical state-side crimes such as robbery, murder, rape to maybe more minor infractions like sleeping on guard duty. For the latter reason, like it or not, I accepted guard duty with major sincerity. (See Addendum.)

On occasion, I served graveyard shift, like the night of September 12, 1948. I was on guard duty at the 25th Division Headquarters in Osaka from midnight to 0600 hours.

(Note here I'm making the transition from American timekeeping to a universal system, one adopted by the United States Armed Forces. Since at this point in my career, I now breathed, thought, and acted as a U.S. serviceman, I shall now write as such.)

Duty was easy. It required sitting at a desk in the lobby of a one-time modest Japanese hotel. If military officers came by during the night, it was my responsibility to assign temporary sleeping quarters. These were in the Headquarters building itself or in the Gas building across the street and down a half block. Two MPs walked guard on the sidewalk, while, on this night, I served inside.

There was never much activity this time of night, making it difficult at best to stay alert. Fighting sleep, I stared at the wall clock across the room and watched the pendulum swing back and forth and back and forth. My head nodded once and snapped back up. After rattling it a few times, the grogginess shook out. I was back in basic training, realizing how this might be the most important practice of all, staying awake, keeping watch. My life might depend upon it.

Later, I dug myself into foxholes at night, reading the dark horizon, waiting for the first footfall, a snapped twig, a misstep in the creek running below. But on one particular night, the enemy was more clever than that. The northern insurgents used the ridge that the captain claimed was safe and clear, and, by the time the first flare hit the sky, the enemy troops were already on our platoon, tossing mortars, shooting up the patchy earth around us. Me and my buddies, we fought for our lives…

The clock struck one, and my head snapped back up from my chest. Those battles were down the road a stretch. I hadn't a clue I'd even be involved in one, much less a fight for my life. No one did. What the hay, there wasn't even a war to fight! The last world war ended all that. For now…

Sometime between 0100 and 0200, someone tapped me on the shoulder. I noticed through a haze this same someone picked up the phone receiver from my desk. I jumped up to see a full colonel calling my duty officer to report to division headquarters at once.

I snapped to attention and saluted, my face heating up like a floodlight was turned on and my heart pounding against my rib cage so loudly I was afraid they could hear it. I waited, hoping beyond hope the floor would open beneath and swallow me whole.

Captain McMullen walked into the lobby minutes later with another MP. A formal inquisition began.

"Your name!"

My name?

"I'm …." I drew a blank.

"Soldier! Your name, rank, and serial number!"

"Private First Class Walter Zweizig, 1 2 3 4…."

I barely recognized my own voice, what with the cords in my neck straining against the stiff collar of my shirt. It was like a third person had entered our dialogue. I could feel huge wet circles forming under my arms and beads of perspiration popping out above my upper lip. Oddly enough, I noticed a cigarette neglected in the ashtray on the desk where I'd been sleeping had burnt down to a tiny stub.

Questions went on ad nauseam. I don't remember what they

were exactly, but it was a long list. Before asking what my favorite top ten movie flicks were before entering the service, McMullen said with a scowl,

"What happened at your guard post earlier this evening?"

How should I know? I was sleeping! Well, of course, I didn't say that. Instead, I cooperated throughout the entire ritual, not wanting to believe where this was leading. Not my finest hour.

The session concluded with firing the biggest bullet in the gun, the riot act.

"Do you read me?" he said when he finished, his hard stare returning to my face and remaining there.

I do. Loud and clear.

"Sir, Yes, Sir!" I managed to say.

My hands trembled as I stood at attention for what seemed an eternity. Humbled beyond belief, I felt no taller than a shelled peanut when it stands on end. There was no getting out of this one.

"That is all!"

They ordered me to return to quarters where I sulked in self-pity, my heavy heart sinking as low as the setting Japanese sun. My world had suddenly turned upside down and inside out. At least an eight on the Richter scale. Needless to say, I spent the night in bed without the least bit of drowsiness.

Next day, they restricted me to the building and charged me with: SLEEPING ON GUARD DUTY. The words were chilling. This was not at all a minor infraction I soon found out. They processed the paperwork to try me under a Special Courts Martial which meant six months in the slammer with loss of pay and allowances. And, oh, no, reduced to private!

A month before my world came unglued, I was re-promoted to private first class. There seemed something fatal about the title private first class. Good grief, considering the speed bumps I might still encounter, this rank could remain mine forever. What a mess! I pulled stockade guard duty often enough to know it was no Hershey Park picnic inside. Yet in due respect, their actions rationalized the old military adage drummed into our stubbly heads, "If you can't take orders, you can't give them!" My grim experience had shaped another brilliant nugget of wisdom for the future.

Of course, I was not without counsel. They assigned 1st Lieutenant Marvin Hess from the Judge Advocate section to prepare for the upcoming trial, an interim period similar to that of a steer awaiting the axe. We arranged a get-together three days before the scheduled court appearance. I am well over seventy at this writing, but I do believe the short walk to the lieutenant's office that particular morning was the longest I ever made.

A fair-skinned, slim man in his early forties with a lined, rather serious, yet kindly patient face sat behind a well-organized desk. He appeared to be writing notes in the margin of a typewritten report. After a minute or two, he finished and looked up.

"At ease, soldier," he said and, without rising, invited me to have a seat.

He began our interview with a long list of routine questions.

"Describe the nature of the charges against you," he said after coming to the third page of a multi-paged form.

I did my best, relieved to hear my own words strong for the rest of my body was weak and felt like a big sponge.

The lawyer listened intently to my answers. At the finish, he twirled his pencil thoughtfully, leaned back in the chair that was silhouetted by yellow sunlight coming through the unshaded window, when all of a sudden he shifted forward again and flipped through the personnel file in front of him.

"I believe this is your first offense," he said, not as a question, rather a statement. He took off his glasses and pinched the bridge of his nose. As if maybe fighting off a headache, I feared.

"Yes, Sir," I answered dutifully. I was grateful that falling asleep at the furnace didn't count. I even prayed some, begging for mercy. It came.

"Because this is your first offense, I hope to plead clemency and convince them to drop the charges."

"How's that, Sir?" I asked, with attached hopefulness. I silently cleared my throat and swallowed what little saliva was left in my mouth.

"Are you willing to extend your enlistment?"

I had several replies, none of which included the word yes. What came out of my mouth was,

"Yes, Sir!"

He nodded.

I smiled.

The lieutenant produced a briar pipe from a top drawer and cradled the bowl, packing it tight with tobacco from a pouch of Standard Clippings. There was a long pause while he lit the pipe and drew deeply on it until the bowl glowed red. He puffed a few times then inhaled a lungful of smoke. Superior officers sit first and stand first. He stood and came around the desk. Assuming our visit was terminated, I stood, too. He deposited the match in a clean china ashtray on the left side of his shiny black metal desk and then parked himself on the corner.

Oops.

"There's something else," he said, looking up into my face.

"Sir?" That's the military way of responding to a superior officer without responding.

"Are you willing to transfer to the infantry?" he said, at the same time filling the air with a sweet-smelling cloud of smoke.

Quick on my feet, it took zero time to reply.

"Yes, Sir!" The only thing holding me to the floor was gravity.

You think it can't get any better, and it does. I wasn't busted to private, thank God. In addition, they removed from my record any mention of the offense. As for the matter of extending enlistment, I knew now what the Oriental expression "save face" meant. We called it "eating crow" at home which is what I did on October 4th revisiting the bald-headed, wrinkled old sergeant in the recruitment office. He sat in his groaning swivel chair and was busy lighting up another one of his stinky cigars. An electric floor fan stirred the foul smoke into the air.

Be nice, I cautioned myself.

"I wish to extend my enlistment, Sir," I heard myself say, mustering as much enthusiasm as possible, all the while fighting a prickle of inner resentment. The ink wasn't dry on my enlistment papers, and here I was on my knees before this hateful person, requesting an extension.

"What did I tell you!" he said, making fun of me in that I-told-you-so tone of voice jerks of his type have.

It was clear he had no idea my request was due to a scheduled court martial for, pardon the time-worn expression, "caught off guard." Bless his cold and steely heart, for no telling what he would've done with that information were it known.

It's interesting to note that ten months prior I enlisted for a three-year tour of duty. Now, October of 1948, I still had three more years and two months to serve. The thought left me numb. Good or bad, and as surely as God is in good and evil is in Devil, I had a much longer row to hoe than originally anticipated. Let's just say the whole incident poured ice water on my overall passion. In particular, my attitude from this point forward would not be totally charitable toward the military police. Yet for the present, I excused the matter as a Dutchman would say,

"Ach, so gaetes yuo alsamol."

We were told at boot camp, that sometimes we fail so we can succeed later. I would get on with things.

They delivered me the following day to the 27th Infantry Regiment, the well-known presidential award winning "Wolfhounds," no less! A new kind of life was about to begin.

First Assignment as a New Corporal

Ours to Fight for...
   Freedom of Speech, Freedom of Worship
   Freedom from Want, Freedom from Fear
                  - WWII Poster Slogan

Sure a door closed, but God opened a window, and the window had a better view. The infantry was more than a job. It was a calling, the stuff dreams are made of, the way I envisioned the Army in the first place. It certainly put a new spring in my step. I was happy. Make that exhilarated. No time for boredom. Nor homesickness. Life was busy and couldn't get much better.

Use and practice with individual and crew-served weapons became a weekly undertaking. Two weeks out of every month were spent in the field with constant maneuvers between regimental units. In between were marching endurance tests. You never walked. You marched. True infantry style. Twenty miles a shot at a hundred and twenty steps per minute: Left pace, Forward march, Route step.... During bitter cold months, instructive classroom study filled in.

Honest hard work and gritty determination are an endangered species in the modern world. But for those rooted in the German culture, these characteristics create success. A Pennsylvania Dutchman, in my day at least, completed a job application as follows:

1. How do you consider Salary?
   ( ) Not Important
   (X) Somewhat Important
   ( ) Very Important

2. How do you consider Benefits?
   ( ) Not Important
   (X) Somewhat Important
   ( ) Very Important

3. How do you consider Hard Work?
   ( ) Not Important
   ( ) Somewhat Important
   (X) Very Important

4. How do you consider Honesty amongst you, your co-workers and employer?
   ( ) Not Important
   ( ) Somewhat Important
   (X) Very Important

5. How do you consider....

I hoped not to be a departure from the common rule and soon earned the reputation for crossing t's and dotting i's and accomplishing these feats in record time. Today, we live in a dog-eat-dog world, clawing our way to the corporate top until we reach our level of incompetence. In the military, promotions are usually well deserved. Granted, I blew it along the way, just like a young fledgling learning to fly. But this time I got it right. Promotion from private first class came within three months of transfer.

In '49, after winter lost its grip to spring and the Japanese cherry blossoms reached full bloom, the new corporal, all full of himself, received his first serious assignment. I'd lead a squad of men to a rifle range in the basement of a large castle near Osaka. (A squad is part of a platoon and comprises six to twelve men. There are four squads to a company and three line companies to a battalion, plus one service company for support.) Our outfit trained at this facility the previous day for a few hours of pistol and carbine firing, a routine exercise to practice shooting and sighting so, should that unfortunate day arrive, we'd hit the enemy target and escape with our lives. Another group used the range after us without cleaning up.

"…get your squad down there, and do a first rate job of putting the place in order," directed my CO. He did not want his unit embarrassed by complaints from the next unit using this indoor rifle range.

"Yes, Sir!" I was on top of it.

We completed our mission in short order. Before returning to base, we were drawn to the Roof Garden, the 25th Infantry Division's main commissary located in an eight story building in downtown Osaka.

Large potted palm trees gave the place a relaxed and pleasant, almost tropical atmosphere, always a favored setting for servicemen of outlying units coming to the city. Like the military's front porch. The snack bar sold lip-smacking varieties of potato chips, hot dogs, ice cream, and candy bars not available back on base. Here we enjoyed food in an inviting environment, viewed the city, and watched ships move in and out of Osaka Bay.

"Just think, Ziggy," my best buddy Baker said one time while we drank coffee and looked over the waterfront. "In two years, we'll be aboard one of those mamas and on our way home."

Home? Not now. Military life as it existed at this moment was a dream come true. Even in my pre-teens, I wanted to become a soldier.

World War II, a popular war, was in full swing while I was growing up. Men enlisted or were drafted. Manufacturing plants switched to war production and flew the "E" flag issued by the Army and Navy for participation in the war effort. Stay-at-home moms no longer stayed at home but moved into the workplace next to Rosie the Riveter. Everyone, regardless of sex or creed, young or old, farm or city dweller, felt the impact of the war and pitched in fervently. All to the rallying cause, "Remember Pearl Harbor!"

In Berks County where I lived (and still do), industry turned out parachutes, military vehicles, and parts for ships and guns. The numerous textile and knitting mills in the area provided clothing for the Armed Services. On the home front, store-bought clothing was not an option. The war slogan was:

"Use it up, wear it out, make it do, or do without!"

BUY WAR BOND ads supporting the war were posted everywhere. "America needs your money—Buy defense bonds!" Here's one by Plymouth Division of Chrysler Corporation:

> The mightiest weapon of war
> Marches on two legs
> Down the road to Tokyo and Berlin.
> This is our fighting man,
> Winner of battles, shaper of tomorrow.
> Guns, tanks, bombers, fighter planes
> Are but tools of this master weapon.
> To give him the best tools possible
> Is today's one aim of Plymouth production.
>
> BUY WAR BONDS!......To have and to hold.

You needed stamps for gas. For some, this meant cars on cinder blocks for the duration of the war. Butcher shop meat, butter, and coffee were also rationed. So was sugar. (Beekeeper specialists and their beehives were transported to Florida's citrus groves to provide sugar for the troops.) Tires were rationed, if you could get them at all. Uncle Herbert tried in vain to buy rubber tires to replace steel wheel treads on his Allis Chalmers so he could access two of his fields from the macadam road. Driving a tractor on the macadam with steel wheel treads was illegal, but authorities now looked the other way. All acreage was required one way or another to help supply the troops. Most every backyard was dug up in towns, cities, and farms across America and victory gardens planted there, making commercial foods more available for men and women on active duty.

Schools also became involved. Military exploits were in all the library magazines. With no TV or computer distractions then, I read every one. Authorities gave lectures in assembly. Teachers charted activities on the globe for students to follow. Schools facilitated the collection of burlap bags filled with milkweed pods for use in life preservers; scrap paper and metal for recycling. We kids saved aluminum foil from gum wrappers and daddies' cigarette packs. Students selected pen pals. My cousins Marie and Shirley wrote letters to families in war-torn Greece and sent care packages of food and clothing as the war raged on. (See Addendum.)

The public was interested in the latest developments of the war. Nine o'clock at night found every ear pasted to the parlor Philco for Gabriel Heater's latest news. Movie theatres preceded main features with black and white newsreels of the war in progress. They showed speeches from desks of great statesmen like Roosevelt and Churchill and displayed chilling scenes of Nazis in gleaming black jackboots, goose-stepping across the screen. Land mines and torpedoes exploded before one's very eyes. The public really admired the courageous achievement of war correspondents risking their lives to photograph and report events, freezing time in history for folks back home to see. (See Addendum.)

Fascinated by all this activity, I could hardly wait to be one of those men in uniform, coveting only the day to join up. But I digress.

Determined not to let things get out of hand with my important assignment, I left the snack bar with my men in reasonable time to return to the base twelve miles away. Baker drove our deuce and a half, and, within ten minutes, pulled onto a crossroad near the edge of town, heading out into the country. In the visible distance wobbled a honeywagon. A carry-over from 12th century Japan, this four wheel oxen-drawn cart collected human waste in an enclosed box with several lids on top and hauled the cargo to gardens and rice paddies for fertilizing crops. (See Addendum.)

"Are you ready for some outhouse humor?" I said to Baker as we were nonchalantly driving along.

"I'm all ears."

"Do you know why they call that stuff shit?"

"Because it stinks!" Baker said, laughing. My best buddy Baker from the Hoosier State could always be counted on for an apt reply.

"That, too, but there's another reason," I said. As a youngster, when I wasn't doing chores, or even sometimes during them, my nose often stuck inside a book. I remembered a nonsense article I read and related it to Baker.

"During the 16th and 17th centuries, most goods were moved by ship from one land place to another, and large shipments of manure were common. It was a time before commercial chemical fertilizer we know today."

"Well, whadaya know," Baker said flippantly and finished with a whistle but was obviously unimpressed. "That it?"

"There's more." I didn't know much about physics beyond the fact that Einstein never wore socks, but I did know from personal experience on the farm that dry manure weighed lots less than when it was wet. I continued sharing my wisdom.

"When seawater hit the bundles that were stored below deck, the cargo became heavier, and it fermented and created methane gas. The first time someone came below at night with a lantern, well, guess what? BOOM!"

"Cripes, Pal! If you had half a brain you'd be dangerous. So, what's your point?" asked Baker, closing in on the wagon. He flicked an ash out the open window, took another drag, and what was left of the cigarette followed.

"Several ships were destroyed before they realized the cause. After that, they stamped bundles of manure with the label S.H.I.T."

"So?"

"That meant 'Ship High in Transit' to the sailors." I turned to Baker to catch his reaction. There was none. Mark Twain was probably right when he said that the world is full of highly informed ignoramuses. I was obviously one of them. I continued. "So, what's my point? That's just it, there is no point—only an explanation."

"How stupid of me. All along I thought it was a pool hall term."

"Hey, y'all see that honey dipper?" drawled the big bony private from the back. Bailey was from Alabama. "Get alongside and blow your horn. I believe he's half asleep."

The wagon containing S.H.I.T. crawled along at the speed of a caterpillar on a turnpike. The guys heckled and joked, and Baker har-de-har-harred in return, drifting closer on a dare.

"Don't get too close," I cautioned, trying to maintain some control over the situation. After all, it was I who was still in charge of this mission.

"I'm working on it." He laughed as if he had just said something witty.

"Careful, you'll hit him!" interrupted a startled voice. It was mine.

Baker honked his horn and said the S word, majorly and enthusiastically focused as Murphy's Law took over. The rear wheel of our truck had caught the hub of the wooden wagon wheel, and things went really crazy after that. The axel broke and spun the rear around toward us just as our truck body caught the box and ripped it open. The left rear wheel functioned like our manure spreader on the farm, throwing you-know-what at least fifty feet in every direction. In case you might be snacking or something, I'll spare the graphic details. But believe me when I say, the intestinal output of livestock is relatively mild compared to this crap that was in our faces, our hair, on our clothes, all over the inside of the cab and back of the truck. On the windshield. Even on engine parts hidden intact beneath the hood.

The driver came back to survey the situation and made a long complaint in Japanese.

"So solly," was all I managed to say in return to the disgruntled little man.

Cleaning up was as difficult as trying to screen out dust with chicken wire. It took seven of us more than three hours. When you do the math, that's twenty-one man hours, plus. Yet in spite of our toil, it still smelled like an over-used outhouse. No, the words "overused outhouse" do not stretch far enough. It was the foulest smelling smell one could possibly ever smell!

We relegated Stinky to the far side of the motor pool parking lot. Baker was told in no uncertain terms it was his truck and ONLY his to drive until it smelled decent again, which if my aging memory serves me correctly was just shy of all eternity. Much like the enterprising days of trapping. Even a one-skunk night, despite much soap, water, and clean clothes, condemned the poor trapper to quarantined living space indefinitely. I know! I was that person!

Of course, the motor sergeant reported the incident to the motor officer who, in turn, reported to the orderly room. Captain Bond was the small intestine of our outfit. As commanding officer, everything passed through him. The captain relied upon the 1st sergeant to manage these types of problems. He was Sergeant Ferrino who had joined the American Army way back when it was founded in 1775. Ferrino, almost five and a half feet tall with closely cropped curly black hair and a Roman-nosed profile, had a nice easy smile. As I fidgeted outside their door, I heard the captain's voice speak to his subordinate, and my name was in it.

"...You handle this matter with Zweizig!"

The door opened.

"Corporal Walter Zweizig!" began the unsmiling Sergeant Ferrino.

I hate it when they say your full name. Like Mom, when she addressed me as Walter Mahlon, I knew I was in for it. There was more coming. I braced myself.

"Who was in command here?" said Ferrino this time with an edge in his voice. He sat down at a small wooden desk while I remained standing.

"I was, Sir. Corporal Walter M. Zweizig, Sir," I said, emphasizing my middle initial. Heat burnt its way from my neck up to the hairline and back down the other side. For an instant, I thought I detected the hint of a grin in the leathery face of this old-line soldier, hoping he'd see it like Will Rogers once said, "It's always funny if it happens to someone else." But if there was any humor present, it was totally suppressed. Through time, I learned the Army doesn't accept any bull crap, intentional or otherwise.

Ferrino leaned forward in his chair. Face flushed, actually approaching heart-attack red.

"We just gave you those two stripes, and now you embarrass me with this bull crap!" he screamed, pounding his fist on the desk.

Gee, sarge, don't sugarcoat it, I thought shamefully. *Tell me how you really feel.* I had the uneasy feeling this wasn't going very well. This was not going well at all.

His next words reduced me to corporal of the guard (not busted to private, thank God!) for four weekends straight and restricted to base for sixty days.

When the tongue-lashing stopped, I was excused and left the office in a display of submission, cowering like a whipped dog with its tail between his legs. I was a little hurt, a little angry, and a little sorry for myself. One more kick in the career for Ziggy boy.

Worst of all, the light in my window went out.

6

The Leadership School

*For I know the plans I have for you, declared
the Lord, plans to prosper you and not to
harm you, plans to give you hope and a future.*
                                    - Jeremiah 29:11

Except for occasional cabin fever due to weekend restriction, life within the 27th Infantry Regiment was business as usual. They say if you love what you are doing, you'll never work a day in your life. I loved what I was doing and reminded myself of this at least once daily, some days more often to make up for those I might forget.

My favorite activity was constant weapons firing with live ammunition. Two or three guys handled one machine gun that was nothing more than a deer rifle that spit out rounds of real bullets at paper targets plastered all over the hillside. Maybe a hundred and twenty rounds a minute. (By comparison, today's machine guns shoot anywhere from five hundred to 1,000 rounds per minute.) We practiced several times a week. I no sooner wished to trade places with anyone else than a farmer would with a desk clerk.

This welcome change was short-lived, however. They farmed out four of us to the 25th Quartermaster Company (still officially

27th Infantry Regiment) at Kanoaka Barracks, a small base ten miles away that also housed the 65th Combat Engineers. The Temporary Duty transfer included Supply and Logistics and Equipment Maintenance School. At first, TDY was sixty days. But they kept renewing our orders, sending us to different schools every time we turned around. A year later, I was still assigned to the 25th QM Company.

During the fall of '49, I attended Leadership School near Shinodayama, Japan where the camp housed the Shinodayama Clap Trap. Anywhere from eighty to one hundred servicemen suffering from STD, along with a host of doctor and medic caretakers, were isolated in a section of this small base. When you thought about it, we were all prisoners of the ward and not allowed to leave base under any circumstance.

Shinodayama was a treatment center. It also served as a place for punishment, rules enforced and no mercy granted for even the slightest deviation to satisfactory performance. No grading on the curve!

Under normal protocol, if a soldier received a demerit or "gig" during inspection and his company or squad got too many gigs, the entire unit was penalized. In this way, the group was encouraged through team spirit. Together was better.

The trap, in contrast, punished abusers on an individual basis. If a clap trap boy received too many demerits during his initial thirty-day stay, or if his treatment of daily penicillin had not progressed according to expectation, he remained on base for an additional thirty days. Gonorrhea would not have been contracted in the first place, per the Army's rationale, had these men adhered to safe conduct rules.

Shinodayama was three times worse than basic training. I wondered sometimes if the stockade where I might have ended up wouldn't have been more pleasant. Leadership class candidates practiced newly acquired skills by running these clap trap boys into the dirt. Anything to keep them occupied, exhausted, and punished. We pushed constant training exercises; i.e. squad maneuvers, infantry tactics, digging foxholes, twenty-mile endurance walks along with any other ridiculous amount of physical activity a leader conjured up. (There was little pole-vaulting for fear of gender reassignment!)

In the classroom, we trainees instructed the boys in a harsh, heavy-handed, sergeant-in-boot-camp manner. I was charged with a group of thirty.

"Sit down!" I demanded when students entered the classroom, some coming early to assure seats in the rear.

We were tough taskmasters at this business and not the least bit courteous. Students were expected to listen and obey, speaking only when requested.

"Today," I said, "we're going to continue where we dropped off yesterday on our review of map reading and land navigation. As a review, the geographic coordinates of a point are found by dividing the sides of the geographic square in which the point is located into the required number of equal parts.

"Corporal DeLong, assuming you've done your homework, if the geographic interval for Kutztown is 5'00" and the location of a point is required to the nearest second, each side of the geographic square must be divided into how many equal parts?"

An officer sat in the rear of the room monitoring and grading my leadership skills. A glance in his direction told me I was on target.

"Sir," said DeLong. "Each side of the geographic square must be divided into three hundred equal parts, Sir. Each would have a value of one second."

"Good," I said. "Did everyone get that?"

The class looked on in confusion.

"Now then, Private Benson, using these values," I said as I chalked the following on a blackboard next to a huge pull-down map, "give me the exact location."

Latitude 32 deg. 15'00" and 32 deg. 2-'00"
Longitude 84 deg 45'00" and 84 deg. 50'00"

"Sir, Blueberry Hill, Sir," Benson said, after sufficient time for me to have three cups of coffee and as many trips to the restroom facilities down the hall.

In all due respect, land navigation was determined by complex calculation. Global positioning systems (GPS) determining location within ten meters were not yet in the think tank.

"Wrong!" I said. "The answer is Toolatenow Cemetery. Sit Down, Mr. Benson. Report to class tomorrow with a typed, five-page, single-spaced essay on 'How to Read a Map!'"

By the smile that tugged at my mentor's mouth, I figured I was doing well.

"Oh, one more thing, Private Benson," I said. "Be prepared to present it to the class, using all of the visual aids and tools available for this project."

The Japanese operated laundry facilities on base. They washed, cleaned, and pressed our fatigue uniforms. Still, there were never enough fresh sets on hand to change into as required. If it was rainy and muddy, like a chameleon, you switched outerwear several times a day. Or, even if we had no field activity, it became necessary on occasion to dress in clean duds before entering the mess hall. A group of us got together to solve this vexing problem and purchased items necessary to prepare extra uniforms so we'd each have a serviceable set ready at all times.

Using noon meal breaks, we washed clothes collectively in a twenty-gallon galvanized tub, rinsed and dipped them in starch until they stood by themselves, then hung them out to dry on a makeshift wash line. A blanket across a footlocker served as an ironing board. It was then I learned how to iron. Mom would have been surprised to know how domestic her little boy was becoming. But I'm not so sure she would have been impressed. Pennsylvania German farm folk, unlike today's culture blurring gender roles, considered a man who did house work a sissy at best.

When classes began October 1, there had been twenty-four students enrolled. Eighteen completed the course by December 1. They sent us back to home base following graduation. But not all. Instead of returning to the 27th Infantry Regiment, several were sent back to Kanoaka Barracks. I was one of them and immediately promoted to buck sergeant, placed in charge of the 27th Infantry personnel assigned there.

7

A Welcome Change

...A well regulated Militia, being necessary to the security of a free State, the right of the people to keep and bear Arms, shall not be infringed.
- Amendment II of the Bill of Rights

Soon after returning to Kanoaka, I contacted Baker and Howart. Al Howart, a big, handsome-faced, bowlegged dude from Plano, Texas, spent his boyhood on the back of a horse until enlisting in the Army. He moved slowly but with staunch purpose and was always puffing on a cigarette that dangled from the corner of his mouth. Wisps of smoke drifted in the air around him like clouds around an idling train. We became fast friends and were fondly dubbed the "three stooges" by our barrack buddies. Plans were in the works even before I went off to leadership school when the three of us applied for a well-deserved ten-day leave. Our leave orders read:

"...assigned to an Eighth Army Rest Hotel near the northern tip of Honshu Island for a period of eight days and two days travel, authorized to begin the day after Christmas."

My second holiday away from home promised not to be as silent night/lonely night as the first. An exciting adventure lay ahead. But we had no intention of going anywhere near the Rest Hotel. Instead, we'd cross the Tsugaru Strait by ferry to Japan's extreme northern island of Hokkaido to hunt bear.

Mackie (soldiers gave Japanese sweethearts American nicknames) was Al Howart's cute little girlfriend. She came along as interpreter. Her eyes, I remember, were deep brown almost black like her hair, and she was small but sturdy, reminding me of the doll my sister Marian drug around by the hair when she was a toddler.

Mackie had relatives in Karuzawa, a small town of six hundred people. Through correspondence, she had arranged to borrow shotguns from their chief of police. Single barrel, single shot shotguns. (When Japan surrendered in 1945, the entire population was forced to relinquish possession of rifles and shotguns except for single barrel.) No matter; we considered ourselves quite the sharpshooters. Shotgun shells and slugs were purchased at the main PX in Osaka.

Before going on, I'll fast forward to a time we were smarter on equipping ourselves for hunting. The Army allowed a furlough of thirty days a year. In spring of 1950, Cecil Cole, Al Howart, and I hunted wild boar with a few Japanese men in the mountains fifty miles north of Kanoaka Barracks. We "borrowed" rifles from the arms room at base, disassembled them, and threw the parts into duffel bags and went out the post gates, arousing no more suspicion than a fox in a hen house at night.

We were even more creative when it came to supplying ammunition. Let me first explain the process of what happens on the firing range. Each person receives a number. At the far end, maybe two to three hundred yards from the firing line, are twenty or so large canvas bull's eye targets on numbered frames. A sergeant with field glasses in a side lane directs the firing, assigns the numbers you shoot at, and records the hits. These targets are run up on pulleys, then lowered after the firing to mark where bullets had struck. If you got a bull's eye, a white disc went up from the operator in the pit below the targets. If you missed, a huge red flag was hoisted. Did I mention the red flag is called "Maggie's Drawers?"

Our moms raised no idiots. We put our brilliant heads together and came up with a plan. To begin with, we received X number of rounds of live ammunition to fire. Okay, now we're at the rifle range and say there are twenty guys on this bank firing at the target. And say everyone gets six rounds of fire, and it goes boom, boom, boom, boom, and this goes on and on. And say you fire twice. The guy at the far end puts up Maggie's Drawers, meaning you missed the target. But technically you hadn't fired. The other four rounds ended up in your pocket. The next series of firing you do the same thing, and you come out of there with twenty, thirty rounds that never fired. Up on the mountain, we reassembled everything and put a clip in.

We never did see wild boar on that trip, but we sure put on a high falutin' demonstration of firepower, impressing the heck out of the Japanese with their antiquated shotguns. At the end of the trip, we took the rifles back in the same way we took them out. And that was the end of it.

My fascination for guns started way back. Pop wouldn't let me touch his double-barrel shotgun. I could only look at it. Admire. Covet. When I was fifteen, I parted with hard-earned muskrat money and bought a .16 gauge. I target practiced, also hunted, on the sly with neighboring buddy Herbie Schaeffer. Afterward, I'd grease the gun, put it in a burlap bag to protect it from rust, and hide it underneath the corncrib.

Hamburg, first whistle stop up the railroad track, boasted one traffic light and one fat pompous cop named Color standing shotgun. A speech impediment earned him the nickname "Billy Tolor the Town Top." His town, population 3,250, served the Norman Rockwell community with a feed mill, three mom and pop corner markets, two banks, two funeral parlors, five churches, and five retail stores. At one of these stores, Nate Balthaser's, I bought my second shotgun, a .410 gauge. Pop found me out and, after exhibiting great verbal annoyance, threw the gun, so he said, into the Schuylkill River flowing past our property. When I came home on leave in '51, he told me to fetch a hankie from his dresser drawer, a request I thought quite odd. My shotgun stood in a corner of the bedroom.

Cousin Shirley lived on the Zweizig homestead across the river. Cowgirl wannabe, she accompanied my Uncle Herbert to Uncle Raymond's feed mill one day, then slipped away to Western Auto where she purchased a replica Gene Autry six-gun pistol and holster set for $5.79, money saved from wild bluebell flower sales on her mother's city huckster route. When she brought the package home, guess what? It, too, was confiscated. In putting our heads together, we believe our families opposed guns, real or fake, as too dangerous for youngsters, our fathers painfully remembering their teen-age brother Charles' fatal hunting accident.

That was back in the days when our parents were not afraid to teach us right from wrong. "Train up a child in the way he should go, and he will not depart from it."

Let's stay here a minute. I don't know how to say this except to just go ahead and say it. We're probably the most mismanaged generation in history when it comes to raising kids. Lack of discipline and consequences run their course, letting our youth who look for love in all the wrong places fall wherever they may. Today, one need only open a morning paper or turn on the evening news to learn the disastrous results. Firearm-related deaths for U.S. children in mid-teens and under is an alarming twelve times higher than that of twenty-five other industrialized countries COMBINED. What a blot on American life!

Now that this old warrior is full of years and a bit more reflective, I still feel the urge to bear arms. At least as in "rifles." At least as in "hunting." I've heard hypocrites say, "How can you shoot a deer? It has such big beautiful brown eyes!" Have they ever checked out a cow's? Besides, a buck in the forest has an eighty percent chance (more for some), escaping the deathblow. The cow in their Big Mac had none! But I say the following with tongue in cheek, allowing enough rope to hang myself should I need a quick escape. My hunting buddies and I are responsible, accountable adults and safety-conscious to a fault when it comes to handling firearms. We treat them with appropriate skepticism and the utmost of respect that is their due...

Forgive me. I seem to have gone off on another tangent. I was supposed to be telling you of our trip preparation for hunting bear and, instead, went off making unconstructive remarks on the ills of parenting, animal rights, and gun control. That is not what this book is about. Yet I've offered a few perspectives of which even I'm confused. I wonder what Paul Harvey would say. "For the rest of the story...."

Before leaving base, we had scrounged up three cases of C rations to sustain us during our furlough. I don't think we were on the train more than half an hour when Baker came back after a trip to the john, his face lit up like a newly decorated Christmas tree.

"Guess what, you guys!" he said. "I found a Jap in the next car back who speaks good English."

"So? Who gives a rat's rip!" was Howie's and my reaction.

"Well, believe it or not, he offered to buy our C rations."

"Why?"

Rhetorical question. We didn't expect an answer. In a case of C rations were cigarettes and chocolate and everything from soup to nuts, and, if you were lucky, Jello, fruit salad, pork and beans, hot dogs in beans, hamburger in beans, beans in beans.... These government-issued supplies—American super market sealed in a can—were foods not available to the Japanese public. C rations at large were envied.

"So what are we supposed to eat if we sell our food?" asked Howie. Howie was a big bull of a guy and needed a full pantry of victuals to keep him running.

"Not a problem, chum. We'll shoot enough game to eat our fill and still have plenty left over."

"Yeah, but what if we don't? What if the bears are already hibernating, then what?" asked the conservative I.

"Simple," said Baker. "We put Plan B in effect. We give Mackie the money made on our deal, and she can go into the village and get stuff."

We agreed. Baker could sell a snowball to an Eskimo. Better yet, convince a polar bear to take a dip in a tub of hot water.

I safeguarded our valuable fare with my life while Baker and Howart fetched the prospective buyer. After minimal negotiation, we sold our rations for 15,000 yen. The rate of exchange was three hundred and sixty yen to the dollar, or $41.66. Not a bad deal. Not a bad deal at all!

The Hunt

...And God took a handful of southerly wind,
Blew His breath over it and created the horse.
                              - Bedouin Legend

We checked in at a small U.S. Army Special Services office in Karuzawa and confirmed lodging arrangements made previously through the Far East edition of the *Stars and Stripes*, daily newspaper serving the military community. We trekked a mile from there to our log cabin located in a recreational area maintained by the Army. Similar shelters were built along the mountainside at intervals of a thousand yards or so. I knew of four different ones in our vicinity under the supervision of the 1st Cavalry Division.

In case you visualize a team of drafts skidding logs, not so. At this point in time, the cavalry was mechanized and running on multiple horsepower.

The horse has been with man since the beginning of civilization. When not pulling a cart or hauling his master over trails, mountains, and deserts, he was often a fierce instrument of war, figuring greatly in conquest and victory. But should you be misled by triumphant equestrian statues of sleek horses beneath captains with field glasses monitoring distant battlefields, let me set you straight.

The warhorses' lot was certainly not one of glory and can barely be imagined. Case in point:

Thousands upon thousands were killed during the Civil War. And during World War I, Lawrence Scanlan, in his introduction to Monty Roberts' book <u>The Man Who Listens to Horses</u>, says that, "... horses used as cavalry and to move supplies and guns numbered 1.5 million, and one-third died. Heavy guns blasted battlefields into gruel. With grooming forsaken, mange and parasites spread like a contagion. Against mange, the Army scrubbed and clipped horses that then shivered in the cold and rain and snow. Water troughs froze, and food supplies dwindled. Desperate horses choked trying to eat the blankets of their stable mates, chewed ropes, others' manes and tails, even...."

More fortunate equine war heroes were the stocky Andalusians, originally bred and trained by the Hapsburgs of Austria and celebrated world-wide today as the dancing Lipizzaners. I've seen these beautiful stallions perform at the Spanish Riding School in Vienna. Innovative maneuvers and "airs above the ground" that contributed to the safety of their riders in battle are truly something to behold. To the best of my knowledge, the Lipizzaners were not used in either of the two world wars, but were highly protected instead. During World War II, the prized stud farm was moved to Czechoslovakia by the Germans, and, at the end of the war, heroically rescued from the Russians under the command of our 2nd Cavalry's "Blood and Guts" General George S. Patton who returned them to Vienna.

The average hayburner's lot greatly improved during WWII. Afterward, he was permanently retired from military use; else, subscribing to President Ronald Reagan's later quote—" the best thing for the inside of a man is the outside of a horse," I would have opted for the cavalry upon enlistment.

Our cabin measured eighteen by twenty feet and was divided into two sections. One for lounging and another hosted two narrow double-decked bunks, each with a lumpy, moldy-smelling pillow and a mat on top of a mattress stuffed with small tree branches. The lounge area had a drop-leaf table, four chairs, and a rough-hewn counter. A wall cabinet stored a few utensils. A small cast-iron wood stove for cooking and a large open fireplace at the far end completed the room. No plumbing. The only running water, excluding rain seepage below the rafters, was a creek behind the cabin. No electricity. The building was crude, even for a rural setting.

When I left home, we had been wired for ten years. I remember the occasion with great clarity. I was eight at the time and received a spectacular licking. No sooner had Uncle Levi finished the momentous task of connecting us to the outside world with the magic of electricity, when out of the clear blue the kitchen light switch broke. It wasn't designed to turn on and off and on and off a hundred times in succession. How was I to know! On the bright side, even though I couldn't sit in comfort weeks on end, I no longer did schoolwork by a dim kerosene lamp once the switch was repaired.

We had running water at the kitchen sink by the time I left in '48. A shower in our newly cemented cellar replaced the galvanized tub where we scrubbed down every Saturday night whether we needed it or not.

No refrigerator. Garden produce, dairy products, and Mom's wonderfully fermented homemade root beer were preserved in an underground arch that maintained a year-round temperature of fifty-five degrees, similar to a cave.

While no indoor toilet, a small building with a quarter moon carved in the top of its door sufficed and stood with age-old dignity in the corner of our backyard. The year's previous Sears & Roebuck catalog lay ready to peruse and use during one's occupation. For certain emergencies, our farm's outhouse sported a two-holer unlike the one pit with no reading material here in the Japanese mountains. But I was in the infantry now. Inconvenience was part of the package.

The northern tip of Honshu, Japan's main island, and the southern tip of Hokkaido are both on the same latitude as our state of New York. Climate is similar. Daytime temperatures ranged from the low thirties or high twenties to bone-chilling teens at night. Except for the first, it snowed every day during our hunting trip. My soul mates were better attired than I for wintry weather conditions. I can't tell you what I wouldn't have done for a visit to the general store.

Every crossroads community had one. In a time when penny

candy only cost a penny, the country store, across from the grist mill in the village of Berne—a mere smudge on the county map, was one-stop shopping for our agrarian neighborhood. I recall with nostalgia, "ching, ching, ching," the brass bells made when you entered through the massive front door with its vertical glass panels. The sweet smell of spices, bread, and pipe smoke wafted through the air. (By contrast, today's convenience stores smell like someone just mopped the floor, or in some cases, need to mop the floor.) Besides all manner of kitchen staples, clothing, and hardware, Clarence B. Kline's store served more than most. Here was a place you bartered milk and eggs for sugar, salt and other essentials, used the telephone in emergency, picked up the Sunday paper, daily mail for some at the little post office in the back, and got a haircut.

Kliney's also functioned for locals and farmers in bib overalls and white shirts too frayed for church to loiter around the pot-bellied stove on cold winter nights and the front porch in summers. They swapped tales, discussed crops and weather, and caught up on news in general, gossip in particular. Numerous card games took place.

The chief reason I wished to be at Kliney's at this moment was for rubber galoshes. *Gumshtivel*, they're called in Dutch. Earlier, I went to a Japanese store, but their largest boot size was much too small for my enormous American feet. Combat boots, about as waterproof as a sieve, were my only alternative. More than once out in the woods, I relived the unpleasant soaking experience I endured during my first hour at basic. Needless to say, I looked forward to propping my stocking feet on a stack of wood by the open fireplace each night. Though wet and cold during the day, they were the only part of my body warmed at night, the glorious bright hearth sending most of its heat up the chimney instead.

Flashes of childhood flooded my consciousness during one of these fireside moments. I watched in silence as the blaze crackled and popped, arousing sharp and colorful remembrances of Christmas past.

On a dairy farm, Sundays and holidays are a day like any other in many ways. Cows had to be milked mornings and evenings and all livestock and poultry fed and watered twice a day. Stables had to be manured, though we didn't haul it to the fields until a day later. Actually, all field work and extra-curricular activities were postponed on these particular days. That included Christmas.

Christmas celebration began with the children's program the night before at our country church. Afterward, each kid received chewy chocolates in a green box wrapped with a red curly ribbon. And a Florida orange. Citrus fruit, very special, was unavailable any other time of year.

By the time I was twelve, me and Barney, our retired draft gelding with hooves big as dinner plates and a back broad enough to spread out and take a nap on, were drafted to ride to the woods for the Christmas tree. With a rope tied around my waist, we dragged a small spruce home through the snow. An assortment of colored lights, strings of popcorn, and fragile softball-size ornaments soon adorned its branches. Gifts lay underneath.

Presents were opened on Christmas morning after the barn chores were finished and a hefty breakfast of ham or scrapple, eggs, fried potatoes and shoe-fly pie downed. We received practical gifts like shirts, over-the-shoe rubbers (that's what we called water-proof, below-ankle boots) or galoshes (that's what we called over-the-shoe, water-proof, above-ankle boots), dungarees, and muskrat traps. Sometimes red or gold hard rock candy was thrown in as a special treat. One year, Pop bought an inflatable PopEye that blew up to a foot high. The more air you inserted into PopEye, the more muscle he boasted. With all the horsing around we kids did grabbing it from each other, poor mister strong guy, with no amount of spinach to save him, burst his guts, breath knocked out minutes after he was born. That was the first and last toy we received.

Dinners at Christmas were out of the ordinary, second, in quantity at least, to feeding a threshing crew in July. My grandparents came, and my mother put out the good china from the corner cupboard that was reserved for company.

Mouthwatering aromas filled the kitchen. Roast turkey and giblet gravy, potato filling like only the Berks County Dutch can make, dried corn, lima beans, peas, candied sweet potatoes, and tomato sauce.

Wait, I'm not done. There were mustard string beans that when still in the Mason jar stood up like soldiers at attention, pepper cabbage, cole slaw, sweet and sour chow chow, (Are you full yet?) and much apple butter and cottage cheese to spread on Freihoffer's snow-white bread—probably the only store-bought goodie on the table.

We kids raced through the meal, keeping vigil over the numerous desserts spread on the sideboard. Bubbly Tapioca pudding, black walnut kuchen with creamy walnut-studded icing, sliced bananas— a holiday treat in red and green Jello topped with whipped cream, assorted fruit tarts as well as the old staples: Mom's funny cake (not funnel cake and not funny like in ha ha but, well, funny in the way she labeled this dry coffee confection), angel food cake, fruit salad, and last, but certainly not least, real mince meat pie (with a dash of whiskey for the grownups).

Glasses of sweet ice-cold milk, pots of coffee or steaming cups of Hershey's hot cocoa washed it down.

Some memories of a bygone era stay pretty much the same, but others, like good cheese, improve with age. I did lots of things on the farm as a kid. I milked, I fed, mucked stalls, stole eggs from beneath squawking hens, rode some, fell off some, *hupta'd* home cows (and charged to the closest fence when a bull charged), and hammered a thumbnail now and then. But stirring fresh milk before placing the cans in the water trough for cooling twice a day was a chore I truly detested. Yet when Mom made ice cream, a time-honored holiday tradition, I went about my arduous task with gusto.

I have yet to find anyone who can explain why, but you required cooled milk for starters even though the milk was heated when cream, eggs, sugar, cornstarch, and vanilla were added. Mom poured the mixture into a metal stanner with a lid and long handle attached. Chopped ice from the crick and rock salt on the top surrounded the stanner inside an oak-planked bucket. We boys took turns cranking the wooden freezer. After a half hour or so, when it became impossible to budge, the ice cream had thickened to the appropriate consistency.

Nothing, I mean nothing more delicious ever passed over a human tongue than the yummy delight of our Mom's homemade ice cream.

Life was good!

We carried shotgun slugs and shot shells the first several days of hunting, until it became obvious the bears were sacked in for a long winter's nap. The black bear I saw at Hershey Park would remain the only one I'd see. As a result, we concentrated on ducks. Black ducks, plumage actually darkish brown, flying against the snowy Japanese sky were as plentiful as goose poo on a park lawn. (That doesn't seem phenomenal until you do the math. One wild goose, for example, can produce two pounds of waste daily. That's nearly six hundred pounds a week from a gaggle of say forty geese.)

A couple of small ponds dotted our hunting grounds. As if someone tapped them with ping-pong paddles, ducks flew from one to the other. While on "stand," I noticed two ducks paired off to the side acting like they were still on honeymoon. Ducks have been studied and noted when one is shot down the mate will circle around, flying too low for men with big guns and hungry dogs, and land beside the wounded.

Sadly, most species of ducks do not re-mate. So, it was with some remorse I shot at all, but we needed the food. Two of us hid in low brush and the other walked about a half mile away and fired a few shots. The ducks winged their way back to the waiting hunters, and "bingo." After those shots, the lucky survivors bounced back and forth from pond to pond until we were satisfied with our kill for the day.

Instead of C rations or bear, what we ended up eating for a week were eggs, hard rolls, and tea from the village, fried duck, boiled duck, roasted duck, duck in wine, and….

Mysteries of War and Peace

We have grasped the mystery of the atom
and rejected the Sermon on the Mount...
...The world has achieved brilliance without conscience –
a world of nuclear giants and ethical infants.
- General Omar Bradley

The villagers invited us to the town hall for dinner on New Year's Eve. Get this, the occasion was held in our honor! Hadn't we just fought a major war? We the victor, they the spoil? I now have a better understanding.

In 1939, immigrant physicist Albert Einstein warned President Franklin Delano Roosevelt that Germany was trying to develop atomic weapons based on an isotope of uranium U-235. The American nuclear program, called the Manhattan Project, commenced under the sharp prod of fear that Germany would win the race to be the first atomic power. It is fully reasonable to assume the first U.S. bomb would have been used against Germany were it available in time. As it happened, the war in Europe ended before the giant explosive was ready. ("Crossing the Moral Threshold," by David M. Kennedy, *Time*, Aug. 1, 2005.)

Allied leaders agreed the atom should be used against Japan as soon as possible. On August 6, 1945, fifteen minutes past eight in the morning, the Boeing B-29 named Enola Gay dropped its deadly payload on Hiroshima, killing 140,000 of the city's 350,000 residents. (See Addendum.)

Only after Soviet declaration of war against Japan on August 8, 1945 and the second nuclear attack on August 9, this time over the city of Nagasaki, did Emperor Hirohito overrule some of his own military leaders. On August 14 (formally September 2, 1945), the Land of the Gods surrendered unconditionally. Thanks to Give 'em Hell Harry and his decision to consider the defense of American troops more important than the enemy, a terrible instrument of war had finally brought peace!

At first, the Japanese civilians' anger was directed toward the American people for dropping the bomb. Later, being further educated on historical circumstances, they redirected the anger toward their own government for having involved the country in such an ill-fated and unprovoked attack.

(At a recent WWII Event that I attended, a member of the audience asked the speaker, a retired fighter pilot from the Pacific war, "How do you feel about the Japanese?" The veteran's answer was, "I like the Japanese people. It's the government I didn't like, and I will never forgive them.")

WWII hero General Douglas MacArthur, assigned the position of Supreme Commander, Allied Forces in Asia, moved into post-war Japan. The independent, assertive, and eccentric general, instead of making the Japanese pay for Pearl Harbor, restored dignity to these fallen people and helped them back on their feet. His strategy carefully worked changes through Japan's existing government, taking great pains to preserve the integrity of the country's imperial family. The Japanese are a homogenous people who place the highest premium on respect and, therefore, fully cooperated with MacArthur's forces after ordered to do so by their emperor.

The general's leadership accomplished many things that made the Japanese citizens hold America in deep regard. The feudal system disappeared; people were allowed to own property; women were given the right to vote. Rebuilding began on ravished, war-torn cities. Factories were rehabilitated and put back into operation. Japanese exports once more played an important role in world markets. The sagging economy began to unsag.

The reduced scale of things in Japan had a way of making us westerners feel ten feet tall and powerful and the Japanese weak and insignificant. Yet we remembered the Army's mandate back in Seattle, "...you are not going to Japan to throw your weight around." As goodwill ambassadors for the United States, we stepped on their soil and respected cultural differences no matter what. Likewise, most Japanese people respected American servicemen. Though, Mackie did tell us later the chief of police and mayor of Karuzawa pegged us as being the cream of the crop.

I like the snow. It makes the world slow down. Not that it needed slowing down in this part of the world. But I think it sounds nice and peaceful to say that beings it was holiday time. On the night of the big event, there was a crusted snow on the ground. A full moon speckling through bare hardwoods lit the path as we crunched our way to the town hall.

From outside, the building looked like nothing more than a cold, dark wooden shed without windows. Inside, however, the hall, maybe eighty feet long by fifty wide, was warm and fuzzy with four lit fireplaces on each side of the two long walls. The floor, covered in deep red carpeting, met with an eight-foot border of polished board on the perimeter. Low rectangular tables, pushed together, filled the room. These were eighteen inches high, similar in size to an American coffee table. *Tatami* of woven rice straw lay next to each for seating. I assume the townspeople brought these since it was customary to roll up their personal mats and take them wherever they went for such occasions.

After an exchange of foreign gibberish with Mackie, the mayor and chief of police and several other notable hosts greeted our group.

In matters of greeting, the higher one's station in life, the lower it's expected one bows to him. Though a breach in protocol, it's sometimes okay to claim ignorance and dismiss cultural courtesy;

particularly, if, like me, you fear butting heads on your way up or down in the process. I judged all men to be created equal and inclined my head just slightly, at the same time extending my large north paw. I did compromise myself, however, and gently clasped my hosts' dwarfed hands instead of giving the traditional American shake as if pumping a five-gallon bucket full of water. (Shame on me! I since learned the Japanese consider the right hand "dirty" and an insult to use in greeting.)

Mackie's father directed a boy-san wearing a pale yellow jacket to seat us. Boy-san bobbed his head as though nothing in the world could give him greater pleasure. He escorted us to the head table, where, as honored guests, we'd pretend comfort, squatting cross-legged on rugs of dark fabric. There were no holes in the floor for lower appendages per typical restaurant seating. I spotted wooden chopsticks called *o'hoshi* at our place settings and became nervous, but immediately relieved to see metal spoons next to them.

We sat.

The feast began.

A host of servers rushed forward with an interesting variety of foods in painted ceramic bowls—rice soup, boiled rice, rice cakes, rice with veggies, rice this and rice that, even the renowned rice mit dumplings. No, not rice mit dumplings. Rice mit dumplings would be about as common in Japan as rice mit sautéed fish eyes would be on a Pennsylvania German's dinner table. Though in all honesty, Germans could well compete with Asiatic neighbors in eating objectionable animal parts.

Kidding aside, plentiful fish heads with marble eyes stared above mouths threatening to snap if you dared partake. And, oh, I almost forgot, there was soup made with dried fish that swam in green stringy seaweed, and batter-fried fish cakes, Rocky Mountain squid balls, octopus pudding, fermented fish heads, raw fish backs prepared both a' la carte and a' la mode—take your pick, fish tails al dente, fish eggs over easy...

Now here's a curiosity. God says He made man in His own image and that, "It was very good." Yet there are those who claim we were first chimpanzees. (Then why are there still chimps?) Others swear we evolved from fish. As much as I detest fish *(sakano)*, I sure hope today's evolutionists are wrong, else God would be out of a job.

There's something to be said about the Japanese' love for art, even in the dining room. At home, Mom mashed, chopped, cubed, or diced carrots, beets, and other vegetables. Here, they carved them into roses or swans and what else have you. Even out-of-season fresh flowers and silk floral arrangements with pretty paper balloons in all manner of color and design graced the tables.

Still, the gracious atmosphere did nothing to stimulate my appetite. Beyond the shadow of a doubt, everything smelled awful. I guess the nose is close to the mouth for a purpose. My problem was I couldn't manage to get past the smell when it came to fishy things. Only out of politeness did I spoon up, most slowly, every morsel from my bowl, which, contrary to everything else in Japan, was about as enormous in size as a toy teacup is small. As I'd finish, a server refilled my bowl. Again, out of politeness, I kept on eating, just like a horse with a belly full of grass keeps on grazing.

You see, there is another cultural strangeness in this strange country of which I was unaware. Each time you clean your dish, they think your hunger is unsatisfied so they fill it again and again. I didn't catch on until stuffed like a pork sausage. With sudden inspiration, I raised a hand, palm out, to block her advancing spoon.

"No. No more," I said to the grinning but uncomprehending face of the little gal who delivered my sixteenth helping. "Please, no more,"

Mackie noticed my distress and gave the waitress a detailed explanation in Japanese. The little gal nodded and giggled behind her hand.

"Ah, so," she said, and moved on to Howart who, between cigarette puffs, continued to shovel it in.

Japan has the world's longest life expectancy, by today's standards anyway. So please forgive me for making sport of healthy cuisine being bad for my American taste buds. Basically a salt and pepper, meat and potatoes, and vanilla/chocolate/strawberry kind of guy (still am), I did discover a remarkable dish while stationed in Japan.

I don't recall if we had sukiyaki *(s'kiyaki)* that night, but it's similar to beef stew and as tasty as dead fish wrapped in soggy seaweed must be disgusting. I even mastered the chunks of meat with chopsticks and, in spite of a few shirt-front stains, slurped the slurry from my bowl as graciously as the best of them.

The Japanese have this thing about graciousness and proper etiquette, you know. Early European missionaries to the Land of the Rising Sun were thought barbaric, not only because they had big noses and more body hair, but also because they touched food with their fingers, for goodness sake. Yet these same well-mannered folk from the East conducted cruel medical experiments on American POWs and chopped off heads, hands, and private parts and made finger food of their livers. (*The New York Times* referred to the war crime proceedings that followed Imperial Japan's surrender as "Cannibalism Trials," p. 460, <u>Flyboys</u>.)

Perhaps we shouldn't go there. Wartime atrocities are past and best forgotten. Yesterday's enemy, today's friend.

The mayor and chief of police spoke following the meal. Mackie made whispering attempts to translate as they went along. Then she stood up and spoke. When she finished, the audience clapped and nodded, sending plenty sweet and generous smiles our direction. We smiled in return even though we hadn't the foggiest notion what transpired.

School children entertained with a songfest after the meal, and, when midnight approached, *sake* (rhymes with rocky) was passed around to toast in the New Year. Thank goodness this is traditionally drunk from teeny-weeny thimble-sized cups. I tasted this warmed alcoholic beverage made from rice once before and very much disliked the flavor. If you've never tasted *sake*, let me tell you it's worse than castor oil, a product Mom made us take that promised to cure everything from flat feet to a broken heart. I drank the wine out of deference and poured it down the hatch in one quick gulp. Much to my relief, unlike with food, that was the end of it. No refills.

We returned to our cabin around 0100. No sooner inside, Baker pulled a bottle of Suntory whiskey out of his duffel bag and said,
"Let's flush out that @#$& *sake* before we all get sick!"

The following day, we packed our few belongings and walked back into town. A train underneath the bay took us through a tunnel leading to the main island, then on to Tokyo where we switched railroads and headed home to Osaka and Kanoaka Barracks.

Oh, yes. There was one other incident during our trip that is worth mentioning. An earthquake.

Earthquakes are a common occurrence in Japan and generally accepted without too much excitement. I had experienced one shortly after arriving in Osaka back in '48. At the time, I had been sitting on the throne, reading *What to Do When You Don't Know What to Do*, when suddenly the single light bulb dangling from a cord in the lavatory ceiling swayed to and fro. My seat shimmied, and I heard a strange noise outside, like thunder, though it was a clear night. Strangely, it was both terrifying and thrilling at the same time. The next morning, the walls of a building across the street were the only thing remaining amidst a heap of crumbled concrete. (See Addendum.)

During the second day of our bear hunt on Hokkaido Island, we experienced a quake, but there was no evident damage as far as we could tell. We dismissed all concern and went about our business. But the day before New Year's, a Japanese newspaper in the village showing photos of servicemen and damaged buildings said otherwise. Large, bold Japanese characters raced down the page. Upon Mackie's closer inspection, it appeared the earthquake from several days before was hardly a tremor. Roads buckled. Power lines snapped and sparked, and bridges and buildings collapsed. Numerous people were injured or killed from falling debris. A search was still on for two fishermen, feared swept out to sea by tsunami-size waves triggered by the quake. Citizens by the thousands were without running water and filled up at our military water trucks.

The most arresting thing about the headlines from that dimly remembered week was the destruction of the 8th Army Rest Hotel—
the same one we were assigned for our leave. Most of the hotel was
leveled and several U.S. servicemen who had lodged there were
killed. (Later, we read the complete story in the *Stars and Stripes*.)

   We had escaped a death trap and were never discovered disobey-
ing leave orders. Did I believe in divine intervention? Fate? Not
really. I was a mere nineteen and such thoughts were beyond my
intellectual comprehension.

   But I would change.

My Best Buddy

A friend is a person with whom one enjoys mutual
affection, esteem, respect, and regard;
A sympathizer, helper, patron, and supporter.
                    - Webster's Dictionary

Gaines L. Baker from Evansville, Indiana was six when his father deserted the family. His mother remarried, became pregnant, and moved out-of-state. In second grade by this time, Baker remained behind with an uncle. At sixteen, he lied about his age and enlisted in the U.S. Army. I'm not sure young folk could get away with that nowadays. In those days, recruiting officers turned the other way if they suspected an underage candidate. They were happy for all the volunteers they could get. If you were good enough, you were old enough. If you were old enough, you were good enough. Whatever.

Baker took basic training at Fort Leonard Wood, Missouri and arrived in Japan in November of '48. Like me, he was assigned to Battalion Service Company (SVC), 27th Infantry Regiment to attend school at Kanoaka Barracks.

I remember well the night he came. It was late. Some of the fellows were already in bed on the second floor where I slept. Slight of build, five-foot nine or maybe ten at full stretch, Baker, but for a street-savvy tint to light-colored eyes, appeared even younger than his mid-teens. Pale brown hair slicked back by pomade creased off center over a face smooth as a baby's you-know-what except for fuzz on a chin that never saw a razor. A duffel bag hung from one shoulder, and a guitar darn near as big as he slung off the other. He looked vaguely lopsided.

"Hey! We got ourselves a singing cowboy," quipped one of the guys.

Baker ran his fingers across the strings, bowed, and pitched his bag on the empty bunk next to mine.

We took an instant liking to this new kid on the block with the boyish smile and apple cheeks. Me, in particular. From day one, we hit if off, really hit it off, going together like the words Noah and Ark, like peas go with carrots. Jam and toast.

"We're always walking," one of us complained when we made a trip to town.

"Yeah," the other said. "We gotta do something about that. We need a set of wheels."

A month after arriving at Kanoaka, I made super guard. A super guard was special in that he stood up to all expectations by the officer of the day; i.e. appearance, polish, finesse. Six months with the military police trained me well in this respect. Being a super guard also meant being an extra. If someone became ill or relieved for one reason or another, you were "it."

The corporal driving for Captain Bond returned to the States on normal rotation. The evening of my appointment, I was asked to drive the captain home and pick him up the following morning. Military officers have their own personal drivers. Believe it or not, there's wisdom behind this irrational government rationale. The Army cannot afford to tolerate nonsense as mentioned before. Since an officer doesn't have time for mechanical detail, he needs someone motivated for safe and efficient operation of his vehicle. Who's to say a mechanic or maybe a half-dozen or so other privates working in the motor pool might not single out an unpopular CO with a practical joke? Maybe even sabotage his jeep?"

Example. One private, name withheld, chatted with me and a

couple other guys in the motor pool one day when Captain So-and-So came by to collect his jeep. As soon as the captain took the keys and walked away, Private So-and-So turned to me, and, after studying his feet, kicked aside a few pebbles and whispered,

"He'll never get it started."

Then I knew why. In a hand huge as a catcher's mitt was the jeep's rotor.

With most things in this world of give and take, there's an occasional negative to this positive tradition of engaging an individual driver. Especially if the officer is a family man. Especially if his wife is a knockout beyond belief and not given to proper morals. Illustration. First, be it known the names are changed to protect the innocent. On second thought, perhaps innocent is inappropriate. Let's just say I'm changing names, and we'll let it go at that.

Captain Merrifield's wife, a curvaceous bottle-bleached blonde of exaggerated proportion, was an avid shopper. The captain sent his driver, Corporal Reed, to take her into the city whenever and wherever her little heart desired. Per the rumor mill, she and Reed spent whole afternoons together. This romance lasted the entire time the corporal drove for Merrifield. Hearsay revealed the captain, a thirties-something man of sufficient wealth it was said, knew of his wife's unorthodox shopping habits and planned on checking things out when they returned to the States. Why wait 'til then? Maybe he took pity and wanted to share military benefits for as long as possible. Maybe, and I don't want to get too radical, maybe he loved her and hoped she'd change her ways.

I participated, so-to-speak, in another love affair amongst the alleged rich and famous, an activity conducive to wagging tongues at a church potluck social. Our mess officer, alias Lieutenant Mitchell, was of average height and had a good head of hair still for mid-forties. His tight physique and well-defined single chin was remarkable for someone who spent twenty-four/seven in a kitchen. Nearsighted, he wore wire-rimmed glasses, but my memory stops there. The lieutenant offered his personal floor model radio for the mess hall.

Mid-morning, Baker and I went to pick up the voice box at his home in Hamadera Park, a neighborhood off base where commissioned officers and their dependents lived.

Allow me to backtrack. In addition to private drivers, most officers hired at token wage Japanese houseboys to assist their families with the cleaning, cooking, or whatever.

Baker and I went up to Lieutenant Mitchell's house and pounded on the front door until our hands bruised black and blue. We smoked six cigarettes each while debating a lengthy research article on the pros and cons of producing burpless cukes or something like that before Mrs. Mitchell finally answered.

She was gorgeous! Despite bedroom eyes, her face was fresh as morning coffee. Flowing honey-colored hair spilled casually over slim shoulders. Lovely figure. She stood two inches above Baker.

"Ma'am. Excuse me, Ma'am," Baker stammered. "Are you Mrs. Mitchell?"

There was room for error. She appeared much younger than expected.

"Yes, I am," she said in a voice soft as warm butter, then smiled in a dreamy sort of way, showing two glorious dimples. Dimples, my forever weakness.

I focused on a shadow behind her where stood a "whatever." He was cloaked in yellow birthday attire and as little and skinny as a Sumo wrestler is big and fat. Mentally, my jaw was dropping. I looked, my eyes taking in the data, my brain a few beats behind trying to make sense of it. I'm sure my eyes were larger than twin moons, for nothing in seventeen years on the farm prepared me for this moment. Baker saw him, too.

"Ma'am," he said, "your husband sent us here to pick up a radio, but it's no problem for us to come back."

"Oh, it's all right. I just got out of the bath. If you don't mind waiting outside, I'll be dressed in a few minutes." She was wearing a robe.

Of course, gossip like this sped through the military system in no time at all. The guys at the base were furious. If this gorgeous gal were prone to misplacing desires, it should at least be with one of them, a handsome American soldier. Not a stunted servant about as macho as an ancient Bonsai tree.

This business of dealing with the opposite sex in an unfitting way calls to mind a dozen different episodes while I stationed in Japan. Few are repeatable.

Sergeant Earl H. Bunter, late twenties, was a long, lanky string bean of a guy, shoulders somewhat slouched. He hailed from Orlando, Florida and could sink a basketball from fifty feet away. Like most sergeants, he had served in the war.

"We heard it so often," he once told me. "The only good kraut is a dead one. I even said so myself. But when you came right down to it, they just looked like kids. My goodness, we all were kids. They were doing what they were supposed to do, and we were doing what we were supposed to do. Under other circumstances, we could have been friends."

While engaging the Nazi death machine, Bunter had fought his way through mud and cow pastures in Belgium as an Army infantryman, narrowly escaping death, only to discover a Dear John letter waiting for him in the rear. He came home following the war and, after a bitter divorce, re-enlisted. He now managed the Enlisted Men's Club at Kanoaka. The club had a bar (beer, no hard liquor) and dance floor where men could fraternize with Japanese women.

"Hey, man, go down to Gate 2 and sign in Suzie for me," Bunter said to Gerald Miller this one day.

Gerry, a smiling, soft-spoken type from the outskirts of D.C., was stocked like the trunk of an apple tree. He was umpteen feet shorter than Earl with legs just long enough to reach the ground. The two hung out together and paired up like Mutt and Jeff.

"Yes, Sir!" said Gerry in a mock salute to his tall sergeant. He clicked his boot heels and disappeared.

Guests became the responsibility of the one who signed for them until they were back off base. Gerry accepted this one with fervor and, by later accounts, had sex out by the swimming pool. Recent activity was obvious when he and Suzie entered the club. I chatted with Bunter, and he just finished a dirty joke when his eyes lifted and moved to the right. Mine followed.

"Miller, you mudsucker! You messed with my girl!" he said, smacking his right fist into his left outstretched palm. A blood vessel the size of a drain pipe swelled in his forehead, and his chin jutted out in stubborn anger while he added a few expletives that weren't too complimentary.

Gerry paled, his round face sagging like melted wax. His lips moved as if they were trying to frame a response. Instead, he made a little motion with his head to say he was sorry for betraying his best buddy and stared at Bunter's feet.

Bunter turned to Suzie and pushed her toward a chair.

"Sit!" he ordered as if commanding a pet Schnauzer.

She was short and wore a short dress that exposed sturdy, slightly bowed legs with calves knotted in muscle, typical physique for Japanese gals. Dark eyes darted everywhere except up at her lover. Tears pearled at the corners.

"And, you! I'll deal with you later!" Bunter said, poking a finger in Miller's face. He stumped off to the restroom.

Miller broke into a stoop.

"It wasn't my idea," he said, blaming the girl. "We weren't more than two yards past the guard booth when she stopped and hugged me and, well, what's a fella gonna do?"

A bystander slapped Miller on the back.

"He'll get over it," he told Miller. "C'mon, have a beer."

"Hey, Chuck," said one of the guys to the bartender, "This time put saltpeter in his beer!" Saltpeter, a constituent in gunpowder, was sometimes added to drinks to subdue the imbiber's sexual appetite.

Everyone laughed.

Minutes later, Earl reappeared and placed a tight south paw on Gerry's shoulder. A tense moment for all of us.

"Listen, Bud," he said, relaxing his grip. "I don't care about any of this, except I got a good dose from her. Take the three quarter and go down to the pro station right away and have the medics give you a treatment."

Miller drained his glass, gulping its contents in one swallow, belched, and took off.

Earl got on the phone.

"I'm sending a guy down who needs a pro. Give it to him good and kick it up a notch or two!" Bunter was a man well wrapped around the axle.

The prophylactic team went along with the sergeant's little game and apparently gave Miller a wicked time, sticking tubes and needles through every hole and crevice they could find. When returning to the club an hour later, our buddy looked a defeated man. Miller had just been put through the proverbial mill!

"For he's a jolly good fellow, for he's a jolly good fellow, for he's a jolly good fellow, that nobody can deny. That nobody can…." we chorused, clinking our glasses in festive toast.

Another incident involving Bunter comes forth from the dark corridors of my mind. Again, more besides spinning the bottle. Fueling their glands with warm *sake* at a house of ill repute, Bunter, Collins, O'Riley, Spinner and two others, one whose name I can't recall and another whose name I'll always remember but choose not to reveal, began copulating by the numbers. They counted cadence, "One, two, three, four…," six women on the floor, six men on top. Similar to the "make love, not war" slogan a generation to come, all thoughts of genuine love in the spirit of procreation were absent from their current lust.

In the midst of this carnal frenzy, Private Collins all of a sudden remembered his sweetheart back home. He jumped up, private part standing at attention. While engaged in a full-blown crying jack, he climbed over the drunken orgy. By the time he… well, on second thought, we best stop here.

The latter is second-hand information, by the way. I was neither spectator nor participant in this decadent activity. It's true in the beginning that moral beliefs, shyness, and a country boy image handcuffed me to a great degree. After emergence, I still remained an exception rather than the rule when it came to the sexual playground. But please erase suspicions this author suffered from GID (gender identification deficit). This hardy virile soldier abstained for fear of potential health problems. As a matter of fact, I drank lots of iced tea mixed with saltpeter. My philosophy: if you don't play with snakes, you won't get bitten.

[The Army held Troop Information and Ed classes once a month. Fifty percent were on sexual-transmitted diseases. This strategy was an attempt to douse the fire before the match was struck, a plan as ineffective for some as opposing rain. Experience in herding the clap trap boys was a constant reminder that only fools dared such risky adventure, a belief I'll hold until the candles are blown out on my

95th birthday cake. The United States has the highest rate of STD of any country in the industrialized world, with 15,300,000 new cases reported each year. (The teen rate alone is the highest in the Western Hemisphere.) We are sitting right now on the verge of something so big nobody knows what to do about it because of its destructive power. It is called AIDS. Three million people died in 2002 of this deadly virus.]

As relief driver, I drove the captain home that evening. His name was Bond, James Bond.

Captain Bond was the CO of the 25th Quartermaster Company. He was commissioned in 1936 and came from the Second World War as a 1st lieutenant and made captain in '48. If you asked him about the war that followed the War to End All Wars, he offered conservative stories about stupid stuff they did, like stealing a taxi to go downtown Paris and getting drunk or how he learned some unrepeatable German phrases. But he never talked about the war itself or his personal accomplishments. He wore but one decoration out of many earned campaign ribbons, including a Purple Heart. That one was a simple combat badge.

Captain Bond was the kind of guy who was comfortable ringing his division commander, Major General William B. Kean, with, "Hey, Bill, this is Red," a nickname he earned from his strawberry shaded hair and smooth, fair-skinned face that burnt easily in a high sun. Short and stocky, (but so is a stick of dynamite), this CO of ours pulled no punches. He stood in front of the company and gave us royal H for this and royal H for that as if we were the worst recruits he ever laid eyes upon. He walked up to someone at attention, examined his rifle and reamed the living daylights out of him for the slightest nonconformance, all the while working his thin lips, his manner of showing minor discomfort. When he'd come to me, he'd wink and look at my gun with the casual indifference of a train conductor checking passenger tickets.

Not only because of his favoritism toward me, but also for many other reasons, Captain Bond was a number one guy in my book. In fact, in spite of being a harsh taskmaster, Bond was well respected and given high marks by all of his men. He lived with his wife and James Junior in Hamadera Park where other family officers resided.

I was busy wiping dust and dirt from the jeep when he walked out to meet me that first morning. I even opened the door like an authentic chauffeur might do. What, specifically, I never learned since he was not one to throw away compliments, but something about me or my actions impressed the heck out of him.

"I'll inform the 1st sergeant that Sergeant Walter Zweizig will be my driver from now on," he said on the way to the Barracks, then cast a side-ways glance I would come to recognize as tricky. He added, "in addition to your other duties [IAOD], of course."

Hooray! Brown-nosing paid off! Actually, two thoughts jockeyed for prime position. But *"Hooray! Now I have my set of wheels!"* won first place.

Within a week, my sidekick received a new assignment, company mail clerk. ["...IAOD, of course."] A three quarter ton truck was available whenever mail clerk duties required the use of a vehicle.

We were proud of our new responsibilities and respected the jeep—The Headquarters One jeep, I'll have you know, and mail truck like they were much more than mere hunks of cold and lifeless metal. They exuded character and gave us transportation and status. The locals custom-made pure white slip-over covers for the seats. Each week, we washed and polished our transports until they glistened like the showroom shine of a new car.

In addition to barracks inspection every Saturday, there was vehicle inspection. This was not a white gloves routine. But almost. We were prepared and focused on excellence, polishing ball joints and removing wires and distributors and distributor caps and wiping each part crazy clean. If the oil level showed low, we drained out the old and added new. If the change date on the radiator sticker was close at hand, clean antifreeze was poured in before it was due. Our fatigues had more grease on them than the engines by the time we finished.

The motor officer corporal doing the inspection carried a pan, and, at random, threw the pan underneath the radiator, opened the petcocks, and drained the coolant through the thin wing nut opening to determine how clean it was.

"If they have any more tricks up their petty sleeves," Baker said afterward, "they might as well forget it. We already thought of them."

A torn piece of canvas cost a weekend pass unless a deficiency sheet indicated imminent repair. Dirty canvas tops, dirt on the cab floor, or muddy tires were serious offenses. All in all, these types of demerit were not in order for Baker and me since our vehicles took turns named Best on Line.

These new toys were meant for official use only. But there were always ways to beat the system by making task schedules coincide with personal activity. This occasioned freedom to dispense work fatigues, don winter ODs or summer khakis, whichever the season mandated, and drive into the big city.

Osaka was full of noises and smells and sights unknown in Pennsylvania. (One exception: A pagoda on top of South Mountain overlooks the city of Reading. But that's another story on how this famous Japanese landmark found its way into the heart of Pennsylvania Dutch country.) An uninspired waterfront displayed a dull vista of fishing boats that looked like over-sized elf shoes. Piers stretched out from the shore where fishmongers tossed around the day's catch to process at nearby plants. Along the dock, numerous warehouses served as transient storage for goods brought in and out by commercial ships.

Although the American government was by far the largest employer, many national factories and industrial shops had come back to life since the war. These included workplaces credited with chintzy "Made in Japan" items little pipsqueaks back at Yokohama's railroad station huckstered to suckers like me.

The city had its upscale neighborhoods but was not without slums. Much of the outlying area where people lived was poor and rundown. Huts made of tarpaper or flimsy wood and no larger than our farm's milk house surrounded small courtyards. Off the courtyard was usually a honeywell where they dumped human slop from a public toilet. It was a semi-enclosed trench at the rear of the village. From there, honeywagons, the kind Baker had the great misfortune to hit, hauled the waste twice a week into the country where gardening utilized every square foot of space. There were few cars, the major mode of travel being bicycles, ricksha, donkey carts, and feet. Electric trolleys took people into the inner city.

The inner city bustled with activity. Neon lights beckoned day and night to prospective customers at bars, dance halls, and brothels. Restaurants and tiny shops lined the many lanes and passageways along the commercial downtown area. Most every corner had an open-air market of some sort, counters and bins abundant with fresh fruit and vegetable produce of the season. Of course, Osaka being a harbor, stalls exhibited fish and seafood of every variety imaginable, some still wiggling in bitter protest. A stink permeated the air far worse than when Mom dressed chickens on the back porch on a hot summer day, (usually chickens that had met their demise on the road out front).

Here and there, a network of canals with heavy boat traffic and bridges (*bashi*), arched high enough to allow long bamboo poles to pass underneath, connected chief thoroughfares. These bridges had character, mind you, for many a GI sloshed his way to one of these and jumped into the drink after a wasted night on the town.

(The acronym GI stands for either "General Issue" or Galvanized Iron," take your pick.)

Evidence of the war was everywhere. Bombed-out neighborhoods abounded, areas where tall prominent buildings once stood. Since we're talking less than four years since Japan's surrender, there was minimal reconstruction. Yet there was some. I saw one lot where resourceful laborers dug through endless rubble, knocked mortar off each single brick by hand, and reused these same bricks to erect a new structure on the spot.

Once in awhile, we saw an American movie at the Kitano Theatre or frequented one of the two downtown U.S. military-sanctioned cabarets *(kyabarei)*. (Any other drinking establishments were off limit to GIs.) Our favorite belly-up-to-the-bar haunt was the Kabuki Cabaret located in a large building just off the main drag. Do not confuse the name of this cabaret with the famous kabuki drama that features Japanese men playing female roles. If there were such performances in the same building, I was never aware of it.

Summers pulsed with life in the cabaret's Roof Garden. In winter, the watering hole moved down to the sixth floor. Inside could have been your typical Saturday night fire company blow-out back home with a bunch of tables and chairs, a jukebox, and dance floor. On a small stage, a two- or three-piece Japanese band entertained.

Here, Japanese girls entered at will. But when parties were back at base, girls waited at the gate for someone to sign them in. This was never a problem, of course, since guys much preferred to dance with girls instead of with other guys. Squat and chunky girls who wore wooden shoes called *geta* were not too popular. But gals visiting the base and cabaret were usually pretty little things, speaking broken English/GI slang *(O Joe-san, pom pom nei?)*, wearing lots of makeup, and dressed to kill in short skirts and spike heels. Successful in their attempt, they impressed the young and lonely GI.

Me? Good grief! I was much too shy to invite a girl to a party. Let alone throw my hat in the ring. The only boot-kicking I ever did, and reluctantly so, was back home at Saturday night hoe-downs in an unused mill shed across from a local hotel called Windsor Castle. And then only in winter. Summers, while guys my age were on dates and doe-si-doe-ing, I was busy making hay or milking cows. Too, knowing me, even if I had city-danced while in the service, I'd have been as graceful on the floor as a bull in a china shop. I preferred the background, opting *gschposs* with my buddies and nursing a coke or rum and coke instead.

One memorable event stands out. Not fortunate enough to drive to the cabaret with our own wheels this one particular evening, we trudged back to Tennojui Railroad Station on foot for our return trip to Kanoaka Village. The mist was thick as pea soup. Still, the first twenty miles of the waiting line were apparent when we arrived. Since servicemen were not required to buy tickets, we jumped the wooden railing and parted the paying crowd like a school of fish swimming upstream until we came to the parked railroad cars.

From out of nowhere, a Japanese national slithered forth with the spirit of a diamondback rattler. He had on a white short-sleeved dress shirt and black trousers, and his black eyes burnt with hatred and disdain as he proceeded to give me a piece of his mind he couldn't afford to do without, shouting through fishy breath obscenities I had never heard before. (Maybe because they were in Japanese?) Before I knew what happened, he blocked me and thrust a sharp punch below the belt that laid me out flat on the slick platform floor like a squashed bug.

Japanese police whistles shrieked.

Ladies screamed.

"Get Back! Get Back...." Baker's voice came as an echo from a distant canyon before it faded into a jumble of muffled sounds. The next thing I knew, my assailant stood over me with clenched fists. At once, a hot bolt of rage shot through me, and genetic demons kicked in. *Little does this dude know how much pleasure, how much long and lasting pleasure, it will give to pitch him above the excited crowd and be on my merry way.*

Quick as a mongoose strikes its prey, I was back on my feet and sprung a real haymaker, picking him up like he weighed no more than the sixty pounds he probably was. But woe, the back of my hand and his protruding teeth collided and sliced the knuckle of my right middle finger. In no more time than it takes to say, "Ouch! You hurt me!" my finger ballooned to the size of a cow's teat at milking time. Mr. Bucktooth, in a rush to attend the Annual Beavers Convention when I came along, was now hurried off by the police and out of my life forever.

When we arrived back at camp, I washed the sticky blood from my hand and went straight to bed. They say there is no bite more venomous to man than a bite from another man. I'd have not thought this possible. Yet by morning, my fist sizzled like fat in a skillet. They gave me penicillin at the dispensary, and those shots were repeated daily for ten successive days. This supposedly small injury took months to heal, and the scar from that brief fight remains to this day.

I received no Purple Heart as you might think I deserved, but did draw workmen's comp. Well, after a fashion. The 1st sergeant put me in charge of the Non-Commissioned Officers Club because of my injured right hand. I moved my sleeping quarters and all my gear to the club.

Since only buck sergeants or higher were allowed membership, Baker could not belong since he was still a corporal. Baker loved the club's egg and bacon sandwiches. Often, he called me to have one made up. Minutes later at the back door, I'd hand him the sandwich and a bottle of beer.

Japanese girls performed at the club. These, of course, were not the cultured geisha introduced earlier. But, they were attractive show girls nonetheless, talented in acting, song, and dance. Still Bond's driver, I had a special pass to go off-limits in Osaka where I made arrangements at Japanese theaters for our shows. The Japanese were always eager to do business with the American military because we paid more than they earned in Japanese theaters with Japanese audiences.

Whenever I went to lay the groundwork, Baker went along as my personal PR agent. My point man. He was a real comedian and did a much better job at price bargaining than I. When Saturdays arrived and a show was scheduled, the 1st sergeant authorized Baker and his three quarter to haul the show people in and return them to Osaka afterward. Baker often sat in the rear of the truck, strumming his guitar, always with a touch of ceremony, teaching the girls to sing "Red River Valley," or "I'm Looking Over a Four-leaf Clover." Or "On top of Old Smoky." Or "Your cheating heart will tell on you." Or some other favorite hit tune of the time.

Baker drew people like a magnet draws metal. A real ham, a jokester, musician, and singer extraordinaire. A class act. One of a kind. He was always surrounded. All who knew him thought he was good enough to be a famous country/western star. I've often thought since, Baker would've made a real hit at karaoke bars. Karaoke was not all the rage at the time we served in Japan, at least I never came across it. In fact, I wouldn't be one bit surprised if this novel Japanese singing expression so popular today weren't an American creation as is our large Italian pizza with all the toppings.

Between 1200 and 1230, they played country/western music on the Armed Forces radio station out of Osaka. Everyone on our barracks floor rushed through chow to hear Baker pick along and sing. It was like tuning in to the Grand Ole Opry on Saturday nights back home. Hank Williams was at the top of the charts at the time, and most of the songs we hankered for were his. Both Baker and I wrote to the station requesting songs. If we wrote too often and they put our requests on the back burner, we called in songs under fictitious names. One time, we petitioned a number from a PFC Joe Boysan. When they announced his name and played it, we laughed to beat the band! "Boy-san" was nothing more than GI slang for a Japanese boy.

They broke all the molds when Baker was made. No German blood, but he couldn't help for that. But what a friend! If I had weekend guard duty and he didn't, he was always on base close by. If he had a trip scheduled to Osaka, he asked if I wanted anything from the PX or the Roof Garden. When I had weekend duty, he showed up out of the blue with a couple of burgers and offered to run errands, like picking up laundry or anything else that needed to be done. Like a man and his shadow, so bonded were Gaines L. Baker and I.

He's given this seventy-six year old man plenty of good memories to dwell upon before walking into the sunset.

Don't Rock the Boat

The whale swallowed Jonah down the hatch
Then coughed him up because he scratched.
                                    - Burma Shave

Asandy beach along Osaka Bay near the city of Sakai was divided into two. One was private and fronted Hamadera Park. West of there, Special Services had boat rental facilities and refreshment stands where peons with less than two dimes to rub together loitered on weekends.

One Sunday afternoon, Leon Brittamy, talkative, amusing barracks buddy from Brockton, Mass slaughtered his piggy bank and rented a rowboat.

"Alright you guys. Let's go!" he said to Baker and me. "Look at all that water out there beckoning to us!"

We looked. Three pairs of eyes followed a vast expanse of blue to a horizon many miles away.

"Yeah, and that's just the top of it!" Baker said with a different take on the situation. "I'd just as soon walk a tight rope across Niagara Falls."

"Don't be chicken now! Navigating those waters is safer than driving a mail truck." Brittamy was that unusual blond type who tanned deeply. His eyebrows and lashes were bleached almost white by the summer sun. He dropped to a bare knee before Baker, and, with a brown arm, removed an imaginary hat with a sweeping gesture. "If you please, my fair one, this dashing, handsome young knight will cruise to far ports unknown if only thee would join me."

Baker laughed.

"Thank you, sire, but I'll remain right here, if you please."

Britt stood, and, with a strong grip on my tee-shirted shoulder, guided me toward the boat.

"How about you, Buddy?" he said, slipping from sophisticated old English to a less yet still somewhat fancy New England accent. "There's a lot more out there to enjoy than there is sitting here on the beach watching others out there having all the fun." He winked back at Baker.

As far as I could see, there wasn't a soul in the water. But I didn't want to make waves, pardon the nautical metaphor. I said,

"Well, I don't know."

"Let's face it," said Britt. "We couldn't have a nicer, calmer day to put into the mix!" Britt would have made a good salad dressing salesman and sold me, thinking it rather important at the time in an unimportant sort of way, or maybe being just plain old stupid and taking leave of my senses. Martin Luther once said, "If the Bible says don't do it, don't do it. If it doesn't say don't do it, do it." It didn't say anywhere in the Good Book that a young whippersnapper from Pennsylvania shouldn't row in Japan's Osaka Bay. Of course, I didn't know this on that sunny August afternoon. Everything that lay before me was new and mysterious and exciting in a way you can't imagine. Japan was full of adventures I'd never dreamed of.

Leon was right when he said it was a beautiful summer day, a picture-perfect day, a meteorologist's can't-go-wrong-on kind of day. If they predicted "Partly Sunny," and there was a meager patch of cloud between here and Mars, they hit the bull's eye right on. If that little puffy cloud matured into a bigger puffy one, covering the sun in passing, they forecast the weather on target with "Partly Cloudy." Whether it was partly sunny or partly cloudy is beside the point. It could have stormed and hailed for all we cared when we pushed our fourteen-foot vessel into the deep. We chided ourselves for not having had the recreational forethought to row on our many previous excursions to the bay.

We paralleled the beach in total control of our aimless destination while engaged in nonsense chatter. This ran the scope from emergency tactics we'd employ should sea gulls deposit their disgusting byproduct on our naked heads to drifting back in time.

"My uncle had a trailer once," said Britt. "Every summer our families took a vacation in it, and one year we went to the beach at Cape Cod."

"Did you row?" Inexperienced in the ways of a bay, I watched him syncopate the oars to the gentle swing and sway of the rippling saltwater.

"No, but we played volley ball on the beach. And we jumped the waves. That was loads of fun, especially when the tide came in, and they bowled us over."

"I'll bet. How old were you?"

"Old enough to know better considering some of the things I did." He looked off into space, remembering, I believe, of another time. "The grownups slept in the trailer, but we kids slept in sleeping bags on the beach. My younger cousin was a spoiled brat and poured wet sand in my bag. I didn't discover it until I crawled in." He closed his eyes briefly and laughed. "But I got even! The next night, we had ourselves hot dogs and marshmallows over the campfire, and I made sure there were plenty of toasted marshmallows left over to decorate the inside of HIS sleeping bag."

"Boy, I bet that was a mess!" I never camped out as a kid, let alone toasted marshmallows.

"Yeah," he snickered. "Sylvester got away with everything. Me, my parents grounded me."

"Grounded?" The term was unfamiliar. I couldn't help myself and said this time, "What do you mean?"

He chuckled.

"I guess the word is sanded. There were two days left to our vacation, and I wasn't allowed to go near the water for punishment. You, did you ever go to the beach?"

"No." I didn't have any memories of my own to share and said, "But my cousin went to Atlantic City every August with a girlfriend and her mother. She always brought saltwater taffy home."

"Hey, I ate some of that stuff once. Hmmmmm! Sticky and yummy! I wonder why they call it that though. I heard they don't even use saltwater to make it."

"They don't?" I never gave it any thought.

"Didn't you want to go along with her?"

"From what she told me. I didn't think I'd be too interested. I got enough sun making hay and shocking wheat and oats."

I mean, like duh, really, no kidding, who in their right mind would drive that far just to do a barefoot chicken walk over hot sand and get a painful burn lying in the hot sun!

"Your feet," he said. "Didn't your feet get sunburned on the farm?"

I was lounging near the tiller, facing him. He glanced at my bare feet with their toes curled around the floor slats.

"Nope," I said and proceeded defensively. "This might come as a shock to you, but I did wear shoes. They were often holey or repaired with cardboard and laced with binder twine. But, yes, we farm kids did wear shoes. Would you want to step in a cow plop without them?"

A fresh breeze picked up over the bay.

Out of the clear blue, Britt said,

"Did you know that sea turtles go to shore to have their young?"

I shook my head. I had no idea.

"And you know what else? As soon as the babies are out of the shell, they crawl into the sea. Only a few survive because the other sea life eats them up." He was a fountain of information. Scientists say we use only two percent of our brainpower. Some of us demonstrate less, but with Leon it had to be more. There was more worldly knowledge in the tip of his little finger than in my whole hand.

"Do you think there's something in here that might eat us if it had half a chance?" I said. The water looked harmless enough, but one couldn't see two inches down.

"Goodness, no!" he said. "There's a shelf life for all of us, and statistics prove we're too young to die."

"Yeah, but what if?"

"What if what?"

"What if our boat tipped and something big was down there?" I was certain the water was full of smelly, scaly, slippery fish, but I thought of sharks or whales and such.

"Well, Bud, you might have something there," he said and paused in his rowing. "Wouldn't that be exciting!"

"What d'ya mean?"

"I mean, think of the adventure of being swallowed by a whale!"

"Swallowed by a whale!" I said. "You're not telling me you actually believe that story of Jonah being swallowed by a whale, do you?" I heard it many times. An allegory, our Sunday school teacher called it, God's way of telling us about the runaway prophet and how we can't run away from Him. He is always there.

"Maybe. I can't exactly vouch for Jonah, but I do understand it coulda happened."

"How so?" This, I decided, was the least-likely-to-be-accepted information he could sell me on.

"I know it's hard to believe. But I read in the encyclopedia once that humans have been swallowed alive by giant sea monsters. And, lived to tell the story, no less."

"No!" I said.

"Yes!" he said. "Certain whales have no teeth, and they feed in an interesting way by opening their big mouths, dropping their lower jaw and rushing through the water at a terribly fast speed. After they strain out the water, they swallow whatever is left."

"Get out!" I made the connection and didn't need to hear this. Not now!

"I'm serious. Check it out for yourself. Back in the thirties, they captured a sulfur-bottom whale measuring one hundred feet long off of Cape Cod. It was not too far from where we used to go. His mouth was maybe ten or twelve feet wide, I forget exactly, and could easily swallow a horse, they said. They said the whale had something like four to six compartments in his stomach, any one of which a group of men could find free lodging inside."

"No!" I said.

"Yes!" he said. "They said these men could even have a choice of rooms, because in the head of this monster was an air storage chamber something like seven feet high and again as wide and fourteen feet long where they could breathe."

"You're making this up."

"Nope." Leon threw back his head and laughed. I was sure he was making fun of me for being so gullible that I would believe this ridiculous tale. "They said if a whale like this has an unwelcome guest on board that gives him a headache, he swims to the nearest shore and spits him out." He puckered up, thrust a good one out into the bay, and began to row again. "Just like that! Just like the whale did in the Bible story."

"Wow! I heard some tall fish tales in my time, but this beats all," I said, staring at him in disbelief.

"Hey, you don't believe me?" he said in a tone that indicated I was not with it. "Wait till you hear this one. I got all wrapped up in this whale stuff after that Cape Cod incident and checked out everything else I could find on the subject."

"Well, what did you find?"

"Several things, but, the biggest impression on me was a story this Englishman back in the 1890's told of a strange experience he had. It happened near the Falkland Islands."

I wondered where they were, but didn't want to reveal my ignorance. Brittamy knew so much!

"Anyway," he continued, "this guy captained a whale ship. Oh, by the way, his report was investigated by two scientists and was found to be true. Just thought I'd say that in case you don't believe this one neither. Anyway, the lookout man spotted a large sperm whale three miles away. After they closed in, they lowered two boats. The harpooners in the one boat were unable to spear the fish. Then the second boat attacked the whale but was upset by a lash of the monster's tail and the men were thrown into the sea. One was drowned, and the other man they couldn't find. The whale was finally killed, and, in a few hours, they got it to shore and dissected it for blubber and for all the other parts they use whales for."

I thought of bio class where we cut up a frog in the name of science and a squashed cat someone peeled off the road.

He went on.

"To make a long story short, they found the missing sailor inside the whale."

"No!" I said.

"Yes!" he said. "He was doubled up and unconscious. But he came to after they poured seawater over him."

Since that day on the bay, I heard my own story, one with a humorous twist from a book written by William Bakus called <u>The Paranoid Prophet</u>. The author interacts as a clinical therapist or psychologist in session with his patient, the biblical Jonah. If you want an idea of what it was like for Jonah in modern terms, read on. First, let me provide some background.

God asked the prophet Jonah to go to the city of Nineveh and "cry out against it for their wickedness has come up before Me." But Jonah didn't want to preach the gospel to the Ninevites. He hated them and fled from the presence of the Lord by boarding a ship to Tarshish. But the Lord sent out a great wind on the sea so the ship was about to be broken up. The mariners became afraid, and every man cried out to his god and threw cargo into the sea to lighten the load. Jonah knew he caused the trouble so he told the sailors to throw him overboard, then the Lord would calm the seas.

"…At first they ignored my solution," Jonah said with a rye bitter smile to the therapist. "They rowed with all their might, but the sea grew worse and worse and their arms finally gave out, and they knew there was no other choice. The sailors cried out to Yahweh for forgiveness and threw me overboard. I couldn't swim. I plunged down through the black water, and it seemed forever. Then kicking and struggling, I managed to find my way to the surface. The sea was already smooth, the wind stopped, and I thought I'd splash my way to a piece of wood from one of the chests the sailors threw overboard…"

But God had other plans and sent a lifeguard to pick him up.

"I turned just in time to see it coming," continued Jonah. "A sea creature the size of a ship raced toward me, it's mouth open. Screaming in terror, I was swallowed whole. I managed to breathe by keeping my head above the acidic fluids in the creature's gut. The stench was so overpowering, I argued with myself before I drew each breath. Finally, I decided to inhale through my mouth, but the sour fumes hurt my lungs. The darkness was total," he said, his voice sinking to a hush. "The noise all around me was like that of a huge machine. The thud of the creature's heartbeat, the swish of blood, the body fluids, the bubbling gases hummed

around me, hurting my ears. I knew nothing but terror. My recollections from this point on are cloudy," said Jonah. "I was buried
alive, in hell without having died, and nothing could get me out.
Desperately, I called to God for help even though hours before I
wanted to get as far away from Him as I could."

"I realized I was gaping," said the therapist. "Even reasonably,
this man was spilling out the most unreasonable story I ever heard."

"I don't remember much else," said Jonah. "I'm sure I was in a
semi-conscious state most of the time. Near as I can figure, I was in
the belly of that thing for about three days and three nights. During my better moments I cried out to Yahweh, and do you know the
worst of it? The fish became sick of me and vomited me up. I was
forced up through that massive slimy digestive tract and dumped on
to a sandy beach...."

God had proved He's a God of second chances.

After a half-hour or so of rowing, I thought my eyes played tricks on
me when the shoreline distanced itself from view. Leon made mention of it, too. While busy chatting, the unthinkable had happened.
We drifted away with the tide!

"You guys are getting too far out!" Baker yelled from shore, his
hands cupped like a megaphone.

Right!

Now the bay looked unpleasant and slate-colored. Soon, choppy
water underneath a sun fighting to keep control bobbed us up and
down like a cork in a washbasin. I grasped one of the oars to assist
Britt and, in haste, managed to pull it out of the socket, yet stabbed
with all my might at the oncoming waves. It was like paddling upstream with only one paddle. Just then, horrors of horrors, the tool
tore from my grip and disappeared.

Lifting and lowering the boat, the disgruntled surf splashed
oceans of water, practically swallowing both of us. I felt the de-
spair Jonah suffered sloshing around in his sleazy underwater
hotel. I'm sure I soiled myself, too, but who would've known the

difference. I tried spooning water out of the boat with my hands but even a table fork would have proved more effective.

While we contemplated our next move in survival technique, deep-throated horns of an approaching freighter gained our split attention.

"HELP! HELP!" We flailed our arms like Methodists at a tent revival. "HELP!" we cried again and again and again. To our absolute disbelief, these people waved from the ship's railing and kept on going. Little did they know we were about to drown. When the boat rose to the crest of each wave, we saw shoreline. As the boat dropped, we saw murky water and more murky water.

"Can you swim?" I asked in a panic.

"Barely. Can you?"

It took me a moment to form the answer.

"No," I squeaked. My only experience was the time Cousin Leroy threw me into Fisher's Dam, the local swim hole feeding the raceway to the village of Berne's flourmill. When I didn't resurface, he knew I wasn't kidding about my lack of fins.

As a couple of young lads still wet behind the ears, literally, we hadn't thought to ask that question of ourselves before we ventured out in the boat. *Ai Yi Yi!* Where had our heads been, anyway? Yet in defense of our innocence, you pitch into the water a ten-week old, run-of-the-mill pup who's never seen the inside of a pond, and it will swim to the closest bank, shake, then trot to the food dish as if this were standard operating procedure. (Could it be man had the same natural ability if he weren't so intimidated by fear of the unknown?)

My partner plunged.

"Hey! I'm standing!" he shouted.

Yeah, and the White House is painted black! I didn't believe until he disappeared underneath the water and came back up with a handful of dirt. I bolted overboard, and, sure enough, stepped on what felt like solid ground. One hand clawing the boat's rim, I pushed myself away into the direction of the beach.

But the bay had a trick up its watery sleeve. Strong currents underneath wash deep gullies in the sand. You could stand knee-deep one minute, take a step or two forward and without warning drop off into a bottomless pit, which, in less time than it takes for me to tell is exactly what happened. After much sputtering and splashing and absorbing salty, fishy seawater like a sponge, I reached the edge of the boat and thrust myself to the surface. This time, white knuckles squeezed with the intensity of a clenched fist. The boat, with both of us clinging fast, hovered inches below the surface, yet, hadn't sunk. Thank God for flotation tanks!

Baker, meanwhile, recognized our plight and attempted to rent a twenty-foot punt from the Japanese who were set up alongside Special Services in hopes of renting to GIs. "Scully" is the nickname we gave these boats. On such a one, the navigator stands at the rear and, using a long thick bamboo pole instead of an oar, propels it through water at a pretty good pace. Like I've mentioned before, canals in downtown Osaka were full of these. Some stretched to thirty feet or more. Baker tried to negotiate with papa-san to go out into the bay and bring us in. The problem was papa-san wanted a two hundred yen rental fee paid up front. That was out of the question since Baker didn't have the money. Unknown to us at the time, he knocked the guy down, took his boat, and left to pick us up.

Between the rise and fall of the horizon, I caught a glimpse of Baker headed our way. He was alone. Twenty or thirty minutes later, his craft slid alongside ours, and we crawled in.

"You drowned rats would be up the friggin crick without me," was Baker's comment without a trace of emotion. "You know that, don't you!"

"Yes, my friend. But now we're all in the same boat," I said, making a feeble attempt at a joke.

Baker gave a small involuntary snort, like when a drink goes down the wrong way. Britt pounded him on the back and the three of us burst out laughing and joked around all the way back to the beach. During a serious moment, we thanked Baker for coming to the rescue.

"We'll pay our share of the fee," Leon promised before we learned the facts.

"Uh, Oh! That's probably why the MPs are on the beach," one of us observed. A military police jeep waited by the water's edge along with three Japanese policemen.

"I woulda never hit the guy if he woulda lent me his boat," pleaded Baker, when the authorities questioned him. "What did you expect me to do? Watch 'em drown?"

Good one, Baker. You were trained well. The best defense is a good offense.

After a dramatic exchange of quibble, the military and Japanese officials escorted Baker to Osaka. As soon as they cleared the beach, I raced over to Hamadera Park to see our commanding officer. James Junior was dribbling a basketball outside their living quarters and stopped to stare at the pounds of sand my legs and feet had collected during my run. I delivered a sketchy report of my mission and asked if his dad was home.

"He's next door with Lieutenant Bowman. I'll get him." The boy took off.

Captain Bond's face creased up in a frown and turned the shade of red earth after I explained what happened and Baker's predicament.

"Give me a few minutes to get into uniform, and we'll go see them."

Within ten minutes, the Captain in tidy dress and me smelling worse than a dog caught in a rainstorm sped to the MP station. Upon arrival, he identified himself and requested Baker's immediate release. A muscle twitched in the captain's left cheek and his lips worked back and forth as they often did whenever he grew tense. He said,

"I'll administer punishment on my own people." And that settled that! The MPs were probably glad to let Baker go and have Bond handle the plentiful paperwork that's necessary in the case of disciplinary action.

"What the @#$%, Baker," Captain Bond said as I drove us back to base, "I didn't know you liked to fight. Maybe we can get you on the boxing team." Our good captain managed a shadow of a grin.

I glanced at Baker through the rear view mirror. His apple cheeks had colored even more.

"Oh, no, Sir. I hate to fight, but this was an emergency."

Beneath our captain's hardened hide was a heart as big and soft as a ripe melon. As far as I recollect, my favorite buddy was immediately back in the saddle and never punished for hitting that guy.

"And you, young man," the captain said, turning toward me. "Stay away from water until you learn how to swim!"

Touché.

"Yes, Sir." Lesson learned. Swimming would top my Things To Do List when I returned home.

We thought Baker deserved a medal for bringing us back to safety. But, of course, there was none, the unmentionable honor being only that he escaped the stockade. Several days later, in the motor pool, we took matters into our own hands and cut, folded, and hammered a small piece of tin to the shape of a military ribbon. On this, we painted several stripes in bright color making it look very official. We made a formal presentation one evening while perched on the edge of our bunks. Baker stood at attention. He was naked except for his GI boxers and two sets of dog tags hanging from his neck.

"We present to you, Corporal Gaines L. Baker," said our spokes person, "the Highest Medal of Honor issued by the Army of the United States Armed Forces for saving the lives of your team mates Corporal Leon G. Brittamy and Sergeant Walter M. Zweizig, both of the 27th Regiment of the 25th Infantry Division. May you wear this ribbon with pride and honor on behalf of your fellow countrymen."

Baker saluted.

"May I be permitted to speak freely, Sirs?" he said.

"Permission granted," said I, in mock salute.

"I accept this honor with the greatest of gratitude. My most gracious thanks to each and every one of you, kind Sirs!" he said and whipped off the salute.

The rest of the guys in the hall clapped and whistled. Each, in turn, came by and shook Baker's hand.

Every time we were required to dress in Class A uniform, Baker wore his ribbon. It wasn't until several months later that an inspection officer questioned him.

"We only allow authorized military ribbons," the officer warned.

Baker removed it. But whenever we went anywhere outside inspection, he wore this pin. It looked so real. No one knew it was home-made. But Baker was just as proud of it as if it were the Congressional Medal of Honor.

12

Back to School

We leave our footprints in the sands of time.
- Henry Wadsworth Longfellow

Not allowing school to interfere with my education, I became a high school dropout at sixteen. Now at the insistence of Captain Bond, I enrolled in the United States Armed Forces Institute in Osaka to get my GED. The captain offered his jeep. Along with a handful of buddies thumbing a ride at the front gate, I went two evenings a week into the city. Classes were scheduled 1900 to 2130.

The school, located in the Gas building, occupied much of my time in January (1950) through June, the close of the semester. Subjects were English, mathematics, history, and typing....

"Now is the time for all good men to come to the aid of their country."

"Now is the time for all good men to come to the aid of their country."

"Now is the time for all good men to come to the aid of their country."

Our typing teacher was a maiden civilian from the States. Her salt and pepper hair was pulled back severely into a bun that resembled Olive's in the Sunday funnies, and her chin came to a peculiar point below her face that gave her mouth a pinched look. She was Blanche Blanchard, if you can believe it, and more ancient than pyramids in Egypt. Long on age but short on tolerance, this woman could stop erasers in mid-air when she entered the classroom.

"Sit erect and keep both feet flat on the floor!" she repeated with rapid fire, glowering over half-moon reading glasses that sometimes hung from a beaded chain around her neck.

I preferred slouching and resting my feet on the table brace ten inches up from the bottom.

"Now is the time for all good man to cme to the aid of thr country."
"Now is the time for all god men to come to the aid of their country."

Miss Blanchard often walked up from behind and slammed her wooden pointer on my worktable, scaring the living juice out of me.

"Noq is the tlme for good mean to come..."

One night, she whacked the pointer so hard a fifteen-inch section broke off and wedged itself between the typewriter and tabletop. I did what any respectable gentleman would do and, with a resounding thud, pulled it out and handed it to her. She snatched it, but the rubber tip remained in my hand. Both holding remnants of her nasty tool, we ended up glaring at each other before she turned and strutted back to her desk. I felt like throwing my typewriter after her. (See Addendum.)

"I got this great idea," Archibald said after class one night.

You need to know about Archibald Nessling. He was the sharpest pencil in the box, yesterday's equivalent of today's Bill Gates. He read Popular Science as a kid while I was reading comic books. Through the years, I've searched page after page in various tech journals for Archibald Nessling's latest achievement. I wondered even back then what a brilliant guy like Archibald was doing in our USAFI typing class. I was afraid to ask. On one occasion, I asked what time it was, and he told me how to make a watch. (See Addendum.)

Perhaps he was more like Robert Fulton than Bill Gates. The famous inventor of the steamboat was held back in grammar school because he didn't do his homework. His mother told the teacher, "He has so many ideas in his head he doesn't have time for those in your books."

"Maybe we can take the meanness out of Miss Blanchard by being nice," was Archie's suggestion.

"What? Her? You got to be kidding!" I said. "It can't be done."

He had a plan. Though doubtful, I went along with it. So did the others.

We started with the traditional apple for the teacher and gifted her with popcorn and chocolate. Even cigarettes to support her smoking habit. One night, we loaded her desk with so many items from the PX there was no room left for lesson plans. Throughout typing class, my feet stayed glued to the floor and my body so rigid and straight you might have thought I was one of those stick people kindergarten kids love to draw.

There really is something to the maxim, "Love your enemies; it drives them crazy," for this particular night we had our teacher both crying and laughing as a result of our kindness. When you throw a couple of devilish GIs together in the same room, there's no telling what can happen.

During breaks, we chatted with the school secretary.

Mai Maknihara was Nissei, second generation Japanese American. In 1925, her father had moved from his native country to San Francisco where he met Mai's mother, also Japanese, and where Mai was later born. She grew up speaking both English and Japanese fluently and had also attended two years at UCLA on the university's San Francisco campus. Life was good, but things would change.

After the Pearl Harbor attack on December 7, 1941, "a date which will live in infamy," Japanese immigrants and Nissei were declared enemies of the state and forced from their homes by order of

President Franklin Delano Roosevelt. The government confiscated properties and sequestered people at relocation camps in California, Colorado, Wyoming, Idaho, and Arizona. Perhaps there were other states as well, but I know of those five for sure. In one sense, you could say American encampment was based on philosophy parallel to Germany's—prejudice. Yet the two differed in significant ways. One fostered experimentation and extermination, the other mere confinement for the war's duration. It's easy today to say our government was wrong.   But we feared the risk of Japanese sympathizers in our midst should Japan invade the West Coast. (The courts later challenged the government, deeming its action unconstitutional.)

You might wonder, what about German immigrants and German Americans?   And the Italians, what about them?   Fascist Italy was involved in the war, too. Why weren't they rounded up?

Some were. It is truly sad, but today's school textbooks are surprisingly vague on both world war histories. But a recent PBS Special claimed 600,000 non-naturalized Italians were classified enemy alien by their adoptive country after the start of the second war in Europe. They were returned to port of entry on Ellis Island or interned. In some areas of our country, imaginary demarcation lines split entire towns and highways in half, "enemy" ethnic groups on one side, others opposite. Young men of eligible age were either drafted to fight the Axis killing machine or sent to prison camp, their choice. If drafted, they automatically became American citizens.

As for Germans and German Americans, 10,000 believed to be security risks were interned at Crystal City, Texas during the rule of the Third Reich.

Nationwide, during both wars, many Americans with German roots experienced strong anti-German hysteria, including children harassed by fellow classmates taught to "Hate the Hun." German American clubs were renamed and German dishes removed from public menus. An example of bringing discrimination closer to home, a cousin-in-law from New York who married into the Zweizig *freinschaft* said his grandparents changed the pronunciation of the family name Riedel (ree'-del) to Riedel (ri-del') to sound Irish as in Rydell to avoid suspicion of German blood.

Started during the Great War, U.S. authorities, fearing a conflict of loyalty, forbade use of the German dialect in public assembly. Strictly *verbotem*! For this reason, speaking Pennsylvania Dutch was not permitted at the Zweizig School, a one-roomer built on the southeast corner of the Zweizig homestead. This was where Pop and my aunts and uncles attended and first learned to speak English. Entire student bodies, including teachers, had German blood flowing through their veins. (Demographics are changing in favor of the Hispanic influx in our country, but up to and into the 21st century, one out of every five Americans purportedly has German ancestry.) Fortunately, they were not harassed because entire communities in southeastern Pennsylvania were of German descent.

In fact, the Pennsylvania German community as a whole escaped prejudice. I'm thinking because we go back to pre-Revolutionary War days (as opposed to immigrant Germans arriving after the Industrial Revolution). Successive rural generations, though still retaining the dialect and culture of the mother country, were considered bona fide Americans and no longer a threat. Anyway, that's my personal theory on the situation. (See Addendum.)

(Interesting to note that back in the 18th century, after the Declaration of Independence was signed and English-speaking England was not a favored ally of ours, the thirteen colonies nearly adopted German as the national language. Also interesting to note that, had we not been victorious in Europe in the 20th century, we might all be speaking German today.)

Uncle Herbert, dutchified as crock-cured sauerkraut, traveled with his family to Canada on vacation just weeks after the second war in Europe ended. The reason I bring this up is that customs officials detained him at the Canadian border until convinced, after lengthy interrogation, his loyalties lay in the heart of Pennsylvania Dutch farm country.

Here's an additional wartime curiosity. The British employed German Hessians during the Revolutionary War to fight against the colonies. At the close of the war, the Hessians on duty and those in prisoner-of-war camps in Berks County opted to stay on rather than return home to the *fodderland*. They were in a land where political and religious freedom prevailed, where people spoke their language, shared the same rural culture, land topography, climate and, in general, an economy far better than in the country they left behind.

Many Germans imprisoned in the United States during WWII returned to their homeland after the Armistice only to return as immigrants in favor to the Stars and Stripes.

Here's another noteworthy incident of how crossing cultural boundaries in wartime circumstance has impact, negative or positive. In Germany during WWII, physical abuse by POW camp guards was for the most part subdued (although there were rare cases of Russian Roulette I've heard.), a positive result of the country signing an agreement in 1929 with the International Red Cross based on the Geneva Convention. Still, there was verbal abuse, constant hunger, filth, lice, and disease to contend with. In spite of these calamities, my neighbor and good friend Charlie—a blue star on a field of white in the Bubbenmoyer family's window—"found favor" during imprisonment compared to other POWs because of a conversant ability with German guards. He even served as interpreter within Stalag 13.

I heard of equivalent experiences from others on how the bilingual tongue aided one way or another. One man in particular comes to mind. He was drafted in 1941 before the U.S. officially declared war on the Far East enemy. He was Japanese American. Following the attack on Pearl Harbor, the military suspended his training and assigned him to menial tasks instead. Later, recognizing the value of Japanese translators and familiarity with foreign culture, they sent this soldier to Military Intelligence School. He then interrogated Japanese prisoners for the duration of the war and translated multiple documents for combat troops. His allegiance to the United States earned him enough medals to do one really proud.

And I'm sure you've heard of the 442nd Regimental Combat Team when an inexperienced officer led an all-Japanese American special attack force on the European front. This unit, combined with the 100th Infantry Battalion, was among the bravest in U.S. military history, receiving more than 18,000 honors.

(Jumping ahead of the storyline, I thought it appropriate to mention here, too, that Nissei Hiroshi "Hershey" Miyamura received from his Commander in Chief the Medal of Honor for heroic battle during the Korean War.)

But, of course, most Japanese Americans were not so well respected. The Maknihara family was one. In the fall of '42, the U.S. Government requisitioned the rodeo and competition grounds located in Salinas, California for a Japanese American internment camp. Out buildings and stables were converted into living quarters and additional dorms and other facilities added to the grounds. This is where Mai and her family housed until Japan's official surrender on September 2, 1945.

Their needs were adequately met while interned, and they were never mistreated in the true sense of the word. Yet after the war, when integrated back into society, they were shunned by the American public. For this reason and because of the humbling and degrading experience of being herded behind barbed wire during the war, the Maknihara family and many others moved to Japan in January 1946. (In 1988, under President Ronald Reagan's administration, congress appropriated $20 million in reparations to surviving Japanese families. The goodwill offering was divided up among those detained across the United States between 1942 and 1945.)

Mai took a liking to me (or maybe it was the jeep). This was the same gal who had been approached at one time or another for a date by every single male in school (except me) and who had refused each offer. In a private conversation between the two of us in her office one evening, I discovered why that was, but only after I told her I had never asked her out because I didn't date anyone. "I came to Japan without VD," I said, "and I'm going to return to the States without it." My confession apparently impressed her, admitting later on that the fear of VD was the reason she turned down all servicemen.

"I'll give you credit for attending class if you take me to dinner on Wednesday evening," she said one time. Mai had a low pleasant voice that sounded close to laughter when she spoke. No accent. It was the first time we had really made eye contact. For the first time I noticed hers were striking and kind of playful. She smelled good, too.

What was it she'd just said? Oh, yes, she asked me to join her for dinner.

Dinner? Me?

"My father's receiving an award at the banquet in his honor," she said and went on to explain that the city of Osaka appointed him chief of police because of his bilingual ability and communicative skills in dealing with both the Japanese and the U.S. military.

How could I resist? Besides, Wednesday was typing class.

Mai showed up that fine spring evening in a trim, black wool sweater dress and high-heeled pumps. She made a spectacular fashion statement. Her soldier boy did, too, if I must say so. I was decked out in dress khakis and a tie I tied three times before the knot suited, a flying saucer hat, and spit-shined brown low quarters. *Looking good.* My heart beat at the rate of hummingbird wings when I escorted the lovely Miss Mai to dinner.

The plush restaurant was in an area out-of-bounds for servicemen except for those with special passes. It was located in an upscale neighborhood near downtown Osaka. A beautiful Japanese garden of miniature Asian pines, waterways, arched bridges, and pagoda-style gazebos surrounded the place. Extended from the impressive entrance, a broad path underneath a long canopied frame wound its way into the building like a giant green caterpillar. From there, a cement stairwell with plush red carpeting stretched to the second floor where the group assembled for dinner.

We dined and enjoyed the evening's festivities while Japanese policemen assigned by Mai's father watched my jeep. I could not afford to have the jeep stolen or cannibalized for parts as sometimes happened to American vehicles. You'd think if a Japanese afforded his own car he would not stoop so low as a snake's belly and steal in order to maintain it. Nevertheless, it wasn't always a matter of sufficient money or lack of it. In some, there still prevailed this underlying resentment toward Americans since the bomb, evidenced by my previous experience at the railroad station.

But not to let other crooks off the hook. One must admit Osaka, like any big city, had its crime. At dusk one summer evening, I walked down Lightning Boulevard, busily on my way to somewhere. The destination is withdrawn from my memory bank, but I recall it was warm, and I wore a short-sleeved khaki shirt. A well-dressed Japanese in a three-piece black outfit approached and pointed to my wrist.

"I buy watch?" he said. It was not an unusual gesture to purchase

American items as I've shown you before with the C rations.

"How much?" I said.

"I give eighty American dollar." Beady eyes that matched the color of the young man's suit stared at me, awaiting an answer.

"Okay, then." I tried not to seem excited about his generous offer. But I was. I hadn't seen greenbacks since we left the States. Here they paid us in military scrip. *Eighty dollars worth? You better believe it!*

"I hide money inside yen and give you," he said this time.

"Okay," I said again, checking the sidewalk traffic. It was not smart to appear conspicuous in making street transactions. I accepted the yen note packed with a handful of paper money and, stifling a whistle, took off in the direction of the PX to purchase another watch.

You know how sometimes something deep inside doesn't sit right in spite of how good it feels on the outside. When I came upon better light, I made a closer inspection. Surprise! Surprise! A bunch of scrunched up notes valued at one one-hundredth of a yen were inside and about as worthless to me as a toothbrush is to a hen; or worse yet, a scope to a skunk. My mind calculated on a Japanese abacus that this sticky-fingered con artist took off with my fifteen-dollar watch for a piddling seventy-five cents in exchange. Zapped again by the Japanese economy! I knew the feeling all too well.

School was a breeze. I was an A student and found myself playing hooky more and more often, attending only half my classes. When I did, I stayed an hour or so then joined Mai on her off nights for dinner or visits with the family in their Osaka home.

Mrs. Maknihara, like her daughter, dressed in western fashion. She was a sweet, gracious little woman who always ushered me to an orange La-Z-Boy brought from the States. The clumsy recliner looked out of place amongst the refined teak furnishings in the small room where they entertained. It was obviously lowered in the legs, perhaps for the ocean voyage, though I liked to think it was to bring me closer to the floor where Mai, no siblings, and her father sat cross-legged on plush pillows while I visited.

Mr. Maknihara was rather tall for a Japanese, maybe six foot one or so. Though I never asked, I assume there was European blood in there somewhere, judging not only by his height, but also by his round deep-set Caucasian eyes. Straight jet black hair, always neatly combed, prominence of frontal facial bones above his eyebrows and the smallness of his mouth and chin portrayed an Asiatic ancestry. In Japanese homes, they don't talk much, but the Maknihara's were westernized. Mai's father, in the States for twenty years, spoke excellent English and liked to talk about Japan from earlier memories. (See Addendum.)

"Me, my parents, grandparents and two sisters and a younger brother were left suddenly homeless when a great earthquake hit Tokyo in 1923. It was a terrible time. It was not the earthquake that leveled our house. It was fire. I am ashamed to admit it, but we joined thousands of other victims in attacking the Koreans living in our city who we believed had started the fires and poisoned our wells."

"Why would they do that?" I said.

"The civilians?" he said.

"No, I mean the Koreans. Why would they burn your homes and put poison in your water?"

"They did not, but it was rumored, and we were angry enough at the time to suspect them and get even. Many, many innocent people were killed that time as a result." He shook his head and stared into space as if remembering, tapping his fingers of both hands on his folded legs.

"I fear," he continued, "it served only to put more salt on a wound that festered ever since Japan took over Korea in 1910. The Koreans hate our guts, especially the communists. Someday, mark my word, those red devils will get even, and the great big bear will come down and help them out. You see, the Russians hate us, too." He said it like the Russians were perhaps justified in their potential attitude toward the Japanese. I thought so, too. Japan had provoked many nations, but I kept that thought to myself.

After a short pause, Mr. Maknihara added,

"It is probably because we were the antagonizer during the Russo-Japanese War. Our country had the spirit to continue, but we ran out of resources while Russia just kept on coming on. Maybe it's because I was imprisoned in California and not able to keep up on current events, but I've often wondered why Russia violated its agreement with Nazi Germany to become an ally of Britain and the United States during this last war. You were worlds apart on philosophy."

I knew the answer to that one. He'd been referring to the Nazi-Soviet non-aggression pact of 1939 that put Hitler and Stalin on friendly terms. In a sense, the agreement had given Hitler permission to go into Poland. As time went on, it became quite obvious that both dictators had lied.

"The Russians ended up becoming our allies only because we both opposed Germany's aggression," I said. "No other reason. We've been on opposite sides of the table before and since."

"The Russians need to be watched. It's my belief they want to spread communism throughout the world." He spat out these last words like he couldn't stand to have them in his mouth.

I nodded.

He continued.

"It's all a matter of control, you see. We've been there. You Americans have been there. Yes, it's all a matter of control."

Americans, control? Well maybe.

"Well, maybe," I said, trying to see it through Mr. Maknihara's eyes. After all, we were occupying his beloved country. "Control and power," I added thoughtfully, thinking in terms of the spread of communism.

He nodded, said,

"There are constant guerrilla attacks from those living north of the 38th Parallel. Your military is occupying both Japan now and South Korea. It's interesting to see what the outcome will be."

"I hope nothing happens. It's nice to have peace for a change."

"Peace?" He sounded skeptical. "No one would appreciate peace more than we Japanese. For as much shame as we bore living in an internment camp in your country, my family was far better off than the people living here. I am not just talking about the bombings over Tokyo and Hiroshima and Nagasaki, horrible as those were, but what the war did to the people emotionally. I often observe that young people here are so serious. There was too little laughter during their bringing up."

"Yes, I can understand it's different from when war is not fought on your native land." I caught mental glimpses of the *gschposs* we kids had Sunday afternoons playing ball, pitching horseshoes, catching minnows, and any number of make-fun activities while our country battled on two fronts.

"After the fighting stopped and the war was finally over, the people began to recognize they could make it through. There were even those who believed Japan would one day recover."

Thanks to MacArthur, it did!

Thanks, too, to Deming!

Dr. W. Edwards Deming, a statistician known as the Father of the Third Wave of the Industrial Revolution, is best known for his post-war work in Japan. There, he worked with management and engineers on his "Fourteen Points for Management," creating a revolution in both quality and productivity and putting Japan on the highway to economic prosperity. Since that time, Dr. Deming has brought his philosophy home to Corporate America to improve its competitive position in the global free market system. ("Reading Teamwork in Action," by Shirley Nestler, *Solid Stater*, May 1985.)

Japan's wealth and prosperity had continued to climb to amazing heights, with multiple investments in American corporate enterprises. I refer to Japan's buying spree in the eighties when Japanese automakers established manufacturing plants and other industries to manufacture their products in the United States. Unfortunately, now, in the 21st century, through a failing social democracy, Japan's public debt exceeds 200% of GDP. (Talk Radio, WEEU, Mar. 30, 2010.)

In the years since World War II, the United States and Japan have become inseparable in many ways. "Japan's ties with the United States are almost a given," says Masakazu Yamazaki, one of Japan's leading intellectuals who studied at Yale and taught at Columbia. "We share similar political systems, freedom of speech, and cosmopolitan cultures. Much of our music has begun to blend, as have our societal structures. I cannot imagine Japan getting as close to any other Asian country as it is with the United States."

There are contrasts. We are a multicultural, immigrant nation scarcely more than two hundred years old. They are an ancient, ethnically homogenous people who trace imperial family roots back more than 2,000 years. We Americans pride ourselves on our differences from the rest of the world and fiercely protect them. Whereas, Japanese tradition is that of a nation/family with strong allegiance to the common good. We settle issues through loud disagreement. They believe in group harmony, preferring internal debate and policies designed to bring the nation together. We are restless, inventive, and quick to discard. They are patient and adaptive with a genius for perfection. Our successes and failures are largely individual. Theirs belong to the group, and, if an individual fails, he quickly accepts responsibility to preserve the group's integrity. ("Reading Japan's Moods," *Parade Magazine*, Jan. 12, 2003.)

During the eighties and nineties, I had the frequent privilege of associating with Japanese nationals who visited the company that employed me. I joined them for luncheons, conducted plant tours of our facility, hosted touristy tours to Lancaster County, and sat in on corporate meetings where I learned much about the Japanese makeup and their approach to problem-solving. Decisions on our side of the conference room table came quickly but took long periods of time to implement. There were always endless layers of corporate bureaucracy to work through. Our friends from the East, while requiring long periods of time to discuss all issues before agreement, moved plans through implementation without delay. Each had its reward.

Frequently, Mai and I shared chocolate ice cream sodas at a tiny teahouse close to where she and her family lived. Once in a while, we visited my old stomping grounds, the Kabuki Cabaret, where again arrangements were made for surveillance of the jeep. Mai loved to sing, so Sundays usually found us worshipping at the Army chapel on base. Several weekends, we traveled to Wakiyama Beach where her father, being of some status, owned a beach house. Baker went along more often than not. On warm spring days, we gathered driftwood, cooked on an hibachi, (You got it— no boating!), and had ourselves a real folksy fun visit with Baker serenading on his Spanish guitar.

Mai's and my relationship you could say was platonic for lack of a better word. True, I found her very attractive. I mean who wouldn't have? She was gorgeously tall in comparison to other Japanese gals, five-foot-six or seven I recall, and had inherited her father's round Caucasian eyes but with ever so slightly up-tilted corners belying her Asian heritage. She was truly a head-turner; a real *tomadachi* with tasteful American-styled clothes and raven hair arranged in short spiffy curls like girls in the States wore before I left.

I must tell you about an embarrassing but sweet experience. One of those cultural experiences you see only performed by comics on the big screen. The master bedroom in the Maknihara home had a States-side double bed in it and was fully visible from the sitting area. I saw Mai turn down the top cover and then disappear only to reappear minutes later wearing brief, frilly night clothes. She slipped into bed. From there, she beckoned with a teasing note in her voice and an inviting smile.

(When Mai smiled, she smiled with her whole face, with her motion, her cheeks, her eyes, especially her eyes. The image still floods my mind.)

I was beside myself with embarrassment and didn't know what to do. Mai's mother giggled and said,

"It's okay."

There was a clumsy silence while I summoned up my courage. I reluctantly removed my trousers and stood in my ugly, baggy, Army-issue boxers while the two of them again giggled and urged me into bed. I went. I crawled in on the side where the top cover apparently had been turned down for me. That was the good news. The bad news was that Mai was between two sheets, and I was between the top sheet and the cover. We awkwardly hugged and then peacefully napped. I was never quite sure if it had been planned that way or if it was a blooper. In any event, it was much too embarrassing to discuss afterward, so I've since chalked up the experience to being similar to the Amish custom for the unwed called "bundling."

Mai was pert and spunky and always had a plan or two up her blouse sleeve to keep things moving forward. Perhaps had I not been so bashful and perhaps if my trusted and treasured friend Baker hadn't usually been with us and perhaps had I not felt some moral obligation to a semi-sweetheart back home, our relationship might have progressed beyond the strong friendship we both enjoyed.

My semi-sweetheart back home deserves introduction. I met Joan on a dare in my later teens. By this time, I had graduated from the total and impossible inept phase of bashfulness to at least a moderate one that would continue to plague me throughout adolescence and into adulthood. In between had its severe drawbacks as you might guess.

A special young lady comes to mind. Cousin Dorothy lived in Shoemakersville where we both attended grade school. One evening, she invited me to stop by her house. We chatted on the front porch glider and watched a family of baby squirrels playing in the maple tree across the street. Aunt Verna happened to mention the brief visit to my father, I'm sure in a teasing way. In turn, perhaps teasing, also, though at the time it hadn't come across that way, he lectured to high heaven that I was not to go to any girl's house after school, cousin or no.

"You come straight home for we have lots of work to do!" he said.

Embarrassed, I think that incident conditioned me to a girls-are-out mode from that day forward.

Pop's admonishment, nonetheless, did not prevent feelings that come naturally to young boys my age. I remember well a crush on a girl in Catechetical Class at St. Michael's. I'll call her Nancy. Thirteen at the time, this boy was head over heels in love. While I was supposed to be memorizing the Ten Commandments, I focused on Nancy's beautiful profile instead. I wished to talk with her and to walk with her. I could dream and pretend we were together, pretend we kissed and hugged. We held hands and walked beneath the stars. It seemed life was all our own, and we never felt alone. But, of course, it was just a dream.

Rip Trexler's was the town hangout after the movie next door let out. One Friday night, my buddies put Joan up to talking to me so they could stand aside and be entertained. My feet went ice-cold from the blood that rushed upward, causing so much heat in my face I might almost have caught on fire. That was the beginning of our courtship.

Joan was still just an ordinary gal; me, except for continual bashfulness, an ordinary guy. I'm not too sure I was in love, at least not by later standards. But at the time, she managed to make butterflies flutter out of control in my stomach. And she was feisty. I liked feisty.

One year, I won a plaster-paris clown from pitching pennies on the Reading Fair's carnival strip. Two days later, I dropped it and a piece broke off in the rear. This left a two-thumb-hole space just big enough to stick in rolled-up dollar bills squirreled away from picking tomatoes at Charlie Levan's and my enterprising days of trapping skunk and muskrat. My parents taught, if you save in the good times, you can weather the storm in bad times. Not sure if this was a good time or a bad time as it turned out, but one day, I broke the clown in its entirety and presented Joan with a rhinestone engagement ring that cost all of $29.95.

Some weeks later, Joan and I got into an argument, I'm not sure anymore over what, and she returned the ring. For some insane reason, instead of trashing it, I cushioned the ring in chick starter mash, sealed the small tin box with tire tape, and deposited the works inside a dead pear tree in a remote field we called North Dakota. The tree was gone when I returned home on furlough in the summer of '51. Someone must have cut it down and drug it into the woods. No one ever said a word about the box. Perhaps it fell out along the way and was plowed into a furrow, who knows.

Truth be told, when I shipped overseas, I can't say Joan and I had anything more than a surface relationship, butterflies flying well in formation by that time, if at all. However, we did exchange letters on occasion and made an appointment for a phone call down the road. But now I'm getting ahead of myself.

Allow me to leap frog back to the future. In October of 1950, I qualified for a GED Certificate. Mai handled the correspondence between the school in Osaka and Perry Township High School in Shoemakersville, Pennsylvania. A letter from Supervising Principal David B. Lander informed me I'd be presented a high school diploma upon return to the States.

In the summer of '51, during my leave, I contacted Mr. Lander, nicknamed Pappy, and scheduled an appointment for the following day.

When I opened the heavy front door to the building, a whiff of lead pencils, chalk, and the smell of rubber rushed toward me. The only thing I can relate to the latter, having one of many senior moments, was the mythical rubber hose Pappy stored in the closet for flogging students who, in his mind, warranted the severest of punishment. As far as I know, and even this is hazy, no kid ever felt its sting or saw it. But the mere threat this mystic tool existed maintained or quickly restored law and order for the most ornery of tyrants.

The walls of the empty hallway leading to his office were covered in at least eleven more layers of institutional vomit green, but otherwise appeared unchanged from my former school years. The wooden floor creaked underfoot the same way it always did when I snuck into class late. Or, when sent to the principal's office for the slightest infraction of established rules of conduct. I went so often they eventually moved my desk into his office. Kidding, of course, but I did have visitation rights.

In case you don't remember how to make spit balls, I'll refresh you. Take a piece of paper, best if it's torn from homework before turning it in, spit on it to hurt more when the target's hit, roll the paper bullet size, then flick behind some unsuspecting victim who's hurriedly finishing up his homework before turning it in. As you guessed, I was caught in the act and earned a few sharp whacks around the head by Mr. Reitz before being marched off to Pappy. Not to mention the blackboard assignment after school. Write one-hundred times: "I will not attack fellow classmates with bees, snakes, spit balls, or any other lethal weapon while on duty in the classroom." That, or something similar. (See Addendum.)

Another time, Teacher asked me to come forward and recite the poem, "Duty," by Ralph Waldo Emerson. I love that little poem, not only because it was written back in the good old days when poetry made sense, rhymed, and had a pleasant meter, but also because it applies to my commitment as a soldier. I'll take poetic license and recite here in black and white:

> *So night is grandeur*
> *To our dust,*
> *So near is God to man.*
> *When duty whispers low thou must*
> *The youth replies I can.*

What ever does this have to do with going to the principal's office? Glad you asked, but I was going to answer the question whether you did or not. There are two things you need to remember. First, I was always placed in the rear of everything by innate alphabetic arrangement. Second, and although I hate to keep harping about this shyness complex of mine, I'll defer one more time; then, may that be the end of it. I failed to understand why I couldn't just stand by my desk instead of speaking at the head of the class. As I walked up the long aisle, Russell Yeager reached out and ripped open my fly, unbeknown to anyone but me. I kept on going and walked out of the room. What the hay! Wouldn't you have done the same?

My last memory of these grand halls of learning was the day I left school for good. I passed from tenth to eleventh in May 1946, but opted to stay home and husk corn rather than return in the fall. After all, I knew how to spell Czechoslovakia. And, really, how much more did one need to be taught about how far participles dangled before considered misplaced gerunds or some other darn thing?

Our principal was a tall, formidable figure already graying at the temples when I left school. A huge stomach strained at coat buttons attempting to hide the crazy-patterned necktie he always wore belted in his pants. It was rumored his ties were made from livestock feedbags, a household trend at the time, because no store-bought could measure to that extraordinary length.

The scary part was the intimidating stern look that never left his face as he peered at you behind Ben Franklins, the wire frames twisted as if they were sat upon once or twice. This look was still present when we met in '51. He sat behind his polished mahogany desk when I sauntered into the office. Acknowledging with a short nod, he reached for a cream-colored document on the desktop, far left, and stuffed the diploma in a 1944 class cover.

"Here it is," is what he said when handing me the package.

Wrong year.

No handshake.

No congratulations.

You may be the more learned one with your big fat degree, but you still have much to learn, I thought ruefully. Not even a curt thank you could form itself in my mouth. In silence, I accepted the package and left.

Count it all joy.

13

The Time Has Come

We make War that we have Peace.
- Aristotle

Guard duty is as mandatory as writing home to mother. For good reason. A soldier not only protects lives, but also secures the immense roster of equipment necessary to perform expected job functions. There were seven guard posts at Kanoaka Barracks, three of them base entrances. The main gate, where two guarded a pro-station operated by a medic on duty, was Post 1. Another gate, Post 2. The gate from which Japanese nationals with proper passes entered and departed was Post 3. I guarded Post 4. Roving guards in the motor pool and the vicinity of a small petroleum, oils, and lubricants dump had Posts 5, 6, and 7.

Shifts were two hours on duty/off six throughout the weekend from 0700 Saturday through 0700 Monday. Detail consisted of an officer of the day, sergeant of the guard, corporal of the guard, and men selected for the watch on a particular weekend. Following Saturday morning inspection, weekend detail carried personal items required for duty and marched to the guardhouse where they slept and hung out between schedules.

No one was required to stay in the guard building. Though, it was necessary to sign out if making a visit to the PX or returning to the barracks for a missing item. Leaving base was forbidden, period! You were either on duty or on call.

Sergeant of the guard managed formation and inspection and made periodic checks to assure all posts were manned in accord with standard operating procedures (SOPs). Whenever Tech Sergeant Harding Basdritch was sergeant of the guard, no posts were checked. If it happened we were both on duty the same weekend, I as corporal of the guard took responsibility for tracking the men and making sure changes were made at prescribed times. I preferred it that way since Basdritch's (aka Bastard) and my relationship was similar to that of oil and water.

Bastard was from Turkey in the star state of Texas and, clearly not a humble man, had grossly inflated notions of self-worth. His head was twice as big as his Texan hat, and he talked a big line, especially grandstanding his sexual prowess following the war.

"…and then there was the time I made love to three sisters in a single night!"

Yeah, and why don't you just shut that big Texas-size hole in your face!

"Talk is cheap," I said to him. "A real man wouldn't stand in front of other men and make statements like that!" The stud muffin's constant boasting nagged at me. I found myself deferring to the old adage taught by my father: you don't increase yourself by decreasing others.

He didn't seem to like my comment. I saw movement in his eyes, and his face was reddish-looking. I thought he might take a swipe at me, but he didn't.

Other than maybe this incident when I burst his bubble, there was no reason for friction between us. Perhaps his nose was out of joint because he wasn't as good-looking as I and spent a lot of money impressing the gals, wherein I had enough clout without spending big bucks. (I'm only kidding. I just threw that in to put a smile on your face.)

On a positive note, and this might be stretching a bit, he was a rather handsome man with tanned skin and a good crop of dark brown hair. Make that dog-turd brown. Erect-postured and wide squared shoulders gave him a look of importance. But in my opinion, he was no more important than the space that's left when you put your finger in a bucket of water and withdraw it. I didn't know too much about him, though, to tell you the truth, but that allows room for speculation. Beneath the surface, there lurked an evil person, one who spent his childhood pulling the wings off insects, kicking the household pet, and snickering when another kid fell off his bike and was rushed to ER.

He was a senior NCO, a five-striper; me, a junior. You can see where that put me in the chain of command when we worked together in the NCO Club. He was the horse and I the donkey, always looking his longer nose down at me. But really, it was Eleanor Roosevelt who said that no one can make you feel inferior without your permission. He didn't know this, but I would not give him permission. Nevertheless, this scornful jerk sat up nights planning ways to be obnoxious, making sure I was victim of the dirtiest grunt detail coming down the military pike.

"Before you're through scrubbing the john, scrounge up a razor blade and scrape the pee drain. It's enough to turn one's stomach," he said one time, with a clear trace of condescension in his voice. Uncouth potty language furthered his point.

Yes, of course, the pee drain; what was I thinking?

"Oh, and by the way," he added, aiming an accusing finger above the bar mirror. "Do you see that cobweb up there?"

I did not, but in a rare display of agreement, I nodded. I knew better than to talk back. We soldiers seemed born with hair trigger responses to everything, and our training honed these tendencies.

"Be sure you get that next time you dust." Having delivered the directive, he sucked his teeth with an air of finality and smiled. Thank goodness my computer has a backspace key.

Even when off duty and in the club as a guest, the arrogant Bastard dripped disdain. Either that, or he had an anal fixation for cleanliness.

"Hey, screwball!" he said once when we were on opposite sides of the bar and loud enough that everyone could hear. I had just served him the mixed drink he ordered of orange juice and vodka, and he was turning the glass around.

"It's time you washed these glasses," he said. "There's a flea swimming around in my screwdriver!"

Other than him, there wasn't a dog in sight. I met pit bulls with better attitudes and waited with bated breath for his next assault.

"...my father can lick your father any day, and, if he doesn't, I will!"

Stop it. I don't get mad, turkey lips. I get even and will go for the jugular, you wait and see.

Connie, his Japanese girlfriend, was a pretty little thing. Her face was pale ocher and framed by short straight black hair. Silky bangs reached almond-shaped eyes that flirted with me on the sly. She took note of the sergeant's manner and told him more than once in my presence not to be so unfair.

It was obvious he was in love with this girl. He bought her a small white frame house in Sakai furnished with a States-side bed and other furnishings to make it authentic American. One weekend, Connie and I ran into each other downtown Sakai. For all the generosity the sergeant showed with material possessions, he apparently treated her as badly as a serpent treats its next meal.

"Sergeant mean," she said. "Do you believe he can be bad man?"

I did. I said,

"Does he beat you?"

"Sometime."

"Where is he now?"

"He at camp and cannot get away."

I smiled.

"Well," I said, "whenever he's on duty, I'd like to come and visit you." In my journey, I had learned the art of making out.

"Wonderful! Wonderful! It is you I want all along." She hugged and kissed me in broad daylight on the main street of Sakai and dragged me to her house.

From then on, whenever the weekend duty roster showed the control freak on guard, I spent time on his private turf, in his house, with his girl, and almost... well, never you mind.

Gotcha.

If someone left base, he passed through Post 3, the most remote gate and least supervised by the sergeant of the guard regardless of who was on duty. I don't believe commissioned officers knew of this practice, but as long as I was at Kanoaka, off-duty weekend guards snuck out to visit a brothel five hundred yards away. The house was located inside a small family compound comprised of five or six huts with a courtyard in the center (or so I heard). Whenever someone left to visit, a star (*) was placed behind his name on the sign-out sheet. It worked fine in emergencies, of which there were few. (We've been here before but bears repeating. I did not engage in such extra-curricular activity.)

I had guard duty the weekend of June 24. Saturday was quiet and uneventful. Sunday, too, to a degree. Around 1800 hours, Baker, off-duty at the time, showed up with a couple of hamburgers and coke. We sat at the guard desk eating and chatting when a jeep barreled up the driveway and came to a screeching halt by the gate. The officer of the day jumped out.

"Where is Sergeant Basdritch?"

"I don't know, Sir." I dropped my unfinished burger and checked the sign-out sheet. As usual, He Who Walks on Water hadn't signed out.

"Where are all the guards?"

"Several are here and the rest signed out for different places."

He hurried on.

"Get all the men together! On the double! Have them in the company street for muster roll call in fifteen minutes!"

"Yes, Sir! Do you want the men at Posts 1, 2, and..."

"Which word didn't you understand? I said ALL men return to the company area for muster roll call!"

Now he had my full attention.

"The North Koreans invaded South Korea," he said, "and that will sure as thunder affect everyone, including ALL the posts! Do you read me?"

"Yes, Sir." *I do! Loud and clear!*

He was gone, my heart racing as fast as his jeep that sped down the driveway. Dirt spewed like a plow turning ground in a drought.

The sign-out board showed five stars. Baker, relieved of duty by this urgent command, returned at once to company unit headquarters for roll call. I dispersed the other available guards to locate and round up missing attendants. Fueled by an adrenalin rush, I hit the ground running.

At a punishing pace, arms pumping, I made an incredible hundred-yard dash on a narrow footpath outside the exit before coming to a still smaller path that wound between two rice paddies. From there, the trail veered first to the left, then right, then straight ahead into the compound where I came to mama-san's infamous dwelling.

Cheap perfume and sounds of giggles and laughter filtered through thin walls as I ripped open the sliding door. The guys inside were self-occupied behind individual cubicles separated by colorful, opaque screens.

"Forget what you're doing and get out of here!" I bellowed.

A squat, flat-nosed madam ran up to me and smacked her lips.

"No shoe! No shoe!" she scolded, beating me on the chest.

I ignored her displeasure at my breaking and entering her nice clean house without first removing my shoes and waited the incredibly long seconds for the men to show their faces.

Here and there, a head popped out from behind a screen like the birdie in Uncle Howard's cuckoo clock. A couple started to ask questions, but I cut them short.

"For crying out loud!" I said. "Do you think I ran all the way over here to play a game of chess? Get your crap together and get back to the company area for muster roll call in ten minutes!" Beads of sweat trickled behind each ear as I continued to snap orders.

Man! This is as difficult as trying to talk a polecat out of a hen house.

"Don't forget to stop by the guard building and pick up your rifles and other gear!" I shouted.

All five would-be guards, in various stages of dress and undress, hopped through the courtyard like chickens with their heads chopped off. Shirttails and shoestrings flew. Some of the men, clad in tee shirts, ran with one arm propelling and the other holding up trousers or clutching personal items. One dropped a boot and was ten strides past before he realized his loss.

God help this outfit, I thought. *We'll never make it.*

That was Sunday, June 25, 1950, outbreak of the Korean War.

Shipping Out

If you want Peace, prepare for War.
- Winston Churchill

Work began in teams, six men each. We dug in our heels, servicing and fueling all the vehicles to capacity, and strapped on two additional five-gallon cans of gas in appropriate places. Everything else was packed and crated. Personal effects were placed in footlockers stenciled with names and ID numbers on top and sides. The lockers were placed in a vacant storeroom for later shipment to the States and, supposedly, our homes.

In mine were a few darting silverfish, several letters from home, a cheap "Brownie" black box camera and two rolls of blank film, and a heavy pullover wool sweater with a slight smell of moth balls my Granny Zweizig had knitted. (I was notified by telegram just days before that this dear old woman had just passed away; the Army denied my return request to the States because grandparents weren't considered immediate family.) And Japanese souvenirs. These impulse purchases included a desk name carved out of some kind of stone, a white china shaving mug labeled "Made in Japan" with a pretty Geisha girl painted on one side, plus other things I don't recall. There were a few dog-eared pocket novels that had made the rounds and that I wished to reread. In addition, four scenic post-cards I hadn't bother to write and mail. That was about it.

Oh, and some photographs of my Fort Dix days and Kanoaka Barracks. Plus, a creased, slightly larger-than-wallet-size picture of Joan in a standing pose on the cement pavement outside the family home. In the background was a huge maple tree with a rope swing hanging from it and the Heinz variety pooch looking on. I planned to keep the photo with me but at the last minute threw it into the locker with the other items. I needn't a picture to remind me of her full-curved figure, her warm nut-brown hair with its hint of laven-der, and a sweet smile she claimed was meant only for me.

The reason I used the word "supposedly" above is because my locker got lost somewhere beyond the blue. I regret the loss since I would love to have included those pictures in this book. Well, maybe not Joan's.

At the time, I was still assigned as NCO club custodian. We NCOs were determined not to leave one drop of whiskey behind. One of the crates in the motor pool was constructed to package an air compressor sized out at four feet long and two feet square. This was also the right size to box and pack all the bottles in the club. We made three boxes and stenciled them "Air Compressor," except one, of course, was filled with newspapers and booze. I don't think more than four or five of us knew the exact location of the liquor when loaded. It didn't matter. As sure as the sun rises every morning, the cache would be with us at least somewhere when we arrived at our final destination.

The evening of our departure, lights were out and the entire base a complete blackout. I remembered another era.

Throughout the Second World War, thick dark curtains at every window made our farmhouse seem sad and abandoned in the day-time hours. But at night, they concealed light from filtering through during the frequent air raid tests. The barn was a different matter. If blackouts occurred at milking time, we ran the embarrassing and painful risk of stripping a bull instead of a cow. Operation had best be postponed until an all-clear strafed the air.

I recall hearing of a particular night during the war when thou-sands filled a sports arena not far from home. At half-time, a display promoted the sale of war bonds. Suddenly, an anti-aircraft gun boomed. A machine gun. A tank arrived. Cracks of a hundred rifles followed. Soon, the ground rumbled, and a full-scale war took place in front of the hypnotized crowd. The noise stopped while steel gray smoke continued to twist its way up through powerful stadium lights.

At first, the people had forgotten it was a war bond rally, but those staging the spectacle knew what they were doing. They knew a man making $37.50 a week couldn't buy many bonds. Their job was to convince this man his contribution, however small, was essential to winning the war.

After the lights were out and the stadium a complete blackout, each person was asked to hold a lighted match aloft. What the drama taught was that every single person participated in lighting the dark, that no one was too insignificant to have a part in dispelling the darkness. Everyone was important to winning the war.

Inside the main Barracks gate was an island surrounded by white-washed stones and filled with a variety of beautiful palms, flowers, and shrubs typical of Japanese gardens. I drove through this gate with Captain Bond for the last time. Beneath a sliver of moon, dozens of Army guys lay on freshly mown grass with Japanese sweethearts, each saying goodbye in their own special way. It would be the last encounter for quite some time. The boys were off to war, an unwelcome distraction indeed. (Mai was not there. She lived eleven miles away in Osaka and would not receive my letter until after we'd left. Actually, she never did receive it, I later discovered.)

A convoy of twenty vehicles and one hundred and twenty Army personnel aboard moved out with Captain Bond and me in the lead. (An officer cannot lead in combat, but we weren't in combat—YET!) Close to midnight, Japanese people lined both sides of the road for the full eleven-mile stretch from Kanoaka Village to Osaka. It was too dark to see tears, but we felt their moisture as people waved and bid farewell. Allies now, we fought the common enemy.

At the railroad station, the unloading and loading of vehicles and equipment began at once. Trucks, trailers, jeeps, and other specialty vehicles and weaponry were lifted on to flat cars and tied down. Box-cars stored smaller supplies. Each individual carried personal gear, a weapon, and C rations. If you got hungry and could squeeze in a few minutes, you heated pork and beans or whatever over a running truck engine.

By noon the following day, before the old steam locomotive pulled out, they assigned several guards to ride on flat cars for the trip to Japan's southern most island of Kyushu. Baker and I volunteered, it being late June and the weather warm and comfortable. Every guard received a one-day C ration pack for a trip expected to take six hours. Our destination was the port city of Sasebo.

After traveling full speed ahead for several hours, I yelled to Baker on the car behind,

"Hey! How do we cross from Honshu Island over to Kyushu?"

"Beats the crap out of me!" he said. "I guess they have a long bridge."

Like the old military adage, "We don't know where we are or where we're going, but we're making real good time."

We finally approached a small hillside and tunneled in. Speak about no light at the end of the tunnel. We kept going and going and going until I darn near died of smoke inhalation and wished I had not volunteered. After leaving the tunnel, I saw the channel and knew the train had just crossed over on to Kyushu. Upon seeing Baker, I roared. From his immediate reaction, I looked the same. We were both plastered with soot from head to toe. Not at all the fair Caucasians we were when we left the States.

We constantly ran on E, hitting on all cylinders, and spent three days in Sasebo loading equipment and supplies aboard a landing ship tank (LST) that would take us out into the Sea of Japan. Afterward, we delayed and waited for other units to arrive and load on this same boat. Baker and I took advantage of the quiet time and spread blankets in an out-of-the-way spot. Since our mission began, we burned the candle at both ends, at no time managing close to the allotted four hours of sack time per day. I lay down my bone-weary, rest-deprived body and sank into an exhaustive sleep.

My original overseas tour of duty started at thirty months, the coming August 1st being the approximate date for return to the States. However, it was evident my departure would not be realized anywhere near this period of time, considering my earlier unvolunteered extension, and now this. Was I anxious about the latest development in my military career? No, I say not and think I speak for the majority. Yet how could this be? We were off to war. I'm thinking, it's because we were young, gutsy, and inexperienced and hadn't the wisdom to fear what lay ahead.

Civilians yesterday.
Soldiers today.
Warriors tomorrow.

As the sun set on July 3, we pushed away from the wooden dock and headed for the Korean Peninsula, Japan's moody coastline receding in a wake of silvery foam. *Sayonara!*

Meanwhile, Back in Washington

You can always count on Americans to do the right thing
after they've exhausted all other possibilities.
- Winston Churchill

Just in case you're not up on your world history or you're in the under-fifty-something age group, or just in case you're a victim of neither, you might still have a moderate curiosity on world events. So, let me catch you up and connect the dots as to where I was at this specific moment in life—crossing the Sea of Japan toward the Peninsula of Korea.

Korea was controlled by the Japanese since its annexation in 1910 on the heels of the latter's continental invasion to the west and north. By World War II, Korea still belonged to Japan. At the Cairo Conference on December 1, 1943, Britain, China, and the United States announced that in due course, after the hopeful and imminent defeat of Japan, Korea should become free and independent.

These same allies affirmed the principles of the Cairo declaration in the Potsdam Proclamation, July 26, 1945. Two weeks hence, August 8 to be exact, the Soviet Union broke a neutrality agreement made with Japan prior to the events of Pearl Harbor and formally joined the Allies in the Pacific war. Several days later, in establishing terms and procedures for the Japanese surrender, Dean Rusk, then a young colonel on General Marshall's staff, pointed to a map and drew an arbitrary line across the waist of Korea with a dark grease pencil. He suggested Russia accept the area north of the line, the 38th Parallel, while the United States accept the south. Russia immediately agreed to this arrangement.

This may not be politically correct in the eyes of some, but, as I'll believe until I push up daisies, had the Soviets not entered the war against Japan—which by the way they did in response to last minute arm-twisting by the U.S., these latecomers would not have been party to sharing the wealth of Korea. Perhaps there would never have been a Korean War. Or even if there were, perhaps no Russian support of North Korean aggression. (Since forming this opinion, I've discovered the great minds of Generals Patton and MacArthur had held similar views.)

The way it turned out, at least in my not so infinite wisdom, the USSR's position was somewhat analogous to a long lost sibling showing up for the reading of the will. But then, what do I know? And what does it matter anyhow? It really comes down to political dealings in the end.

While history in our schools today is skewed and textbooks revisited and watered down, possibly even flawed, the truth of the matter is that history itself cannot be erased in spite of being whitewashed. It was what it was. So, back to the portents of history, as it were.

The one hundred and ninety mile demarcation line made no sense from an economic viewpoint. The southern zone covered 37,000 square miles and contained some 21,000,000 people, two-thirds in farm families. Although the South contained twelve of Korea's twenty largest cities—including the capital of Seoul with well over 2,000,000 citizens, it was primarily agricultural and supplied rice for the entire country. The northern zone, larger with 48,000 square miles, had only 9,000,000 in population. But because of its highly developed hydroelectric works, the North claimed most of Korea's industrial plants—chemical, steel, cement, and fertilizer, products that complemented the South's agrarian economy. (Korea, The Untold Story of the War, p.20)

Looking at the big picture, neither zone had the capacity for economic self-sufficiency. To add festering insult to an already blistering wound, this geographic partitioning frustrated the Korean people in their continuous strife for independence and unity. Namely that of Syngman Rhee.

Rhee converted to Christianity through Methodist missionaries. At an early age, he moved away from ancestral veneration and other centuries-old customs followed by his parents with the Buddhist and Confucianism belief systems. In addition, new Christian ideals distanced Rhee from the medievalism of Korea's social and political structure. While attending a missionary school, he led lively demonstrations demanding the Japanese be given the tip of the boot. These radical anti-imperialistic activities sent Rhee to prison and earned him brutal torture even beyond any known Oriental cruelty, so horrid I refuse to go there no matter if only on disposable paper.

With Rhee interned, American missionary friends visited and reinforced the notion that Christian principles were essential to political freedom. The church sent him, upon release, to the United States where he schooled and stayed some thirty years before returning to his beloved homeland. There, the "old man," convinced of a God-granted mission, achieved a life-long ambition. He flexed political muscle to lead the Korean people, at least those south of the 38th Parallel, toward peaceful reform and independence. He was elected president of the Republic of Korea (ROK) on July 20, 1948.

Unlike Rhee, many stayed on in Korea during Japan's occupation and, through public protest, opposed the Japanese. They promised not only to evict these intruders from across the sea but also created what they felt was a better society. Communism. Communism promised equality as well as an end to the old hierarchical systems of Korea and Japan. Both farmers and factory workers received communism with favor and managed demonstrations and rent strikes even in the face of harsh police measure. Further, exiled Korean communist guerrillas fought the Japanese military across the Manchurian frontier as part of the Chinese Communist People's Liberation Army. (Do not confuse this group with WWII Allied Chinese Nationalists under the leadership of Generalissimo Chiang Kai-shek who, like Syngman Rhee, was Christian.)

One such guerrilla was Kim IL Sung. Kim's success in guerrilla warfare convinced even the Soviets of his usefulness during the postwar period; clearly, a man they could trust and control. He was appointed premier of the territory north of the 38th Parallel known as the People's Republic of Korea.

Meanwhile, back in Post-War Washington…. The Joint Chiefs of Staff, after extensive study on how to deploy America's limited military strength around the world, wrote off South Korea as having little strategic value to the United States. The attitude, "If it ain't broke, don't fix it," prevailed. The U.S. was determined not to defend South Korea in the unlikelihood North Korean communists invaded. Because the U.S. focus was presently in Europe, Korea fell by the wayside.

Even knowing the probable withdrawal consequences, the JCS had made this well-thought-out perfectly bad decision. One of their staff groups, the Joint Strategic Survey Committee, had reported back in January 1948 that withdrawal of U.S. forces might result in communist domination. In spite of this drumbeat for war, the last American troops sailed as scheduled on June 30, 1949. A corporal's guard of advisers were the only soldiers left behind.

On the 38th Parallel, June 25, 1950 dawned gray and damp. Periods of light rain began to spread over the area as the morning progressed, hiding the sun behind low hanging clouds. The ROK army, after months of false alert, was enjoying a long overdue weekend vacation. Frontier defense forces of four infantry divisions and one regiment consisted just shy of 38,000 men. In actuality, one-third of that number occupied defensive bunkers that particular day, the remaining either in reserve ten to thirty miles below the 38th or on leave. Army Headquarters on June 24 authorized commanders to give fifteen-day leaves to enlisted men from farm communities to work the rice paddies. Another event drawing away ROK officers and not to be taken lightly was the festive opening of a new officers' club in Seoul that same weekend. (See Addendum.)

Such was the calm, sleepy circumstance that Sunday morning when the NKPA launched an all out attack against blood relatives to the south. Now I've never heard or read this anywhere. So, please allow me one more daring probe. I hazard a view that North Korea's tactical surprise achieved a striking resemblance to the military state of unreadiness when the Japanese awakened a sleeping giant that fateful Sunday morning on December 7, 1941. By some accounts, even the NKPA's timing was similar...0945 local time. The second horrific wave on Pearl had occurred at 0930.

While Seoul burned, Washington fiddled. Empty suits in the Pentagon believed the news to be just another false alarm, life going on as usual. When he heard the news, Truman—the president who spent his first six months in office wondering how he got there and then the next six months wondering how the others got there—was vacationing in his home town of Independence, Missouri. He dropped plans to repair the garage door or some such domestic chore and rescheduled a return to Washington, but not until the next day. It's been said that before midnight (Saturday night, Missouri time) he bid the family good night and was sound asleep seconds after his head touched the pillow.

But not all doubted the seriousness of the situation. John Hickerson of the State Department immediately sent telegrams to members of the Security Council of the United Nations, putting them on alert on these latest events. As a first order of business, a United Nations resolution was approved by a 9-0 vote (the Russian delegate being absent) around 1800 hours Sunday evening. The resolution called for the immediate cessation of hostilities and the withdrawal of North Korean forces to the 38th Parallel. Truman arrived an hour later and ordered U.S. air and sea forces to give the R.O.K. army support and cover. On June 30, he ordered MacArthur, commander of U.S. forces in the Far East at the time, and now General of the Army, to advance with U.S. ground troops to assist in halting North Korean aggression. After all, he could not let the North Koreans come down and take over South Korea. That would make a laughing stock out of the U.S. and a laughing stock out of the U.N. as well. Learn from history or be destroyed by it.

Okay, then. When did we officially enter the war? It's a question I kept asking myself when I did the research. Perhaps a better question would have been, "Not when, but rather DID we officially enter the war?" The answer still eludes me. You can figure it out for yourself. Let me quote here from Korea, The Untold Story of the War (p.86) Truman's answer the first time he met with reporters after the start of the Korean conflict.

"Q: Mr. President, everybody is asking in this country, are we or are we not at war?

"A: We are not at war.... The members of the United Nations are going to the relief of the Korean Republic to suppress a bandit raid on the Republic of Korea.

"Q: Mr. President, would it be correct under your explanation to call this a police action under the United Nations?

"A: Yes, that is exactly what it amounts to."

Yes, politics as usual.

With the foregoing discourse, I hope you feel better informed on the eccentricities of military and political personalities involved as well as activities, sometimes non-activities if you will, that led up to the grinding Korean Conflict. Or Forgotten War, as it was later accurately dubbed. Other than thin, fragmented FYIs we received after leaving Japan, I knew very little of why we were where we were, much of it remaining a mystery to this day until I read up on the subject for purposes of this book. If you thirst for detail, there are more materials on bookstore and library shelves, (though sadly far less than on the "other" unpopular war—Viet Nam).

Here again enter Baker and Ziggy, liberators crossing the Sea of Japan toward South Korea on the eve of July 4, 1950, the 174th Anniversary of U.S. Independence.

PART II

16

We Have Arrived

The highest obligation and privilege of citizenship
is that of bearing arms for one's country.
- General George S. Patton

There were two World War II vets in our unit with combat experience, Captain Bond and Lieutenant Bowman. The rest of us were late teens or early twenties. I was twenty. Baker, who lied about his age, was eighteen. We were young, adventurous, and bold. Strong, proud, and arrogant was our common denominator, and, the novelty of what was happening so great, there was little concern for the future as we knifed through the Sea of Japan toward Korea. Korea, where we'd kill or be killed in a remote northern cornfield or some stinking rice paddy in the south.

To kill time, we exhausted topics central to our lives, like girls, religion, cars, and who came from the greatest state, then turned to sharpening bayonets and cleaning and rechecking rifles. We bragged with overbearing confidence:

"When I get a darned gook in my crosshairs, I'll knock 'im flat like a dummy in a baseball arcade!"

Yes, fight we would and loving every hateful minute. That's what soldiers do.

In a pale predawn glow, shore lights appeared. It was Tuesday, July 4, 1950. There was little thought to celebrating freedom. Instead, we prepared to join up in a war unfolding in the East. We had arrived. (See Addendum.)

When the sky threw light ahead of us, we could see the misty outline of most any type of military equipment and supplies one can imagine. Many ships had preceded us to this same area during the past several days. Two freighters at the harbor docks and another landing ship tank unloaded cargo not far down shore. An LST is an ocean-going vessel anywhere from five to six hundred feet in length. The front of the boat opens up like a giant yawn, spitting out armory through its metal jowls like a cherry pitter spits stones.

Inside the bowel of ours, drivers readied the engines for exit. Exhaust gases were stifling. The deck stank of sweat, oil, and other obnoxious odors of a troop-carrying landing ship. First off were troops strapped with whatever seemed appropriate as a means of killing or staying alive, anything from bandoliers of ammo, M1 30caliber Garand rifles, to weighty backpacks of seventy pounds or so.

In a pack was a raincoat, boots, steel pot and liner and camouflage cover for a helmet, standard fatigue jacket and trousers, underwear, personal hygiene and "housewife" kits, an accessory packet including salt and halazone tablets, bandages, sulfur powder, morphine, smokes and matches, toilet paper, entrenching tool, two or three water canteens, plus other miscellaneous essentials for combat field survival, including a two-day's supply of food. Most rations were the old C or K kind left over from World War II. But there was also a new box called the 50-in-One. Everyone tried to get his hands on one of these. They contained scrumptious Hershey Bars and Milky Ways and full-size packs of cigarettes with, of all things, twenty sticks apiece.

Grateful for fresh air, I approached the water's edge with eagerness, until I noticed the men moved awkwardly under the unaccustomed weight and bulk of packs and equipment. Some were in up to their armpits, struggling to maintain balance. The extra burden on the body was enough to make anyone sink, even an Olympic hopeful.

"Hey, man. That water's deep, and I can't swim!" I reminded my good captain standing close by.

"Oh, this won't be a problem. All my men are eight feet tall," was his cocky response.

I didn't comment further, but continued observing the situation with utmost care. While the waves surged in and out, the ramp synchronized as if on cue. Perfect timing, the water came no deeper than up to my waist.

Numerous trucks and a flotilla of jeeps plus a host of specialties on wheels followed. It's mind-boggling how a sea-going craft of such magnitude and tonnage stays afloat! The answer is buoyancy, of course. Buoyancy is created from the surface/weight ratio and surface tension itself. Most landing vehicles are flat-bottomed for this reason. They float with great weight, skipping over the water much like a surfboard. In contrast, ships cut the water like knives to allow both buoyancy and speed.

Hours before landing, we received specific tasks to perform upon reaching shore. I was assigned to Service Company (SVC), a trucking outfit, if you will. The basic function of a service company is transporting equipment, ammunition, and supplies such as fuel, water, food and so on, and, most importantly, troops. In short, we'd provide mobility for the regiment from one hot spot to another.

On shore, we loaded seven trucks under my responsibility as platoon sergeant in support of the 1st Battalion. At least three of those trucks carried small arms ammo and 60mm and 81mm mortar ammunition. Mind you, that's a lot of fire!

By 1400 hours, our unit set up on the main supply route (MSR) in three separate convoys. Two guards on each truck, it was "wagon, ho" over what some might call a road toward the town of Taegu fifty miles to the north. Enormous clouds of dust stirred in our wake.

The Korean Peninsula is one hundred and fifty miles across at its widest point with small towns and villages scattered throughout. Although Korean maps showed highways linking major cities, legends were generous beyond a doubt. These roads were designed for oxcarts, not marching armies of the 20th century.

Know, too, our equipment was not what you called mint condition, rather, hand-me-downs from World War II, having been no new weapons experimentation since mid-1945. Hence, six-year old tires and tubes with worn, dried-out rubber would not pull their weight on rough Korean roads for long. The main highway running north and south connecting Pusan and Seoul was unpaved, rock-strewn, chuck-holed and, in many places, single lane with jagged steep shoulders requiring extra cautious driving to avoid ending up in a ditch. (See Addendum.)

Sure, we had assistance from the ROK army. But its troops were hastily mustered, inadequately trained, and poorly equipped. Graft and corruption among higher officers was a problem, too, and the desertion rate high. It was difficult coordinating an attack with the ROK when you consider WWII radios were corroded or malfunctioned for a variety of reasons. If communication was mastered from a technical standpoint, the interpreter made himself impossible to understand because of a poor command of the English language.

The 24th landed in Korea five days ahead of the 25th Infantry Division. A full strength combat division comprises at least 18,000 men. Neither of these added up to that volume, our division itself only 9,000 strong. There were never any peacetime maneuvers in Japan larger than battalion size. The Japanese Islands' countryside did not offer the space, terrain, or roads for large-scale maneuvers. At best, the American occupation force of Japan, now in Korea, led a soft life.

In addition to this downside, many an American officer had a cute little "moose-a-may," GI slang for Japanese girlfriend. She cooked his meals, mended socks, kept his bed, and, coming from a culture where women shadowed men, obeyed in all aspects as if he were MacArthur himself. This for $25 a month. Because they were spoiled and because they assumed the United States after possessing the atomic bomb would never again fight an infantryman's war, officers in general were lulled into false security, becoming complacent and dangerously lax.

Such were conditions upon arrival in Korea. In sum, we're talking crew-served weapons and used equipment—most obsolete, personal training level at forty percent (an uneducated estimate), and both American and allied forces caught unprepared in an unexpected war. Our greatest asset, perhaps our only one, was individual determination to get into a scrape and prove our worth. Do or die, we'd make it happen, just like our fathers and grandfathers in WWI and II.

Wherever my trucks moved and whenever possible, Baker's

truck drove behind mine. Down the road, often two or three trucks were used and the remaining sent to other locations. In such instances, Baker and I traveled together. Some of the truckers assigned to me worked with different companies or other battalions within the regiment. As much as two weeks passed before we'd see each other. But, for the most part, Baker and I, like twins joined at the hip, were inseparable.

Another obstacle we hadn't counted on, as we traveled north, refugees traveled south. They were fleeing Seoul and the villages beyond and were a major nuisance. They came in droves, choking the narrow roads with life-long belongings strapped to A-frames on their backs or bicycles, or on hand-pulled, donkey- or oxen-driven carts. Or anything else that moved, including old pickups that when broken down were pushed into the gutter.

These civilians dressed in multiple layers of baggy trousers and shirts or vests in spite of the blazing heat of the sun. The ancients among them were further distinguished by black horsehair hats and long stemmed tiny-bowled brass pipes held in their teeth. Quiet children, women heavy with young both in and outside the womb, and the elderly supported by walking sticks shuffled onward, dragging their little feet. Herds of bony livestock paddled alongside.

Most of the people bowed their heads or, if they looked forward, were silent, their faces worn and expressionless as we struggled past. Slow humanity hurrying to survive. There were incidents, few worse than frustrated troops shoving civilians into the ditch to provide us with adequate passing room.

Another deterrent to progress, though somewhat covert, was the North Korean warrior disguised in civilian dress moving on foot with the refugees. Just like a guy from California looks the same as a guy from Pennsylvania, there was just no way you could differentiate between a friendly South Korean or an aggressive Korean from the north. They looked alike. They dressed alike. They spoke alike. But they didn't think alike, making it difficult to tell who's naughty and who's nice. Infiltration was a big thing for the commies. They broke through lines and disrupted communications, wreaking much havoc and mass confusion. As a result, we kept every Korean suspect and our senses always on the alert.

A steady breeze turned a blistering afternoon heat into a blast furnace when we arrived on the outskirts of Taegu. We immediately dispersed our vehicles, camouflaging them with scattered brush or whatever organic materials we found. The "front" we prepared ourselves for and awaited eagerly, much as Cousin Marvin anticipating his first solo flight, was about to become reality.

Full of you know what and vinegar, our entire unit went on guard at once, digging foxholes on the slopes surrounding the vehicles in all directions. Four men called forward observers (FOs—a polite label for spies) went forward a mile and established listening posts on the hillsides several hundred yards in from the road. It was their job to warn the unit by radio of any activity, or, if need be, call in the artillery to assist our infantry.

In the foxhole, one man rested while his partner stood guard. This rotation of duty throughout the night afforded each person a standard pack's worth of smokes and four hours of sleep. Truth is, we were so hyper few of us slept. Yet all was quiet, the night as exciting as a label on a tube of toothpaste. At daybreak, what I wanted more than anything else in the whole wide world was a good strong cup of hot coffee. Things being what they were, I settled for warm water tasting of tin and chlorine and a can of boring C ration. I nibbled on a saltine while our convoy traveled further north.

Early morning of the second day, we moved through Kinchon and on toward Taejon. We were advised the 34th Regiment and units of the 25th Division had spread out along the road ahead. What we weren't told was that a North Korean division supported by heavy, twenty-ton and upwards Russian T34 tanks that clinched the war in Berlin was charging toward us in double column. Had we been closer, we'd have recognized soon enough the clanging rumble and the accompanying roar of engines these giant monsters made as they advanced. Ground troops would have to be within two hundred and fifty yards of these remarkable tanks in order to immobilize them, and, during these early days, air cover was not available on a moment's notice as would be the case later on. Another detriment, our unit did not possess the 3.5 rocket launcher, only the older World War II version, a 2.3.

A rocket launcher is carried by one person who might also carry two rockets. At least one other person carries three or four rockets. Together, they become the bazooka team. You put the round in the back and hold the tube on your shoulder. There's not much recoil when you fire because the blast comes out the rear, sending this good-sized projectile on its merry way. But let me tell you, it doesn't take a rocket scientist to know a 2.3 rocket launcher is no more effective against a monstrous T34 than a broken wing is to a Canada goose outside a fox den.

On the third day, we received orders to withdraw and return to Taejon. Advanced infantry units had taken the brunt of assaults, apparent by the number of casualties hauled through our ranks. In Taejon, four GIs lay dead behind a small mud-brick Christian church that witnessed a horrendous slaughter the night before. The act was committed no doubt by North Korean snipers who passed our forces undetected. There was a lot of behind-the-lines activity when men lost their lives for being complacent and letting down their guard. Or they were caught in booby traps set at night in rear areas.

Our CO instructed Lieutenant Wilson, two other men, and me to bring them in. When receiving the directive, we exchanged looks of denial, then nodded agreement, and proceeded to execute our orders. Wilson and Bellamo, visibly shaken, coughed up their guts before the task even began. Small wonder. It was a helpless, pitiful sight.

One of the men lay stretched out full length on his back, his open eyes staring vacantly at the hot morning sun. Stainless steel ID tags were visible where a gaping wound from a bayonet slice had torn the shirt. A crumpled figure lay next to him, and a huge red stain flowed underneath. The two remaining men, limbs helter skelter like broken toys, were soaked in blood that stuck to our hands when we struggled to ready them for the ugly wrap of death. Tears formed behind my eyelids until anger overtook when I thought of the enemy holding our lives in their wicked murderous hands. These were ordinary men who were asked to do extraordinary things. Lives, like a vapor, here today, gone tomorrow. This carnage was a grim, sobering reminder that war is serious business.

From the day Cain killed his brother Abel, the world has known very little else but war. Someone estimated that in 5,560 years of recorded history, there have been more than 14,550 wars. Three hundred and fifty of these have been fought between WWII and the current age. By the time this book is published, these statistics will probably be hiked a point or two given the ongoing Middle East crises.

After delivering four litters to Graves Registration in the town of Waegwon, we returned to Taejon. There, they advised a general withdrawal of all units, mine moving west to Masan. If you were assigned to another unit, from this day forward you remained with that particular one until Masan, another hundred miles away. Captain Bond told me to turn over my two and a half ton truck to another driver and take him in a three quarter to battalion headquarters.

The temporary command post (CP) was less than a mile away, leaving precious little time for conversation. I had already learned that if you asked questions you only got answers that led to more questions. Yet I hoped for at least some indication of how things were going. But the captain seemed deep in thought. He never said more than he wanted me to know and asked only what he wanted to know. For now, he was silent and studied the worn hands in his lap, analyzing every wrinkled detail. His face was ashen and grim.

Earlier, I noticed new furrows in his brow, and the dark shadows under his eyes had deepened. The day-in/day-out pressures of war, combined with his son James Junior now serving with the 65th Combat Engineers in Korea, were taking a fearful toll on this remarkably rugged man. (Engineering units generally prepared the way for the Army to follow. They served at the front lines and were first to penetrate enemy territory. It was the most dangerous possible assignment.) Roman armies of old disallowed marriage and families as too distracting. Figures. Bond was a family man and had been through this kind of thing before, knowing well the perils of war. (See Addendum.)

The reason younger men are less afraid is because they haven't lived long enough or experienced the hazards of previous warfare to fear the dangers ahead. Me? A rookie, but no longer a pimple-faced stick in the mud, reminded of massacred compatriots, a torturous scene branded in a memory that would never forget.

Most of the brass were present when we arrived, each with paled expression before disappearing under the tent flap. It was obvious the situation was grave and that things were not going well on the front. After a half hour meeting, Captain Bond came out.

"I'm traveling with some of the other officers to attend a division meeting in Taegu," he told me, his lips twitching nervously and his brow corrugated with worry. "I'll see you in Masan."

"I have a few trucks loading supplies from a drop point just south of Taejon," I said. "I can help finish and then travel on with them."

"Good." He spoke the single word in absence.

On The Road Again

We don't have anything to fear but fear itself.
- Franklin Delano Roosevelt

The small supply dump was empty. I started south along the MSR, once again at the mercy of the dirty road and an oppressive sun, when a deuce and a half came on my tail throwing voluminous clouds of dust. The horn blew as if virtually stuck in place.

My pursuer came alongside.

"Hey, Zig Zag! Fancy meeting you out here!" It was Dolly Jackson from my unit. His blond hair was the color of dried cornhusk, and every pockmarked groove on his jovial face was packed with dirt. Only his trademark smile, one that disarmed a drill sergeant, was the same.

"Hey, yourself! Where you going?" I shouted back, making a mental note to add Dolly to my Christmas card list.

"Maybe the same as you."

"Oh? Who you assigned to?" The roar of our idling motors through the open cab made conversation all but impossible.

"The 25th Signal Company. There was six trucks in our convoy, and I broke away to return to the dump to fuel my truck. Turns out everything's cleaned up and gone." He must have been at the same site I just came from.

By the way, a dump is not Roadside America where irresponsible passersby discard anything from coke cans and mattresses to broken toilet seats and rubber, rubber like in worn-smooth tires as well as those things that block the passing of genes. A military dump is a supply site for a regiment's ready use. They are well organized and hidden. For obvious reason. If the enemy targets gasoline and ammo happens to be next door, well, need I further explain?

"So, where you headed?" I asked again.

"My truck's loaded with commo spools, and I'm supposed to re-join that same convoy in Taegu for the trip to Masan." Communications wire, called commo, is double-stranded and plastic-coated and was laid along roads, through valleys, and over mountains to maintain extensive telephone contact with units and outposts. The enemy cut this wire whenever possible, but most of the wire was simply broken by being blown up by artillery fire. The safest and fastest way to replace breaks was to forget the old wire and lay new stuff.

"How about you?" he said this time. "What are you up to?"

"I'm on my way there, too," I said. "Well, you go ahead of me but hold down the dust." It hadn't rained since we set foot in Korea, and dirt on the roads flowed like flour down a mill chute. It was difficult to see or breathe.

A large steel bridge straddled the Naktong River near Waegwon. Dolly drove south instead of turning to cross. The dust was so thick, he never caught on that I was trying to flag him down. Nor was it safe to overtake him. After several miles out of the way, I gave up and turned around.

A mile before the bridge was a small cove where eighteen fifty-five gallon drums of gasoline stood ready for the taking. If it had been someone from our unit who dropped them there, I wasn't aware. Seizing this opportunity for extra fuel, I surveyed the situation. If you think one person can't lift and load a full fifty-five gallon drum—all four hundred pounds, I'd manage quite well, thank you. What with my excellent physical condition, plus being a stubborn and determined Dutchman who between you, me, and this book cover was kind of scared and alone, it turned into a simple task. I was out of there in less time than it took to open a pack of cigarettes. To illustrate how fast that was, but to give you the benefit of the doubt, we're talking of days before plastic wraps were hermetically sealed and impossible to remove without first firing up the chain saw.

At the Waegwon Bridge, a lieutenant colonel of the 25th Division Artillery was parked in a jeep installed with an Angry-9 (AN/GR-9). This type radio occupied the entire back seat and was used to call distant units, FOs, and, when necessary, air support. Overhead were two straight-winged jets, both Lockheed F-80 Shooting Stars.

"Are you planning to blow the bridge?" I asked, squinting up at the aircraft. Bridges strong enough to support heavy tanks were prime target and often destroyed on both sides of the line. This was more or less a nuisance obstacle to an army's advance that bought the opponent time. Road graders, front-end loaders, dump trucks, and bulldozers were not shipped in until a month or two into the war. After that, engineers rebuilt roads to bypass blown bridges.

"Yep!" he said. "If you want to cross, pal, you best go now, because it's history in a coupla minutes."

I put the truck in gear and told the officer about the seventeen drums of gasoline. He immediately radioed the jets to set them afire. American stock or no, fuel was never left behind for enemy hands.

At every river crossing in South Korea, there's a small group of crude shacks usually supported by long poles on the bottom side of the bank. To watch the show, I paralleled one, a weather-beaten red-painted frame building with a white cross on top maybe a hundred yards in from the bridge. I was reminded from history studies how earlier folk pitched chairs and picnic blankets on hillsides to observe battles below. Killing people was big sport in ancient Europe. Americans carried on the tradition during both the Revolutionary and Civil Wars. I was lost to thought when the colonel came by. We stepped out of our vehicles.

"You have more faith in those flyers than I do," he said. The senior officer was a good-looking man of middle age, well built, dark glinting eyes, and had a day's stubble of black beard. He reached in his chest pocket for a cigarette.

"Yeah, I guess they don't always hit their target, do they?" I said, striking a match. I held it cupped in my dirt-stained hand until his cigarette was lit before lighting my own.

Like a hawk zeroing in on its prey, one jet made a single pass over the gas dump and fired two rockets.

SHWOOSH-SH-SH!

Seconds later, black smoke mushroomed above the small up-grade that hid the dump from view. I lean back from my keyboard and shudder to think of that precious commodity going up in smoke. I remember the gas crisis in Carter's administration in the late seventies. Lines of vehicles typically snaked thirty deep at gas stations with some fuel-thrifty drivers pushing their cars to the tank. Some motorists even got into fights over what little gas was available. And there was the gas rationing during WWII. One of the posters illustrated the need by saying, "When you ride ALONE you ride with Hitler! Join a Car-Sharing Club TODAY."

Then there was the traumatic Katrina, the hurricane of epic proportions that exposed extremes in human behavior when it struck America's nerve center the end of August 2005. Oil refineries shut down and price gouging began immediately, shooting gasoline to $3.40 a gallon and fuel oil to $2.50. God got the blame as He often does for allowing such a catastrophic event. But we should've looked at ourselves. We lacked refining capacity. Yet we hadn't built a refinery in thirty years. Also, we lacked steps to make ourselves fuel independent.

We failed abysmally through decades of presidential administrations to put more effort into seeking alternate fuel sources or even drilling in our own country, or just off-shore, rather than depending on foreign oil. And most important, we ignored warnings to re-shore century-old levees that held the water back from partying New Orleans built six feet below sea level. Hundreds lost their lives, and a million people were displaced due to man-made mistakes.

But that is neither here nor there. In wartime, economic situations are assessed differently. The gas drums needed to be destroyed.

Both planes made a swoop over the steel structure without firing, then another, this time each firing two wing rockets. One rocket missed and dove smack into the river, while the other three hit the bridge with a spontaneous explosion equal to that of the Reading Fair fireworks but without the spectacular colors. Dust, smoke, and debris cluttered the air surrounding it. The bridge trembled with terror and swayed before tilting to one side. A deafening silence, except for the roar of the planes circling above, followed. The second jet fired two rockets. After a direct hit, the mid-section fell into the river. One end of the north section teeter-tottered, so fragile the weight of a sparrow's feather might've dunked it at will. An unforgettable moment, one as overwhelming as when I learned that Great Grandfather Elias Zweizig had helped to build the Brooklyn Bridge, the longest suspension in the world (at the time).

The colonel remained talking to the pilots, and I continued south toward Taegu.

I felt like a big rock in a cement mixer as my five-foot ten and a half frame vibrated around in the driver's seat of my truck that bounced and lunged from pothole to pothole. The drive in this sometimes beautiful but mostly unforgiving landscape had been tan and parched, the hillsides littered with large beige stones. Every once in a while a tiny funnel of wind ran up a dry wash and spiraled a handful of dust across the partially graveled, partially tarmacked road. I saw no wildlife and little vegetation other than lifeless looking scrub. Occasionally, abandoned fields and dry rice paddies, their cracked faces turned to a hazy blue sky awaiting the rain, presented themselves, then it was onward through a succession of charmless, deserted villages where vegetable gardens were up in weeds and workshops empty. Neglected clutter lay at random where goats once browsed before refugees hurried south.

As the miles ticked by, I further considered the landscape. What I couldn't take in at the time I made it my business to research later.

The principal feature of Korea's military geography is the great north/south mountain range that forms a wall down the entire length of the eastern side of the peninsula. This central spine and the lateral spurs extending west and southwest into the flat country beside the Yellow Sea are bleak and rugged. Flowing westward from the main range is a number of broad rivers creating serious obstacles for both communications and north/south movement, yet less discouraging than the formidable east coast where, in most areas, the treeless mountains drop abruptly into the Sea of Japan.

The country's half-decent roads and railroads, at the time of this story, were concentrated in the west. Only one road plus an antiquated train on aged tracks running part of the way shuttled along the east coast where I traveled.

"Hi, Mac! Having trouble?" I asked the driver of a stopped vehicle.

He was a freckle-faced soldier in fatigues about my age and had a pug nose sprinkled with beads of sweat and grit. Red kinky hair sprouted from beneath his cap. He drove an American two and a half ton empty troop carrier.

"Yeah. How do they expect you to fight a war when they give you crummy junk like this!" he griped around a cigarette. With a booted foot, he stabbed the left front tire pasted to the rough road surface. The breeze kicked up a dirt devil alongside which then dissipated into thick air. All the while, the sun beat bright and heavy.

After we changed the tire, I stayed behind for a smoke to give him a head start because of the dust.

At Taegu, I expected traffic and servicemen at the supply dumps. Wrong again. The two sites from which we drew supplies days before were cleaned up and vacated. I continued toward Pusan.

On the outskirts of Pusan, still along MSR markers, were several rice shacks, some leaning and looking kind of tired. I pulled up to one with a peppermint post poking from the corner of the building. In the ancient past, this universal shingle served also for surgeons. I hoped this owner was first a barber. My hair was a far cry from the crew cut of basic training days. In fact, I'm sure I looked more like a sixties beatnik than an all-American farm boy from a decade before.

On the porch, a rickety chair leaned against the wall and served as a playground for two little boys who disappeared when I approached the shop. Somewhere in the distance, a dog barked once, then was silent. A mournful donkey brayed. Rats the size of rabbits sent a shiver down my spine as they scampered behind the building.

I hated rats. Still do. Mice have their day in court, especially on the farm, but at least they're cute. There is nothing redeeming about a rat. My hatred stems from the time Uncle Herbert was approached by an army of them. He had snuck into his chicken house with a twenty-two late one night to determine what was eating the feed and discovered soon enough who were the thieves. He was darn lucky they didn't attack him.

Let me tell you something else about the rat. This is free, by the way. You don't have to pay for this. It's a bonus for buying the book. Did you know that if we were to exterminate ninety percent of the rat population, it would replace itself in one year? Did you know that this vicious rodent is the greatest menace to human health? They carry numerous diseases, probably the most destructive in history from the bubonic plague in Europe to typhus across the planet. To bring this topic closer to home, thousands of these repugnant beasts took up residence amongst famous urbanites near Hollywood and Vine some years back. I'll bet you didn't know this and are glad now you didn't skip to the next page when I brought up the loathsome subject.

I ascended an assortment of mismatched steps that had no master design while a hound of mixed ancestry met me by the door, gazing in disbelief at my huge truck. A creamsickle-colored cat, obviously unaware of the rats that had been nosing about, was deep in slumber and nestled next to him. The dog's wrinkled lips exposed sharp eye-teeth in greeting, and a growl resembling distant thunder came from his throat that aroused the cat. The cat quickly disappeared. Deciding not to charge, the dog resumed a sleeping position.

On either side of the door was a short window of paned glass. Thin faded curtains hung in both windows, and the curtain on the right moved as I passed cautiously by Rover and entered the shop.

Spending more than two years in Japan, and since Japan occupied Korea more than forty years, I felt confident the barber and I could communicate. The shop was empty except for him. His short black hair was wet with perspiration. Slanted dark eyes stared intensively at the rifle I carried in front of me.

I turned up the volume like I always did when speaking to someone schooled in another language.

"Haircut!" I said and removed my cap, pointing to my head to make myself better understood. Filthy with road dirt and grime, I was grateful to be in a regulated environment, if only in a room measuring two by four.

"Okay. Okay," the little man in baggy white cotton trousers said.

He bowed three times, in sync with the dangling waist cord that looked like the twine we wrapped straw sheaves with back home.

My cap flew to a wooden bench nearby. With the loaded M1 pinched between thighs, I sat on a backless stool while the little man worked and critically studied my face in the small mirror on the otherwise bare wall. The mirror reflected my image only too well. The skin lay firm against the bone in a deceptively healthy-looking tan, or was it dirt, but, from my lack of sleep, the eye sockets were so deep you could've planted potatoes in them. My shadowy jaw revealed growth of a beard from what seemed months ago, but in fact was only maybe 48 hours. It was difficult to remember the last time I put razor to skin since one day blended into the next.

Oh, what I wouldn't have given for a shower, too. It was a dirty, sweaty day, a real scorcher, with the temperature locking in at three figures. I smelled as ripe as an old Billy goat because of it.

When he finished, I picked up my cap.

"How much?" I said. My pockets were empty, but I had thought it proper to ask.

"Five hundred won."

Five hundred won? That's about thirty cents. I gave him two cans of C ration. This seemed to please him a lot. He bowed thirty-one times. I counted.

There was a crossroad several hundred feet from the shop. Using my hands, I beckoned the barber outside and asked the direction to Masan. He pointed to the way I should go, but I trusted him no farther than I could pitch a Holstein bull. For all I knew, this guy was a commie and had the owner tied up in knots in the back room.

"Will the real Mister Barber come forth?" Sorry, I made that up. "I'm taking you along," is what I really said, motioning him into the cab. There are things in life you can't afford not to do. This was one of them.

"No. No. No, I no..." That's Korean for no.

"Get in!" I said, sealing my intentions with the butt of my rifle. I moved the truck forward before he was even seated. Advancing toward a sinking sun, I felt certain we were on the correct road. The time was 1800.

We passed a refugee camp while still inside the Pusan Perimeter that was supported by the Americans. A noisy sprawl of lean-to tenting made from tarps was visible from the road. As were clotheslines loaded with sheets and sundry items hanging at random between scrawny trees. Trillions of smoky campfires dotted the area, and the air was saturated with the smelly odors of boiled cabbage and fish.

I took my eyes off the road for a second to observe humanity in its most submissive state when suddenly two skinny, moth-colored mutts locked together in romance filled my windshield. Of all the six billion people on this planet and of all the roads and of all the dogs, these two chose this moment to cross this road in front of this person and this person's truck to propagate another generation of skinny moth-colored mutts. My companion turned to me wide-eyed and mumbled major Korean mumbo jumbo after I made a one hundred and eighty degree swerve to avoid a near death experience.

Following this same avenue into a stern and harsh landscape, my complaining transmission groaned and shuddered its way through ruts and bumps for at least twenty miles before heating up. I stopped and signed my hostage to get the five-gallon water can from the rear bed. When he returned, he held the can up in the air.

"Emptee!"

"Horse dung!" From the rugged roads, or was it the lovers, the can tipped and the water leaked out. No streams were apparent since several miles back. Nor were there any ahead as far as I could tell from where we were which was near the crest of a long sloping hill. I decided to restart the truck and drive until we came to water, somewhere. When I switched the ignition, there was the wincing whine of a starter giving its best, but the engine wouldn't turn over. I waited and tried again. And again.

Road filth had mixed with hundreds of insects flinging themselves into the windshield since the start of my journey. On a few occasions, I made a hurried swipe with a ragged tee shirt I carried in my truck, widening my visible space to the size of an opened wallet. It was like looking through a tank turret. While I waited for the overheated engine to unheat, I squeezed a few remaining drops from the empty water can and applied them to the windshield. But that simply turned everything into a brown sludge. I further attacked it with a generous portion of precious canteen water but that just converted the mess from a brown sludge to a brown slurry. Now I couldn't see through at all. It mattered little. After a half hour's wait, the truck still didn't start. Sometimes I was the bug. Sometimes I was the windshield. That's just the way life was that particular day.

My best guess was we were in mountains halfway between Pusan and Masan. It would be dark soon. No vehicles passed since my breakdown, and, if there were, most likely no one with whom I'd risk thumbing a ride. Movement at night was not a good thing, ambush and sniper fire always a possibility. Considering all options, there was little choice but to continue on foot. I hand-signaled the barber to return home. He had a good hike ahead, but that was his concern, not mine. I had better things to think about and gave him a few C ration cans for the road. He bowed several times and left.

In the truck, I carried a 30 calibre M1 Garand and a 30 calibre M2 Carbine. A .45 calibre pistol was fastened under my left arm. Like a Bible is to a preacher, an M1 is to a soldier. It was considered the finest military rifle available. It weighed ten pounds and was top-loaded with an eight-round clip that had to be pushed down into the magazine holder in one quick motion or else your thumb slammed up against the chamber, resulting in an M1 thumb injury. "Knuckle-buster," they called it. This semi automatic was gas-operated, meaning each shot operated from gas produced by the last shot. The M1 was the only weapon I had with me when we arrived in Korea. Soon afterward, Baker donated a carbine (a lightweight known for its fast-firing capability) and the forty-five. If anyone could scrounge up stuff, it was Baker. His only remark at that time was, "I look after number one and number two, and that's you and me!"

The tanned hills were full of long shadows while I walked carrying tools of war, my canteen, and two cans of pork and beans in a leg pocket. Before dark, I spotted a pheasant and thought I just might have use for it. I fired a single round with my carbine and twenty yards away retrieved the bloody hen lying by the road. She was hit all right. Half her chest blew away in the process. I strapped her on anyway and kept walking as fast as possible, meanwhile, chuckling to myself. I'd been in Korea for at least ten days, America's wonder fighting man, and all I managed to kill so far was an innocent little game bird.

Somehow night came on without my planning on it. The sun

dipped below the horizon, and only a faint orange glow in a purple sky remained. Just before darkness smothered dusk, I heard an approaching motor and jumped behind some bushes concealed by a copse of short trees. I crouched to a tiny opening and made out a small Korean pickup loaded with bags of some sort and six people on the back. One had a rifle slung over his shoulder. They might well have been friendly, but on the other hand, venturing forth could prove as dangerous as playing catch with a hand grenade. Moments passed uneventful. I breathed a word of thanks and hurried on before sitting it out in brush near the roadway for the rest of the night.

The temperature dropped at least thirty-five degrees after the sun disappeared. How foolish not to have grabbed a jacket from the truck for my trek into the unknown. In spite of the fatigue shirt pulled tight around me, goose bumps chased each other up and down the spine like my cousin's fingers on the accordion. I tried to catch some ZZZs, but the chill and anguish allowed a mere fifteen winks at a time.

I was not alone. Crickets chirped in the tall dry grass, and when I closed my eyes and heard the steady metallic chant of the cicada (*maemi*), I was back home on a warm summer's night.

The back porch, moths busily fluttering around the single electric light bulb in the ceiling, is where the family, except for Pop, gathered after the outside farm chores were done for the day. It was where the girls shelled peas, snapped beans, or shucked sweet corn to jar the next day. Mom worked on tomatoes or some other seasonal produce from her large vegetable garden. Cooking and canning were done in a summer kitchen behind the big house so that sleeping rooms would remain as cool as possible. Window shutters were closed to keep out the daytime sun and opened at night.

Pop was not around. My mother, Laura, was an "at the store widow" as was Uncle Herbert's wife Florence and many other women in our farm community. Their husbands were at Kliney's General Store in the village of Berne each weekday night after a late supper, playing cards or chewing the fat.

We boys who had done men's work all day long hung around the porch for a little while, teasing our sisters and playing with Sheppie, then hit the hay so we could start all over again early the next morning. I remember being lulled to sleep many times by the ghostly schlopp, schlopp, schlopp the cows made as they stepped through the swampy meadow alongside our backyard. And there was the time…

A breeze or something rustled in the brush. I popped open my eyes in time to see a pair of the same darting through the blackness in front of me. Too low for man, too high for skunk or possum or whatever nocturnal creatures they had in this part of the world. I reached slowly for my rifle and the eyes disappeared. Now I was fully awake.

The moon was nowhere in sight. But as I zeroed in on a clear sky, it wasn't so dark anymore. The constellations provided a nice escape from my uncomfortable circumstance, and I found the big dipper and little dipper with relative ease. Their individual stars hung perhaps since The Beginning when God spoke the heavens and the earth into being. (The Bible says six days and six nights, though I have a feeling He spent most of the week with His feet up!) They blinked down at me and glistened like jewels studded on a black velvet cloth. When I left home, the already developing cities raped the sky of its sharpness. Still, it was more brilliant than today. What with pollution in the mix and a trillion electric lights up and down the eastern seaboard, you are blessed if you see a handful of sparkles in an eye's view. Even so, they are on the move to the closest airport. (See Addendum.)

Silently, my experience with the night sky turned to dawn, and, just like Willy Nelson, I was on the road again. By now, the pheasant didn't look too edible so I threw the carcass away for some lower form of animal to feast on. Besides, enough things hung off me without carrying excess baggage.

After sunrise, the air starting to warm, I sat down on a log and contemplated a can of cold pork and beans I opened with my bayonet. This fare looked and smelled like commercial dog food our fancy neighbors back home fed their pets, kept inside the house for goodness sake. Nevertheless, my mouth tasting like the bottom of a birdcage as it were and my stomach growling "Feed me!" I couldn't afford to be too fussy. My stomach felt otherwise. "Oh, no, not beans again! All I ever get is beans!" it complained. "This is disgusting. I want some real food. I want ham and eggs and blueberry pancakes on the side with lots of warm butter and syrup. Really, this is just too gross for words."

While continuing to displease, I imagined a doleful whistle in the distance. *Could it be…*

In the direction of the sound were long reaches of pale rock, strewn with dwarfed bushes and drifts of thick tough grass. A solitary tree, its thirsty branches dipping toward the parched earth, broke the landscape that seemed to suddenly end with no visible mountain on the near horizon. Still in the days before Lady Bird Johnson's "beautification on highways and byways" stressed in the homeland, I tossed the empty tin into the undergrowth, gathered my few belongings, and hurried to the hill. At the crest, a rocky, scrub-choked cliff cut into bottomland, revealing a small village with a railroad station in its midst. An engine spewing steam waited on a track that wound through the valley in the direction of Masan. Four cars linked behind. I was determined to be on one before that train left the depot.

Thickets of savage brush hosting tangled vines cost my footing. I rolled twice and, over rocks and stones, slid on the seat of my pants to complete a stupendous descent. My arms were scratched as if I'd been shocking bundles of wheat for a day.

The train had clearly seen better days. Four wooden boxcars, named coffins on the other side of the globe because of their hazardous construction, and two flatbeds in between were loaded with baggage and people, plus chicken coops, goats, and barking dogs.

"Me go Masan!" I said to no one in particular and hoisted myself up into the engine's compartment, the only room left.

Both the fireman and engineer looked at me as if I had dropped from outer space. "Me go Masan!" I said to them.

"Okay. Okay. We go Masan," agreed the little men.

The engine coughed and shuddered and belched black smoke from the stack as it prepared to leave. After ten minutes, a sudden hard jolt started the train into motion. We hadn't gone far, maybe a mile or two, when up on the same roadway where I walked earlier was a big brown dot, stirring puffs of dust. When we drew closer, a three quarter ton truck emerged. It came into the valley and traveled in our direction. On the back of the truck was a fifty-five gallon drum.

THAT'S MY TRUCK! *Someone got it going, and now I want it back!*

The locomotive snaked through a steamy rice paddy. By following the footpaths, I could run to the roadway and still meet the truck.

"Stop the train!" I shouted to the engineer.

"No, no. Must go!" the engineer said with equal conviction.

"Stop this train!"

"No, no. Must go!"

Why must everything be repeated!

With the carbine slung behind my back and the M1 in my left hand, my right hand was free to pull the forty-five out of my shirt. Jamming the gun hard against his neck, I shouted once more to stop the train.

"Okay. Okay," he said, attempting to bow before slowing the engine. These little folk from the East could be polite even in the most awkward of situations I observed in a fleeting moment.

Iron wheels shrieked as they resisted the brakes, slowing the train to maybe ten miles per hour. I jumped off into the muck and ran toward the road. Two servicemen in the truck waited. It was the doggonedest thing—as weird as finding a bowling ball in a snow bank. (I know someone who did!) This was not my truck after all. It was the same type and had a drum on the back and a windshield in front with road dirt and slime of battered insects. But it belonged to the 35th Infantry Regiment.

"We're stationed near a small village outside Masan," the driver said, pointing ahead. He was assuredly Italian by makeup and spoke with a "Joisy" accent.

Hey, did you know a fella by the name of Larry Viscardi? Oh, never mind....

"Did you see a three quarter ton truck along the road several miles back?" I asked, jostling between the shoulders of my two new colleagues.

The dust billowed thickly behind us.

"Yeah, we tried to start it, but nix," said the driver. "Is that yours?"

We beat the slow-moving train into the village. When we pulled up to a small CP tent, a captain who looked vaguely familiar approached our vehicle.

"We found this poor soul five miles out hitching a ride to town," the corporal told him. His dirty face had split into a wide grin at the telling, like a cat proudly showing its master the mouse it just caught.

Small world! Jonathan Mackley was my CO during basic training at Fort Dix, a thirty-eightish WWII vet, soft-spoken, reasonable sort of training officer who wasn't pushy as some tend to be at his level. In fact, I never heard him swear and never saw him ruffled. He had a quiet leadership and always respected those under his command. He had been a 1st lieutenant back then.

"I thought I trained you better than that," Mackley said after I revealed the events of my past twenty-four hours. "Hungry?"

"Truman's a Democrat, ain't he?" You better believe I was hungry. This would be my first hot meal since Kyushu.

Mackley smiled and asked, "What's for dinner?" of the 1st sergeant whose bushy eyebrows stuck out to the scraggy Korean hills. He had more hair below his forehead than above.

"Same as always, cap'n. Beans fried in axle grease." He hawked up a good one and spat toward the mess tent.

I laughed.

"Whatever it is will be better than what I had the past coupla days," I said, feeling a sudden thump behind my belly button.

The captain laughed.

Captain Mackley had arrived in Japan in the fall of 1949 and was assigned to the 35th Infantry Regiment at Otsu in Japan. He poured two cups of very black coffee that was simmering on a gas stove, while I collected a dollop of meatloaf and mashed potatoes from a steam table. Between gigantic bites, I asked Mackley how things were going. My host chewed on the mouthpiece of an empty pipe and studied the question.

"Well," he said, removing the pipe long enough to take a swig of coffee. "The last casualty figures from one of the morning reports indicated fourteen wounded and three dead." He paused, took another swallow of coffee and added, "This happened in the Taejon area just west of the 27th Sector."

My stomach gave a small lurch as I recalled the dead we removed the day before.

"I think that first contact caught everyone by surprise," Mackley said this time.

While buttering my dinner roll, I chewed thoughtfully, then said,

"Funny, during an orientation period on Kyushu before we left Japan, we were told that most likely the Koreans wouldn't fight when they saw us Americans."

Mackley seemed to consider that and plucked absently at his unshaven chin.

"Yes," he said. "We were told the same thing."

We both retreated into our own thoughts. I concentrated on the rest of the food on my plate while the executive officer's focus appeared to be on something a long way off. He swilled his second cup of coffee.

"Unfortunately, it was a real disservice," he finally said, "since many of the men expected just that to happen, and it didn't." With a slim index finger, the captain pushed his glasses up on his nose and resumed his stare into space with pale blue worried eyes before saying this time, "That may have cost many lives."

Neither of us said more, our silence acknowledging the lie in any intended optimism.

From the mess tent, we walked to the small station where the train had arrived. Grownups and children huddled together, encumbered by bundles and boxes tied with string, and, again, dogs, goats, and chickens. They were bound for Masan and points west.

"It seems the refugees from the north are heading south, and the ones here are heading west," I observed.

"Yes, they are people on the run. It's sad. But this is war. There's no safe haven for any of us, really."

"Thank God it won't last long!"

We checked all six loaded cars. Few passengers had departed since the train pulled in, and five times as many piled on in the vacated spaces.

"I guess the only room left is the cow-pusher," suggested Mackley.

I thanked him for the hot meal and elbowed my way through the remaining hopefuls on the wooden platform before climbing in front of the locomotive for the last five miles to Masan.

When we neared the station siding in Masan, I spotted trucks with 27th Infantry bumper markings. Home at last! I walked into the CP tent of my service company, 1st Battalion, and noticed Lieutenant Bowman. He wore captain bars.

Bowman, an infantry line company officer during the latter part of WWII, was promoted and transferred to one of the line companies in the 2nd Battalion. The most I can tell you of the red-nosed Bowman is that he drank too much. Single and unlike family men at Hamadera Park, he lived in the bachelor officer quarters when we were still at Kanoaka Barracks. He spent off-duty hours at the club's infamous watering hole. Captain Bond enjoyed his drink as well.

Prior to sundown, I related my story to Captain Bond.

"We've got to get our hands on that truck," he said afterward. "Vehicles and parts are scarce. Take a mechanic and another truck at dawn and get that thing started and bring her back, even if you have to tow it." Then he yelled to the orderly room clerk, "Is there any more beer out in the lister bag?" The lister bag held thirty gallons and had four taps at the bottom. It was intended for drinking water. The captain also used it to keep his beer cool. Every now and then he slipped in a couple of chlorine tablets. I guess he assumed that would purify the water from dirty hands retrieving a beer. The clerk, a quiet thin lad with a crew cut and wire-rimmed glasses, came back empty-handed.

"Beer's gone," he said.

"There are too many people who know where I keep my beer," complained the captain. He turned to me. Long before now, we were on a first-name basis. "Hey, Ziggy, how about taking my jeep and running down to the end of our company area and look for the beer truck. It's numbered SVC-17."

It was night. We were in a complete blackout zone, making it tricky business driving through the tented maze to the service trucks. When I reached what I thought was the right truck, I climbed over the tailgate and felt around in the dark for cases of 3.2 beer. My eyes must have widened to the size of headlights when my first touch was a shoe. I let go and returned to the jeep and retrieved a flashlight (covered with layers of blue cellophane) clipped to the dash. Again I crawled over the tailgate and into the canvas-covered body and cautiously turned on my blue-lensed light. I now saw several litters with dead Americans tagged to be moved in the morning. A closer look at the bumper markings after wiping off dried mud revealed "SVC-19."

"There should be another truck in that same area with bodies on it," the captain told me after I returned with the beer. "The 3rd Battalion lost eleven men."

I didn't comment but shook my head in sympathy.

After bedding down in a small supply tent, I sighed with great relief. I hadn't slept more than two hours at any one time since arriving in Korea. Now would prove no exception. For just before nodding off, a small plane motor droned overhead. A loud boom followed and seconds later another. I lay wide-awake until morning.

The guys laughed when I asked what the heck went on during the night.

"That's just Bed Check Charlie throwing out some fire-crackers!"

"He shows up every night," Captain Bond told me. "We have strict orders not to fire at him."

As long as I was in the Masan area, Bed Check Charlie made a nightly visit, throwing out a couple of bombs from his single engine plane. He was just enough of a nuisance to wake us up if, indeed we got to sleep at all.

So ended my first two weeks in Korea.

18

No Korean Dunkirk

...We shall fight on the beaches;
We shall fight on the landing grounds;
We shall fight in the fields and in the streets;
We shall fight in the hills.
We shall never surrender!
                                        - Winston Churchill

Bruce Griffin, a mechanic who came from our country's most northern state, was a big burly guy with shoulders as broad as those that span a paved road. He and I took the company's five-ton wrecker the next morning to my abandoned truck, sure to find it cannibalized or, at minimum, tampered with. I did a walk-around to see if any parts had been appropriated. Or worse, if anything lethal had been added.

Surprise! Surprise! The truck was intact, at least on the surface. By now, we were aware of Koreans slipping past guards and into parked vehicles at night. They set booby traps by planting mines and then leaving undetected. So far this had not happened within the 27th Regiment. But we received reports from other units experiencing the problem. To be on the safe side, we carefully checked the engine, the front of the truck, behind each wheel, and also around the base of the body. We filled the radiator, added gas. I climbed into the driver's seat, put the gearshift in place, turned the ignition, and it kicked over immediately. We were fortunate. Beyond fortunate. The truck hadn't exploded.

That same morning, I took six trucks and fetched food supplies and ammo in Pusan. As soon as our convoy returned, we picked up a hundred and twenty men who had just arrived from Japan and moved them to the 27th Regiment's staging area. By this time, I could have maneuvered the MSR in my sleep. Come to think of it, I wonder why I hadn't thought of that back then. I certainly could have used more shuteye.

Most replacements came from the 8th Army Stockade (The Big 8) in Japan near Yokohama. Since all units of the 24th and 25th Infantry Divisions, as well as some from the 1st Cavalry, were on their way over, many witnesses to scheduled trials were now in Korea and no longer available. Therefore, MacArthur released up to 2,300 criminals of all stripes who had served at least a third of their two to ten year sentences. He sent them to Korea to bolster U.S. Forces.

We hauled some of these released prisoners. On one occasion, I remember a tall, tough-talking buck sergeant walked up to my truck to accept two men assigned to his squad.

"I'm the SOB in charge here!" he announced. "You screw up in my squad, and, if the Koreans don't get you, I will! Get over there with the rest of the men where we'll give you a twenty-minute dry run on the use of our weapons!"

Back in the States, President Truman extended everyone's enlistment for one year. There was rumor, too, the draft was extended.

These were perilous times. The North Koreans had a force ready since day one of, and research numbers vary, anywhere from 90,000 to 138,000 troops in addition to possessing well over one hundred T34 tanks. Talk about being unprepared. Even with the units coming from Japan, our troops fell in the pitiful low range of 28,000 to 29,000 with no American tanks in the country to date.

Some of the darnedest things do happen! In the midst of all this gearing up, I was instructed to take two trucks to Pusan to pick up Al Jolson and his troupe. Baker caught up with us several days before, and we went together on this assignment.

At a waterway near Pusan, we had a couple of spare minutes before catching up with the entertainer. We fished. Well, sort of. We threw hand grenades in the water and stunned the close-by fish while hundreds of others floated to the surface. Why did we do these things! We're lucky we weren't reported, since it could have been viewed as a courts martial offense, and times were tense.

It was a courts martial offense just to walk around without a weapon in hand. All Koreans were viewed with suspicion. We never knew if they had weapons concealed beneath their gowns. Even when eating C rations, you did not sit in a group. Small arms fired in the background, and you constantly heard the muffled drum roll of distant artillery.

People were dying. I remember walking along a dirt road and up ahead someone, most likely a sniper victim, lay by the side of the road with a medic in attendance. Another medic ran past me, and, when I came alongside, I saw the soldier was in a pool of blood. He screamed the most awful scream as the medics tried to take his hands away from holding at his stomach. I'm sure he died minutes later.

No, these were not fun times, and there we were, in the name of fun, doing idiotic stupid stuff like targeting fish with hand grenades!

People tell me I'd have a photographic memory if only the lens cap weren't screwed fast. Yet in spite of this technical detriment, I can still picture me and four others struggling for all we were worth to unload the upright piano at the dock warehouse where the shows would be held. Too, I visualize Mr. Jolson at the piano, a little beanie sitting on top of a face blackened and barely distinguishable in the fading light, singing his renowned version of "Mammy." He always ended each program by leading with his sensational voice the military medley honoring our Armed Forces. Would you believe his first voice teacher said he'd have no future in singing?

Unfortunately, few attended the performances. Maybe no more than thirty at a time. If the guys weren't working, they were on guard duty, leaving precious little time for something as frivolous as Hollywood entertainment. This is certainly not to say Mr. Jolson's efforts were unappreciated. Under normal circumstances, there would have been nothing better than an opportunity away from responsibilities and worries. But these were not normal circumstances.

Every night was blackout. Every night Bed Check Charlie dropped by for a boom-boom as faithfully as a grandfather's clock strikes at twelve. Jolson's stay lasted only two days after which his group with all its bells and whistles was promptly hauled back to Pusan.

Did you know he pioneered sound in the movie industry? His given name was Asa Yoelson. Born in St. Petersburg, Russia, he began his career in the circus, then Yiddish theatre on Broadway and, finally, Hollywood where he starred in the first all-talking production, "The Jazz Singer."

Al Jolson continued on to fame and fortune when World War II came along. Another first, he entertained troops under the auspices of the new United Services Organization (USO). During the Korean War, USO funds for entertainers' travel expenses were exhausted. But Jolson, now a tired old man, paid his own way. He wanted to be with his favorite audience, the American Armed Forces, and performed forty-two shows in sixteen days throughout war-torn Korea. Sad to say, three short weeks after returning to the States, the famous jazz singer passed away. (*Good Old Days*, Sept. 2001.)

Around August 1st, Lt. General Walton Walker came through our area to hold a meeting at our regimental headquarters. Walker was the 8th Army's Commanding General. All forces in Korea were under his command. On the day following Walker's visit, officers and NCOs were summoned to an outdoor meeting. The meeting was conducted by Colonel Michael Michaelis, 27th Infantry Regimental Commander.

Colonel Michaelis, a hotshot West Pointer hailing from my neck of the woods—neighboring Lancaster County, established quite a record as a lieutenant colonel during World War II. Following the war, he went to Japan and took over the 27th Regiment. He became a full colonel within just thirty days. Six months later, he was promoted to Assistant Division Commander of Brigadier General.

Funny, I can't remember whether I had oatmeal or dippy eggs for breakfast this morning. Yet I specifically recall the colonel's presentation five decades back. One of the more profound phrases (I'm not sure this was originally his or Walker's, nonetheless, he said it) was:

"There will be no Korean Dunkirk!" We would not be pushed off the Korean Peninsula.

The terminology was a throwback to the seaport of Dunquerque. This city in northern France was badly damaged during WWI and almost completely destroyed in WWII when, in June 1940, German forces surrounded and trapped some 380,000 allied troops in this sixty square mile area, then pushed them out to sea.

A large fleet comprised of brave Brits from both the public and private sectors sailed in small boats (naval craft, fishing boats, barges, virtually anything that floated) across the English Channel to the French shore and rescued 350,000 men while still under enemy fire. This daring and noble endeavor became known as the Miracle of Dunkirk. The Church of England and its people, under the head of King George VI, prayed all the while for God's protection of their nation and troops during this risky rescue mission. God followed through and provided wind to their backs, both coming and going across the channel. The Miracle of Dunkirk.

Here are more excerpts from Colonel Michaelis' speech:

"...Effective at once, orders are to stand and hold. (Later, I read he was quoted as saying, 'Stand and fight or die!' But, being a stubborn and unyielding Dutchman, I'll stand by my stand and hold.) There will be no further withdrawals.... From this day forward we will strictly hold in place defensive action. ...This information must be relayed to every man in your command...."

Here's an additional item somewhat significant spawned from my recollection of the colonel's meeting, although he didn't specifically say it. Like me, though, you might find this remarkable quotation remarkably interesting.

Winston Churchill, Prime Minister of Great Britain at the time of the Second World War, was known for his long powerful speeches. At a commencement exercise during the most discouraging days, he walked to the podium to give an address and stood silently for a few moments, then looked to one side of the student body and boomed, "Never give up!" He looked toward the middle of the audience and boomed, "Never give up!" He turned to the opposite side of the room and boomed, "Never, never give up!" and sat down. Churchill inspired these young people to new hope and new belief all the while bombs rained on their beloved city of London.

At present, our lines extended from Pusan to as far north as Potsung on the northeast coast to slightly north of Taegu in the central portion of Korea and south and west of Masan near the southwest section of the peninsula. This was no small undertaking. Still, ours was merely a toe-hold in comparison to the enemy's. Colonel Michaelis said General MacArthur needed time to recruit additional men and supplies from the States and that some supplies were moved "as we speak" from the Philippines to Korea. It was at this time, we received a Combat Infantryman's Badge. Along with it came an automatic fifteen dollar-a-month raise. A big deal! A very big deal!

The day after the meeting concerning our "stand and hold" orders, two trucks rolled into camp with six dead Americans on each to turn over to Graves Registration. All of a sudden yesterday's instructions had much more meaning as things slowly but surely intensified.

Casualties were from the 29th Infantry Regiment and not the 25th Division, though, at the time, they were under the jurisdiction of the 25th as I remember it. During the last ten days of July, the 29th Infantry Regiment moved to Korea by transport from Okinawa. It should not have been called a regiment, rather, a reinforced battalion, since it only had two battalions for a total of seven hundred men. Of these, four hundred had just come from the States. Upon their arrival in Okinawa, they left their ship, drew weapons and combat gear, and re-boarded the same transport for passage to Korea. These GIs completed basic training with no advanced infantry training whatsoever.

Several officers had flown to Okinawa to accompany these men and gave instructions and weapons familiarization during the flight to Korea. When these troops with last minute training crammed down their vulnerable throats landed in Korea, they were dumped on line near Hadong before even test firing their weapons. Within twenty-four hours, they were ambushed. Surviving such an encounter was as likely as a hog walking away at butchering time.

When this same area was retaken three weeks later, we picked up three hundred American dead. One can only speculate what had happened. You see, another North Korean trick was to walk up to the Americans with hands raised in surrender. Several feet away from capture, they dropped to the ground while hidden comrades fired away.

More than one hundred allies had been taken prisoner. We found some of these same prisoners later in North Korea, massacred. It appeared whenever the allies pushed too hard or moved too fast the prisoners became a burden and were shot. (Some POWs ended up in Russia's Siberian labor camps, but were not located until years after the war. Some still MIA.)

It's an eerie feeling to deliver fifty or sixty men to a sector on one day and return two days later to move that same group minus ten percent. I was never officially a part of Graves Registration but did participate in some of their activities during the early days.

What a sobering experience! Each soldier wears two dog tags. One is removed, and the information is recorded on site. The other tag remains with the body that is moved out on a litter and hauled away by truck to the Graves Registration office.

This was the most gruesome work I ever had the displeasure of being associated with. I remember at times the sector was not stabilized for a week or even longer, and dead bodies would lie out in the hot summer sun and bloat to twice the normal size. The smell of rotten human flesh struck me with as much force as if someone had shot hardened clay up my nose. And the worms! Oh, man, the worms! To this day, my senses are as gut-churningly and putridly sensitive when I thumb through my mental scrapbook as if it had happened yesterday. I had witnessed the tremendous cost of war firsthand. This was quite different from the glamorous myth of men of old falling in battle as seen in library books!

So it was in late July and August of 1950. Many lives and much blood were sacrificed holding this small area until a buildup of U.N. manpower equaled that of our enemy's to the north.

The Boys From Gifu

…We hold these truths to be self-evident,
That all men are created equal…
                    - Abraham Lincoln

Ever wonder why some folks are white, others black? I have. When God destroyed the Tower of Babel, He scattered farmers, bricktossers, janitors, and cup stackers over the face of the earth and provided those who settled closest to the Equator with darker pigment full of natural sunscreen. The farther north people settled, the paler the skin to absorb more light. Of course, their clothed bodies added to the situation as having less sun exposure, hence, requiring more work to synthesize Vitamin D. To add to this last tidbit of wisdom, northern folk are generally more industrious caused by a dire need to provide for the long cold winters ahead, like the busy squirrel hustling to store a cache of nuts. I realize this insight is just a blip on the radar screen and has no scientific basis. Yet that doesn't make it less valid.

Three infantry regiments plus a host of support companies comprised the 25th Infantry Division. Regiments included the 35th formerly from Otsu, Japan, the 27th from Osaka (mine), and the 24th stationed in Japan at Gifu. The latter was an all African American regiment whom the Japanese called Chocoletto Boys.

At Kanoaka Barracks, we had African Americans on base, a single platoon, with one of their own sergeants in charge. Top officers were Caucasian. Black soldiers always worked under the command of white officers. They stayed in a separate building at the far end of the facility. Jointly, yet separately, they attended reveille, were involved in retreat formations, and participated in close order drills and police calls. (Police calls are demeaning tasks such as picking up cigarette butts, cleaning johns, and taking out the trash or something similar. We all participated, regardless of the color of our skins.) They were scheduled fifteen minutes behind us in the mess hall. Each morning during calisthenics, I saw them at the far end of the parade field doing the same. Separate but equal?

I don't ever recall fights or racial slurs between whites and blacks, but I must admit it was obvious in some non-obvious ways that they were often shunned and scorned and treated as second-class citizens. It's amazing these people were asked to fight as part of a team when the government for which they fought to protect democracy and risk their lives oozed in unconscious racism, eighty some years after emancipation.

Still, you can't blame the government alone for this equal yet separate mentality. Just as one assumes the color of a horse named Black Beauty is black, one assumed segregation no matter where one went back in the forties and fifties, whether school, bus, theatre, restroom, public outhouse, you name it. Even in the Roman Catholic Church, people of color sat in rear pews and took communion last. This is just the way it was. Until Rosa Parks.

Miss Parks, a seamstress, was an ordinary person who acted in an extraordinary way one particular day in 1955. She not only confronted a bus driver and a sheriff when she refused to yield her front seat to a white passenger, but also history itself by sparking the Civil Rights movement.

Before that, an old German proverb well depicted life in these United States:

"Take the world as it is, not as it ought to be."

A decade later, Martin Luther King put it differently:

"I have a dream…that my children will not be judged by the color of their skin, but by the content of their character."

A fourth grade teacher started one school day by asking students to each take an egg from a mix of brown and white in her reed bowl. Owners of white eggs giggled behind cupped hands while fellow students cleaned chalkboards, emptied wastebaskets, swept the floor, and sharpened pencils during recess—police calls, if you will. Roles were switched in the afternoon session. At the end of the school day, they cracked open the eggs. Whether brown or white on the outside, the insides looked the same.

John Howard Griffin in his 1960 book, titled <u>Black Like Me</u>, demonstrates similar testimony. Griffin was a white man turned black through a series of experiments and treatments that changed the color of his skin. Then he moved throughout a number of states in the Deep South and experienced the ugliest side of prejudice ("prejudge"). Even though he himself was the same man inside, even though he treated people the same way as before, with kindness and thoughtfulness and courtesy and hospitality, the same ones who treated him that way earlier didn't recognize the altered Griffin and turned on him in a nasty way. They judged him by his shaved head and black skin, and it changed everything.

When the 25th Division went into positions north of Taegu in the Naktong Valley around July 20, it was the 24th that drew the first assignment to defend the small town of Yechon. I had contact with them through my constant shuffling of men from the 27th and the 35th Infantry Regiments to the front line reinforcing the above sector. It was then I learned of the 24th's collective attitude: "Why should we get our butts shot off for a bunch of people who don't give a hoot about us?"

Justified or not, this attitude caused the unit's downfall. After a few hours of fighting, the troops broke rank and fled. They insisted a superior force of the North Korean Peoples Army came down upon them. An officer from the 35th Infantry Regiment who led a scouting party the following day found no evidence to support such claim.

In fact, he discovered the town burnt due to American artillery fire.

I remember at least three more occasions where they withdrew from positions in anything but an honorable manner. Feeling prejudicial guilt in wording this, I wish to remind you that, right or wrong, we cannot change the chronicles of history.

(While there may very well have been white units who deserted their posts, I had no personal experience with such, nor any knowledge thereof.)

On one occasion, two battalions from the 35th were placed behind and in reserve of the 24th Regiment. When the 24th broke and ran, one black lieutenant given a direct order by a bird colonel to get his men back on line refused and said he was scared. (For those of you less enlightened, a "bird" colonel bears no resemblance to our fine-feathered friends other than the silver pin he or she wears on the collar is shaped like an eagle. A major wears a gold leaf, lieutenant colonel a silver leaf.) A sergeant from the 35th Infantry Regiment then took fifteen men back on line after being told that they could and most likely would be shot for desertion in the face of the enemy.

The lieutenant received a death sentence in his court martial but was later committed to twenty years of hard labor by President Truman. It's hearsay, or I might have read it somewhere. I can't be sure.

On another occasion, a major was placed at a check point to examine all vehicles leaving Sangju around the time final units of the 27th Regiment moved to Masan. He averaged seventy-five stragglers a day from the 24th Regiment, once as many as one hundred and fifty. Several other truck drivers and I continually transported men back on line.

Still, another happened during one particular night in late July. An entire battalion of the 24th left positions of defense, leaving a field artillery company and one company of the 65th Combat Engineers holding down the fort. Thanks mostly to the artillery, the line was secured by firing more than 3,000 rounds of 105 and 155 ammo to defend their current position.

The 24th Regiment, dubbed the bugout unit, never overcame its reputation. Sight alone of the regimental shoulder patch brought jeers and sometimes embarrassing lyrics of Bugout Boggie. Evidence against the 24th became too strong to ignore. Late 1950, though it pierced the Army's soul, these folk were moved offline and lost their colors in disgrace. The entire regiment was disbanded and reformed into the 14th Infantry Regiment.

Remaining members of the 24th were reassigned and integrated into previously comprised all white units. From that day forward, aiming for unity in diversity, at least in the 25th Infantry Division, all black units ceased to exist. Out on the line, it didn't make any difference if your neighbor was white, red, yellow, or black as long as his rifle fired in the other direction.

And all God's people said, "Amen!"

(President Harry Truman had desegregated the Armed Forces I believe in 1948.)

Where are we going with this? It's a proven fact that blacks integrated with whites, equally trained, educated, and accepted as equal can and will work or fight with exceptional achievement. Unfortunately, several decades since Civil Rights, if you talk to an African American, the playing ground is still uneven, be it in the North or South. Add it to the long list of growing pains our country has had or still has. Let me count the ways: overcoming the slave market where people were bought and sold like pieces of property, enduring the hazards of the Pennsylvania coal industry that fueled the industrial revolution, pioneering the West, engaging in numerous wars to protect our freedom, and, last but by no means least, the challenge of moving forward in love for one another, regardless of race, color, or creed.

Exhibit I:

A chapter largely ignored in the history of slavery is that most African slaves brought to the New World were purchased from Muslim slave traders. The slave trade ended in the British Empire in 1807. Slaves were emancipated in 1833 largely due to the efforts of John Newton, slave trader turned born-again Christian, who wrote the familiar song, "Amazing Grace." Importation of slaves was stopped in the United States in 1807. During the War Between the States, 600,000 Americans lost their lives defending or opposing slavery. Slaves were finally emancipated in 1865 under Republican President Abraham Lincoln's watch. (<u>What Every American Needs to Know About the Qur'an</u>—A history of Islam & the United States, by William J. Federer.)

Exhibit II:

More than 200,000 African Americans served with the Union during the Civil War. The pay of black soldiers was raised to the same level as whites late in the war, but promotions were extremely limited, and regiments remained under command of white top officers. Soldiering was one of the few professions open to African Americans. Following General Lee's surrender, all-black regiments traveled throughout Texas and northward with the U.S. Cavalry in its conquest of the west. They were nicknamed buffalo soldiers by the Indians who noted a similar texture between their hair and the buffalo's. (American Experience, WHYY, May 2, 2006.)

Exhibit III:

Following the Great War (WWI), an encampment of angry vets both black and white marched on Washington, known as the Million Man March, protesting the lack of benefits promised to them and their families. In 1944, President Franklin D. Roosevelt signed the GI Bill of Rights in response to the annual bonus marchers to benefit all veterans of war. (American Experience, May 29, 2006.)

Exhibit IV:

Up to and including WWII, the Army War College in Carlisle, Pennsylvania trained officers in the ideology that blacks were careless, shiftless, and irresponsible and should by all means be treated disrespectfully. But the college's academic face would someday turn red. The U. S. Government in 1941 began making Alaska the northwestern bastion of North America's defenses. Naval and air bases and secondary airfields were established and communications strengthened. In 1942, the Army Corps of Engineers took on the Alaska Highway Project. Twenty-four/seven, eight months and 1,500 miles later, a team of black and white pulling equal weight in both will and muscle power while battling blizzards, downpours, permafrost, forty-five subzero temps, ninety degree highs, mountains, forests, mud, and eagle-sized mosquitoes completed the Alcan Highway. Construction of the road that stretched from Canada across the Alaskan territory would provide an inland supply route should control of the sea routes be lost to the enemy. (American Experience, WHYY, 2005.)

Exhibit V:

In spite of tremendous trials and tribulations experienced by the 24th Regiment, some individuals distinguished themselves remarkably. Private Thompson, skin rich as coffee without cream and whose first name I don't recall, was awarded the Distinguished Service Cross and later, posthumously, was a recipient of the Medal of Honor (our country's highest military award) in 1951 for bravery on the Korean battlefield. I am proud to have known him.

Sangju, The Last Three Days

Do the thing you fear,
And the death of fear is certain...
*   - Ralph Waldo Emerson*

"...The crash of the stick of bombs was loud, and I felt the earth jerk with the impact. Clods of dirt came showering down. When the last carrummp had sounded, I waited a few seconds, then got up a bit shaken and looked across the grassy field at a row of fresh, clean-cut bomb craters. The ground everywhere around was strewn with small, cube-shaped clods of earth. I measured off the distance to the nearest crater. It was not much more than one hundred feet.

"Tonight, I heard cheerful reports of an action between our Naval forces and the Japanese somewhere near Guadalcanal. Torpedo bombers from one of our carriers had attacked the...."
(Guadalcanal Diary, Richard Tregaskis, pp126,127.)

As a youngster, I thrilled to Westerns at the local Strand with good guys like Gene Autry, Tom Mix, and Roy Rogers in wide-brimmed white hats and silver badges, knocking off bad guys in black shirts and black hats as they galloped through the wild and wooly West. (And yes, they did have talking picture shows by then.) Later, I graduated to more serious stuff rated GW (Gee Whiz!) by enthusiastic audiences. One such advertised was <u>Guadalcanal Diary</u>.

Just to admit my naïvete, the word "diary" had not yet been recorded in my memory bank. I doubted the screenwriter's accuracy and assumed an inadvertent transposition of "a" and "i," this then being a story about a particular dairy. Seeing this movie, I'd learn how other milking operations, albeit Hollywood, functioned in this vast country of ours. Having eager expectations, I clip-clopped two miles to town astride Barney, tied him to a steel rail behind the National Bank of Hamburg, and entered the theatre four doors up to reap my reward. It was the start of a journey that would eventually land me in Korea.

While the 27th Infantry engaged the North Koreans between Sangju and Ulsong, plans moved forward like a loaded hay wagon without brakes. There's a little saying on the farm that two draft horses teamed up can pull four times the weight of one. On the battlefield, you're no longer one. You're a team, a family, bound together by the thread of disaster. You're emotionally and professionally dependent upon each other. Staying alive requires it. Baker and I were such a team and, by late afternoon this particular day, we had trucked two entire platoons of E Company from the 2nd Battalion to an area a good mile distant.

The men were deployed and dug in on opposing slopes above a well-worn foot trail. Meanwhile, we refueled, picked up small arms and 60mm mortar ammo from the supply dump, and returned to the same site. Even though I was in the business of trucking and not a front line infantryman, many times after dark, I joined the infantry squads on line, always keeping my vehicle close by for emergency.

A young corporal from my unit and I occupied the same foxhole. Two men partnered to our left. The enemy would have to pass our dugouts before coming to the trucks that stood ready for whatever. Baker followed three guys to the opposite finger ridge where other infantrymen dispersed along the hillside.

The prospect of meeting the enemy eye-to-eye was exciting to say the least. But anyone who says he's not scared when confronting an opponent with lethal weapons is either a fool or a liar. My stomach spun and tied itself into a hundred tiny knots, and my heart thumped so hard I could feel my temples hammering against the inside of the helmet that enclosed them. I felt a pain in my hand and realized I was pressing my fingernails into my palms. I forced my fingers to relax and, simultaneously, a light feeling prevailed in my head, fluttery and taut, as I looked out into the dark night filled with danger. I felt giddiness and doubt and awe. We could likely die. You know it could happen. It would not, of course, you told yourself. But it could. You wonder if you're dreaming, or sitting in the movies.

Other than revisiting a war zone seen earlier from the safety of a theatre chair, a million questions swirled through me on this hot summer night like leaves in a late autumn wind. Would I come off the hill with blood running down my face? Staggering as if drunk, leaning on a buddy like members of the 24th Division when we passed them early July? Could I walk at all? Moved out on a litter or in a black zippered bag?

Could I kill a man? I didn't know if I was capable of it. It was years since I had so much as even hit anyone and that was only friendly tussles with my brothers. Wholesome upbringing taught: Thou Shalt Not Kill. But in war you cross the line, and things get mixed up. You don't dare think of it as shooting someone. The other person is only a target. You're trained to maim, destroy, and preserve the attitude, "It's either you or me!" This fight for survival point of view took me into my first encounter.

The air was charged and everything as quiet as an arrangement of flowers in a funeral vase. I looked at my wristwatch in the glow of my cigarette. It was two minutes before midnight, everything still silent, when suddenly all hell broke loose. A spine-chilling fusion of screams, whistles, and bugles pierced the hot night.

Minutes passed in silence.

I glanced at my foxhole partner. He appeared calm enough, but lit a cigarette and drew hard on it.

Butch Fletcher was a rough and tumble guy, built short—maybe five foot five plus whatever boot heels added, and strung strong and tight like a bulldog. He spent life before the war herding cattle from horseback and building fences in eastern Oregon.

"You all right?" he whispered in a shaky voice.

"Yeah," I answered, hoping he hadn't noticed my discomfort. Transfixed in horror would have been more like it. I wished I were watching a war movie at the Strand in Hamburg and eating gummy bears instead. I stubbed out a freshly lit cigarette and released the safety on my M1 for the fortieth time. I thought back of what my Glen Gery co-workers who had served in WWII said about the frontline. They said it's ninety percent boredom and ten percent terror. I was well within the ten percent terror range when a pebble bounced off my helmet, a pre-arranged signal from our neighboring foxhole that something was up.

"There's movement down there," I whispered to my partner.

I heard Butch's safety click off.

The horror of what was happening began to fade and my fear diminished as action began. There were things to do.

An explosion of orange and yellow streaked the darkness, sending a fascinating glow across the sky, and revealed bent silhouettes of Korean troops with Russian automatic "burp" guns (machine pistols) scurrying through the shadows. They were coursing the trail below that meandered along a creek amidst a jumble of boulders and fallen trees. Once the firing opened, bodies dropped down and out of sight much as moving targets in a shooting gallery. Some crept into a roadside ditch. Our other platoon, maybe a hundred and twenty-five feet away, tossed several hand grenades after them. High-pitched screams mixed with orders shouted in Korean followed the blast. Before I could discharge a second round, a series of whistles blew and the attackers fell back and disappeared.

During the long night, we heard moans and groans, and, in the morning, found three Koreans on the trail left behind by comrades to die. In the ditch, eight mangled bodies in a bloody heap filled the watery grave. No casualties amongst our troops.

While we perched outside our holes, drinking warm coffee from blackened canteen cups and eating cold C rations of one sort or another, comments mocking last night's ambush sprouted faster than corn after a summer rain. Joking around was a way of deflecting the fear we felt. We were afraid of dying but even more afraid to show it.

"I guess we kicked the spit out of gol-durn Charlie, didn't we!"

"Yeah, the dang coward took off like a dog with its tail between his legs."

"Those gooks can't fight for sheet," drawled a southern hillbilly.

Bill Rutherford, nicknamed Cowboy, a rugged maverick from Chicken Lip, Colorado, likened the enemy to a horse in danger, an animal of flight instead of fight like we did.

Some made obscene gestures.

A hopeful said,

"Pucker up, babe. Your ole man's coming home!"

"Knock it off, you guys! Don't get cocky," Captain Bond warned.

He and 1st Lieutenant Donald Dunkleberger, a refined-looking gentleman were it not for an unlovely mop of curly hair, moved from one foxhole to another checking on the men.

"Believe me," Bond added, "the North Koreans are not cowards. I'm sure this was only a probing action to determine our strength. Expect a heavier force tonight."

"Hey, they come back they're dead meat!"

"Yeah, well, maybe you'll be dead meat if you don't prepare," said the lieutenant.

Preparing for the worst, hoping for the best—a statement I would come to think of many times during the ensuing months. Three additional 60mm mortars were set up in anticipation of the upcoming attack. Let the battle begin.

I had survived my first action with enemy fire and felt pretty doggone good about that. Yet dread of a possible repeat sustained.

In mental debriefing, if a lowly buck sergeant's permitted to speak his mind so far as he understands, the Koreans ran too close to each other. This had given us the opportunity to focus on their single group. If there had been greater intervals between men, they might not have suffered eleven dead. We, in turn, may not have been so fortunate. Too, the enemy's noisy signaling to advance alerted our troops as well. In basic training, they taught that deception is the art of war—"Figure out what your enemy is going to do next, then do something else."

On the upside, for the enemy I mean, their unique means of communication was perhaps more effective than our walkie-talkies which COs complained failed to operate in almost anything but flat terrain.

Like clockwork, just as the captain predicted, the Koreans came down the trail. Again minutes after midnight. Again those spine-chilling blasted hair-raising bugles blared and flares blazed as I watched in hypnotic fascination. Soon, I heard a sudden spattering of sharp rifle reports to our left and ahead. Deeper toned rifles at rapid fire took up the chorus, and we joined in.

Bullets cracked and leaves thwacked, and each side hurled grenades like they were on a handball court during a dead heat. Submachine and machine gunners fired full tilt. Now and then, ear-shattering mortar shells exploded at close range, pelting the loose earth in front of our hole. Once, I felt a bullet whiz by so close I could feel the disturbance in the air. And, more than once, I ducked to avoid flying shrapnel. I would become expert in ducking and diving and digging.

Rather than on the trail this time, the Koreans hung out on the brushy hillside where our other platoon dug in, making it difficult to shoot. After a while, mortars concentrated on the trail to prevent friendly fire on our own men. It was Catch 22. We couldn't drop ammo toward our own people. Still, it was critical we did so to protect their positions. In many cases, we saw Koreans approaching an American position when members from the other platoon could not. Color-coded smoke grenades (red for enemy contact, green for general signaling or tactical deception) and illumination flares flew constantly to light the area while pounding from both sides continued.

This second skirmish lasted at least an hour.

At daylight, my partner and I made out the twisted, lifeless body of a North Korean just spitting distance from our foxhole. Neither of us realized during the intense heat of battle that the enemy was that near. Close inspection revealed a smooth young face, white and drained of color. He wore a stunned expression. The slim man's chest was poorly muscled and split in two like a ripened melon. The blood looked thick and greasy. Whose bullet had killed him? Fletcher's? Mine? I wouldn't think about that. What was important, I made it unscathed through yet another night of conflict.

Some didn't. There were two wounded and one fatality from each platoon. Near the end of the battle, I had heard a loud voice, urging and commanding:

"Get down!" followed by a stricken call for, "Medic!"

Vinny Harabach had just lost his best buddy, Bart Kowalchuk. When I saw him afterwards, tears spilled over. He covered his face with his hands and his shoulders shook. The sounds he made were like none I ever heard before. The Army discouraged tight friend-ships, but it was impossible to heed such advice. These two served together since basic training and were attached ever since. I felt so bad for him and couldn't begin to imagine how I'd feel if I lost Baker. Why, Baker and I were as close as any two buddies could possibly be.

Baker was a cool breeze on a hot summer day. I always felt more comfortable when he was around. Tasks were easier. He was de-pendable, conscientious, responsible, and mature far beyond his eighteen years. Above all, he was a heck of a lot of fun and made this horrendous war tolerable for most anyone fortunate enough to be in his company. I'm not a poet; far from it. But sometimes when I write things down, words come out in a poetic way. Here's an ode to our friendship:

> *Good friends are hard to find.*
> *Good friends are easy to love.*
> *Good friends are presents that*
> *   last forever and that*
> *   feel like gifts from above.*
>
> *Good friends are one in a million.*
> *Good friends have stories to share.*
> *Good friends know the path to your*
> *   happiness, and they walk with*
> *   you all the way there.*

If my memory serves me correctly, of the adversary, a total of thirty-nine would never fight again. We stepped over the crumbled bod-ies lying across our path and left them behind to rot, feeling little remorse to do else, considering recent massacred GIs fresh in mind.

Both our dead and wounded were rushed to a mobile Army surgical hospital (MASH) near Taegu.

The jovial mood of the previous day was absent.

Harabach, how did he fare? When a dramatic turn arrives in anyone's life, say psychologists, the affected character passes from the emotional to the cognitive before a decision or course of action is made. Sometimes this process is quick. Other times, the emotional factors resound for hours, days, even years, before thoughts channel into rational paths to follow. Death lends itself to the latter. But Vinny would not have adequate time to work through his emotions. The military is skilled at keeping combat soldiers moving for this very reason, to not think about death around them. He'd have to function in his grief before rationalizing what had happened.

The following night, a storm of Genesis' proportion broke the drought. Skies rumbled. Jagged lightning bolts ripped a bruised sky, illuminating ghostly outlines of gnarled trees and tall, spear-shaped grasses. Adam's ale showered as lavishly as the village of Berne's water wheel dumping its load over the millrace. I shivered from the dampness and sudden temperature drop. Staying dry was impossible. You could feel the grizzly, cruddy crud coming inside your boots and crawling up your legs underneath your pants. Butch and I dug a small trench around our hole, but it poured so hard, our efforts were a sum exercise in futility. They say when you wrestle with a pig you are bound to get muddy. Well, the enemy was absolutely the pig, and Butch and I crouched together in a flood of mucky Korean pig slop to a degree that was unbelievable.

A chicken, when a storm comes, will continue to hang out in the rain and get itself all soaked. When an eagle sees storm clouds coming, it uses the winds to drive him on until he's above the storm. We had enough of being the chicken. At the hint of morning light, we loaded our few ground supplies and, like the eagle, soared to a higher and drier position, getting there as fast as humanly possible. Maybe a little faster.

Anxious about Baker, I filled with a ton of joy when he showed. A playful smile wrapped his boyish face.

"…The mean bastards ran into the mailman, and I sent them packing, but good!" Baker always came out on top. Thank God!

Neither of our orders had changed. We both remained with the same platoon. I continued patrolling with Butch who compared the bleak, brown, brushy Korean hills to the lush green forests of his beautiful home state. If he said it once, he said it a dozen times, "This place can't even grow a tree with a straight trunk!"

On the third day, we moved farther west to another hillside, one looking down upon a stream twenty feet wide and eight or ten inches deep by eyeball measurement. It seemed every day you dug a new foxhole or slit trench or reconstructed an old one. I now realized the wisdom of Dix's Foxhole 101 and placed a period at the end of the sentence where once a question mark had been. There was one big difference. On the frontline, an entrenchment spade with the cute little fold-down handle that hung from a back-breaking back pack dug a little bit deeper and a little bit faster than at basic. Correction. Lots deeper! Lots faster!

There's something else I'll add about foxholes. I defer to a WWII expression, "There ain't no atheists in a foxhole." How often during the course of the war I thought of my paternal grandfather's desire for his grandson's ministry or of the need to read the Bible my mother had sent along instead of playing matchstick poker, drinking whiskey, and doing all those other silly things young soldier boys do when they aren't sweating it out in a foxhole.

A Pennsylvania Dutch adage comes forth. There are three things a man does in winter: One, he reads the Word; Two, he loves his wife; Three, he hauls manure. (Not necessarily in that order.) I don't put this in to amuse you, or myself for that matter, but rather to show the importance of the Good Book in the Pennsylvania German culture when I was growing up. Yet I must say, while we might have been considered religious, we weren't, by today's definition anyway, what you called spiritual. At least not outwardly. Lifestyles reflected faith, but nobody talked about our far-away God or even mentioned His name except for the reverend high in the pulpit. Maybe it was a German thing. Maybe it was like the Old Testament Jews who didn't verbalize the Hebrew God "Yahweh" because the name was too holy.

Still, there was formal prayer before meals and bedtime, regular church attendance, and lots of church social activity. Church was a way of life. These memories gave great comfort during my perilous hours in a foxhole.

An hour after dusk, Lieutenant Greeley slipped up to our hole and said it might be a good idea if someone set up a listening post by the stream. John, our senior officer, a forties-something soldier from upstate New York, was a charming and infectious enthusiast. I just knew what he was going to say next.

"I want the two of you to go down and get as close to that stream as possible," he whispered. "Conceal yourselves. There's lots of tall grass down there. Stay low and tell me what you see. Don't talk on the radio unless you have something definite to report or if your position comes into jeopardy."

We nodded agreement. What else could we do? By the way, you never ever saluted a superior officer in combat situations. In fact, there is not a lot of formal military training used in combat.

The evening was absorbed in moonless dark, and there was a humid stillness in the air that precedes rain. With only the twinkling of firefly butts to light our way, we crawled at a snail's pace down the hill into the damp evening grasses, rifles cradled under sticky armpits, our helmets slick with perspiration. A couple of years before, I stalked game in the mountains of Pennsylvania. Now, several continents away, I hunted people. How things do change. When a twig snapped below my right elbow, my ticker nearly stopped in place. Even so, unable to suppress a feeling of dread, some courage maintained as I inched closer and closer until a prone basketball player's length from the water's edge.

It seemed a little odd to me at the time, but the water rippling across the rocks and gravel sounded so peaceful, almost like the aura one gets in a graveyard's eerie quiet. Yet this did little to still the other noise in this strange dark Korean night. My stomach. It rose up to meet my diaphragm then flip-flopped back into place. And not to mention the dreadful drone of Korea's national bird zeroing in for attack! The Good Lord didn't create anything without purpose, but mosquitoes come close.

It was July and, not unlike in Pennsylvania, the hot and steamy day had turned into a hot and muggy night, and the mosquitoes were fierce. They buzzed around my head like entrapped bees circling in a jar with no place to go. As much as I hate the smell of fish, I'd have given anything to coat my body with fish oil like the American Indian used to do. Or a blast of OFF or whatever pesticide was in vogue at the time to murder the vicious little beasts. Cigarette smoke might have helped against this horde of bombers but striking a match was much too risky. And the itchiness, oh, the wretched itchiness—much worse than the scratchy long woolen underwear I endured as a kid! No, I was totally at their mercy, and the whine around my ears about drove me crazy.

As if all this weren't bad enough, I no sooner knelt semi-comfortably on my knees when I felt them getting wet, and, within minutes, saturated in water several inches deep. I was as miserable as a barn cat in the middle of a farm pond, pushing last night into second place for the most awful of my life.

After a few hours, my legs and butt past numb from being in this awkward position, I saw Charlie through blades of grass. I counted figures until I ran out of fingers. Probably a squad. They were on the far bank, perhaps thirty feet away, and stood there for the longest time. If they talked, it was in low whispers because I couldn't hear a thing. They finally moved out of sight, and I let out my breath, realizing it had been checked for a very long time.

After swallowing what little saliva was left in my mouth, I thirsted for that chief sustenance in life called drinking water and thought back to another time. The past always seems attractive when you are in trouble.

One roasting August day on the farm, I chopped thistles in the high corn crop. My sister Catherine was supposed to bring me water but claimed later she couldn't find me. In desperation, I drank out of the wide shallow crick similar to this one. There, cows cooled off, loitered, and relieved themselves during the hot daylight hours. I never got sick, but then again that was back in the good old days before we knew anything about pollution.

I shifted my weight and heard a soft splash. The men had returned and strolled into the stream. Two bent over to fill canteens, murmuring weird gobbledygook in hushed tones. They walked a few steps further and, at one point, headed directly toward us. I drew a deep but discreet breath and wasn't this frightened since my second day at basic when the colonel read the Articles of War. *There's no foxhole to protect me now,* I thought with a flash of fear.

There's a reason knees bend only one way.

"God, please," I breathed. My prayer was short and cut to the chase. They say when God is in charge, mortals can relax, but who was in charge? I was positive they'd come ashore and step on us. We were under strict orders not to fire or make contact unless urgent. Still, I maintained a tireless preoccupation with my clammy trigger finger.

For sure, I had a snowball's chance in hell to get out of this alive and envisioned leaving my bones in this hostile, warring environment far, far away from home. I did not want this to be. Instead, I tried hard to concentrate on determination and hatred, remembering Captain Bond's sage advice: "Stay sharp! Always keep your wits about you, and never let your emotions be in control. You always have the upper hand when you know where the enemy is, and he doesn't know where you are. Try to relax. Forget you even have a home back in the States. Instead, concentrate on what's before you!"

A couple of days ago when we were under attack, I knew what was before me and released my emotions to some extent while engaging the enemy. Now? Bond's counsel was like telling a person not to panic while a cougar advanced with visions of pot roast in its eyes. Hours later, in reality maybe ten minutes, the Koreans moved out of the stream and up the bank where they remained until close to daybreak. After they disappeared, my partner whispered his findings to Lieutenant Greeley on the radio.

Soaked, emotionally drained with anxiousness shedding off me like old skin, and punctured with a million mosquito bites, I was never so grateful to see the sun peek over the hilltop. My tension faded in many happy ways.

Luck Was With Me

It is the Soldier not the president who gives democracy.
It is the Soldier not the congress that takes care of us.
It is the Soldier not the reporter who gives us freedom of press.
It is the Soldier not the poet who gives us freedom of speech.
It is the Soldier who salutes the flag, who serves beneath the flag,
and whose coffin is draped by the flag.
                          - Father Dennis O'Brien, Chaplain

A soldier generally served on the frontline three to four days before being replaced. A week at the most or maybe two in critical circumstances. Encampments were set up several miles to the rear of the battlefield. Here one caught up on rumors, hot meals, a shower, and gained some decent rest. The pause that refreshes, if you will.

The day we moved from the stream and our listening post, Baker's platoon returned to its parent company. The platoon I transported drew an assignment eight miles away to cover the 35th Infantry Regiment. They were hit hard the night before, and their battalion commander required assistance, considering all the casualties they suffered.

At this new location was a portable shower and mess tent. Like after a long morning of threshing wheat, I was hot, dirty, and hungry and needed both as much as a flag needs a pole. We were parked next to a stream with a 15 kW generator for needed electricity. The shower was a squad tent with wooden pallets on the floor, and a gas-fired tank heated water that came out of nozzles hung from tightly strung pieces of black commo wire. I used far more than the allotted ration of hot water, my skin as pinched and shriveled as sister Marian's face at birth.

We had choice of new duds from the several bales of clothing in the tent. Old clothes were generally left behind to launder, or so they said, but I can't recall ever being provided any used. The downside was there seemed no attempt to size garments other than maybe petite or extra large, including ill-fitting underwear. There were plenty of socks, but we're talking here of days when socks were sized and had a left and a right. It was the luck of the Irish if you drew equal partners. Many abstained from turning in dirty laundry for these reasons. Korean soldiers attached to each unit in the rear were often eager to earn money and washed and pressed for perhaps fifty cents or an exchange in cigarettes or rations. Not a bad fit this day.

Chaplains of various Christian/Judeo faiths served bravely across Korea throughout all branches of the Armed Services. They encouraged weary soldiers by saying, "Pray as if everything depends upon the Lord; act as if everything depends upon you." They performed worship services, administered sacraments, aided the wounded, and honored the dead, often in enemy fire. They wore military uniforms but never carried a gun and distinguished themselves by a small gold cross on the left side of the collar. A helmet with a white cross in front was worn on the battlefield. Generally, one chaplain was assigned to each battalion (three line companies plus one support) and constantly circulated amongst the regiment, never remaining long in any one place.

Catholics conducted Mass daily. Other denominations held field services more sporadically but always short prayer sessions before soldiers returned to the front and often on the front itself. "Tell it to the chaplain." was a familiar phrase. It was the only time you heard Jesus' name mentioned outside of cursing. I stood in briefly this particular morning at a service conducted from a jeep.

Chaplain Brady was a bear of a man who, I heard later, had been a chest-thumping preacher in West Virginia's mining country during civilian times. In spite of his strong exterior, he was a genial, smiling fellow who moved easily amongst the troops. A rumble and boom of explosions could be heard in the distance while Chaplain Brady read from Psalm 91:

> *He that dwelleth in the secret place of the Most High shall abide under the shadow of the Almighty.*
> *I will say of the Lord, He is my refuge and my fortress; my God; in Him will I trust.*
> *He shall cover thee with His feathers and under His wings shalt thou take refuge: His truth shall be thy shield and buckler.*
> *Thou shalt not be afraid for the terror by night; nor the arrow that flieth by day; for He shall give His angels charge over thee, to keep thee in all thy ways....*

Feeling squeaky clean, both bodily and spiritually, I was ready for some hot chow. Plus, by all means, good, strong, honest-to-goodness, home-brewed coffee. It smelled so darn good as I approached the mess tent, I inhaled my first two steaming cups as quickly as I drank the intoxicating aroma.

Breakfast was canned eggs, for goodness sake, but there was real dairy butter for toast and all the tomato juice you could drink. And the freshly baked cinnamon rolls were to die for. Besides what I ate inside the tent, three more got stuffed in my leg pocket "to go."

After leaving the mess tent, I glanced at the blank space where my deuce and a half had been parked.

"Looks like my truck got wheels," I said to Lieutenant Lolschou who was cleaning his rifle's trigger assembly.

He was a towhead, maybe six feet tall, with beautifully carved features and blond Nordic fairness. I heard he'd been a hotshot tennis player in peacetime.

"An urgent call came in a few minutes ago for transportation to move some wounded men," he explained. "That truck there was the only one available."

The ignition in an Army truck is an on/off switch. No keys.

Our platoon, or more correctly, our partial platoon from the 27th, waited almost an hour until my vehicle hastened back into camp. A captain and major followed in a jeep.

"Get that truck loaded PRONTO!" one of them yelled, tires crunching on gravel as the jeep performed a quarter circle on the camp road. "Follow us! Let's Go! Let's Go! On the double!"

As he spoke, men loaded ammo, and I scooted into the front seat with the driver, a young corporal from the 35th. He had already thrown the floor shift into gear before turning to me with a big question mark on his face.

"Stay put," I said. "You drive."

We shot forward like a horse given the spur, plowing through a thick cloud of dust that hadn't yet settled from the truck's arrival.

"What's all the fuss about?" I wanted to know.

"Not sure," he shouted back.

We gunned down the bumpy dirt road at a reckless pace to keep up with the jeep. Soon the terrain became steeper. Ahead, through a depression in the low-lying hill, a jeep with a litter came toward us, and my driver moved slightly to the right to avoid it. The last thing I remember was asking if he wanted a smoke. I reached in my vest pocket and then held out the pack.

She was oh, so pretty, even from behind. I wanted to touch the gorgeous black curls as they fell gently over her narrow shoulders. On the bench where she sat, a skirt spilled off to both sides from a small waist I longed to put my arms around. If only I had the nerve. If only I had the nerve to talk to her. Interrupting my drooling thoughts, the minister picked on me to recite the Ten Commandments. I opened my mouth to speak, but try hard as I might, nothing came out. I knew every one by heart, even in numerical sequence. Still, I drew a blank. Ronald raised his hand, nearly touching the ceiling, then stood and rattled them off in perfect order. My dream girl turned toward him and smiled. Her hero!

Oh, what a stupid idiot I must be. Before I considered the disappointing result, Nancy did a surprising thing. She stood up and an-

nounced to our catechetical class of twenty-four confirmants that we were going to be married. I was delirious with happiness! In a blur, figures moved around in front of me like passengers on a ship in heavy seas. Each, except for Ronald, congratulated both of us on our forthcoming marriage. From the sideline, the minister began reciting the wedding vows until a younger male voice drowned him out, and my pretty bride-to-be drifted softly out of sight.

"Welcome back to the land of the living," the voice said.

I shook my head in bewilderment and looked around, wondering where I was. Then I knew.

"Can you tell me what happened?" I asked, suddenly feeling like I'd been run over by a ten-wheeler.

"Sure," said the medic. He was a tall, thirties something guy with big hazel eyes and a toothy smile and had a disposition as gentle as a St. Bernard's. He stuffed a cold thermometer under my tongue and said, "Let's just say you had a rendezvous with a land mine. They brought you in three days ago around noon."

"Good grief, a land mine," I mumbled indistinctively, recalling now the events of the drive and the explosion that followed. It certainly gave new meaning to the term real estate boom.

"Yeah. Pretty lucky you are."

"Anything else you care to share?" I asked after he withdrew the thermometer. I had already felt my arms and legs in place.

"Well, I can get a mirror if you'd like to see those two black eyes of yours," he said.

Without enough energy to lick a postage stamp, I raised myself up. A bandage on my right leg below the calf covered ten stitches over a deep, shrapnel cut. I realized, upon further self-inspection, that my hip was sore to the touch and painted every shade in the rainbow.

Later, an Army captain walked toward my bunk. He was rather short, not a bad nose, dark-skinned with glasses framing intense slightly slanted dark eyes and heavily marked eyebrows. A stethoscope hung from his neck.

"How do you feel?" he said in an accent I couldn't identify.

He lit a cigarette and stuck it in a mouth as dehydrated as a farm pond sucked dry by the sun. I sank back into the pillow and took a long drag. It made my aching head feel dizzier, but tasted splendid all the same.

"Been better," I replied.

When the doctor finished, I asked the first question that came to mind,

"Are they going to send me back to Japan?" Usually wounded recuperated in Japan.

"No. Your injuries are not that serious. As a matter of fact, you should be out of here today."

A mixed blessing! Of course I was overjoyed to be okay and wanted to stay in Korea and fight alongside my buddies. After all, going to the safety of Japan would be missing out on the action, somehow like watching a broncobuster at work from the top rail of the corral fence. On the other hand, I'd be fibbing not to admit some letdown that I didn't have a ticket out of this forsaken place and this miserable war.

"Just lay there until you feel like getting up," he said. "When you're ready, I'll give you a hand."

I finished the cigarette and, after the room stopped spinning, pulled myself up again. For a good while I sat on the edge of the bunk before the doctor returned.

"How about removing this sugar water needle and giving me some real food," I said, focusing on the humongous pipe that stuck out of my left arm.

He regarded me with some contemplation.

"I'm thinking that rather than have an orderly bring food in here, maybe you can make it to the mess tent instead?" It was a question.

I'd certainly give it a try. First, they needed to clothe me. I lost one combat boot in the accident, so they brought me a new pair as well as new fatigues. Granted, I was sluggish as a fly at a sunny window in spring. Yet walking went relatively well.

Outside, the sun shone bright, gleaming in puddles of stagnant water. Men in combat fatigues were coming and going as though nothing had happened. These ordinary goings on seemed out of place to me after what I had just witnessed. But I felt better once I traded the sick room environment for fresh air. One of the medics followed me to the mess tent and ordered the cook to make me something. I asked for a full works breakfast. Instead they gave me thick beef stew, biscuits, and enough coffee to flush a radiator. Anything was better than sugar water and needles!

I've never been good at the sight of blood and needles. You may recall how upset I was back in Seattle when they made me retake those shots. Here, since my waking moments, I endured and witnessed plenty of shots and blood and pain in that short time. Field hospitals were always close to the frontline and had a huge red cross on top in a square white field visible from the air. By International Agreement through the 1929 Geneva Convention, war combatants honored these hospitals. This one, hardly a comic California hills MASH production, had a real bad atmosphere about it, most soldiers suffering far worse injuries than I. Some moaned and screamed and were wrapped up like mummies, waiting to be shipped out to a standard hospital. Some walked around on crutches, one with his leg blown off. Others sat up in bed smoking cigarettes and exchanging vulgarities, while others just stared, pondering the battle they had just survived.

A sergeant 1st class who lay next to me was cut by piano wire across the neck and required over forty stitches. He drove a jeep without a wire catcher and was lucky he didn't have his head severed from his torso—a likely result of just one more of those nasty Korean tricks. The enemy tied piano wire, one-eighth inch thick, from tree to tree across roadways at a height of about sixty inches. Most vehicle movements were made with a jeep in the lead, and, in most cases, windshields laid down to prevent glass shards from flying into your face if shattered from small arms fire. Just clearing the top of the steering wheel, the wire was set at the right height to cut the driver and passenger up front. My division welded an angle iron to the front bumper of each jeep to a height of six feet with another ninety-degree angle iron welded on top to snare and tear the wire. The sergeant next to me was not from my division.

Before leaving the mess tent, I heard a familiar voice.

"Vacation's over. Time to get back to work." It was Captain Bond. He heard only that morning of the mishap when the hospital called my unit for someone to pick me up.

"You're going to have to check with the doctor. I think he wants to send me to Japan," I said as sincerely as I could fake it.

The captain winced and raised a skeptical eyebrow. Through the dim light, I saw his lips twitching from side to side as he viewed me with some suspicion.

"What the (censored) you talking about? There isn't a thing wrong with you!"

"Well, I feel pretty good, but maybe the problem's internal," I said, milking the situation.

Bond rolled his eyes, and the small smile he had allowed to play on his lips faded. He grabbed me by the arm.

"Come on! We're going to talk to that doctor of yours."

Easy, Sir. Remember, I'm wounded, and my legs have been out of commission for three days.

When we left the mess tent, we ran into the doctor, and Captain Bond inquired about me. I just kind of stood back and smiled. Doc nodded thoughtfully, and it looked like what he was about to say would be of interest.

"I think he has a girlfriend in Japan," he said, "and wants to look her up."

Before leaving camp, I went to the administration tent to clear and close my record. An orderly handed me a bundle of blood-encrusted clothing I had on when they brought me in. I stood by a fifty-five gallon trash drum and discarded things I didn't want anymore. I'd likely lose a tooth on the dried-up cinnamon rolls. They, too, went into the barrel. The orderly also handed me my holster and .45caliber Colt automatic, but I never saw my M1 or carbine again. Bond stood there, striking a thinking pose as he scratched the stubble of his red beard. A wrinkle formed between his eyes as deep as a rut in a Korean road.

"You're not authorized a forty-five automatic. Where did you get that thing?" he asked.

"I found it hanging on a tree branch near a slit trench a couple of weeks back." *My goodness, why do I say such things?*

Bond made no further comment, but surely knew I lied through my unbrushed teeth.

"I need you to initial this form," a clerk inside the administration tent said. Bond stepped up and signed it. When we started to leave, the clerk stopped me and said,

"Hold it. You're entitled to one of these, too." He handed me a small box and saluted, saying, "For the blood shed for your country, it is my honor to give you the Purple Heart."

I humbly accepted, and my eyes watered up a bit. It was a great day to be alive. Somehow I ended up losing the medal before leaving Korea. (Later, I was given another.)

On the way out, Captain Bond informed me of some pretty tragic news. We had been rushed to a sector to reinforce a weak spot. Four of us were hurt; the other three left the same day they brought us in. The 35th Infantry driver who had taken my place behind the wheel was killed.

This latest news socked me between the eyes. Of course, I felt the usual compassion for those downed in battle but considered the irony of this innocent young corporal dying in my place. Was it dumb luck? Was it fate? Divine intervention? Suddenly the minister's words in confirmation class came alive:

"Jesus died in your place so that you might be saved..."

The date was July 31, 1950.

The Marines Have Landed

We can't guarantee success in the war,
But we can deserve it.
    - General George Washington

Rumor had it that the marines assigned a photographer and a public relations specialist to every unit. If they did, I never saw them. This is one guy who will always have the highest regard for the Marine Corps and believes their eagle soars higher than any other military branch. Why do I say that? I saw results. I saw wounded. I saw their dead.

One reason the salty marines are an exceptional fighting force is they maintain their people in top physical condition. Plus, each receives combat training regardless of rank or assignment. The marines, nicknamed jarheads because of the high and tight haircut, came to Korea as cohesive units in which officers and men served together for months (though some might take issue with that timing), not weeks or days as was too often the case with the rest of us. Army rifle companies in many instances were thrown together at the last minute, combat training as a unit often next to zero.

Another success factor: the marines controlled their own support aircraft. In contrast, the Army Air Force was abolished in 1948. The Air Force, instead, became its own branch of service. If the Army wanted air support, it now called on the 5th Air Force. Those planes did not always respond unless the area in jeopardy was accorded highest priority. (Today, each infantry division has aircraft assigned directly.)

The U.S. Marines landed on Korean shores on or about July 26, with one brigade, and met the enemy in our area around Chinju and Masan. Within days, their wounded straggled back through our ranks, gaunt, pale men with distinct memory of death in their eyes, limping along, clothes torn, cigarettes drooping from ashen lips, one man supporting another. The worst off were hauled to the rear by truck along with the dead. The marines remained for a month when all of a sudden the brigade moved lock, stock, and barrel to the rear and headed for Pusan.

A part of the 27th Infantry filled in where the marines vacated. It was then we realized with great awe and respect the incredible damage our military counterparts accomplished during occupation. On one hillside alone were four hundred stinking, worm-infested, decomposing North Koreans. Even with noses covered by handkerchiefs, we found the odor absolutely unbearable. Like an ocean full of rotten fish.

We came to a site where the awesome gull-winged Corsairs with their powerful guns protruding from the forward edges of each wing caught enemy trucks, jeeps, and motorcycles, destroying more than a hundred vehicles. I counted at least sixty, maybe seventy, cycles run down during crossfire. Some of our guys tinkered with them and had a couple up and running and did figure eights and fun spins back and forth on the dusty dirt roads by camp.

Prevalent were the 1946 Ford pickups. They were painted green and yellow. We had one exactly like those at the place where I was reared. That was in the good old days when a Ford was a Ford was a Ford in both make and model. The only differentiation being "machine" or "truck," chrome or no chrome, some red, some blue, some black, some green and yellow. Shortly after WWII, the United States exported these truck models to Russia. Seeing them in battle was another overt sign of Soviet support to the North Koreans.

While the marines' quick departure was questioned, we later

learned they joined the rest of the 1st Marine Division preparing for the Incheon landing. Incheon is approximately one hundred and seventy miles north of Masan on the Yellow Sea west of Seoul. Of course, unbeknownst to us, the plan would sever North Korean supply lines, isolate the enemy in our sector, and prefigure in the retaking of Seoul.

We were told once the Koreans saw the marine invasion force at Incheon, they'd quit fighting in our sector and return to the north of the Peninsula, totally and unmercifully demoralized. Ours would be a simple mop-up task. But as the best laid plans of mice and men often fail, the North Koreans chose the same day of the Incheon landing, September 15, 1950, for a new offensive of their own—OUR AREA! Was this an intelligence breakdown? We didn't know.

Baker and I and a third truck driver, Jim Mellon, transported ammo to the 2nd Battalion. We came to a small village in our travels and saw trucks up ahead blocking the road. As we approached, the heavy cough of an M1 followed by mortar shells whistling through the air caught our attention real fast. Two exploded in the rice paddy alongside the road and erupted into white and black geysers, sending smoke and debris into the already murky atmosphere. The three of us got the same idea at the same time and placed about eight yards between vehicles, grabbed weapons, and rushed away from the trucks loaded with ammo. Volleys of rifle fire bombarded us from every direction as we high-tailed it to the closest truck, dove underneath, hitting dirt like a ball player at home base.

"What the Sam Hill is going on?" said Jim.

"A war! There's a war going on in case you didn't know it," joked Baker nervously.

"Well, no kidding!" Jim said, giving Baker the middle digit.

"Whew, that was close!" I said. "Maybe we better stay put for a while and see what happens." I laid my rifle alongside and propped my upper bulk on my elbows, fists pressed into my cheeks, and observed the dramatic goings on. Every time mortars whizzed our way, they fell just short and landed in the foul-smelling mud. The sharp stutter of machine guns came from our left, and in between we heard the hills beyond echo with rifle fire and artillery explosives.

"Sticking our friggin heads out right now is friggin suicide," said Baker.

He was right. We'd only draw friendly fire.

"Hey, what's that?" said Jim. Thirty yards or so in front of us plopped something big and black from the sky. "It's a bird!" he shouted.

"No! It's Superman!" said Baker.

"Must have been hit, poor thing. Look! It's still moving." The stunned hawk shook its head and struggled forward a couple of inches through the furrowed ground. Though it tried, become airborne it could not. "I bet its wing is busted." Jim was from Michigan, a well-muscled son of a Detroit mechanic who inherited his dad's skill to fix things. He was the first to get a cycle up and running back at camp. "I'm going out and get it," he said.

"You will like the devil!" I said, grabbing him by the belt as he started to crawl forward. "That's suicide!"

"Yeah, Jerk!" added Baker. "If you think I'm gonna risk my neck to go get you, you have another think coming."

"Okay. Okay."

"Besides," said Baker, "I'm about out of smokes, and I notice you got a full pack there in your shirt. That won't help me any if they're splattered out in the stinkin' rice paddy!" He was right about the stinking part. The stench of the paddy mixed with the acrid smell of gunpowder was truly nauseating.

"Ditto. I'm about out, too," I said, reminded of the full pack rotting away on my truck seat.

"Okay. Okay. I got the message." Mellon peeled cellophane and foil from the mouth of his fresh pack, tapped out a cigarette, tapped the cigarette itself, and lit it between two days' growth of rust beard and passed it on to Baker. He lit one for me and one for himself, all the while keeping his eye on the bird.

"Thanks, Bud," said Baker. "Wow, sparks from the matches and the three of us puffing away like this would be enough to ignite a good size explosion were we under our own trucks."

"Y'know, at home we shoot 'em," I said, returning to the topic of birds. "Chicken hawks, we call them. They drop out of the sky like a helicopter and swoop up the ducks and chickens and carry them off. Most farmers have a hawk nailed on their barn siding as a warning to others to keep their distance."

"Does it work?" Baker wanted to know. He was a town boy.

"Well, now you got me on that one," I said. "But don't get me wrong; farmers do like birds. They're great at eating insects and mosquitoes. The barn swallows especially. You should see them flitting back and forth while you're cultivating corn. It's supposed to be good luck to have swallows build nests in your barn. We actually record their arrival on the post right inside the cow stable."

"When do they come?" asked Jim.

"Anywhere from the last week of April through the first week of May comes the first pair. Then the others follow in dribbles. I guess it depends on what the weather is like down in Argentina where they're supposed to be spending winter. "

"It's awesome how birds can migrate for thousands of miles and then return to the same nests," said Jim. "They actually navigate by using only a very tiny piece of their brain."

"Next time some one calls you bird brain," said Baker, "bow and say, why thank you." He laughed at his own joke.

I laughed, too, and was reminded of the smart crow in Aesop's Fables. The crow was thirsty and couldn't reach the water in the bottom half of the pitcher, so it dropped pebbles in until the water level had risen high enough for it to drink its fill.

"Yeah, swallows are smart and strong," I said, bringing the conversation back to me. "They usually have two nests of young, and the kids are all trained and on the run south by the third week of August. Imagine that!"

"Birds are strong, that's for sure," said Jim. "I rescued a pigeon once with a broken wing. My old man scolded me for taking care of it. Said they were dirty and messy birds and not worth saving. After that, I hid it in the neighbor's outhouse they weren't using anymore. After awhile, Pidgie got stronger, and I let him out, and he flew away. But before he did, I spent lots of time with him and studied him, along with reading about birds in an article a school chum loaned me."

"Yeah? Well, what did you learn?" I wanted to know.

"I learned that big heavy birds like your domestic chickens can't fly and get away from hawks because they don't have the same feather structure. It's mostly in the feathers, you know."

No, I didn't, but was soon sorry I asked.

Jim went on.

"A single pigeon's primary wing feather has more than a million parts, believe it or not, stuff like barbs and flanges and tiny hooks and so on. They all work together so that when the bird flies, its feathers automatically adjust for every bit of change in the air flow. And then there's the nervous system that controls the feathers. In the skin near the quill of each flight feather are nerve endings that convert the feathers into sensory receptors. They actually record the exact position of every feather. And then by way of the spinal cord, they bring about constant adjustment in the thousands of tiny muscles that are attached to the base of the..."

"Cripes, Mellon! You talk like a college professor!" said I.

"Yeah, anyway. But please don't hold back. Tell us what you really know," quipped Baker.

Neither of us would ever look at a bird quite the same way again.

Jim went on.

"The flight feathers of the wing tip act just like the prop of an aircraft." He paused for a moment and rubbed his right eye. "Here," he said, reaching out for a small flat stone he found. He wiped the dirt off, and holding the stone forward, illustrated his point using a thick blade of grass. "They change pitch to cope with the changing stresses that the air pressure puts on them. And the base part of the wing acts just like the wing of an airplane. And the secondary and third wing feathers act as flaps. See?" he said, this time adding a precious cigarette to his model.

"Excuse me, did you say something?" said Baker, faking a yawn.

Jim ignored him and moved on.

"Then there's the circulation part, plus they have the highest body temperature of any wildlife, and they have small light hollow bones. Some birds can even breathe through their bones. But nobody knows how they do that. The bird's respiratory organs act kind of like two cycle pumps. You know, like a turbocharger. As the bird inhales, fresh air bypasses the lungs and is stored somehow. As the bird exhales, air is pumped into the lungs under pressure, and, as the bird inhales, the stale air is sucked from the lungs into rear air sacs and then exhaled through its beak..."

"Like this?" cut in Baker, expelling the air in his lungs to demonstrate disinterest.

"Come to think of it," I said. "I've never seen a barn swallow short of breath.

"Neither have I. Well, yeah, sorta, kinda. I did see a blue jay pant once," said Baker. "I think it was a male, because the other one was smaller and cuddling up to him."

"Okay, hang on, you guys," said Jim. "I'm about done. I'm just trying to show you how all these things work together so the bird can fly. It's so amazing how strong and well equipped they are and on so little food. I read that if a small airplane could do as well, it would get about a hundred and sixty miles to the gallon."

Speaking of planes, we heard the characteristic whine of two P51 props and birds were forgotten. The first of these single engine Air Force fighters skimmed the far side of the field and threw white-streaming rockets that tore up the ground at the Koreans' position. The second plane raced into view and dropped a pod of napalm. The big black canister hit the ground, skipped a few feet above the surface and exploded into a wall of flame, something Hollywood orchestrates with its thundering sound system on today's wide screen. The ground beneath us trembled like before an earthquake. A wave of searing heat followed.

"Jiminy Crickets!" said Baker, or something slightly more evocative. "What are they gonna do for an encore!"

Strafing followed for another twenty minutes before they left.

"I wonder what the folks back home think when they hear about days like this," said Mellon.

"We interrupt this news bulletin for a special announcement...," mimicked Baker.

I said,

"They'll say 'Oh, that's terrible' then go on and finish their supper."

"Naw, you got that wrong," corrected Baker. "By the time they hear the news, it's been painted rosy by MacArthur."

In the beginning, MacArthur was our boy. Then, you couldn't help but like the guy whose colorful character ranged from exceptional brilliance to the oddly eccentric. Now the tide of both military and political attitude gradually changed as the police action (Give 'em Hell Harry's term, not mine) continued.

"That pompous old SOB would probably tell them how he killed all these gooks single-handed," I said.

"Look! It moved!" Jim said.

"What moved? What are you talking about?" It was Baker again.

"The hawk. It moved."

"Forget the hawk. Let's get some shuteye, if that is possible."

Night came, and we still hid underneath the truck.

It was too dark to check my watch, but I guessed a wakeup call within the hour by the diminishing distant rifle fire, yellow blasts, and red streaks on the horizon.

"Hey! What the…!" Something silky and soft lay beside me. Mellon had snuck out after all while Baker and I dozed. Fitfully, I might add.

"He's dead," said a quiet voice out of the darkness. "A piece of shrapnel is stuck in the right wing, and it must have penetrated his breast each time he moved."

"Oh, great! Now we have to do another burial!" said Baker.

In the stillness of a new morn, we came out of hibernation and noticed our truck looked similar to the one that collided with the honeywagon back in Osaka. At least this time the substance was only mud. Trust me, it didn't smell as bad either. But here's an amazing fact. The truck beneath which we took sanction was loaded with twenty-two drums of gasoline!

"Whose idea was it to jump under this truck anyway?" Baker said. It could have been like snuffing out a cigarette in a can of paint thinner or slightly worse. "Why the @#$% didn't we stay with our own trucks?"

"You know what the old man {Captain Bond} always says when someone screws up," I said. "'Act now and think later!'"

Within two days, the 27th Infantry moved north along the west coastline near the city of Kunsan. There we came across a university. We searched the grounds of choked-up weeds and vacant buildings for an appropriate place to unload supplies and set up a temporary command post. While exploring the dorms, we found an old hand-cranked Victrola and one thick seventy-eight RPM platter labeled "Mule Train," sung in English by our very own Frankie Laine. It was as scratchy as a cow's tongue. The flip side was even worse, and we didn't play it for fear of ruining our only needle. Whenever breaking for lunch, we wound up the old phonograph.

"...mule train, klippity klopp, klippity klopp, klippity kloppin' along....ghost riders in the sky, yippee i yoh ki yay... HA!... ghost riders in the sky...."

The record player lasted until we reached North Korea a month later when it conked out and died.

"Some Korean will come along and find that thing," I said. "They'll fix it up, and it'll be around for another ten years."

"Wanna bet?"

Baker blew the music box to smithereens.

During our third month in Korea, I believe it was September 25, we moved north toward Seoul. It was this date, or maybe several days later, when the marines recaptured the capital. At Incheon and Ascome City, near Seoul, good hard blacktop roads enabled real headway. Outside Yongdungpo, we set up a bivouac area. The marines had crossed the Han River on a pontoon bridge not substantial enough for our truck traffic, therefore, causing some delay. Now the 65th Combat Engineers planked the railway bridge for our unit's crossing. They also constructed a floating footbridge.

Time to kill during this construction, a rarity, some of our men nosed the area and discovered a wooden beer vat one claimed as huge as his hometown municipal water tower. These thirsty guys scrounged up anything they could lay their hands on that might hold beer, anything from a canteen cup to, would you believe, five-gallon gasoline cans. I was there for at least three days before seeing this enormous vessel for myself. It left me unimpressed.

You see, I disagreed with Ben Franklin and his maybe not so famous quote but nevertheless his words, "Beer is living proof that God loves us and wants us to be happy." I didn't need beer to make me happy. Atypical for a German, I hardly cared for the stuff. I tried it once or twice. At best, it had the nauseating appearance of a urine sample and the likely taste and consistency of five-day-old cut-flower water.

An intoxicating thing happened following the jubilant discovery of the vat. There was a kicker. You see, there's always a kicker. Jakie Fox found a ladder, stood it alongside the vat, and, out of curiosity, climbed up to see how much beer remained. His reaction was one for the Guinness Book of World Records.

"Hey! There's a dead gook in here!" he shouted, after the cigarette that dangled from his lower lip fell into the vat.

"Yeah, right! You want it all for yourself!" snorted one of the men, throwing his head back in a goofy laugh.

Nobody believed Foxie. Like in liar's dice, several Doubting Thomases checked it out before confirming the disgusting condition. We took an axe after that, chopped several holes in the side of the vat, and the last two or three feet of yellow beer gurgled on to the ground. As you might well imagine, so did the sobering guts from those who earlier imbibed. Only in the Army!

But we were talking about the stars and stripes of the illustrious Marine Corps, weren't we? Yes, have at it, marines. Kudos. My cap goes off to you!

Hauling Ammo in South Korea

A man's life is not measured by what he does,
Rather, by what he gives back.
                                    - Unknown

During the early stages of the Korean War, all units were on the move from place to place, town to town like peddlers hawking their wares. We holed up in tents, camped in wide spots on the open road without cover, or, if fortunate, moved into vacant buildings. In August, when the U.N. Command held on by a small toehold around Pusan and Masan, called the Pusan Perimeter, our unit set up housekeeping in a wooden schoolhouse. At this location, I received orders to take six trucks and pick up 81mm and 60mm mortar ammunition at a dump near Pusan fifty miles away.

We left after dark, the windshield wipers slapping away in a moderate rain that continued to fall, and traveled with blackout lights only. Blackout lights are tiny bluish-colored slits on the front and rear of each vehicle that enables one to follow another. No fourways. As with nocturnal critters, after ten or fifteen minutes into the dark, your sight adjusts to the small amount of light, and you're able to move along at a reasonable pace. Occasionally, the rain came so thickly it overwhelmed the wipers. Yet we made decent headway on the MSR in spite of it and arrived at the ammo dump about 2200. We loaded manually, no tow motors or weight-lifting equipment being available. We were out of there around midnight and planned arrival back at camp by 0300.

I rode shotgun with Cardoza at the wheel.

John Cardoza was a dark hairy guy with a picture perfect smile were it not for a space between his two front teeth that he claimed was wide enough to stick a cigarette through in a pinch. He came from a suburb of Schenectady. There, he cleaned floors, washed dishes, and cleared tables in a small restaurant owned by his Sicilian-born parents.

"So, how come you enlisted?" I asked.

"And wash dishes the rest of my life?" His tone was incredulous.

I nodded.

"No way!" he said. "Not this *paisan!*"

"I can think of worse things."

"Yeah? Tell me."

"Driving truck in a war zone."

"Well, Buddy, you got me there. Except there was no stinkin' war going on when I enlisted."

"Ditto." I often wondered if I would have volunteered my services to protect this great country of ours after war had been declared. My guess is I would have accepted the challenge in any event. Moot point. Things were the way they were.

We were forty-five minutes outside Pusan. Our convoy, with Cardoza in the lead, pulled over at a pre-arranged spot and switched from headlights back to blackout for the remainder of the journey. By now, the rain had quit.

"Hey, Bud. I can hardly keep my eyes on the road. How about you taking over from here?" He hadn't slept in two days. Now would be no exception. Normally, one didn't sleep while traveling for fear of being shot at. Still, as a passenger, his customarily darting eyes could relax somewhat.

Thirty minutes later, a small mountain range loomed ahead. The narrow road with no guardrails angled toward the left. It was not a good thing to have the trucks get separated since ours was the only one with a .50 caliber machine gun mounted above the cab. The other trucks had only canvas roofs and one driver each. I took advantage of the curve and leaned out looking backwards to spot the other five trucks, something I would soon regret, like miscalculating a stair step.

"Ziggy!" Cardoza yelled. "Look out!"

As if recovering my footing on thin ice, I swerved sharply to the right to compensate. But the rear wheels had already slipped over the edge! My partner jumped free from the doorless cab while I continued on my merry way. I would like to say that because I kept my wits about me and was cool in the face of a crisis, managing a series of delicately performed maneuvers, I came to a smooth halt on the floor of the ravine, twenty-five feet below.

Yes, I would like to say that but it would be mostly a lie. While in reality that's what happened, it was purely accidental. As soon as I started down, I had closed my eyes, maybe even screamed curses as one of the guys told me later, but I don't remember doing so. Living in an era before lap belts, harnesses, and air bags, I recall gripping the steering wheel at nine and three and holding on for dear life. At least I got that right. The truck rolled over once, then again, and, wonder of wonders, came to rest right side up.

Have you ever experienced a car accident and come through it fully conscious? Obviously, you survived or you wouldn't be reading this, but I'm talking about your recall of the audible impact. If you have, you'll know exactly what I'm talking about when I say there was this brief but overpowering, noisy, undulating roar and clamor, like a percussionist caught up in his own dream world. It ended with a sudden bomb-like thump. Then deafening silence!

Was this a mirage? Maybe the result of some new form of driver training ed I was involved in? When reality hit, I shook out my head and squinted warily, then took mental roll call of my faculties. The only thing out of order was a tow chain we kept on the floor in front of the passenger seat. It was wrapped twice around my neck! I squeezed and pulled like the ancient rhythm that draws milk from a cow until I got myself unlassoed. When I exited the cab, the engine started to burn from the oil that had spilled over the hot manifold. In much haste that startled even me, I extinguished the flame by beating it with a ragged fatigue shirt that had been pinched behind the bench seat.

The others came running down the bank. Cardoza got there first. "You okay?" he asked.

"I'm upright, ain't I?" The only thing injured was my pride. It took an awful blow.

"If you're trying for your wings," scoffed David Wetzstien, "you joined the wrong outfit." Dave was from the Bronx and as Jewish as pastrami on rye with a Kosher pickle on the side.

I shrugged, said,

"I didn't know any other way to play it."

"Right."

Ammo boxes were scattered everywhere.

"Well, don't just stand there gawking!" I ordered of Joe Martin and of Speedy Jernigan, who normally moved as slow as molasses in January. Their mouths opened and closed like fish gulping air or whatever fish do when they do that. "You two stand guard while the rest of us clean up." No time for wit. No time for pity.

By collective muscle, we removed the machine gun from the damaged truck. It was certainly a different way for a gun to help. Without it mounted on top of the cab, the truck would have crumbled like an empty paper bag, let alone the more valuable content inside, that being me, of course. Despite slipping and sliding from the wet grass on the steep incline, we had the entire load spread out amongst the remaining five trucks in no time flat and arrived back at base only thirty minutes later than originally scheduled.

If I didn't have bad luck I wouldn't have any luck at all. To tell you the truth, when a man loses his truck, it's how a diver under water must feel without air. Or how a firefighter feels when he's on top of a burning building without water in his hose. There was such a void I cannot begin to explain. Captain Bond raised a questioning eyebrow but didn't seem too terribly upset when I reported the incident, at least no more than if I'd have told him it might storm two days from then. His nonchalance was somewhat comforting. Nonetheless, he cautioned,

"We can't afford to lose any more vehicles since the supply chain from the States isn't filled yet."

Orders the following night were a repeat of the previous one. Again, six trucks were sent to Pusan for more ammo. Captain Bond walked up to me before we left.

"I suggest you don't lose any more trucks!" he said, with a dart in the middle of the sentence. It wasn't exactly advice, rather a command, his voice revealing a core of military toughness while the corners of his lips worked back and forth.

Again, we traveled on the open road with blackout still in effect and headlights only within city limits. While driving through Pusan toward the ammo dump, we passed a small snack bar and mini PX run by the Army. Here sodas or 3.2 beer, cigarettes, and mediocre coffee could be purchased, but little else. Because our small convoy crawled through heavy rush hour traffic, a contradiction of terms, I had time to notice a two and a half ton truck parked outside. According to the markings, it belonged to the 25th Military Police Company of the 25th Division. The engine was running.

I don't know what got into me. Normally, I can't think myself out of a paper bag. But a thought cropped up in my head I was as powerless to stop as the wind is to stop itself from blowing. An epiphany moment. An idea so simple it was almost profound. I turned to Cardoza, who was driving.

"Hold it here a minute," I said. I ran back to talk to the driver of the next truck.

"Get going!" I told him. "Run down to the ammo dump, and I'll be in with my requisition as soon as possible to start loading." I waved the other trucks to follow and went back to Cardoza. "Go around the block and come by that PX again."

"Now what're you up to?" he asked suspiciously.

"We just hit the mother lode!" I said, not without some cockiness. "If the MP's deuce and a half is still parked there, I'll jump from your running board to their truck and bring it to the ammo dump."

By his facial expression, you'd have thought I brought a girlie magazine into an Army chapel.

Sure enough, the truck was still there and the motor running. Without further adieu, I confiscated the truck as planned and followed Cardoza, keeping my eyes fixed in the rear view mirror.

I headed for the nearest mud hole at the dump, drove through it recklessly, and stopped. Hands-full of mud smeared over the bumper markings and USA numbers covered all previous identification. That accomplished, I helped to unload the trucks. When we were finished and ready to leave, the starter wouldn't start on my truck. It became suddenly obvious why the engine had been left running back at the PX. We towed it a piece way by chain for a kick start and returned to camp without further incident. That was the sum of it.

Later that morning, I reported to Captain Bond without preamble.

"Our lost truck from yesterday has just been replaced," I told him, mentally polishing my halo. "I figure we have more use for that truck than the MPs loitering at the PX." I couldn't be sure he'd applaud my cunning for this most unorthodox manner of acquisition or have me court-martialed for theft of military property.

Bond screwed his brow and shook his head as if to clear it. He started to say something, but then hesitated. Frowning, he squinted at the mud-caked truck and walked away without a word. But when he directed the motor sergeant to paint our numbers on the truck, I figured I done good. A Zweizig moment.

Here's something else that's a little bit crazy. The captain promoted me to staff sergeant that very same day.

Since, I've often wondered how the military police explained the loss of a two and a half ton truck to their superiors. But I have a good idea. They left the engine running because the starter didn't work; that, or the battery was dying. The Koreans then stole the truck. Credible story. Theft was common.

Fallen guard duty always fresh in mind, I'd be lying if I denied having derived at least some small glee from pulling one over on these worrisome people. Like the satisfaction one gets when scratching an itch.

The date, August 25, 1950.

Crossing the 38th Parallel

Freedom is not free!
{Somebody's got to pay for it!}
   - Korean War Memorial

S eoul lies three miles north of the Han River in a basin among granite hills of 2,000 to 3,000 feet fringed with craggy peaks and barren slopes. Historically, this city was the capital of the Yi Dynasty. Following the annexation of Korea to Japan, many changes came about. Under Japanese influence, old, crumbling dynasty walls and gates were often torn down or restored, though some are still found throughout Seoul and the environs. A railroad center and streetcar system were developed. Residential areas sprang up, spilling out into outlying areas. Commercial buildings were constructed, and educational establishments opened—all signs of a city on the rise to meet the ever-growing demands of an expanding population.

In the post-war period, after the division of Korea at the 38th Parallel, this thriving metropolis became the command center of the U.S. Military and, late summer of '48, the capital of the Republic of Korea. Because of its strategic location and because of its huge population growing daily as refugees arrived from communist-dominated North Korea, Seoul became an immediate target for attack. Communist forces overtook the city the day they crossed the 38th Parallel. From then on and throughout the war, occupation was batted back and forth between North and South like a tennis ball at Wimbledon.

Soon after the marines recaptured Seoul, MacArthur planned a triumphant entry at the side of South Korean President Syngman Rhee. The Han River flows between Kimpo Airport and the city. Since no bridge existed, the marines were ordered to take time out from mopping-up operations and build one so the chief could travel by limo rather than the more practical and economical means of helicopter.

Baker and I, as well as other members of the 27th Infantry Regiment, the renowned "Wolfhounds" if you recall, were sent to Kimpo Airport for guard detail. The forenoon of September 28, mere hours after the bridge's hasty completion, MacArthur arrived in his plushly-furnished C-54 named Bataan piloted by Colonel Story. As was typical for the senior military officer, the lineup was fully stocked with four staff cars and twenty jeeps, probably supplied by the South Korean Government. Each vehicle was loaded to the gills with lower brass, and, not unlike today's mainstream self-serving media-driven culture, numerous reporters who would expand, diminish, exploit, and create.

"Bull crap! That's total bull crap! He needs all those reporters to crap up the people back home," complained Baker.

"Yeah, over here, he knows we know it's all a bunch of crap!" I said.

"The press don't know jack about what it feels like to kill people or get shot at or sleep in the rain or watch a buddy's life get sucked out of him. They'll just paint things rosy so that Truman can say it's not really a war."

By the time our escort guard arrived in the city, the streets, rain-slick from an all morning drizzle, were empty. Most inhabitants had taken earlier flight south and west. It was a different atmosphere for a parade. Only a few die-hards remained, waving miniature Korean flags and calling out half-hearted greetings as our motorcade snaked past alleys choked with trash, burned-out vehicles, and barricades thrown up by mop-up crews.

Sometimes tourist as well as soldier, I was amazed to see so much Christian influence. Several churches dotted the area, their pointed steeples reaching skyward toward the Heavenly Gates. Actually these plain little places of worship looked curiously out of place in this land of large temples, shrines, and monasteries. I can still hear the mystical mantra Buddhist monks chanted. Reflectively, I wonder if their strange singsong had anything to do with our presence—a threat perhaps of invading their culture with just one more step toward westernization.

The capitol building was nothing more than a fire-blackened shell when we arrived for MacArthur's conference. I know little of what these people discovered when they disappeared behind the top steps and inside the rotunda. But I can bet their experience was fraught with surprise. An horrendous smell of death permeated the place. Just close your eyes and imagine a mid-summer road kill multiplied a hundred fold. No, a thousand fold! U.N. forces rise to the height of compassion and carry their dead and wounded off the field of battle. It seemed the enemy cared less about collecting the misfortunate if doing so impeded their advancement. Or rapid retreat as was this particular case.

The day following special guard duty for MacArthur and gang, our unit shifted north of Seoul to the town of Uijongbu. It's truly amazing how efficient and organized the Army executes commands, never a minor undertaking. Within a very short period of time, hundreds of truckloads of supplies moved our entire base of operations to this forward area where we scattered around in various stages of readiness.

On October 7, 1950, when American units crossed the 38th Parallel into North Korea, perhaps thirty miles from Seoul as the crow flies, our 25th Infantry Division was halted. By the time we were authorized to proceed, the British had already captured North Korea's capital, Pyongyang, on October 15. We had the job of transporting men from this same British brigade to their temporary base behind the line.

"Indeed, it was decent of you to come," said one of the tommies following the last haul. He invited Baker and me to have "a tea" and opened the tent flap against a gust of premature winter wind.

"Brrrrrr!" I uttered between chattering teeth as we ducked inside.

"Yes, quite frigid out there, I say. This country's climate can't make up its mind. It's broiling hot in summer and bloody cold in winter. In England, we stay comfortably in between." He rubbed the cold from his ungloved hands and poured three cups of brewed tea from a kettle simmering on a gas hot plate.

"Thank you," Baker and I said in unison.

"I'm afraid we have no scones," the Brit said, "but here's powdered milk and sugar." He placed two china bowls on the small folding table where we sat. I wondered how such dainty glassware survived bumpy Korean roads.

"That's okay," I said, not knowing what the heck scones were anyway. "I drink it black."

He snapped his head toward me and wrinkled his brow.

"Black?" he said, his six-foot fit and trim frame pulling up a chair. He spooned milk and sugar into his tea and stirred. "So tell me, old chaps, how are things in the colony without us? Getting along all right, are you?" He lit up a cigar and, protruding his lower lip, released a plume of smoke then pitched his match on the ground floor. Baker and I lit up smokes as well.

"Smashing, Sir!" mocked Baker, cracking an uneasy smile. I'd never seen Baker so quiet, reserved, perhaps intimidated, yet, still hanging on to humor.

Our host laughed. By the looks of things, a gold-encased crown in his smile and thinning reddish-blond hair, he'd been around much longer than Baker and I. He had the presence of an executive officer, but I couldn't be sure exactly what rank judging from his royal insignia and was too polite to stare and much too shy to ask. At the risk of saying something foolish, I decided to change direction.

"We're with the 27th Regiment of the 25th Infantry Division," I said. "Service Company." Mom's meadow mint tea with honey was just the cat's meow. But this hot store-bought variety was a new experience. It was bitter. My host noticed and pushed the powdered milk and sugar bowls toward me. I took some of both and sipped.

"Thanks," I said, sipped some more, wiped my mouth politely with the back of my hand, and smiled pleasantly.

"Fine of you to pick us up, I should think," the Brit reminded us again. He raised his teacup and looked thoughtfully into the dark liquid, took a sip, sat back, and rubbed his chin with his cigar hand. "What a time of it!" he said, as though speaking to himself. "Would you believe the bloody fools mistook us for Russians? The bloody blokes came round us, offering cigarettes and red stars from their caps and slapped us on the back like we were long lost buddies during old home week." He chuckled.

"What did you do with that?" Baker said or something similar.

"I say, we were quite stunned at first, but then stepped back and poured fire into them...."

Terrible business, but such are the spoils of war, my friend!

We spent the next several weeks trucking more supplies and established a large dump twenty miles north of Pyongyang. During one of these trips, I received the painful instruction to take two trucks and pick up massacred Americans several miles away. When Baker and I arrived at what was a destroyed railroad tunnel, officers and other trucks were already at a site steeped in allied blood. It appeared that when U.N. forces pressed too hard, these prisoners became a liability. The NKPA, having absolutely no compassion for POWs or adherence to the Geneva Convention if indeed they were so obligated, finished them off with machine guns.

In a gully nearby were seventeen more bodies. These, too, were loaded on to trucks and stacked like wood in a cord. Several officers with fixed expression motioned to us from a small cornfield bordering the railroad. Here was the most pitiful scene of all. Fifteen Americans lay in a semi-circle. Some had come from the 29th Infantry Regiment captured near Hadong back in July. It was obvious they were murdered while sitting on the ground expecting food. Their rice bowls had been blown into a million pieces. Too, some of the bodies.

Experience something often enough and even the shocking becomes strangely familiar. Yet no one ever gets totally immune to the seriousness of war. My throat tightened and my breath shortened into quick gasps while I moved slowly past the lifeless, crumbled forms. I was stunned into anger and silence and never felt so helpless and frightened as I did on that particular day.

Overall fatalities, including the tunnel massacre, totaled seventy-two. Seventy-two young men whose hopes and dreams ended in the vicinity of a remote North Korean cornfield. Some like me had enlisted for sense of adventure, some for sense of purpose, others for escape from tough life experiences. Whatever reason, they came. They came to Korea in unison, soldiers willing to fight and sacrifice in the name of duty, honor, and country. And freedom for the oppressed. But freedom is not free. At any moment, one might be killed by a random circumstance. In fact, that is the game, to kill more of them than of you. To quote General Patton from the previous war, "...to break things and kill people." Yet throughout the ages, futility of war has been proven over and over again, most wars leaving more questions than answers at their finish, especially since the start of the Korean. What fools we mortals be!

For several weeks running, there was rumor of Communist Chinese intervention. My mental note was a trifle sketchy on the basis for such hearsay until researching corrected my knowledge gap.

At first, the Joint Chiefs of Staff saw no objection to penetrating North Korea. On the other hand, China's foreign minister warned that if U.N. forces crossed the 38th Parallel, Communist China would put them on notice. But why would China get involved in this conflict? I alluded to that in an earlier chapter, but failed abysmally to make myself clear. I'll try once more. Meanwhile, grab another cup of coffee, flip the phonograph record, and get set for a comfortable spell under the lights.

Remember when I said Russia entered the Pacific war in '45, something like a week to ten days before we dropped the A bomb? Well, in that short space of time, they launched a massive, successful attack on Manchuria. Manchuria was a vast area of China occupied by Japan.

After WWII, a couple of things happened. Actually, a number of things happened to change the text in the atlas, but only a few relevant for purposes of our discussion. One, the Japanese withdrew from Korea as well as from Manchuria. Another, after decades of civil war, China's People's Liberation Army kicked butt with Chinese nationalists and drove the latter out of Manchuria and on to the island of Taiwan. An historic moment, China, Korea's neighbor to the north, was now a new communist state as of October 1949 and allied with the Soviet Union in terms of expanding communism to the world.

But China had a priority. It wasn't enough that the nationalists withdrew to Taiwan. Premier Mao Tse-sung wanted them back, as well as the entire island, and, don't you forget it, UNDER HIS DICTATORIAL RED THUMB! Hold this thought; we'll return.

Three weeks after South Korea declared independence, North Korea followed suit as the People's Republic under Premier Kim Il Sung. In spite of two years of communist agitation and guerilla fighting throughout the peninsula, things were going nowhere for Kim. His dream to reunite Korea in the shortest possible time could only be accomplished with a full scale out and out invasion in order to bring the south under HIS dictatorial red thumb, thus, making Korea the third newest communist state in the world. To do this, he needed support of his commie allies—the Soviet Union and Red China.

In December 1949, Mao and Stalin met to create a new alliance between their socialist regimes. Kim's request was also on their paper agenda. By the meeting's conclusion, however, neither premier was ready to give the North Korean warrior the green light. Earlier, Stalin promised weapons for Mao's Taiwan campaign. Mao was now afraid these weapons would be diverted to North Korea if Kim Il Sung invaded the south. Stalin on the other hand, while already armoring North Korea, was unwilling to risk Russian troops in a direct conflict with the United States should something go wrong with the young Korean's aggressive plan. Rather it should be the Chinese. After all, what difference could it make to over-populated China if she lost a million or two on the Korean battlefield!

By spring of 1950, North Korea's president convinced both to move forward. He insisted his army would defeat the ROK so quickly the United States would not have time to join in. (Bear in mind, U.S. troops had earlier withdrawn from South

Korea.) Plus, the political grapevine revealed statements like, "The United States will not supply troops to back South Korea if the North invades."

In the interest of protecting the Manchurian border, Mao reluctantly agreed in May to back the North Korean People's Army with troops if need be. Stalin gave the plan his blessing, things working out just the way his devious, deceitful mind had hoped—China assumes the risk, Russia the reward!

China Intervenes

China is a sleeping giant.
When she awakes, the world will tremble.
- Napoleon Bonaparte

On November 24, 1950, the same day MacArthur had made a press statement, "The boys will be home for Christmas," a U.N. offensive began to rid North Korea of all enemy fighting units. In this plan coming down from MacArthur's Tokyo headquarters, the marines would continue north to the Yalu River, the border with China. In the east, an Army division and some ROKs had already advanced that far against light opposition. Far to the west, the 8th Army received similar orders. There would be a grand sweep up the peninsula.

The rumor of China's intervention was valid. In fact, November 25 was a day to be reckoned in the annals of history. Not only did the Chinese hit our sector but also attacked all divisions including the marines at the forefront near the Manchurian border, one of the world's harshest landscapes. Baker and I secretly hoped to get to the Yalu River and into China just to say we were there. We were crushed when word came down that our mission had changed. (See Addendum.)

The chicoms pressured the 8th Army's flank on the west side of the peninsula, and, within two days of fighting, our units moved further south toward Pyongyang, each taking up new defensive positions. As we moved, P51 props and F4U Corsairs, the Navy's single engine fighters, flew close air support and dropped incendiary bombs within a thousand yards of our new location. The infantry line companies had napalm dropped several hundred yards ahead of them as well. On the evening of the third day, we were not allowed to unload trucks for fear of being overrun.

That night, after dark settled in, the communist's calling card of bugles and whistles that gives me a coronary whenever I think about it broke the eerie silence. Immediately, the sloping hillside in front of us came alive with flares; the enemy moved in our direction like a raging forest fire driven by the wind. We were under attack!

"Here they come," my foxhole partner, a sturdy, steady East Coaster, muttered with a quiver in his voice. He added a stretch of expletives not found favorably in a church school lesson book. Men always acknowledged God before battle, either in prayer or cussing. There was lots of cussing.

"Let 'em come," I returned. "We're ready." Were we? We were scared witless is what we were! An unfamiliar fear had gripped my throat.

Within seconds, a heavy barrage of mortar fire erupted and the sky was filled with the arcing red streaks of artillery shells that blossomed into fiery, ear-numbing explosions. Tracers sent out from both sides, brilliant lines of red and orange and green, illuminated positions as grenades flashed by. While the flaming bursts of machine guns painted the night in fluorescent hues, burp guns and rifles filled the air with the hot stench of weapons on full automatic. Amidst the deafening roar of battle were the agonizing screams for help. This light and sound show turned into the longest and most intense battle since our arrival in Korea. So much for China's age-old strategy, I later learned: "Defeat the enemy without going to war."

Fighting the Chinese was a different experience, even for seasoned veterans. First, their strength was in numbers. Second, like the North Koreans, apparently a communist thing, they attacked mostly at night, a military tactic we had yet to perfect. And always with incredible speed! They tied brush and branches to their bodies for camouflage and were all doped up, ballistic, and half crazed, often, no weapons on them at all. Having no regard for human life, not even their own, they intended that we, their foes, burn up our ammo on the warriors in the fore. During the second wave, oncoming soldiers picked up guns from fallen comrades.

They surprised us on occasion with sophisticated stuff like U.S. Thompson submachine guns and Model 1903 Springfield rifles, thought to be booty from the defeated troops of Chiang-Kai-shek, our allies in the Pacific war.

I saw later, in a U.S. Army photo, that commie knives and spearheads were made out of steel supports from shoes, of all things. They cut daggers from oil drum metal, and rifles were frequently fashioned from discarded wood. And, check this out. They made hand grenades out of C ration cans! Interesting to note, their resourcefulness has withstood the passage of time. Today, we Americans provide China's exploding economy with basic raw materials such as cotton, scrap paper, and scrap metal. In turn, the Chinese manufacture and export to us the finished product: clothing, cardboard, and machinery. (Hopefully, the Chinese won't turn the scrap metal we sell them into weapons to use against us like the Japanese did with the scrap iron we sold them in the thirties.)

"If the chinks were smart, they'd stay home and beat their weapons into plowshares so they could feed all their people," Baker said. If the population of China walked past you in single file, the line would never have ceased because of the prolific birth rate. (See Addendum.)

"Yeah, and we could go home and leave this crummy war for the Koreans to fight out."

"I'd be willing to bet all the tea in China that's not going to happen."

"Why not?"

"No contest. Why those southern gooks would run and hide the minute we split."

"Yeah, I suppose you're right," I finished. We saw much evidence of that early on.

Autumn faded all too quickly, transforming into a cold Korean winter. Daytime highs stayed in the low twenties. At night, temperatures plunged to the bitter single digits and sub-zero. Several inches of snow continuously blanketed the landscape. Except for supply points, we had no tents. It makes my throbbing joints throb even more today when I think how we attempted sleep by pulling ourselves as far into our coats and caps as possible, sleeping bags if lucky. We bedded down inside trucks, underneath trucks, in shell holes and trenches, or out in the open elements. As once was heard: "They're in the infantry; they can sleep anywhere!"

On one occasion, while negotiating sleep that wouldn't come, I reflected on my on-again/off-again relationship with Joan. There was not a lot going on emotionally when I shipped out, but we did exchange a few letters. One time back in Japan, I followed through on a phone call reserved well in advance through the military system. Today, the mind-boggling click of a mouse speeds a message around the world in no time. Back then, communication depended upon snail mail or crackling, complex trans-continental telephone calls. The problem was, by the time they connected me to Hamburg, Pennsylvania, I was red-lined. Red-lined means they found an error in my pay record. Until straightened out, a ten-dollar bill had to tide me over until the eagle dropped its next load, one long month away.

Minus sufficient operating capital, I reversed the charges.

A disinterested switchboard operator with an accent intoned with,
"Go ahead."
Joan: "Hello."
Me: "Joan, is that you?"
Joan: "Is …(static)….. Walt?"
Me: "Yeah, it's me. What's happening?"
Joan: "…. (static)…….Did you say I was babbling?"

I listened for a smile in her voice. It wasn't there.

Me: "No, I said, what's happening? "

Joan: "………….. (static)…………"

Me: "What? I can't hear you."

Joan: "……… (static)……….Paul………"

Me: "What did you say? Did you say Paul? Paul who?"

Joan: "………….Lengel……"

Me: "Paul Lengel? What about Paul Lengel? Is Rascal okay?"

Operator: "You have one minute left."

Me: "Huh? What happened to the first four minutes?"

Joan: "What?"

Me: "Never mind. Is Rascal okay? I couldn't hear you."

Joan: "………..(static)……………..…..I can't ………….."

Me: "I can't understand you. What did you say?

Joan: "……………..(static)……………………"

Me: "I'll see y…." My words were shorted out and replaced by a hum and a click. I jiggled the receiver. The line was dead.

Frustrated beyond belief, I sat down after the call and penned a letter.

"…I am not sure exactly how much the call cost but at my end they pre-estimated $20 dollars. I'm sending you $25 dollars after my next pay to be sure I give you enough to cover..."

Like two ships passing in the night, perhaps literally, our letters crossed. Joan's cussed me out big time, saying I had a lot of nerve reversing the charges. That angered me to no end! For spite, I waited until September 1950 before mailing a money order for the amount due.

Mail delivery was an important event. Morale shot upwards unless the news was bad, and, even then, it could be tempered. In South Korea, we averaged mail call up to three times a week. In North Korea, it was sporadic. One day when they brought the mail forward, fifteen issues of the Hamburg Item arrived.

The Item, a small-town weekly paper, reported on big-time local news. Oh, nothing like the tabloid shockers of today where a mini mermaid is found in a sardine can. Rather, I'm talking important down home kind of stuff. Stuff like:

"In Tilden Township, Samuel Balthaser's Guernsey bull broke out of the pasture this Wednesday past and inseminated Calvin Geiger's registered Holstein heifers."

"Wanted: Part-time Adult. Apply Greasy Spoon Diner anytime but Sunday."

"Family, friends, and neighbors created major gschposs, banging pots and pans, clanging cowbells, and playing the bull band beneath Harold and Mary Schlappich's bedroom window. They continued far into the night until the young newly weds produced enough food and drink to serve the many uninvited guests. People from miles around were said to hear the ear-screeching rosin over the wood saw and came to join the shindig." (Authors' note: Today, such revelers are arrested for disturbing the peace. Back then, authorities crashed the party.)

In the event of leftover space, the remotest of possibility, the editor filled in with church service listings, who visited whom and when, obituaries, births and marriage announcements. Sometimes a photo or two. While I fingered through the third issue of the Item with frost-bitten digits, a picture of Paul Lengel popped up. He's the fellow who took my pet coon when I left for the service.

Allow me to tell you about Rascal. There was this old rotten tree along one of the line fences my brothers and I pulled down with the Farmall. During this traumatic maneuver, a bunch of baby raccoons emerged from a dried-out hole in the trunk. They were the dadgumdest cutest little devils you ever laid eyes on. We couldn't help but adopt them.

Being a small community, word gets around at the speed of lightning, with or without the Item. A game warden came by shortly and made us release the coons. Except for one that was missing. Everyone blamed me for hiding it. I would have if I could have. But honestly, I hadn't. After the warden left, confiscating our new babies, I went into the horse stable to muck out, feeling all kinds of sorry for myself. There on top of the door track watching me crouched the missing culprit. This time I kept my mouth shut.

Rascal's fur was a rich mixture of gray, black, and brown with broad bands of gray and black adorning his tail. White eyebrows above and black patches under his eyes gave him a masked appearance. His ears were held erect and prominent. He spent daytime hours usually curled up in a ball on top of a beam in the horse stable after he outgrew the door track space. At night, I put table scraps in a pan next to a dish he and the barn cats shared. Mom complained something was stealing eggs from her hens, but I never let on about Rascal. Occasionally broken eggshells were in the water trough where apparently he tried washing his meal. Either that, or he ate them right then and there.

I never found out how the little stinker fared after I gave him away. Nor would I. You see, the guy in the Hamburg Item decked out in formal attire stood next to my pretty Joan garbed in lacy white. While her boyfriend risked arm and leg on the dangerous Korean warfront, she thoughtlessly discarded him like an old worn-out shoe!

All that sympathy wasted when she overslept while a home perm fried her light brown hair to a crisp orange from the rusted bobby pins!

All that sympathy wasted when she tripped over my foot and fell face-first in the theatre aisle on the way to the restroom during the feature!

All that sympathy wasted when she came out of the restroom at Rip's after the movies with toilet paper anchored to her right shoe heel!

I confronted myself on that cold bitter day in Korea: *I don't know if I had ever loved Joan, but I was definitely infatuated. Was I still?*

A wise man once said: "There are several things a man needs to know about a woman, but nobody knows what they are."

Someday, I promised myself, I'd publish a book entitled <u>What Men Know About Women</u>. It would be a fat book, a book with lots of white space like readers want. In fact, there would be nothing but white space between the covers.

In quiet rage, I threw the Item as well as the stack of other read and unread papers into the bonfire. In olden days of swords and armor, open-air fires were built so soldiers could find their way back to the battlefield after a night's sleep. In even more ancient cultures, huge outdoor fires offered human bodies to the sun god, hence the name bone-fire. Ours, fueled by Korean corn shocks, prevented the plain and simple occurrence of freezing to death. Even though it was daytime, we huddled around the fire, men no more than boys, boys spending the winter like thousands of other boys all across North Korea—alternating between battle and off-time, shivering, blowing on frostbitten hands, pacing, stomping or any movement that helped to keep us warm. At least the papers would help a little.

"Hey, Bud," said Rock Preston, a dark-haired city slicker from Chicago. "What are you doing with them newspapers?" With mittened hands, he rummaged through his own pile of mail scattered on the white frozen ground.

"I'm finished with them," I lied, staring at the leaping flames throwing their warmth toward me.

"Well, maybe someone else would like to read them. Ever think of that?"

I shook my head.

"Too bad!" I said, scrunching up the last one before tossing it into the red inferno. "Small town stuff. No one would be interested anyway."

"Well here's something you might be interested in," said Gerry Miller, waving a penciled sheet. "How about a God joke?"

"God joke? Hey man, I don't wanna hear no blaspheme," Farwell drawled in an accent thick enough to support a cotton bale. "The Man upstairs just brought me through a scrape with death. Y'all don't read no blaspheme to me!" Billy Joe Farwell came from the Bible Belt. He had just gotten through passing around Christmas cookies with red and green sprinkles on them that the ladies' social committee at church had sent. Mine was stale.

"No, don't worry," said Miller. "I already read it, and God's the good guy, honest. It's from my sister, and she would never blaspheme. Says she ran it by her husband and said that even though the joke picks on men, her Luke thought it very funny and suggested she send it to me to make me laugh. 'God loves laughter, and so do you,' she said."

Hearing no further objections, he began,

"God was just about done creating man, when …."

"Sounds like some preaching coming on," interrupted Marvin Wayne who spat toward the ground for emphasis. His spittle froze in mid-air. "I'm outta here!" The man burdened with two first names pocketed his only envelope and ducked inside the closest truck.

"God was just about done creating man," Miller repeated, wiping his runny nose with a dirty coat sleeve, "when he discovered there were two things left over in his bag. He couldn't quite decide how to split them between Adam and Eve. So He thought He might just as well ask them.

"He told them one of the things He had left was a thing that would allow the owner to stand up to piddle. 'It's a very handy thing,' God told them, 'and I was wondering if either one of you had a preference for it.'

"Well, Adam jumped up and down and begged, 'Oh, please give that to me! I'd love to be able to do that! It seems like just the sort of thing a man should have. Please give it to me! Pleeeez?'

"On and on he went like an excited little boy. Eve just smiled and told God that if Adam really wanted it so badly, he could have it. So God gave Adam the thing that allowed him to piddle standing up.

"Adam was so excited he started whizzing all over the place. First on the side of a rock. Then he wrote his name in the sand, and then he tried to see if he could hit a stump ten feet away, laughing with delight all the while.

"God and Eve watched him with amusement. Then God said to Eve, 'Well, I guess you're kind of stuck with the last thing I have left.'

"'What's it called?' asked Eve.

"'Brains,' said God."

That got a pretty good laugh. It was either that or cry.

"That joke wasn't half bad," said Red O'Riley, popping a stick of gum in his mouth. O' Riley chain-chewed like most of us smoked cigarettes. "It was all bad. Hey, what's up with Pers?"

Percival Hampden sat propped against a truck wheel. One hand covered his eyes. The other held on to a yellow piece of stationary like it might try to blow away.

"I don't know," I said, wondering if he received a Dear John. I decided to find out.

"Did your girl ditch you?" I asked the dejected-looking soul.

I wondered about parents who would name a baby Percival. I wondered even more about the young man who used that name. From what I knew, he was a quiet gentle person from a small town in Ohio who usually kept to himself, normally displaying the personality of a failing flashlight battery. He rarely smiled, but when he did I noticed his teeth were small and crowded.

"What's wrong, Pal?" I said.

He shrugged.

"Nothing," he said and dropped the eye shield, rubbing his thumb against his fingers. His gloves lay empty alongside. He had small slender hands, almost like a young boy's.

I sat down next to him and stared at the bonfire. The dancing white and orange flames spirited high and wide, evoking images that reminded me of those I'd seen in clouds as a kid. Many a hot August day, my brothers and I took breathers and sprawled in the shade of the huge straw pile out in the field.

"D'you see the underside of a turtle up there?" one would say.

"No, but I see an Indian chief over there," and I'd point to a feathered profile that transformed magically to an angel in flight.

"Naw," answered a brother, "That's not an Indian. That's Old Saint Nick. Can't you tell by the fluffy white beard?"

"Oh, look! There's a horse. You can make out the shape of its head, and the tips of its ears are looking at each other." Grempop Zweizig said that was a classy feature.

"That's not a horse, stupid. There aren't no legs."

"Sure, there are. He's just laying down."

"Horses don't lay down."

"Maybe he's old and tired."

And so we went on.

"My girl just dumped me for someone else," I said, leveling my sight back at Pers. "It doesn't feel too good. But hey, there's other fish in the sea." I hated fish, but I was ready to offer any sympathy I could give on his behalf. My male ego had taken a major hit.

"I never had a girl back home to lose," he said and creased the letter into six folds, then stuck it in his vest pocket.

"Guess it looks like I'm being nosy. I'll leave you alone." I shivered to my feet.

"It's alright. It's only news that the old man died. Nothing to get excited about." A stray tear trickled down his left cheek, threatening to ice up.

"Oh, I'm sorry," I said, but my words were inadequate.

He took in a long slow breath through his nose and then let it out. He focused his empty gaze toward the bonfire and shook his head.

"Don't be," he said. "It's something I wished on him many times. It's as if I pulled the trigger myself."

I was shocked and found things to do with my freezing hands. I looked away and tried not to think.

He continued.

"I'm not sad because he's gone. I'm only sad because I don't have any good memories to be sad about."

The relationship with my own father flashed before me. It wasn't much of a personal one. Pop was a decent though somewhat distant father. He was rarely at home. He spent weekday evenings at Berne's general store cajoling with the rest of the neighborhood men. Daytimes were spent "on the road," going to farm sales, auctions, dealing with cattle dealers, fetching feed and equipment parts, and running a whole host of other errands that could only be accomplished behind the steering wheel of a Ford pickup. He was the business manager while the laboring was left to us boys. He treated us each fairly, though, when it came to boasting about his beautiful dairy farm, always giving credit where credit was due to his young and able work force.

Memories? No exceptionally good ones that stood out about my father. No bad ones either. No affection, but no blame attached there either. He was a product of the rural German farm folk generation. It was simply the stuff of life on a Pennsylvania German *bauerrei*.

"Is your mom okay?" I said, venturing forth once more. I cupped my hands and blew into them. Dang, it was cold!

He shrugged, said,

"My mom died when I was born. This letter is from my stepmother twice removed. Says they buried him back in August and that she put off telling me because I had enough things to worry about." That was four months ago.

"I see," I said. I did not.

There was an awkward lull in our conversation when O'Riley called from the fireside circle. He was shuffling a stack of playing cards.

"Zig! Get over here. We need a fourth. Chop! Chop!" Red was

an outgoing sort and enjoyed the spotlight, one usually in the midst of organizing *gschposs*.

I leaned over and put a hand on Hampden's shoulder, then stood and resumed my place of warmth.

James Bond, Jr. was a spitting image of his dad and two years my junior. He and I were good friends. Often Baker and I were the captain's dinner guests at his home in Osaka, and we developed a fine relationship with the family. In fact, James Junior, following his enlistment, wished to serve with me in our unit. The captain felt that was unwise, considering the seeming possibility of favoritism under his command. For that reason, he suggested signing up under the 65th Combat Engineers, the outfit next to ours at Kanoaka Barracks. Young James trained with them when the Korean War broke out.

Serving with the combat engineers was a heck of a job. There are streams all over the place in Korea, and the engineers were continuously building bridges and roads to cross or bypass these waterways. Existing bridges were often blown to deter the enemy's advance and then later rebuilt. Harassment by enemy fire was constant both day and night as they worked. A lot of combat engineers got killed on the job. James Bond, Jr., pulling planted wires and explosives out of a bridge one day so the infantry could cross, was one of them.

Someone once said, "Losing a soul mate is hard. But to bury a child is totally unnatural in the order of things. It's like putting a period before the sentence is finished." Every man has a breaking point. He can't go on. He can't rationalize and does the unthinkable, whether consciously or subconsciously. The devastating news of losing his only son drove our captain over the edge. Days before, we had brought in several truckloads of a new type of overcoat. These bales of clothing were on the ground, and you could walk up, find your size, and take one. Also at this time, there was constant movement of refugees through our area. They took note of these coats, and, from forty yards away, Captain Bond pulled his forty-five automatic and killed a would-be coat snatcher. Of course, all the other would-be coat snatchers immediately scattered. That same day, my good captain was relieved of command and returned to Japan where his wife still lived in Hamadera Park outside Osaka. I never saw him again.

Eight days following China's entrance into the war, the chicoms barnstormed our forces with a vengeance. Being a fairly low man on the totem pole, I was not in the know of things on why we did what we did or when we'd do them. Seemed like odd timing, yet the infantry war was put on hold once more, then ordered to withdraw. We were located south of Pyongyang on a large level plain at this time and retreated southward while the thundering racket and screams of Navy Corsairs accompanied us overhead. They circled the air, swooping and diving repeatedly at Chinese outlying positions in the nearby hills like barn swallows after insects released from the grass machine. They dropped earth-shaking pods of napalm and strafed the city itself with rockets and heavy caliber slugs. Before they vanished over the horizon, four Air Force F80 Shooting Star jets zoomed into view and began their runs.

I pushed my cap back for a better view. At least ten miles behind us, the burning city billowed fire against the late afternoon sky while we continued toward the 38th Parallel and on toward the city of Seoul. It wasn't over yet!

Withdrawal to a Point

...We will celebrate this Christmas Day in our traditional American way – because of its deep spiritual meaning to us; because the teachings of Christ are fundamental in our lives; and because we want our youngest generation to grow up knowing the significance of this tradition and the story of the coming of the immortal Prince of Peace....
- Franklin D. Roosevelt's Address to the
Nation on December 24, 1944.

Energy was high. Gale-force winds drove snow horizontally while we made continuous runs, setting up supplies at different locations for the withdrawal of all 25th Division units. Onslaught of the Red Chinese became so great that sometimes we ended up moving the same company twice in one day.

On the third day at a new location, after an overnight snow ceased and a raw biting cold set in, we set up new defensive positions fifty miles away. Several officers held a roadside discussion and stopped our convoy on one of these trips. While waiting, I heard the deep throaty hum of a plane motor. To my right, a P-51, tank busters they were called, a plume of exhaust trailing from behind, made a dramatic wheels-up belly landing in a yet unfrozen rice paddy. Slushy snow and mud splashed everywhere much as sludge from a broken-down honeywagon. After the craft halted, two captains, one riding on the lap of the other, emerged.

"Medic!" someone shouted.

"Medic!" someone echoed. Several men rushed to the scene.

The way I heard it, one pilot crash-landed after hit by ground fire. The other swooped him up much as a hawk grabs a mouse. During this heroic rescue mission, the Air Force single engine fighter stopped at least thirty enemy bullets while remaining airborne until the fliers saw our convoy. Neither suffered serious injury, but they did bear urgent news.

"Thousands of Chinese are crossing a river just a couple miles back and headed this way!"

They came all right! Night after night after night! As soon as the sun disappeared over the horizon, the chinks were over us like fleas on a hound dog. Most of their vehicles and equipment were well camouflaged and hidden throughout the day. But we knew they were out there. Tire tracks, bent grass, and branches cut from trees, making them misshapen, were only a few overt signs of enemy movement seen by a sharp reconnaissance pilot.

Under normal circumstances, the artillery lives behind the frontline, whereas the infantry is the frontline. But the frosty, foggy December weather shrouded everything in a cold raw mist from day one, preventing adequate visibility for our aircraft to direct us. As a result, we relied entirely on the artillery boys, using the heaviest equipment available, the 155 and 275mm Long Tom field guns. That was the bad news. The good news was that, the further south we traveled, the enemy's supply lines became longer; ours became shorter!

One gray and chilly morning, when snowflakes floated down like biblical manna, I moved a squad of men from one ridge to another a mile distant. When I arrived, the men were picking up their ambush bags. In basic, we studied, "Know your enemy; don't fight the enemy until you know his tactics." We were learning. Earlier, the squad scrounged up every spare sleeping bag they could locate and stuffed them with snow or other materials, arranging them in a circle to give the Chinese the impression GI Joe was tucked inside. At the painful cost of many casualties, Fox Company of the 2nd Battalion caught on to the enemy's trick of shooting troops while they slept in their bags. Fox's payback technique worked. In a two-acre area alone were the splattered remains of more than sixty green-padded Chinamen from the previous night's skirmish.

The only good thing about sub-freezing temps was that bodies either froze or filled up slower with gas, avoiding the terrible stench that managed to bring up your last ten C ration meals. Though, there were times I could've challenged that final statement.

During an arms combat on the frontline, a courageous soul on the German side of the offensive shouted in stunted English for the Americans to hold their fire. It was Christmas Eve. The year was 1943. Forever suspicious of the conniving enemy, the Americans were reluctant to lay down their weapons until they heard a familiar German Christmas Carol fill the air.

> "*Stille Nacht, Heilige Nacht....*"
> Soon the yanks joined the celebration of Jesus' birth.
> "*Silent night! Holy night!*
> *All is calm, All is bright.*
> *Round yon Virgin Mother and Child,*
> *Holy Infant so tender and mild,*
> *Sleep in heavenly peace, Sleep in heavenly peace.*"

I am going somewhere with this. On Christmas Eve 1950, when Baker and I were on guard duty (We were always on guard duty!), one of the guys in Baker's foxhole sang out:
"*Silent Night.*"
From another hole came:
"*Holy Night.*"
From another came the third phrase:
"*All is calm.*"
The latter was followed by still another tune, less resonant

from the former.

"All is calm, my butt! Knock it off, you guys!"

Nonetheless, there seemed to be a more peaceful air throughout. Especially noticeable was the fact that there were fewer curses ringing in the air.

To keep us warm, someone usually came once or twice during the night with coffee in green mermite cans. These were canister-shaped containers with a metal lid about two inches thick, something like a thermos. When a guy went to a foxhole, or any gun position, he had better know the password. The password was changed daily. One particular night, the password was "Lady/Butterfly." From your hole, when you heard someone coming, you'd say, almost like in a Shakespearean play, "Who goes there?" The guy with the coffee then says, "Lady." You reply, "Butterfly." On Christmas Eve, somewhere between "Silent Night" and "Knock it off," I overheard the following:

"Halt! Who goes there?"

Silence.

"Who goes there?"

No response.

From the foxhole:

"If you're the guy with the coffee, you better say so NOW, or in ten seconds, I'll blow your @#$%& head off!"

"Hold it! Hold it! I have the coffee, but I just can't think of today's password!"

Christmas Day, inside a twenty by sixty foot tent, tables set up on snow and frozen ground were topped with steaming hot servings of roast turkey, bread stuffing, mashed potatoes, and a few other holiday trimmings.

Chaplain Stoudt entered the tent just as we were about to eat. Our chaplain was well named for he was a stout man, fair-haired with strong Germanic features, tight skinned with a broad square jaw and firm mouth. After God's blessing on the feast before us, he led us in a few Christmas Carols. (See Addendum.)

Here we are in the midst of combat, I thought, *mouthing words of love, forgiveness, and peace on earth!*

When we started to eat, some of the guys complained.

"My first good hot meal in weeks, and I had to let it get cold to sing a few songs."

"Yeah, anyway. Why couldn't it wait until after we ate to sing?"

We discovered why that would not be fitting. Our holiday feast was not meant to be joyous. While we ate persimmon pie without whipped cream, our new CO, Captain Bond's replacement whose name I've long forgotten, walked over to another table where Chaplain Stoudt was seated. He whispered something in his ear and handed him a slip of paper.

The unsmiling chaplain slowly rose and tapped a spoon on the table for silence.

"I have an announcement to make," he said and paused to clear his throat. "We just learned that General Walker's driver was passing an ROK convoy on a narrow dirt road thirty miles from here. One of the Korean trucks turned out to pass and forced Walker's jeep into a deep ditch."

Lieutenant General Walton H. Walker, a rather chunky man who spoke with a twang and walked with a swagger typical of native Texans, was the 8th Army Commander since 1948. He carried a deserved reputation as one of the best fighting generals the Army had.

Stoudt stared into space, his eyes shiny, maybe a little damp, and returned his gaze to the paper. Following a deep breath, he continued in a voice that was barely audible,

"Walker died of head injuries before reaching a hospital. This happened three days ago."

A murmur rippled through the camp.

"Let's bow our heads in a moment of silence for our great leader."

Ergo. The whole dinner affair lasted less than an hour. The Chinese were not taking Christmas off and, obviously, neither were we. We were back on alert as soon as the bad news was digested and dessert swallowed. So much for MacArthur's promise the boys would be home for Christmas.

Walker's reins were turned over to Lieutenant General Matthew B. Ridgway, a handsome fifty-five year old West Pointer with a brilliant military record. The three-star general cared little about taking real estate but insisted on an aggressive, offensive campaign. His goal was dead Chinese. Lots of them! All of them! During the first six weeks of his new assignment, soldiers moved around in the field like pawns on a chessboard. A host of top echelon officers, mostly WWII veterans, were put out to pasture and replaced with younger, more assertive COs. The 25th Infantry Division, 24th Division, 1st Cavalry Division, and the 7th Division now had new commanding generals.

Ridgway was a no-nonsense type of guy and disallowed staff officers to sit in the rear smoking cigarettes and making decisions without knowledge of what happened at the front. He liked to visit a forward area, then back out and ask questions. He soon learned whether the CO led up front or issued orders from behind. I remember on at least two occasions an officer flagged me down to wait while Ridgway's observation craft descended from out of nowhere and landed on the roadway ahead. Unlike MacArthur, the pipe-smoking absentee commander who was around for photographs but rarely the fight, General Ridgway was close by whenever your unit was in a scrape!

Much later, while returning home aboard ship, I talked to an MP whom I knew in Japan. (Yes, there actually were MPs I took a liking to.) He was a security guard with Ridgway and recounted the following incident:

While traveling toward the front one day, they met an ROK convoy. Ridgway ordered his driver to stop.

"Let's find out where these guys are headed!" he said.

"Chinee come! Many, many!" the ranking Korean officer said. "Must go! Must go quick!"

"You're right! But we're going that way," said Ridgway, pointing north in the direction the Koreans retreated from. "Not south!"

"No, No! Must go!" the colonel insisted. The ROK convoy was high-tailing it back to safety like a rabbit fleeing the fox.

General Ridgway got on the radio and called for a replacement. With his jeep, they blocked the roadway and stood guard with Thompson submachine guns while waiting for the replacement. The American KMAG Team (Korean Military Advisory Group, better known as Kiss My Butt Goodbye Team) arrived, and, twenty minutes later, an L17 landed on the roadway with a Korean brigadier general who took immediate command. The entire ROK convoy turned around and headed toward the front. When they arrived at the forward defensive line, not one lousy red commie was encountered.

Perhaps you're wondering why American officers had such clout on the Korean battlefield. While the war was a United Nations collective effort, the Americans had by far the largest investment of military personnel, equipment, ammunition, and other resources. Sure, there were fifteen or more U.N. members involved in the war besides us, but their contribution in most cases was merely token, maybe a brigade or one company or a small hospital ship. It behooved the United States military to take charge, including authority over U.N. newcomer South Korea. The U.S. paid ninety percent ROK expense. We trucked their troops. They moved on our ships. We fed their refugees. We fought the common enemy.

Seoul Lost Again

…Then the dust will return to the earth as it was,
And the spirit will return to God who gave it.
                              - Ecclesiastes 12:7

New Year's Eve was a night like any other. The whiskey stored in the air compressor boxes when we left Japan was long gone by now. If there was 3.2 beer available, who can say. I never touched it. I went to sleep early that night and woke up in 1951 to a thick coating of new snow and an icy wind blowing from the distant hills. About five hundred yards away, a shell exploded into a cloud of smoke and debris. The chicoms wished us a Happy New Year!

By mid-month, our unit headed toward familiar surroundings and hung snowcapped hats in the Suwon area, a short distance from the K-6 Airfield. Ridgway didn't give a darn about losing Seoul; he didn't want to fight an engagement with the river at his back. Where we were, the Han River lay south of the big city.

Skirmishes continued throughout February while Ridgway attempted to firm up this southernmost line of defense across the peninsula. A tremendous amount of ordnance was fired to hold the

Chinese at bay. I recall our unit expending as many as 4,000 to 5,000 rounds on any one night. Shrapnel fell continuously from the sky like hail in a thunderstorm.

The Chinese concentrated in the west and central portions of the peninsula while the North Koreans fought in the east. Not once did the two conduct joint operations, probably due to a language or communications barrier. Or maybe some other unknown factor, like motives for fighting the war being different. Perhaps they just plain old didn't like each other, who knows! I, for one, would bet my cards on the latter, because I can't for the life of me comprehend how anybody could have liked either one.

The 25th Division fought in the west and west central region, confronting the Chinese. The 2nd Infantry (Indianhead) Division's 23rd Regimental Combat Team aided by a French battalion moved into the Chipyong area. The Twin Tunnels battle was fought and resulted in an actual count of more than 4.000 Chinese dead. For the first time since they entered the war, China's offensive was broken.

We continued to shuttle troops and supplies back and forth. In the Osan area, supply and gasoline dumps totaling fifteen acres were combined. Not known to us at the time, we prepared for something big, confirmed later in the *Stars and Stripes* as Operation Ripper. The combat operation controlled by Ridgeway cut MacArthur out of his beloved limelight. But he tried. In Tokyo news conferences, MacArthur, through his typical unmitigated outspokenness, made statements on plans in the works. Many wanted to execute him for such treason and placed the responsibility of American casualties on his non-calloused, lily-white hands.

"Is it true normal folk get three squares a day?" asked Baker. We were always on the move, seldom getting a hot meal.

"Yeah, and what's really odd is they sit on a four-legged chair at a four-legged table when they eat." I parked my butt on a sandbag close to Baker's.

Earlier, we had heated pork and beans over the manifold next to the truck engine valve covers. Sometimes the guys forgot to puncture the hole large enough or left the can on too long, and the explosion spit contents all over the engine. While the end result was no gourmet delight, not by any means, it was hot and tasted a million

times better, I'm sure, than the smelly canned sardines the ROK soldiers smelled of if you had the misfortune of being within smelling
distance.

Standard rule of thumb was fifty percent of the total force served
as guards, alternating throughout the twenty-four hour day. Like the
start of a mystery novel, "On a cold dark night in February…," while
posted on alert, I walked from my watch area to the command post a
hundred yards away to learn what was planned for me and my trucks
the following day.

As I approached the squad tent, the outline of a pint-sized body
took shape in the shadows behind it. I felt a sudden adrenaline surge
as kill or be killed mentality took over and continued surreptitiously
toward the entrance. Instead of going inside, I snuck round to the
opposite end and came up from behind, jamming the muzzle of my
M1 so hard into the small of my victim's back, the force knocked
him flat in the snow. Before he could grunt, "Hey, I'm the coffee guy,
please don't shoot," I fired into the frozen ground no more than two
inches away from his right foot. He rolled over and raised skinny
little arms in the air, crying,

"No! No! Me ROK! Me ROK!" He was bony-faced, bareheaded,
and short.

Soon, a ring of the curious collected around my catch.

"What you got, Ziggy?" someone asked.

"I found this SOB snooping behind the tent," I said. The SOB's
clothes were an odd assembly of civilian and ROK. I grabbed the spy
by the jacket and yanked him to his feet.

"Let's see what we got here," said Sergeant Hanson, one of the
other guards.

While I stood shotgun, rough hands frisked the trembling
slant-eyed sneak.

"Well, well, well! Look at this!" said the frisker, after discovering
an American hand grenade pocketed in the dark cotton trousers.
"You didn't have the guts to use it, did you, you coward!"

The prisoner caught the meaning and stretched his mouth into
a forced smile.

"No! Not hurt *yangki!* Not hurt!"

"What else does the bastard have?" asked a big rifleman from the
2nd Platoon. He found a six-inch blade hidden deep inside our cap-

tive's worn boots. The guard inspected the knife and drew it across the little man's throat in a cutting gesture. "And just what did you plan to do with this?"

"Me ROK! Me ROK!" the spy insisted.

There was no identification to prove the frightened sleaseball belonged to any South Korean unit. One thing was certain though. He shook like a leaf in a windstorm and had the dread of death in his eyes.

"Well, if you're an ROK, I'm a chink!" said the tall, blond, blue-eyed Hanson, shoving the runt toward the tent flap.

Several of the guys wanted to take him out back and shoot him, including Clerk O'Neill who didn't want to deal with the cumbersome paperwork involved with POWs. But Major Gibson raised the red flag.

The major was a dark, tough customer with a thickset jaw and pursed lips and had been a professional boxer between the wars. He took pause from working on an assignment chart clipped to a board on the field desk and scrutinized the prisoner.

"You're wasting time, gentlemen. Get him out of here, and get back to work," said the major in his quiet, authoritative manner. He dismissed us with the wave of a hand, like catching a spy was maybe an ordinary event. He sat back down next to O'Neill who started punching keys on an old black typewriter.

"Come on! Let's go! Move it!" ordered Hanson.

"Oh, Zweizig," said the major when I was leaving the tent. "Good job! You know what to do."

We chained our prisoner to a truck bumper and in the morning took him to G-2 Division Intelligence Section for intensive interrogation.

Later, we had another infiltration incident. Eighteen of us shared the same living space in the three days spent at this site. Two stoves fueled by gasoline heated our squat tent (more correctly said: attempted to heat our tent). A few of us congregated around one of these, playing matchstick poker, when in walked a *yoja* who hadn't seen bath water for quite a time.

She was a gaunt, unhappy-looking woman, nudging the mid-life mark, I'd say, and had untidy hair and thin features like a tired old mare. She wore open sandals and a threadbare overcoat, and the homespun scarf around her neck was road dirt brown.

By sign language, she willed her body in exchange for food to fill the empty cloth sack in her hand. The one who walked in my boots and slept in my bag tossed in two cans. There were four or five others who did the same. The rest took the woman in trade, one after the other, until the bag was filled.

I have mixed feelings about people like her. It's impossible to imagine the devastation they endured. Wherever our trucks passed through cities and small villages, children surrounded our trucks, begging for food and water. War destroyed their country, and these people were living in abject poverty, hanging on the apron strings of the U.N. military and American camps, maybe taking in washing and sewing, or, in this woman's case, prostitution. People in desperate times do desperate things in order to survive. One wonders, do you give them a fish or teach them how to? (See Addendum.)

The next morning, a change of plans placed my trucks on hold. Baker, six others, and I attended funerals and assisted in burials at a temporary cemetery close by. Four numb and broken American families received "The Secretary of War regrets to inform you..." telegram. The men were laid out in plain wooden coffins for later removal to a permanent site or sent home, unheralded, for burial beneath a modest headstone in some windswept plot in downtown USA. (See Addendum.)

No inverted M1 with bayonet stuck in the ground before each coffin. No helmet and dog tags topped the M1 that wasn't present. The slow grief-stricken sound of Taps echoed only across the bleak plateau of our minds while we stood in work fatigues—numbed, empty and angry, braving sub-freezing temperatures and biting sleet. The chaplain took a Bible from the make-shift altar, a jeep hood draped in a brown woolen blanket with a small gold cross in the center, and brushed off frozen water particles from the Book's cover. He conducted a brief ceremony including a few words to eulogize the fallen heroes and a long prayer.

"...Greater love has no one than to lay down his life for others, it says in John 15," spoke our man of cloth to the few of us in attendance. "When they took the oath, they knew and accepted the fact that Army life could put them in harm's way. Each of us here understood that. Our fallen brothers understood that, willing to sacrifice their lives to make a difference for you, for me, their families, and for our country, and now their battle is over. It's difficult to understand the grip of death and its reality. It's wrong. Yet it's natural. We are born into this world and then enter into that gray zone called life. And we cherish life even more because we know that death as we know it is always at the end, regardless of when it comes...."

I am not normally a good listener of words from the pulpit, and I tend to drift, but this day I hung on every word.

"...Dear Heavenly Father, loving God of mercy and grace, we humbly stand before Thee, the One who embraces each of us in fellowship with an everlasting love. Through Thy Son's sacrifice for our sins on the cross and His glorious resurrection that followed, Thou promises to all believers a life in Paradise, a place so marvelous it transcends all manner of human imagination, a place where there is no more pain, no sorrow, no war, no death. We're reminded that life as we know it is Thine alone to give and to take. Receive our thanks for victory over death and the grave through our Lord and Saviour Jesus Christ. Because He lives, we, too, shall live and shall one day reunite with our loved ones. Neither death nor life, nor things present nor things to come, shall ever separate us from Thy gracious love. We pray this in the name of Thy Son, Jesus the Christ. Amen."

The chaplain removed his right glove and, with an index finger, made the sign of the cross. He repeated over each coffin:

"Inasmuch as it pleases our Creator God, we commit thee to the ground, dear brother. From dust thou art to dust thou shalt return, and Jesus Christ our Saviour shall at the latter day raise thee from the dead."

The sleet stopped, and the sun broke through cracks in the cloud cover like a benediction. While solemn and sorrowful still, the atmosphere became strangely uplifting in a way, beautiful in a tragic way, like dying for the country was maybe a fine thing.

I could deal with that. Or so I thought.

R&R

Treasure today, for tomorrow never comes.
We hear this so often. Still, it's true.
- Source Unknown

A rest and recuperation program started soon after the first of
the year. R&R was a five-day rest period spent in one's previously assigned area, in my case, Japan. Everyone was ready
to leave, but, of course, no more than five percent of unit strength
could leave at any one time. (Down the pike, the percentage changed
to eight.) In our section, we drew six or seven names out of a box,
depending upon the number allowed. When those people returned,
the next group was drawn. There were cases in our unit where men
were assigned as recently as a month before. Those in Korea since
the landing date on July 4, 1950 were selected from a separate box.
FIFO. First In/First Out. Others followed in due time.

Neither my name nor Baker's was picked on the first four draw-
ings. On the fifth, mine came up, but not Baker's. We wished to
leave together so I stepped aside. The next time, my name turned
up again. Again, I passed my spot to another. And fortunate for me!
This particular group, transported on a C-82 Flying Boxcar out of
K-6 Airport near Suwon, went down in the Sea of Japan, cause un-

known. (K-6 was a designated Korean air base constructed for military use.) All passengers and crew perished. Few names remained, and, on the next to final drawing, my name came up again. So did Baker's.

A chaplain who earlier lectured that Japan offered more than alcohol and women sat next to me on the back of the troop carrier en route to the airport. I have vague recollections of a friendly sort in his thirties with charisma that filled the room. He was dark-haired and reddish-skinned with high cheekbones and said to be Irish and Cherokee in makeup, and, regardless of circumstance, forever neat and clean-shaven. Comforting to know, we'd have spiritual influence on our behalf for the journey, thoughts of the C-82 incident fresh in mind.

"Sure hope the guy at the control panel has God as his co-pilot," I said to impress him.

Twinkling blue eyes behind wire-rimmed glasses turned toward me.

"If that's the case, they need to switch seats," rebuked the man of cloth.

A pelting rain greeted us at the airfield, but the good news was we'd fly the newer C-119. The Air Force twin-tailed cargo plane had two huge props up front with sword-like blades to propel this heavy craft to Japan. We'd be piloted by fliers who I'm sure were far more "pilot" than today's information systems techs who are surrounded by hundreds of digital avionics in the cab.

We climbed aboard and sat for the longest time, listening to shouting, doors banging, and chutes opening and closing while the engines rumbled like distant thunder. Suddenly, the noise of the engines grew louder, and I felt a lurch as the aircraft moved forward. After another few moments, there was a heavy knocking sound, and we lifted. The whole experience gave an uneasy sensation in the pit of my stomach, and I was reminded of my fitful first day at sea. Another maiden voyage.

Earplugs might have been optional; I don't recall. I just remember that the engine was so loud, so roaring and consuming that it ruined little chance for conversation. Yet the chaplain who must have noticed me turning green asked,

"First experience?" We sat next to each other again, this time against the plane's fuselage.

"I was never higher than the top of a loaded hay wagon," I shouted back over the roar of the motors. "Oh, yeah, I almost forgot the roller coaster at Hershey Park."

"Yes, it can be a bit frightening. Probably because we have no control in the situation."

Karl, whose last name I can't recall except that it sounded like one long sneeze, was a veteran flier. He overheard us, said,

"So true. Except why do they have to tell you just before landing that you're on the final approach!"

Everyone's a comedian.

Eighty minutes later, we floated safely into Osaka in spite of a displaced March wind that whipped up over the sea and another heavy, repeat heavy, April shower on this late February day.

At Itami Air Base where we ought to have boarded something sea-worthy, we got on buses and sloshed our way to the Gosho building downtown. I was grateful for one thing, no, two—first, the weather hadn't precipitated in the form of white stuff, and second, I wasn't out in a foxhole.

Our weapons, carbines for Baker and me, were stored in a locked arms room until our return to Korea. My priorities included a hot shower, barber chair, and shave, in that order. Afterward, I shuttled to a large supply room and exchanged damp inner and outer clothes for a brand new outfit, brass insignia, and a spanking newfangled pair of low quarters. Dress trousers cut to a variety of sizes were available by choice. Shirts were ironed and starched. At the time, I was a staff sergeant, and, within minutes, the Japanese nationals working in ready rooms had stripes and patches sewn onto all of my outer wear.

I was a shadow of my former self and slim as a carrot. Little wonder! How sustaining is a tiny can of pork and beans every other fortnight for a growing lad of twenty? When I left Japan at the outbreak of the war, I tipped the scales at two hundred and fifteen, all muscle and fit as a fiddle. On this day, I weighed in at one seventy-four. That's forty-one pounds in eight months! What I wouldn't trade for that today—right arm, eyetooth, maybe both.

After squeaky clean and pressed, we settled down to real food, a top sirloin steak dinner served by a friendly and obliging Japanese staff in a new dining hall recently annexed to the Gosho. Oh my! How novel to sit in honest to goodness real chairs at a real table topped with a green-checkered oilcloth. And, of all things, electric lights beamed overhead. And there were see-through panes in the walls that were trimmed in green-checkered curtains to match the tables. And imagine this, dairy fresh ice cream for dessert with chocolate, marshmallow, and peanuts on top—the coveted CMP at the Adams and Bright drug store back home!

"Not bad," Baker said around a mouthful of gooey hot fudge, but added wistfully, "We were so busy surviving, we forgot what it was like to live."

He got that right! It had been forever since we lived like human beings instead of like animals. In those eight long months during which friends were wounded or killed by Charlie, constant concerns were food, water, and survival. It was hard remembering and controlling one's emotions in this totally revamped environment.

The assigned sleeping rooms were unique, spacious, and decked out with as many bells and whistles as any stateside Conrad Hilton, or so I'd heard. This was truly a luxurious and much appreciated experience after all those cruddy months on the cruddy Korean battlefield.

I had no pocket cash since June 1, 1950 when agreeing to delay my pay until my return home or to Japan, whichever happened first. Both Baker and I signed for an advance of a hundred and fifty dollars at a small payroll office. We were ready to do the town!

Japan waited with open arms. The city had come to life in spite of the foul weather. The streets were already jammed with car and foot traffic and crowded with vendors, the air full of good and bad smells. Block after block of shops merchandizing anything from cheap knick-knacks to precious gems beckoned to hundreds of men in uniform hitting the streets. I bought a double strand of cultured pearls, anticipating a girlfriend in the wings, and a small battery-operated radio. Baker purchased a wristwatch and a 1951 calendar made out of rice parchment that was bordered in an Oriental design. Inscribed at the top in English with a Japanese flair were the words, "A Year to Remember."

"Someday, Zig," Baker said, rolling up the calendar, "when I get out of this miserable war and settle down, this will hang on my parlor wall to remember our good times together."

And to remember the bad times, too, I thought. Those times when we held up each other while in the thick of war. Like General Sherman said, "War is Hell," but you made it tolerable, my buddy, even fun at the most awkward of times. Like the time we spent underneath a truck loaded with umpteen drums of gasoline in the heat of battle and had to listen to Mellon's boring saga on birds.

I never had so much fun in my entire life as in the space of two years that I've known you. The jokes, the gschposs, the singing, and playing that humongous Spanish guitar of yours. I'll always remember, too, my best buddy, how you saved my life. Once from drowning in Osaka Bay and again from going down on the C-82 into the Sea of Japan. I'll always laugh when I see your silly face with the black soot from ear to ear when we crossed from Honshu Island to Kyushu. And never, never will I forget the stink you raised by hitting that stinking honeywagon. It sure wasn't funny at the time, but it proved quite the conversation piece later, didn't it? The guys never let you forget it, mainly me. (I still laugh at the memory of it.)

There were plenty of sad times, too, like the time we experienced our platoons' first casualties back near Sangju. Curt Bennings and Bart Kowalchuk. Bart's best buddy Vinny Harabach never talked about it. The Army doesn't allow time to grieve, but the bounce was gone from his short quick steps. We knew he hurt deeply, and we hurt right along with him. And soon there were others who came and went. And there was James Junior and the memories you and I shared with Captain Bond's son during a happier time back in Hamadera Park. And how about all those horrible assignments we pulled together, like picking up the dead at Hadong and Hoengsong and stacking them like wood in a cord. And those silent, never-ending hauls to the Graves Registration Office, never knowing which one of us would be on the next load out.

Most of all, I'll remember our companionship, our plain old ordinary constant companionship. No, not ordinary. Nothing is ordinary about you, my friend. From the day we met at Kanoaka Barracks to the war in Korea and back again, you made life exciting to the hilt and anything but ordinary. Yes, Gaines L. Baker from Evansville, Indiana, I'll remember you, too. Maybe not reminded by a Japanese calendar on the parlor wall. But in my heart, my mind, and in all my years to the end of time, you'll always be there. I'll always re-

member you, my dearest friend. Always.

We took our souvenirs back to the room, and, to avoid the shops and more temptation, walked to the opposite side of the road. But there a long row of bars and strip joints greeted us with inviting prostitutes at every entrance.

"Let's get the heck out of here, or we'll be broke before the sun goes down," said Baker.

"If it ever comes out," I added.

The sky was gun-metal gray and full of cold rain. In this windswept downpour, like turtles, we pulled our heads into our jacket collars until we reached the main PX on Lightning Boulevard that reopened since R&R began. Upon entering, we shook off water like wet dogs, then gobbled California cheeseburgers and French fries doused with ketchup. We finished by jamming candy bars in our mouths like logs in a sawmill. Stuffed and satisfied for the first time in months, we flagged a cab to visit Kanoaka Barracks for old times' sake.

Many changes had taken place since we left. Japanese nationals now occupied the base at Kanoaka. No longer decorating barrack walls were posters of undraped female figures or figures in various stages of undress. Or Hollywood pinups like Peek-a-Boo Marilyn Monroe. Or Betty Grable, showing shapely legs said to be insured for a million bucks. Gone were the double bunks with wrinkled fatigues hanging from bedposts and spit-shined boots and shoes parked beneath. In their place were row upon row of sewing machines and short tables. The motor pool buildings were converted into a factory for cooking and bottling some kind of Japanese (obviously) steak sauce.

Yielding to further nostalgia, we stopped at Mama-san's beer and tea garden at the Sakai White House where we often sat evenings past. Her name was Tatamuchi or something like that. But we called her Mama-san for short. She always wore fancy kimono. Her thick hair was piled high in a black hornet's nest and held in place by colorful combs, giving the appearance of inches taller than her already tall frame as Japanese women go. Subtle signs of aging around eyes slanted like a Siamese cat's made me guess she was old enough to have sons our age. Yet for all her years, she moved with the grace of a swan.

A local said Mama-san was once a geisha but compromised the profession by marrying her keeper. This disrespectful, unforgivable act cast her out of geisha society forever. The husband, a high-ranking officer in the imperial army, widowed Mama-san twenty some years later. He was one of 70,000 who had died defending Okinawa, an island three hundred and sixty miles south of the Japanese homeland. (12,000 Died trying to take the island when on June 22, 1945, it fell to the Americans.) Following his death, she reopened the beer and tea garden they partnered before the war.

When we came by that evening, she went half crazy and clucked over us like a mother hen with a brood of chicks.

"Good to see! Good to see! Come, you wet. Get sick."

She ushered us to a back room and insisted we replace our damp outer jackets with long-waisted, baggy-sleeved silk tunics wrapped with a sash. Of course, our shoes had been deposited at the front door where we had slipped into sandals.

Mama-san never once accepted a yen. She never had. Were we special? I'm not sure, but I suspect it was Baker's magnetic personality. Baker always came mit guitar and jammed with the Japanese entertainers, patrons enjoying him every bit as much as she. Then, too, it might have been the *pan* (bread).

My first memories of store-bought bread came when Ralph Becker with his blue and yellow Freihofer's van drove into our farm driveway on Tuesday afternoons, scattering chickens in every direction. Mom put a dollar bill in the tin pan on the dash above the step and, in exchange, received ten crusty loaves of *weiss brodt*. (Contrast this with a similar time in pre-war Germany when it took a wheelbarrow load of German marks to buy one loaf of bread.) Oh, there were many other goodies for sale: sliced bread wrapped and sealed in blue and yellow wax paper (up to 1943—after that, sliced bread was banned for the duration of the war to save steel that would be used in slicing blades), plain and iced chocolate cupcakes, sticky buns, cream puffs, and powdered donuts. But these were Depression days. Extras were done without.

I drove the bread run nine months in '49. My truck had a special enclosed body stacked with trays twelve inches deep, two feet wide, and three feet long to haul fresh bread, not much unlike Ralph Becker's. Mornings, I picked up a load at the bakery in the ancient harbor city of Kobe and hauled it to Osaka. On the way, the driver, that would be me, treated himself to a continuous nibble during the forty-minute trip. I ripped the end and pulled out the delicious warm stuff from inside and, except for the crust, had a fifteen-inch loaf consumed by the time I reached my destination. It is written that man cannot live on bread alone. But I tried!

Belly full and distended, I parked at the PX and waited. Within the next two hours, trucks came from Gifu, from the 27th Regiment, the 35th from Otsu, the Signal Company, and the Military Police Company to pick up bread for their respective units. When my truck was empty, my day in, and roster checked off, I headed home via Sakai and gave Mama-san two or more fresh loaves.

{The last time I saw Mama-san was the day we left Japan. She had traveled twelve miles by bus from Sakai to Osaka and stood alongside the tennis court fence where we assembled to board buses. I spotted her easily with her towering beehive hairdo and waved. The dear woman always laughed easily, her slant eyes crinkling merrily at the corners. This day, they glistened shamelessly in the early afternoon sun. *Sayonara, my dear beautiful friend.*}

We left the Japanese cab driver waiting outside the White House since the plan was to hit several old haunts along the way. But after a couple of drinks, it became obvious we'd be planted for a time. We invited him in.

"Yes, yes," he said, grinning from beneath the bill of a battered American soldier's fatigue cap. It was parked on top of an excessive amount of black hair streaked with gray. His shrunken flat-nosed face beamed, his smile flashing an uneven set of teeth yellowed by time and tobacco. "I leave cab, yes?"

"Yes. You leave cab. C'mon."

Before the night ended, he was three sheets to the wind and totally incapable of stoking a cab. There is something you need to know about the taxi in Japan. Open up the trunk, and you were in for a big surprise. There was a funny little stove inside that did a funny little thing. As amazing as an electric light, it burned charcoal to fuel the automobile, hence the nickname "charcoal burner." Gas is so high at the pumps today it would seem an excellent alternative. But not without compromise. Top speed at best with these CBs was between twenty to thirty miles an hour.

We left for Osaka around two in the morning with Baker behind the wheel of the tired old taxi and the cab driver passed out on the back seat. The following morning, I looked out the fourth floor window of the Gosho building. The cab was gone. A question comes to mind as I write this. Except for the drinks he got on the house through us, he was hardly paid. Let's see, from the Gosho building to Kanoaka Barracks, then to Sakai, then back to Gosho again adds up to thirty miles plus. With three hundred and sixty yen to the dollar at the time and at a compound interest rate for fifty-five years, not to mention a tip, this calculates to roughly.... Good grief! Speak about unforgiving guilt! I shall forever have this financial shortcoming on my mortal conscience.

So solly.

The following day, we looked up the chief of police to locate his daughter, Mai Maknihara.

"The Armed Forces Institute in Osaka shut down soon after you left for Korea," he said in his usual good English. "Then she transferred to the same school in Tokyo."

"What do you hear from her?"

He stared at me for some time before answering.

"We haven't heard from Mai in months."

This news struck me as rather odd. They were a close-knit family.

Tracing his lead, we boarded the train around 0600 the next morning and arrived in Tokyo, home of Hirohito's Tokyo Rose, eight tiring hours later.

The old trolley rumbled through a busy thoroughfare, swarming with celebrants of National Teeth Brushing Day, and on through a crowded downtown of markets, shops, and renovated buildings of a modernized Japan on the rise. We then passed a neon-lit amusement district before coming to an intersection where the USAFI awaited our visit.

A moderately attractive middle-aged woman hinting of jasmine welcomed us to her study just inside the entrance.

"Mai Maknihara?" she repeated after me as if searching her brain for a spark of recognition. "Name not familiar. I check."

She opened a wooden file drawer with a deep rack of fawn-colored folders and thumbed through them one by one.

"You say she secretary?"

"Yes, ma'am. A darn good one, too," I said, remembering how Mai fudged attendance records so I could do the town instead of slaving over square roots and algebraic equations.

She nodded as if that information classified something for her, but then said,

"I so solly. I find no record of such lady."

I'd been had! Her father liked me, or so I thought. But then again, he didn't like Americans as a whole because of their treatment during the war. Probably now, he even feared the loss of his daughter to the States if our relationship were to flourish. For all I knew, she was in the back room when we called on him the day before.

We left her office and walked down the steps and on to the rainy plaza.

"Wait a minute," said Baker thoughtfully, reaching out and grabbing my arm. "We're at war!"

"We're at war? You coulda fooled me! What's your point, Buddy?"

"My point is we wouldn't have men getting their GEDs when they could be fighting a war, now would we?"

Made sense.

I nodded.

"So, how could Mai be a secretary for a school that probably ain't no more?"

Simultaneously, we double-checked the small billboard outside the building we had just left. It read:

UNITED STATES ARMED FORCES INSTITUTE
(The rest of the message was in Japanese.)

"I'm going back in there," I said, starting for the steps. That woman knew more than she let on.

Baker grabbed me by the jacket.

"So what do you expect her to do? Tell you where Mai went when she doesn't even know where she was in the first place?"

"Well, I'll call her father, then!" I was not one to give up easily.

Three phone stalls later, we found one that functioned, and I was fortunate enough to connect with Mr. Maknihara.

"You won't believe this," he said. "This morning, we received a letter from Mai. It came from Kyoto." Our connection was nearly as bad as when I called Hamburg, Pennsylvania. I was limited in Japanese tokens and hurriedly scribbled the address on my wrist with a pen I bummed from Baker.

"C'mon, let's go get drunk," Baker said after I hung up.

Baker had always rather patronize a bar where indigenous folk gathered rather than one set up for servicemen. Even though he didn't have a guitar this time, he entertained all the same, joking around and singing to endless applause. In broken Japanese lingo, followed by that big toothy grin of his, Baker had the locals buying drinks for us left and right. The drunker he got, the better the show...

Earlier we had stopped at a hotel and reserved a room. Now during the wee small hours of the morning, we couldn't figure out the way back. Nor did we recognize the name in Japanese scroll on our room receipt. Nor had it occurred to either of us to hire a charcoal burner with a driver who might recognize the name in Japanese scroll on our room receipt. Desperate, we hailed an MP patrolling the district. While I made a reasonably coherent attempt to describe the area and street fronting our hotel, Baker, drunker than a sailor on his first leave, plowed around me.

"Why the @#$% are you guys here in Japan?" he hiccupped, clucking his tongue against the roof of his mouth. "Who's your CO, anyway? I'm gonna get your butts shipped over to Korea where you can do some good!"

Hotel? Moot point. We didn't need one after all and were kindly escorted to the Military Police Detention Center. This wasn't all bad as it turned out. Besides free overnight accommodation, we ate a top scale American style breakfast mid-morning. Not only that, an MP lieutenant drove us to the Tokyo Railroad Station in, believe it or not, a full-sized military staff car.

On the way to Kyoto, we stopped for an hour at the base of Mt. Fuji and had lunch inside a cozy little tea garden. They're called that even though they are indoors in winter. An icy steel fog surrounded the summit and blotted out the mesmerizing view I had seen on my first train trip through the mountains. From there, we continued on toward the city.

Kyoto, a city of shrines and temples, was left undamaged by the Pacific war. Along the narrow streets and amongst the tidy shops were stonewalls topped by long rows of paper lanterns that piqued our curiosity. We were told that inside the walls were gardens and Buddhist temples and that the lanterns with vertical Japanese characters painted on them were prayers.

"You know why the Japanese write from top to bottom, don't you?" asked Baker while we viewed the passing city from the inside of an electric trolley car.

"I do not."

"It's because a man's head is at the top and his feet are at the bottom. Fact."

"Brilliant! What would I ever do without you to keep me in the know of things!"

"What would you do without me, period!"

Life without Baker was unthinkable. I changed the subject, said, "I believe this is where that policeman told us to get off at."

We were at the main entrance to the famous Garden of Kyoto and were told to get a charcoal burner from there to Mai's address. It was a long Japanese name and the spelling not easily committed to memory. I had taken great care that morning not to wash my wrist. Actually, that was not a problem with our stark military accommodations. In a Japanese hotel? Different story. The natives were anal about cleanliness. After you washed thoroughly from head to toe at a small basin, it was expected you participate in the customary toilette that followed: total immersion in a public bath. No way! Not this dude!

The name is long gone from my memory, but, whatever it was, I verbalized as best I could and showed the script on my wrist to the first CB driver who pulled over. The little man shook his head.

"Don't you know where that is?" I asked.

His slant eyes stared at my round ones. Again, he shook his head.

"Oh, boy," I mumbled and looked to Baker for help.

Baker gave it a try. He was much better at this sort of thing and gave the long word a Japanese twist.

"So solly. No speak English." The unsmiling, wrinkle-faced driver took off.

"Where the H are the MPs when you need them?" It was Baker again.

Frustrated, we walked until our shoes were soaked and thread-bare and our feet blistered and sore. It had been drizzling off and on throughout the day.

"I have this fantastic idea," said my buddy seemingly hours later. "Let's try another taxi."

The cab driver repeated the address with a question mark, raising a thick black eyebrow.

"Okay, I take you."

We rode past a sharp contrast of western-style buildings on one side of the street and primitive huts with tin roofs on the other and, from there, wound in and out of alleyways until we came to a dirt path lined with small pine trees and barely broad enough for our cab, small as it was, to pull through. Forty yards in, our driver stopped in front of a long vertical sign with Japanese symbols carved into the wood. Beyond stood a square mound dominated by a roof in the style of a Shinto shrine. A priest walked around on it, chanting bless-ings and shaking his sacred wand adorned with folded paper strips.

Close by was a postage stamp-sized playground with a jump board, slidie, and two swings. A boy about seven climbed a swing rope, giggling as one hand over-reached the other while he pulled himself higher and higher. Mama-san sat on a bench, nursing an infant. The dank air was saturated with the smell of fish from a nearby market.

"Don't look like a place a classy young dame like Mai would hang out at," said Baker, viewing through the opened side window of the cab. "Then again, how long did her father say she was gone? Nine months?"

I pointed to my wrist and then the sign and asked the cabbie if these were one and the same. He smiled and said something neither of us understood.

"I wonder what he's saying," I said.

"He says it's going to cost you nine-hundred yen to sleep with a mama-san."

"Very funny."

Why would Mai's letter come from a male shrine or a kiddie's playground? Or weren't we there yet? We'd wasted most of our leave time pursuing someone who was obviously not pursuable. Enough of this wild goose chase. We directed the driver to move on and drop us off at the nearest bar.

Neither of us had been to Nara. The old section of the city was Japan's first permanent capital going back in time to the 8th century called the Nara Period. It is locked in another age and maintained by the Japanese government, similar in a sense to a national park in the States. After a long walk from the train station, we made our way down a slender cobblestone street and past quiet little shops with open fronts, attended and visited by people wearing traditional Japanese dress. Women in bound feet, a custom slowing them down to demonstrate respect, shuffled several paces behind their mates. Alone, men scooted about in ricksha, hand-hewn oxen-drawn carts, or canal boats. Everywhere there was an unhurried atmosphere, not the noisy city sounds of modernized Tokyo. A war carried on across the narrow sea, but here there wasn't a care in the world.

Since we landed in Japan, it had rained or had threatened rain, but we lucked out this particular day. Japan did have its moments. The sun shone gloriously on gold-domed palaces and medieval castles of the old aristocracy that still dotted the hillsides. Manicured grounds, the grass from recent rains recovering from winter brown, surrounded them. Trees and gardens lined principal thoroughfares, and, in the center of the old downtown, a path bordered by ever- greens clipped into strange shapes meandered through a delicately landscaped park. Small Japanese deer and domestic geese crested around the park's lake like ceramic lawn ornaments, making one question where nature ends and art begins. Nara was a fascinating spectacle.

There were numerous Buddhist pagodas with colorful tiers, Shinto shrines, monasteries and temples, many in Chinese archi- tecture and boasting great imperial wealth. Tourists in action, we visited a few. (See Addendum.)

Having no tour guide and attempting to recall an event over fifty years in the past, I can truthfully say the only memorable thing in- side a temple was the removal of my shoes and walking past a large stone statue. He was a fat-cheeked man with heavy-lidded eyes wear- ing a funny-looking hat. He sat kind of funny, too, legs crossed in an awkward, painful position. People placed flowers and fruit and other things at the base. Later, much later, I made it my business to learn what this was about.

First off, it's important to be familiar with the terminology of these strange Eastern customs. Let me tell you what little I know about a topic I hardly know anything about. With the assistance of Daniel Webster, a book by Osho titled <u>Buddha, His Life and Teachings</u>, and a Christian relative turned Buddhist, I'll try to pull it together.

Japan is a nation steeped in spiritual smorgasbord. Shinto, a tra- dition incorporating the worship of ancestors and nature spirits or deities, is unofficially, at least at the time of this story, the religion of Japan in spite of MacArthur's prohibition as a state institution. Hindu, too, had a foothold early on. (Our present day New Age movement is founded in Hinduism.) But Shinto pretty much allied itself with the Buddhist cause as far back as the Nara Period.

Buddhism is a widespread Asian philosophy founded by Gauta- ma Siddhartha in the 5th century BC. Legend has it the young prince escaped and left home on the proud white steed Kanthara to meditate and preach throughout India. His followers nicknamed him Buddha, "the enlightened one." His enlightenment came at a personal cost of later abandoning wife and child for twelve years while searching for truth and an explanation for human suffering. His followers believe that life is filled with suffering, but, through meditation, they can achieve the state of nirvana (cessation of suffering) by controlling desires, overcoming ignorance, and leading moral lives. They claim purism in peace and harmony with the universe.

There is another term to reckon with on the Buddhist's path to enlightenment called karma. Karma is the "action" bound to one's desire "to be, to grow more and more, to become more and more, to accumulate more and more." Buddhists are devout in building their karma {dubbed meritorious good works by western translation that determine one's destiny} and devote great energy and wealth as they advance cycle by cycle toward nirvana. Are you with me so far? Okay, then, moving right along…

In the shadow of temples glistening with real gold, you can witness the faithful prostrating themselves, lips moving in prayer, or recitation, if you will, of Buddhist law called "sutras." In other spots of the large temple yard, a young person may be seen praying with the aid of beads to the sound of a gong or bell. Temple visitors, except for the likes of Baker and me, bring gifts and lay them on the altar in praise and thanksgiving. Within certain sects, the food first passes through incense before placed on the altar. Others burn incense when praying, the smoke supposedly taking prayers up to Buddha (of which there are many) in heaven.

On this matter of heaven, Buddhism teaches that heaven is not the soul's final resting place. Instead, it is believed different heavens exist that lead the believer not to God but to nirvana. Buddhists are born again and again, living many different lifetimes. Behavior on earth determines the quality of their next life and whether they return reincarnated as a lowly animal or as a person; i.e. transmigration like a horse soul in a human body. (Tibetan Buddhists believe that the Dalai Lama, whom they call His Holiness, is god-like, the 14th reincarnation of a semi-divine being. It is said, to see the Dalai Lama is to see God himself. Says the present day Dalai Lama, "They {the people} believe in me and have faith in me.")

The original Buddha followed an earthly path much like Jesus. Both were teachers of compassion, love, and wisdom. But, of course, Gautama Siddhartha lived five hundred years earlier, and, though deified in some minds, never claimed divinity. It is said you can match these two figures right down the line, even to the roles and characters of their immediate disciples. One major difference: Christians claim Jesus Christ created the world, and, when incarnate, remained sinless and died for the sins of others so that they might be saved. But that's another story.

[Some say that Judeo, Christian, and Islamic faiths are spiritual, their followers worshipping the same God, and that Confucian, Hindu, and Buddhist principles are only ways of living.] (See Addendum.)

Oh, yes, we were wondering who the big fat-cheeked man was. I mean no disrespect, but that is how I perceived him at the time. He was, in fact, one of many Buddha figures in meditation throughout Nara. Something else about that visit many years ago comes to mind. That is the chant of monks reverberating across the airwaves of this quaint city. It's my present understanding that their rhythmic sounds spoke of careful surrender in their determination to walk the eightfold path to nirvana.

"If I see one more temple, I'll puke," Baker said at the close of the long day.

"Me, too!" I said. Except for some being more grand than others, if you saw one, you saw them all.

After a bowl of disgustingly fishy *Odong* soup at an old ultra Japanese hotel, we retired to our room and slept the night away atop scratchy rice straw mats. The next morning, we had tea and rice biscuits in the lobby, and, starving, ordered a box lunch "to go" for the last leg of our trip to Osaka.

Baker sat by the window, seat reclined and his cap pulled down over his eyes. He was in deep slumber. Or so I thought. Out of the blue, he raised himself up, removed the cap, wearily combed his fingers through damp hair parted in the middle, and replaced the cap.

"So Ziggy, what did you think about all that ceremony yesterday?" he said.

He produced a pack of cigarettes, knocked one out, lit up and flicked the match out the opened window.

"What ceremony?" I said. "What are you talking about?"

"I mean, all that praying and chanting stuff. What's all that about?"

"I'm not sure." He caught me off guard. I had dozed off, and my thoughts were fuzzy.

"Well, as I see it, it don't seem like they are praying to the same God we have, if there is such a one."

"You wouldn't think so. The way they kept putting food at the statue, it looked like they were trying to feed him, whoever he is." I chuckled at the thought of a stone figure munching on apples.

"I heard a guide tell some tourists in English that that was Buddha who was born a long time ago, and his followers are called Buddhists. They place things there out of respect for him."

Baker must have been listening while I searched in vain for the statue's feet.

"Do you believe in God?" he said this time.

"Of course," I answered my personal friend and confidante. "Don't you?"

He shrugged.

"I don't know," he said and took a drag on his cigarette, blowing a thin stream of smoke toward the ceiling.

For several minutes, neither of us spoke. Then Baker said,

"Pop forced me to go with him and Mom to church on the rare Sunday mornings he was sober. Things would go good for a few days, and Mom would be cheery as all get out. Then sure as midweek rolled around, Pop would come home drunker 'n a skunk and beat the living pulp out of her. If I was near by, I got it, too. I remember one time we were expecting some people from church for a visit, and I had this swollen black and blue eye. Mom said I should tell the people I got stung by a bee. It just never made sense why we went to church if things just kept getting worse and worse at home." Another cigarette went out the window.

I lit one up and took a long slow drag and kept silent, letting Baker go at his own pace. The iron wheels continued to rumble as they propelled us toward Osaka. Then Baker said,

"Where was God in all that?"

I nodded as if I understood.

"Yeah, I see what you mean," I said, recalling the story of how my God-fearing Grempop chained Uncle Herbert to a kitchen table leg. It was punishment for restlessness during company. *Schuslich*, we call it in Dutch. "Children should be seen but not heard" was the household philosophy. I was a believer, but, too, had questions. "Did you ever ask God?"

We smoked.

I waited.

His head tilted to one side, and he said,

"Ask Him what?"

"What you just said, where was God in all that? Did you ask Him?"

"Well, now, what am I supposed to say, Zig? Hey You up there in the command center! Where were You when Pop pushed Mom down the cellar steps?"

"Why not? We're supposed to be able to say anything to God." At least that's what I learned in Sunday school. That's what is so great about a relationship with the God of the universe, the teacher explained. We can speak to Him directly anywhere, any place, about anything. False gods are not flexible like that.

Baker shrugged. He lit another cigarette and slowly waved out the match.

I went on, amazing myself at the brilliance coming forth.

"It's a way of getting a conversation going with Him. That's how you can find out what He's thinking. Or like finding out where He was when your Pop beat up you and your Mom."

Baker seemed lost in the memory and inhaled deeply, blew smoke out the window and what was left of that umpteenth cigarette followed. He turned toward me.

"Yeah," he said. "You might have a point." He appeared to ponder that theory and went back to a reclined position, pulling his cap down low.

I stared ahead in thoughtful silence while the conductor strolled down the aisle toward us. He stopped to chat with a passenger in front of our seat.

"Too late now," said Baker then, "and who cares anyway? I wouldn't know Pop even if he was the one collecting tickets on this train. And Mom, she got herself knocked up by some salesman and

left me behind with her brother. Yeah, who cares anyway."
    Closed parentheses.
    End of discussion.
    Period.
    Baker snored.

R&R was six months of social life, shops, hide and seek, and touring squeezed into five short days. Each day started early and ended
late. When it was over, we were broke and tired. We spent the final
night in our lovely staterooms at the Gosho building. Ninety percent
of the other rooms were untouched. We checked. On the morning
of our departure, after a full American breakfast of bacon, sausage,
fresh eggs, and dehydrated fried potatoes that were delightfully hy-
drated with fat, we visited the NCO Club in Osaka and purchased
twelve bottles of whiskey to fill requests back in Korea.
    The bus to Itami Air Base was scheduled to leave at 1300 hours.
Following a noon meal, we assembled in the tennis court outside.
The atmosphere was extremely noisy, and a tempo built. A captain
showed up and read names from a roster.
    "As I call your names, answer 'here' and board the bus."
    Nine guys made it quite clear they were not returning. To be ex-
pected, the end of leave was a problem for many. Who would want
to return to Korea other than those who felt the strong call of duty?
For some who witnessed so much death, that wasn't enough. In fact,
they'd had enough.
    "We are not going back! We are not going back!" they protested.
    The captain ignored their chant and continued roll call.
    "No!" yelled one disgruntled soldier. I lie. His verbal response
was far more emphatic than what I wish to express in black and
white. He gripped his rifle by the front sight and hurled it over
the high tennis court fence and onto the street where trolley cars
ran back and forth. Eight additional rifles followed, flying like
discuses I imagined in the ancient Greek Olympics.
    Baker and I and several others volunteered and retrieved the ri-

fles from the street. When we returned, the MPs were already on the scene. A lieutenant colonel read a few select Articles of War from the Uniform Code of Military Justice Manual. One by one, the men boarded the bus. The bus left, all quiet aboard, and headed to Itami Air Base where we took the C-119 return flight to Korea. It was a sad day.

After the plane landed, we walked to a large tent that served as a holding area and waited for vehicles from our respective units. We rode from there with Sergeant Magaldi in a three quarter. Magaldi, our mess sergeant from Biloxi, Mississippi, was one of the fellows who ordered whiskey.

In ready expectation, he brought a large can of grapefruit juice to make mixed drinks. While we were in Japan, our unit had relocated twenty miles from K-6 Airfield. Every two or three miles along the way, we stopped to make a couple more drinks. At one point, Baker halted an eight-truck Aussie convoy and insisted each driver have a drink. I rarely drank much, but that afternoon I imbibed enough to float a good-sized raft. I don't even recall coming into the new campsite. Equally unremarkable is that when I awoke next morning, my clothes were still on, and my head felt like a giant wad of chewing gum.

A month earlier, we were assigned a new 1st sergeant. 1st Sergeants are the most senior NCOs in a rifle company. These men usually have vast field experience and an over-abundance of barracks wizardry. They are strict disciplinarians, and it is their utmost purpose in life to maintain order amongst the troops. Just to let you know how much I didn't like this southern rebel, on a scale of one to ten, I'd have given him a minus three and then only out of charity. We never hit if off. He constantly pushed my button for reasons I don't recall.

Anger is one letter short of danger. I have a blurred memory of inserting a thirty-round clip in my carbine when we left K-6 Airfield. Provoked in my drunken stupor and spoiling for a fight, my only excuse since I don't know what else could have raised my hackles to such a height, I chased the new first sarge into the drink with my ready rifle.

Proof of the pudding was in the photographs Sergeant Bunter snapped during this notorious act. When I saw them a month later, the poor guy was pictured standing fully clothed in waist-deep, Ides of March H2O, fifty feet from shore. I, the guile-ridden Sergeant Ziggy, had put him there. So they said. Fortunately, no shots were fired.

Part of you is surprised that this didn't result in some sort of punishment. It could have. Perhaps a special courts martial or, at minimum, a three hundred dollar fine. But the incident was squashed by my CO who wouldn't have wanted this to reach Division Headquarters. Men got drunk and did foolish things. It was a reality of war. I've heard of other stories with no harm done that were glossed over on the "battlefield." It reveals the general fatigue of war. Everyone has his limit, and this was mine. I wanted at least one snap of this award-winning performance. Bunter kept promising one before I'd go home, but when that happy day arrived, the picture was forgotten.

The next day was also eventful. Because of a hideous hangover, I wasn't as alert as I normally would have been. I took a convoy out and crossed a pontoon bridge, not noticing the sign that read, "No more than two trucks at a time." We darn near swamped the bridge as well as ourselves with all six trucks at once. A colonel on site gave me royal H, zinging out cuss words like targeted pumpkin ball shots, and his hard-lipped mouth snapped shut like a trap when he finished. He looked a wiry sort with a tanned leather-lined face partly covered by a sparse, spiky growth of grayish beard. His light blue eyes were tired and red-rimmed in appearance. No doubt weary from long days of fighting the enemy while constructing the bridge I was about to destroy. But I was quick on my feet and told him I thought the third truck would wait until the first two of us had crossed. Hmmm.

The Supreme Sacrifice

It is noble to die protecting your own freedom,
But even more noble dying to protect the freedom of others.
- Mark Twain

Two days following our return from Japan, the 3rd Battalion was held in reserve while the 1st and 2nd Battalions moved back on line. Our task was tiring and endless, two men to each truck twenty-four/seven. Sleep was sporadic (dangerous, too, when you risked a swinging fist if you awakened someone). Or it was absent since it's darn hard to nod off while bumping down a winding Korean dirt road. But I tried.

On one occasion, I almost lost my life. Jack Lengel, a fair tousle-headed guy my age from one of the Carolinas, drove while I took my turn dozing. I was zipped fully clothed inside an arctic bag to keep warm. As was the case this stupid day, neither doors nor safety straps were in place in order to facilitate an easy exit in the event of an emergency. While I was off somewhere in la-la land, Lengel made a rapid swerve to the left that sent me in a swift trajectory to outer space. I landed with a severe jolt on the frozen ground, but was none the worse off when he collected a totally revived mummy out of the hole he tried to avoid.

After several days on this new assignment, Baker and I were pulled off and sent to Hoengsong twenty-five miles away, engulfed by a swirling snowstorm. Baker sat behind the wheel, battling punishing winds. A bitterly cold air was thick with spiraling snowflakes that transformed into crystals of ice in the sweep of the windshield wipers. Every couple of miles, we'd stop, and I'd get out and scrape away the freezing crust.

"The weather was stormy and blizzardy like this when I was born," I said after my umpteenth trip outside the cab.

"My, you have an extraordinary memory!" said Baker.

"I heard it so often I guess I feel like I was there." *Come to think of it, I was.* "We didn't have a phone and, the roads being closed, Pop hitched the team to the old sleigh and drove to the Berne store. He called Doc Potty in Hamburg. Then, he back-tracked to Clouser's Gas Station near Shoemakersville to pick him up because the road was blown shut to the farm."

"By the looks of things, everything came out okay."

"Yeah, one dressed chicken and two smoked hams later. You, what about you?"

"Yeah, I was born, too. What's up with that?" Baker reached in his pocket for a pack of cigarettes. He extracted one, lit it, and deposited the match in the ashtray.

"All right, silly. Tell me what you know," I said.

"This could take awhile."

"Well, just hit the high points then."

"I mean this could take awhile to think about it."

"Well, then just give me the low points that you know of."

"I know nothing," he said and then seemed to go inside himself for a moment or two. "I told you before that Pop was the town drunk. I'm sure he went out and laid a good one on when he knew I was coming along. My grand entrance into this world was probably no more ceremony than when I bite the dust."

We both fell silent.

Baker vigorously wiped at the freezing fog accumulating on the inside of the windshield with the back of his gloved hand. Our truck had no defroster, but the random smoke inside the closed cab helped a little.

"At least Mom was there," he said, breaking the silence. "If I make it through this @#$% war, I'm gonna look her up and find out the details for you, Bud."

We transported supplies to an artillery battery supported by an infantry company for the Republic of Korea's 8th Division. When we arrived, they had just finished preparations for the night when the Chinese communist forces attacked. Luck was with us. The allied forces repulsed the assault with great expediency and ease.

I remember the next morning feeling fairly comfortable with this new assignment and the units we serviced. But the Chinese, as well as the Koreans, were like winter storms. You were certain they'd come but never quite sure from where or when. When they blew in, they sometimes quit before getting into the heat of things, leaving the impression they no longer wished to fight or had no resources to carry out a sustained attack. More often than not, these touch and go skirmishes were considered probing actions only. Was this the case that first night? No one knew.

The following night, while we made a run for ammo, the CCF stormed again and within the same hour counter-attacked. Similar to a horse in the midst of danger, the ROK broke and ran, and the Chinese swarmed all over our artillerymen like hornets from a disturbed nest. Six P51s and the 3rd Battalion were brought out of reserve during the early daylight hours to stabilize the situation. Unfortunately, much too late. May I interject that in civilian accidents one is either injured or dies. In war, one is wounded or slaughtered. It is what it is. Here at Hoengsong, it was slaughter, with only two men surviving. One was a private who had helped load and unload fuel during this traumatic episode. This is his story:

"The chinks hit us about 0200. There was shooting all over the place. They sent me and a dozen other riflemen to help secure the guns. We helped to get them hooked to trucks and prevent their capture, but only three of us came back. About 0300, the artillery convoy started moving out of the area to escape the Chinese, but we soon ran into another ambush. The chinks hit the driver of the first vehicle, and that stopped the convoy. The roadway was blocked, so no one could pass. We tried to push the truck into a ditch, so we could pass on this narrow road, but the gooks were on top of us. Everybody got rattled. As soon as someone fell, they picked up the fallen comrade's weapon. Somebody hollered, 'There's one!' and we fired into the darkness. Sometimes, it was only a tree we fired at. The whole world seemed to explode at my feet."

The most concentrated loss of American lives during the entire war happened at Hoengsong. An overwhelming count of five hundred and thirty men! Five hundred and thirty widows or mothers were presented a folded flag!

"I give you this flag on behalf of a grateful nation…." (See Addemdum.)

Because the carnage was of such high magnitude, we moved the Graves Registration people directly to the site for identification and removal of bodies, now swollen mounds of white from more snow that fell through the early morning hours. The dead were everywhere. Some lay in piles. Some lay alone. Some dismembered. Some nearly cut in half. One, I remember, looked like he was peacefully snoozing, but when I turned him around the skin on his face stayed stuck in the ice of his own blood that came from a dime-sized penetration in the center of his forehead. Another kneeled and was frozen in prayer.

We worked in teams. Identifying, tagging, loading. When you work in the vicinity of so much death, a strange aura of quiet spreads over the area. Words are spoken in whispers. No joking. No blasphemy. Never a curse word is uttered. No unnecessary conversation exists. What does is brief and to the point. This atmosphere prevails long after the chore is ended.

It's hard to explain, but there is complete and total respect and affection for these fallen comrades who made the supreme sacrifice. As the chaplain quoted earlier from the Good Book, greater love has no man than he who lays down his life for another. More than once, I witnessed men losing self-restraint, dropping to the ground, bodies wracked with uncontrollable sobs, grieving those who had lain down their lives for them. For their families, their country.

I never understood much about dying. Sure, I lost grandparents and endearing pets. But while the ravage of war continued its untimely toll, awareness of my own mortality surfaced. Like the secular song made popular by Peggy Lee, I wondered, "Is that all there is?" What had I contributed? Did I make a difference? Or was Sergeant Zweizig merely a number who always drew the end of the line? At a moment's notice, was I ready to meet my Maker when all the stops were pulled? Was going to heaven after death a given as most people thought? Or would I simply sleep until the Lord returned like Granny Zweizig believed? But then what? Someday, I promised myself, I'd check these things out. No, not through experience, of course not, but by searching the Holy Scriptures.

The dictionary is the only place where success comes before work. Both Baker and I were as eager to push forward as a dog team is to pull a sled. On March 10, we were summoned to the company CP tent and informed we'd receive an attaboy medal, a bronze star for the offensive that began January 25 and ended February 15. A Meritorious Service Award made all those endless, sleepless days and nights trucking back and forth, often through enemy fire, worth it. *Good job!*

The following day, overcast and raw, it started snowing lightly, an onion snow we called it back home. We stood in a muddy flat below a Korean hillside graveyard of earthen burial mounds as none other than Brigadier General Michael Michaelis landed in a chopper. Michaelis was Acting 25th Infantry Division Commander at the time after the removal of Major General William B. Kean by the new 8th Army Commander, General Ridgway. His presentation took less than seven minutes, but I hold a life-long remembrance.

The next day, Baker and I traveled to Taegu with six trucks and picked up artillery ammo for the 25th Division Artillery's rear area. Upon return, an officer of this same artillery outfit halted our convoy near the 27th Regiment sector.

"Do you gentlemen have any white phosphorous?" White phosphorus was useful for many things, like sending white smoke screens to block areas from view and, for the opposite, marking targets. It was especially useful to signal low flying air support. Illumination rounds fired at night lit a diameter of one hundred yards with high-intensity light for twenty seconds. White phosphorous was also effective to start a burn. The Chinese feared WP because it burned at a phenomenally high temperature (2,000 Deg. F.), eating through metal or anything in its way. Miniscule bits tortured through flesh and uniforms without a moment's hesitation. (See Addendum.)

"We do," was my response.

"Good! We can sure use you. Pull over best you can!"

Below the road and a couple hundred yards in was a tiny settlement, maybe fifteen houses. The whole place was about a short city block long with a courtyard in the middle across from a solid, sturdy building that stood well above the rest. The other dwellings at quick glance were old and weather-beaten. Weeds trimmed the exterior. The village, surrounded by untilled bottomland and pinched between two sloping hills, connected to the outside world by a wooden bridge where a wide stream flowed beneath. A thin fog followed overhead.

Through earlier scouting, the infantry encountered an undetermined number of Chinese in hiding. Two squads had already moved toward each ridge when Baker and I came on the scene.

The artillerymen set up a 105mm howitzer on the roadway edge as we scrambled to unload boxes of white phosphorous. As soon as the infantrymen were in position, the firing began.

The ammo had found its target. I noticed a brilliant white spot of fire and watched, fascinated, while it burgeoned into a spreading sheet of red flame. Soon, flames licked the sky like from Uncle Herbert's burning barn four years before. The air filled with soot, and splintered shreds of rice straw seared by heat sailed heavenward from the taller building's thatched roof as if on a kite Koreans write their sins on. After about six rounds, it appeared no one was in the village. But as the fire intensified, screams and the horrific sound effects of popping skulls and stomachs reached my ears.

Soon, Chinese soldiers came running outdoors, fully ablaze. I saw raised hands from my position, but the Hoengsong blood bath was still so fresh in our battle-hardened minds that, within seconds, anyone who appeared in the open was dead meat. The enemy had no mercy. Nor would we. This was war! At the finish, dirty black smoke hung over the valley, and all that remained below was a blackened, burned-out replica of a village, now reduced to a pile of rubble, and the sickening, stinking charred remains of forty one-time enemy warriors.

The above action may seem shocking when you consider the

Chinese had surrendered. But these types of atrocities happen in every war. The enemy on both sides of the line is often killed because fighting personnel cannot be taken off the front to guard or escort prisoners-of-war to the rear. Or for whatever other reason, like in the case above. Only the idealist would make an issue of it, which, of course, they spare no occasion to do. It is a dirty heinous business, this business of war, and that's just the irrationality of it.

Minutes before, this looked like an ordinary sleepy hamlet amongst Korea's poor agricultural countryside. Where were the civilians while the burning and shooting was going on? There were none. We came across few civilians no matter where we went. People were either on the move to keep outside battle zones or holed up in some refugee camp supported by American taxpayers. Houses were vacated. Whole towns were vacated, and fields lay dormant.

Under normal circumstance, the farmer in baggy white pajama-type trousers, shirt, and vest tilled his two-acre plot by hand or with oxen, preparing an upcoming rice crop. Older children in the household cared for the communal goats, pigs, rabbits, and chickens while school-age youngsters played outside the sturdy one-room schoolhouse, having a gleeful romp on the jump board at recess. Little boys, too young to work the paddies with parents and too young for school, flew kites to keep the birds out of the rice field. From an assortment of preservation jars, mother gathered fixings for the household meal of dried chili, soybean paste, rice, or mushrooms. Or kimchee, Korea's national dish, a pungent aged cabbage concoction that smells multitudes worse than German sauerkraut.

Cooking, even in winter, was often done at a stove in the village center by the water well. For good reason. Their shacks were generally made from rough-hewn boards of native birch or pine, dried out from hot Korean summers, and topped with straw-thatched roofs, especially vulnerable to fire. Like the village we just burnt.

The village center also functioned for harvesting rice. They lay a huge homespun cloth on the ground, spread bundles of rice and beat the heck out of it to collect the grain. The straw itself had multiple use.

Something else that took place in a communal setting, not unlike rural Japan, was the common privy. A Korean farmer hauled buckets of human waste with the aid of a *ji-gae*, a frame for trans-porting goods shaped like the letter A (the type refugees carried on their backs I referred to earlier), and dumped in fields for fertilizer.

Kids fretted about surly spirits said to dwell in the primitive out-house. Legend said to prevent a child from falling through a hole into the filth below, steamed rice cakes should be placed in the vicin-ity to appease traditional gods. Ill-tempered ghosts were also be-lieved to inhabit toilets. Some people cleared their throats before entering to give spirits time for flight.

Far-fetched? I venture to say most cultures, including yours and mine, hold on to some degree old world traditions regarding spooks and such things that go bump in the night. Even Chris-tians. We Pennsylvania Germans, steeped in superstition from our beginnings, had a whole host of remedies for warding off evil spirits or accommodating good ones. In the thirties and forties, while I was growing up, negative folklore was very real in our rural community. But because of a world made small through technology, younger generations know little or nothing of such omens today.

The Korean people's belief system has changed down through the centuries. They've gone from the indigenous Shamanism (animistic nature worship where the Creation is worshipped rather than the Creator, somewhat similar to the aboriginal Native Americans, but don't quote me) to mostly Confucianism and Buddhism. And lastly, but fortunately not least, post-war Christianity. Best guess is in a country so timeless, so rooted in tradition, today's Korea contains a nebulous blend of all of the above, letting continued spiritualistic influence wide open. In the final analysis, could free-floating spirits from beyond the grave still be very much alive?

It was late afternoon now, the sun sinking behind the barren Korean hills by the time Baker and I approached headquarters. The mess tent was our first stop. We sat around folding tables and drank coffee, shooting the breeze, in no particular rush to service vehicles. Sergeant Bunter entered. He looked tired. I suppose we all did.

"Two trucks are broken down," he said to me. "We need one of yours to go along to the railway depot for gasoline." By now it was dark, and the driver was expected to return from Osan midnight or thereabouts. Baker volunteered. One of the other drivers seated said he'd go as well.

"That's okay, I can handle it," Baker said and left.

In the meantime, we serviced and refueled the rest of our trucks for the next day. They were always made ready for immediate use, first echelon maintenance being standard procedure, and always backed into space so they were facing forward and prepared for a quick escape under fire. Sergeant Washko came by at 2330 and said he was going to the mess tent for coffee. I tagged along.

Wash was a well-built young man in his mid to late twenties with a smooth round face and greenish brown eyes. He was third generation Polack. His folks immigrated through Ellis Island around the turn of the century and settled in Pennsylvania's Schuylkill County north of Berks. The family lived in a company row house outside the city of Pottsville and, like his father and his father before him, Wash worked in the anthracite coal mines. He was a breaker boy, earning little more than his father did starting as a breaker boy years earlier at two cents an hour. When World War II broke out, similar to Baker, Wash lied about his age and joined the Army. Following the war, similar to Bunter, he re-enlisted to escape a shotgun marriage gone sour.

We sat and talked until midnight when Bunter's trucks rolled in and dispersed for the evening. The trucks were not unloaded since they'd be moved early morning to another location. As usual after a run, everyone came into the mess tent for coffee.

I watched for Baker. I lit a cigarette then crushed it out impatiently.

"Where's Baker?" I asked, lighting up again and checking my wristwatch for the umpteenth time.

One of the drivers was drawing a cup of coffee. He was wearing a bandage on his neck where he'd been grazed by a bullet a week ago and then circulated back into the combat pool. He stopped and his eyes narrowed and focused on a spot above my left shoulder.

"Why, I don't know," he said. "He was right behind me."

I scanned the group.

"Did anyone see him pull into our area?" I sensed a terrible feeling in the pit of my stomach that seeped its way through, just as a stain spreads across cloth. Hurried glances the drivers swapped told me more than I needed to know. My buddy was in trouble. Simultaneously snuffing out my last smoke and swallowing the rest of my coffee in one gulp, I ran for the closest vehicle—the old man's jeep. Bunter jumped in and folded his length beside me. We headed toward Osan, each with our own private thoughts.

"Was Baker the last truck in your convoy?" I said, breaking the silence after a jarring five miles down the MSR.

"Yeah, he was."

We traveled several more miles.

Neither of us spoke.

After a while, Earl said,

"He can't be back this far. I'm sure I saw him on the road beyond this point."

"You sure?" I asked, after I trusted myself to speak.

"Positive."

I did a rapid one eighty and headed back the way we came.

"Please be okay! Please be okay!" I pleaded, to whom I'm not quite sure. I willed my words to find Baker alive and well, as much as I willed to believe it myself.

A mile later, we spotted light off to the side of the road. We stopped, kept the jeep lights on, and recognized Baker's truck down a deep ditch. I grabbed the flashlight clipped to the dash and leaped down the bank.

What I saw curdled my blood. There were massive holes and scrapes on the hood where bullets had hit. The guitar Baker sometimes kept on the passenger side of the cab was lodged in the shattered windshield. The neck was broken, and the strings fanned out like antennae searching for a live signal. Inside, blood was splashed all over the ripped seat. There was no visible sign of Baker.

Apparently, when the truck hit bottom, the weight of the twenty two drums fell forward. We muscled several barrels out of the way and found a warm flexible body pinched between a twisted steering column and the dash.

It was not Baker after all. This was just a lifeless corpse that bore no resemblance to the dear friend I knew so well. I remember the helmet was gone, and the body's head fell forward onto the chest, and the right arm dangled down the side when I carried the body up the bank and laid it on the flat cold ground. The left arm seemed to be held in place only by the torn jacket sleeve.

Bunter focused the light. It was like a bomb had exploded. The forehead was open and the skull completely smashed, and the neck was barely connected to what was left of the head by a mass of bloody, splintery tissue. The left eye stared at me vacantly, and the right eye, ear, cheek and cheekbone were nearly gone. Baker could not be dead, but this thing could not be alive. I looked away and looked back. It was Baker, and he was dead.

Bunter got unit headquarters on the radio at once. Fifteen minutes and fifteen cigarettes later, a jeep arrived with a litter. Both Baker and I experienced much of this in the past, losing buddies we trained with, laughed with, shared foxholes with in the face of the enemy, then trucking them away at life's end. Yet nothing, nothing prepared me for this moment. An event impossible for him to remember. A scene impossible for me to forget.

Bunter took the wheel and followed the litter. No moon or stars that night, the leaden sky wept with me every inch of the way to Osan. I heard of body parts amputated and phantom pain felt long after they're gone. That's how it was with me then. That's how it's still with me now.

Diagnosis confirmed that enemy fire did not kill Baker. It was the crushing blow of the gas drums.

"He died instantly and never knew what happened," said the sergeant who had met us.

I hoped so, but who would know about those final moments?

"You all right, Zig?" Earl's whisper had penetrated my muffled senses, but his words strangled any response, no matter how hard I tried to force it out. We sat in the side room of the Graves Registration office. I propped an elbow on the table and rested my forehead in my hand.

"Why? Why? Why him?" I repeated over and over as I burned cigarette after cigarette. "What did he do to deserve this? He was such a good person, so much fun, so talented, and had so much zest for life." A memory flashed by, crisp and clear, of Baker strumming his guitar and teaching the Japanese girls back in Osaka to sing "Red River Valley."

"Now he's gone, and he wasn't even nineteen. Why...?" I let my words trail away as they choked dead in my throat.

Earl said nothing. He knew I didn't expect an answer. At some point, he stood up and patted me on the shoulder.

"I understand," he said in a thick voice, turning his head to conceal his emotions. He left the room.

Understand? How could he? How could anyone know the pain of relinquishing that which bound Baker and me together—the essence of life itself. Remembering him was like writing a song that would never be sung or a poem never read.

"WHEN SOMEONE IS IN YOUR LIFE FOR A REASON... It is usually to meet a need you have expressed. They have come to assist you through difficulty, to provide guidance and support, to aid you physically or emotionally, or spiritually. They may seem like a godsend, and they are! They are there for the reason you need them to be. Then, without any wrong-doing on your part, or at an inconvenient time, this person will say or do something to bring the relationship to an end. Sometimes they act up and force you to take a stand. Sometimes they walk away. Sometimes they die. What we must realize is that our need has been met, our desire fulfilled, their work is done. The prayer you sent up has been answered. And now it is time to move on." (Source Unknown)

Bunter returned with two cups of coffee. Damp eyes full of compassion met mine. He leaned against the wall, let out a heavy sigh, and took a swig from his cup.

"Pal," he began, his lips drawn as if framing a difficult question, but no sound came. Then he shook his head and walked away, not returning until sometime later. "Let's head back," he said this time, softly.

No! I was not going to leave the area where Baker's body remained so close. I couldn't leave. The world was too big out there without him. Yet I did. I had to. Now more than ever, there was a war to fight.

The date was March 12, 1951.

PART III

The Good News

I have fought the good fight,
I have finished the race....
　　　　　- I Timothy 4:7

The third week in March, our unit crossed the Han River as part of Operation Ripper. Operation Ripper would drive a wedge through the central portion of Korea toward Chunchon, separating Chinese in the west from Koreans in the east. Chunchon is approximately twelve miles south of the 38th Parallel. We established our command post halfway between there and Seoul. For the third time since the start of the war, Seoul was retaken. The capital was so battered by now and so slight in population its possession was mainly symbolic. We remained in the western sector for the remainder of my Korean tour.

Mid-April, rumblings of MacArthur's relief spread like wildfire in dry brush. Of course, no one fully believed until copies of a week-old *Stars and Stripes* floating through the company bannered the breaking news in bold black type:

COMMANDER IN CHIEF FIRES SUPREME COMMANDER IN CHARGE OF UNITED FORCES IN KOREA

It didn't make much difference one way or the other. Most didn't like him anyway. "He should go home in a box rather than return to a hero's welcome," was popular opinion.

The last time I saw MacArthur was in the early days of March 1951. He appeared exhausted, depressed, and low as a rug, a beaten man slumped in the front seat of his jeep. Times had turned sour for the five-star general. But it hadn't always been so. From the time North Korea's communist troops crossed the 38th Parallel in June of '50, he was prominently in command, flexing verbal muscle with statements like: "I can beat the North Koreans with my hands tied behind my back!"

Except for a pompous attitude, "I'll do it my way, thank you," for the most part General MacArthur was highly regarded by Washington. He stopped the communist advance near the port of Pusan despite heavy odds and, with the arrival of fresh U.N. units, planned a strategic offensive. This would be a massive amphibious landing at Incheon, a port lying directly west of Seoul. At first, subordinates and other high military officials raised doubt on the general's risky plan. Still, his persuasive skills won out. On September 15, 1950, U.S. Marine and Army units sailed north on the Yellow Sea and landed at Incheon. There, he successfully accomplished the military element of surprise by coming in behind enemy lines. At the same time, U.N. troops to the south broke out of the Pusan Perimeter and traveled north to join the amphibian forces. They all but destroyed the North Korean army during the weeks that followed.

Yet this successful operation wasn't enough for MacArthur. After crossing the 38th Parallel, he kept going and going until he neared the Chinese border. Now, the people in Washington were getting excited and feared an incident with Red China. They even told MacArthur he could bomb only half the bridge, the half on the North Korean side of the Yalu River. In October, Truman personally traveled to Wake Island to confer with the general, instructing that in no uncertain terms was he to cross the border.

There's a fly in the ointment. China enters on her own accord.

Intervention of the Chinese communists in late November forced U.N. troops to withdraw to south of the demarcation line. A new war was taking shape.

MacArthur got gutsy and returned to the drawing board. In direct conflict with President Truman's policy that the U.N. stay out of China, he urged the bombing of communist bases in Manchuria, a blockade of the Chinese coast, and employment of Chinese nationalist troops. This opposing view was the general's demise.

For the man who originally dismissed the June 1950 invasion as a mere border incident, the Korean War would become the undoing of a long celebrated military career. His replacement was General Ridgeway who took over on April 12, 1951.

The new Far East commander earned everyone's respect. When fighting took place, he was somewhere close by, not sitting comfortably back in Tokyo talking to the press.

On or about the 1st of May, we received a directive from headquarters that would change my life forever. Servicemen with the 25th Infantry Division since its arrival in Korea, July 4, 1950, and who had completed more than thirty-six months in the Far East theatre would rotate back to the States. First, unit strength had to be maintained and replacements made before anyone could leave, a discriminate determination based on power overall.

Things happened quickly! Forty-eight hours later, a truck unloaded sixteen unfortunate replacements. One had to be mine since in our unit only four GIs surpassed me in service time. The following day, an official list posted fourteen names. Mine was included. Immediately the sergeant in charge ordered us to prepare to pull out. We'd depart the next day. In no time at all, I'd be headed in the same direction as the Canada goose in spring—HOME!

Our group reported to Ascome City for shipment back to Japan and on to the States. We spent the evening gathering personal things, few as they were, and bidding farewell to friends, many with whom we rubbed shoulders for three years running. Serving in Korea together under major unpleasant conditions and fighting to protect one another forged a strong bond that stands to this day.

You never saw such a happy bunch of guys. Even those not on the list to ship out were elated, knowing their turn was mere weeks away.

In the morning, the lucky fourteen boarded a two and a half ton truck for Ascome City some forty-five miles distant. We spent two days there awaiting word to move to Incheon Harbor. As night settled in on the second day, we expected to be there yet another. At approximately 2200 hours, a sergeant entered our temporary quarters, surely with the dreaded news of a change in military orders, and we'd be moved back on line. Fortunately, this was not the case.

"Okay! Move it! Chop, chop!" ordered the sergeant.

Some of the guys had already sacked in. Others wrote letters or were reading comic books and dog-eared pocket novels for the umpteenth time. Several, like me, played poker to kill time. A hearts full house was a work-in-progress when I threw in my hand, grabbed my gear, and loaded on a truck a half block down. We were on our way to Incheon.

I didn't realize so many men from so many different units would join us. They kept arriving and arriving and arriving I wondered if anyone stayed behind to fight the war. On the dock itself were at least four hundred.

The waters were much too shallow for a large ship to enter port. Hence, we were transported via LCMs from the dock to the USS Thomas Jefferson, anchored out in the bay. I was in the last boat to ride to the waiting destroyer, but then what else is new. Mesh rope hung over the side as our small craft pulled underneath. Like the other home leave candidates, I scrambled up the wiggly ladder with a weighted-down duffel bag and a rifle hanging from my shoulders, fully conscious one miscalculated step would send me into the murky yellow muck aptly named the Yellow Sea. The experience was a subtle reminder for swimming lessons when I got home. At 0130, they raised the anchor.

It was sleep as the sleepy may sleep come time to hit the roost. No bunks. Considering crowded conditions, even standing in place was an option. Sure, fine if you're a horse. They have an internal locking mechanism that allows REM without lying down. Still, no one complained. We were used to roughing it and didn't expect Conrad Hilton accommodation. Besides, we were going home. Little else mattered.

The deck was wall-to-wall men and bags. As I remember it, one had to leapfrog over another to get to the coffee and donut table Navy cooks had set up after sunrise. This was our only food before pulling into Sasebo Harbor on Japan's island of Kyushu the afternoon of that same day.

When we arrived, things settled down to a dull roar as we lined up to disembark. The sailors were glad to see us leave since we created much congestion and noise from a sugar hype caused by nothing but Twinkies coursing through our veins.

Several hundred more GIs waited at the docks when we arrived. Our ticket home, the Joe P. Martinez, a small victory ship, was parked nearby. We spent only one night, thank goodness, in a large dockside warehouse. What if any blankets one had in his personal possession was the only protection against the nippy air. Even though it was May and even though we were indoors, an unseasonable cold snap made for mighty uncomfortable sleeping. I don't know about you, but to me it's always colder inside an unheated building because of a mindset that it should be warmer, and it's not.

Next morning, we had coffee and hot biscuits. If things were to continue this way, I'd find myself down a couple of more sizes and thin as a zipper. After our excuse for breakfast, they held a debriefing session. My thinning hair, though relatively not bad considering my age, still stands straight out today when I recall with contempt a certain lieutenant colonel. The officer stiffened up with his own importance while he glowered over a warehouse full of frozen servicemen from a platform of wooden crates.

"Now don't go home and tell the people how rough you had it in Korea," he shouted through a bullhorn. "I can tell you, the veterans of World War II saw much more and endured far more than you have ever in Korea."

We hissed and boo'ed the villain and would have thrown rotten tomatoes, but they were out of season. One guy's voice rose clearly above the protests.

"I served in the infantry in both World War II and Korea," he shouted. "You have not earned the right to make such a statement! Maybe you should get out of Japan and spend some time in Korea!"

A standing ovation followed, my hands hurting madly from the pounding they got. So ended the debrief.

We went through a complete shakedown before boarding ship. All items were dumped on tables to be inspected. It was amazing how many guys attempted smuggling out weapons. Yours Truly was not one of them, by the way. I hadn't even thought about it, so I can't say whether I would have tried or not. Most likely not. Why, that would be stealing. I wasn't brought up that way. Though I'm wondering if you are wondering if I didn't steal a truck from the MPs. The truck I cleverly removed from under their stuckup noses was nothing more than taking from Peter to give to Paul. Weapons stolen from the U.S. Government for personal use is a different matter entirely, if I'm allowed to say so.

There were carbines, American forty-fives, Russian burps, and, remarkably, Thompson submachine guns. Weapons had been disassembled and their parts hidden deep inside duffel bags similar to when we went boar hunting back in the Japanese hills. Big difference, however. Back then, we had simply borrowed the rifles for a few days and returned them to the base intact.

There was one smuggling success story aboard ship I heard of afterward. Servicemen were permitted musical instruments. They were great morale boosters amongst the troops, just like Baker with his guitar. Anyway, this guy had an accordion and removed the wooden panel behind the keyboard. He stored a pistol inside, replaced the panel, and continued to play the accordion flawlessly.

As usual, we boarded ship in alphabetically-ordered chaos. As usual, I was the last man on the roster. Number 2019. On May 21, 1951, our ship headed out to sea. Uncle Sam's nephew was coming home! (See Addendum.)

PHOTOGRAPHS

Sergeant Walter M. Zweizig in Korea

Left: Zweizig (right) and buddy during Korean tour
Right: Private Zweizig following basic training at Fort Dix

Sergeant Walter M. Zweizig

Zweizig (center) was the first Berks Countian to be awarded
the Pennsylvania Commendation Medal.

In their cold weather gear, soldiers of the 25th Infantry Division watch phosphorus shells hit enemy held areas in February 1951.
US Army Photo.

Infantrymen of the 25th Division shield themselves behind rocks from exploding mortar shells during action in Central Korea. US Army Photo.

A grief-stricken American Infantryman whose buddy was just killed in action in defense of the Pusan Perimiter (August 1950) is comforted by another as a corpsman in the background fills out a casualty tag.
US Army Photo.

Our nation honors her sons and daughters who answered the call to defend a country they never knew and a people they never met.
Korean War Memorial.

31

Journey Home Begins

Yesterday is history; tomorrow is a mystery.
Today is a gift from God; will we use it wisely?
- WBYN, 2008

Our sleeping quarters were low in the belly of the overcrowded victory ship, the Joe P. Martinez. Berths were made of canvas, held taut by steel rods and stacked five high, eighteen inches apart. There was barely enough room between mattresses to turn over. The idea for modern-day time-sharing spawned from the following arrangement. Two men were assigned the same bunk. It was mine between midnight and twelve noon. Upon leaving, I took along my single sheet and, sometime during the wake period, dropped by the supply room for a clean one. The guy I shared with did the same.

Usually after 0200, when most shifts were in place, a strange quiet settled over the sleep area. The ship's constant creaking and surging and steady roll through the water was relaxing and lulled you toward sleep. Few talked about combat experience, but most every night, a high-pitched piercing cry from a dream taking someone back on line broke the mood. Muffled sobs followed. One or two guys were instantly alongside.

"Hey, Joe. Let's take a walk for a cup of coffee or go on top for fresh air and a cigarette."

No one ever complained. We all understood. When daybreak arrived and you headed for breakfast, the previous night was never discussed.

There were two meals served daily, all day long. If you didn't mind shuffling along in line and chewing the fat with others before and aft who didn't mind shuffling along in line and chewing the fat with others before and aft, you could occupy your whole day or night just approaching, then satisfying endless nutritional wants only to begin again. Who would know? Besides, there was little else to do.

On one of these frequent trips to the galley, I ran into an old buddy I hadn't seen since basic. When first meeting Mark Wolfen, two years my senior, I figured I'd forgotten more in my eighteen years than he had ever learned. Maybe it was the way he spoke in that laid-back, south-of-the-Mason & Dixie twang that made me want to say, "Hurry up and spit it out!" Then, though I loved him dearly, I pegged him as slow. Now, more than three years later, he returned a field-commissioned captain and me only a staff sergeant in spite of a relatively good track record. We both served in the 27th Infantry Regiment, but in different companies.

Wolfie had aged. Lines cut deep into his brow when he spoke. The skin lay loose against the bone, and his bright hazel eyes were dulled like maybe they saw too much. He had grown gaunt. But, the unhurried gait most men of length have was still the same.

Mark was a thoroughly nice person, and, once we passed the language barrier, our renewed friendship enriched my voyage home. We got together on several occasions and skipped the short volleys of useless quibble like "Hi/How're you doing/I'm fine/Thanks/How are you/Fine" and went directly to sharing and comparing experiences. We told funny stories and sad ones, and occasionally ones laced with hints of the horrors we survived. His ambition was to return home after the service, marry, and settle down on the family farm. Like with so many buddies, we lost touch since then.

Everyone needs a happy place, whether an abstract state of mind to retreat to or a quiet tangible nook where one can be alone with his thoughts. To reminisce. To meditate. Lowest deck starboard was my special spot. There, on many an evening, I enjoyed the swishing of water and watched the timeless, endless waves slapping against the hull. I had no fear of water as long as I was safely on deck. Actually, I became quite fascinated with the sea, feeling safe and far less vulnerable, the water far more intriguing and mystic than during the wide daylight hours.

While seeking a pod of whales or school of dolphins or a great white shark, I tip-toed back in time. You know you're growing older when you have more memories than dreams. I was getting on in years, nearly twenty one and a half. Prior to induction into the Army, I was an innocent farm kid who saw life through a rose-colored glass. Now, things were tinted a few shades darker. I'd visited magical places and experienced unbelievable things in my journey, things that sometimes fascinated me from a distance, but, when moving in closer, I wasn't so sure I wanted to see them.

It was without doubt the most exciting time of my life—the happiest, the saddest, the most terrifying, witnessing events that would cause uncomfortable flashbacks and midnight sweats for many years to come. These experiences became an integral part of me, including those who died and those whose names I can't even recall, but whose faces linger on in memory.

Baker? I managed to keep the door closed on that one. The mind must do that, to hide things too painful to remember.

You see, war changes people. It's the excitement, fear, terror, the dirt, hunger, the heat and cold, frustration, death, pain and suffering. And the survival attitude, "It's either you or me." These things can really mess one up, the effects of war lingering long after the shooting stops. And what about the physically infirm who admit dying might have been easier than staying alive? I needed only to be reminded of that in talking with a few returning home on ship. Some without arms, some with only one leg, others in wheelchairs for assorted reasons, all a memento of the horrors they survived. They were now going home to a challenged life-style.

Sure, I reflected, fate had slapped me in the face. Yet there's no denying God's abundant mercy when my parachute opened in the nick of time. I counted the ways:

• The 8th Army Rest Hotel on the northern tip of Honshu Island, to which Baker, Howart, and I were assigned, was destroyed by an earthquake while, against orders, we blissfully hunted bear and duck on Hokkaido Island.
• The frightful boating accident on a bay near Osaka, Japan where I was rescued by my best buddy Baker.
• The rendezvous with a North Korean land mine, and the driver who took my place behind the wheel was killed.
• The time I rolled my truck in the mountains of South Korea and was saved by a machine gun mounted on top of the cab.
• The time Baker, Mellon, and I waited out a night of heavy fire underneath a truck loaded with umpteen drums of gasoline.
• The time I survived an airborne incident when my sleeping bag exited a moving truck.
• The C-82 flight out of K-6 Airfield I passed up to be with Baker had taken a fatal dunk into the sea.

As I leaned over the deck's railing and reviewed the occasions my life was spared while others perished, I got tired thinking how tired my guardian angel must be.

"Lord, I know you move in mysterious ways," I prayed, "and that some ways are more mysterious than others. But just in case you might be stumped when it comes to helping me out of any future jams, please grant me one more favor as soon as you can. Could you send in a replacement to watch over me?"

They say God has a plan for each of us. Would I, now that I'm metaphorically shrunk and shriveled, spend the remnant of my finite self to ponder His purpose for sparing my life? Was He saving me for future battles? Was it to write this run-away bestseller?

Besides the battlefield, military life was more than hurry up and wait, peeling potatoes, or spit-shining shoes. For me,

I became more worldly. I'm not sure if that is a good or a bad thing. Perhaps both. I would never again be content to spend the rest of my life on the farm, maybe not even in rural Pennsylvania. Like the boys said when they came home from WWII, "How can I go back on the farm after I've seen Paree?"

At the same time, I'd never shed the integrity of hard work or family morals and values learned at home. There is always place for those attributes, even within the world. After all, how do you know where you are going if you don't give honor to where you've been?

Of course, a minus that comes from worldliness, at least when you serve in the military, is the multitude of lewd words that creep into your everyday vocabulary. (Now that I'm older and grayer and shut my hearing off at night, I've pretty much cleaned up my act and am, for the most part, a golly/gosh/gee-whiz type of guy.) The plus in worldliness is that never again would I strain to understand my peers, thanks to Wolfie and those who speak with a southern drawl.

32

Tell it to the Chaplain

This Book will keep me from sin,
Or, sin will keep me from this Book.
                    - D. L. Moody

Things got pretty boring so when I wasn't reflecting in my quiet place, standing in chow line, or playing matchstick poker, I occasionally attended a Bible study for something to do. I did so surreptitiously so I wouldn't be pegged as a religious fanatic by others less inclined. A few such groups convened, usually facilitated by a member of the Chaplain Corps. (See Addendum.)

On my first visit, the chaplain brightened noticeably when I entered and greeted me with a wide, friendly smile. He gripped my hand with both of his and invited me to sit down. One by one, others arrived and filled in the floor space against the wall. We met in the supply room outside the laundry located on the main deck to the rear of the boat. There was constant traffic in and out of the room with men exchanging sheets, and it was small and hot. Most, like me, sat pinched between two other scholars, our backs pushed up against the gray-pimpled, however cool, cement partition. Two men at opposite ends seated in wheelchairs completed a semi-circle of fifteen.

"If this is your first time in one of these sessions, let me explain how this works," our man of cloth said, pulling up a stool.

"A few of you were in the past couple of meetings when we zeroed in on specific Bible topics. While those were meaningful, for most it seemed to generate many queries that time never permitted answers. I thought today we'd try something a little different. Perhaps a Q&A session using the Bible only for support."

Chaplain David Berman distinguished himself by a small gold cross in his shirt collar, left side. He was medium-sized and had a rather large nose, sparkling blue eyes that seemed to blaze with intelligence, and a receding hairline. Premature streaks of gray ran through a thin maze of dark wavy hair. Curiously, he looked both young and old at the same time. He was a Messianic Jew, I later learned, with a faculty for plain talk, and his guttural accent was similar to a dutchified Pennsylvanian's.

"Okay, let's open her up," he said, tipping his stool backwards. He leaned against a laundry cart that was fortunately without wheels and parked inside a tray bolted to the floor. "Something you always wanted to know, but were afraid to ask."

I'm not normally the first to speak up in these kinds of things, but I had to for Baker's sake and raised my hand. Chaplain Berman pointed toward me with his glasses, then put them on.

"Go ahead."

"Where was God when my buddy Baker was killed?" A lump swelled in my throat and tears threatened to release emotions held in check far too long. I hoped he wouldn't see the mist in my eyes.

He surprised me.

"Who would like to answer that?" he said, scanning our motley group. "Where was God when our buddy's buddy was killed?"

"He was back in the comfortable churches in the States," said one.

"Any other thoughts?"

"I can tell you where He wasn't," said the invalid at my end of the semi-circle. "He sure as H wasn't with me!" A patch over his left eye and a purple scar that puckered one corner of his mouth served to emphasize an otherwise handsome face that screwed up into an angry knot when he spoke. A dark brown Army blanket covered the young man's lap and gathered in empty folds on the steel footrest.

"What is your name?" the chaplain asked.

"Mike."

"Granted, life isn't fair, Mike. But God is, and He often puts us in a place where we need Him more." A tone of compassion showed in our facilitator's eyes and voice. He paused for a moment as if to remember something in detail. "Let me tell you a little story about a young Jew who grew up along the Polish border of Germany."

He adjusted his wire-rimmed glasses and began.

"When still a teen, he escaped with an aunt to America before the war. His parents and siblings were never heard from again. He married and, against the reluctant wishes of his new bride, joined the United States Army to help fight the Third Reich. Enlistment would give him automatic citizenship. After the war, he returned as a survivor of two injuries, minor as injuries go," he said, specifically addressing both wheelchair occupants, "and embarked upon a successful door-to-door sales career, selling Watkins household products. Profits skyrocketed, his beloved got pregnant with their second child, and life was good."

The chaplain stroked the bridge of his nose in thought, and moved on.

"Then the bottom fell out. His wife, young daughter, and unborn baby were killed in a car crash after a drunk driver hit them head on. To escape the pain, he turned to the very thing that caused his pain. The bottle. During a rare sober moment, he reviewed sympathy cards received after his family's passing and rediscovered one sent by a Gentile friend. That particular day, this young Jew, he being me, met another Jew who changed his life forever. His name was Jesus."

He paused a moment and stared into space, as if lost in the memory of it.

"It was then I realized Jesus was all I had. It was then I realized Jesus was all I needed."

With a trace of emotion, he retrieved a white card from inside a black-leathered Bible cover and cleared his throat before saying, "Allow me to share some prose with you."

I settled back and, for the first time, relaxed.

"One night a man had a dream," he read. "He dreamed he was walking along the beach with the Lord. Across the sky flashed scenes from his life. For each scene, he noticed two sets of footprints in the sand; one belonged to him and the other to the Lord.

"When the last scene of his life flashed before him, he looked back at the footprints in the sand. He noticed that many times along the path of his life there was only one set of footprints. He also noticed that it happened at the very lowest and saddest times in his life.

"This really bothered him, and he questioned the Lord about it. 'Lord, you said that once I decided to follow you, you'd walk with me all the way. But I have noticed that during the most troublesome times in my life, there is only one set of footprints. I don't understand why when I needed you most you would leave me.'"

As he read, I felt a flush coming into my face and a curious burning sensation that made the room seem even warmer. With an index finger, I wiped away the perspiration that accumulated above my lips. The words seemed to pound straight at me.

"The Lord replied, 'My precious, precious child, I love you and I would never leave you. During your times of trial and suffering, when you see only one set of footprints, it is then that I am carrying you.'"

My neighbor to the right, a fair-haired, fresh complexioned young man who wore glasses over inquisitive dark brown eyes, broke the silence that followed.

"Fine, but then why do innocent people like your family get killed in the first place?"

"Yeah, anyway. How could a God who is supposed to be so good let such bad things happen?" asked Jim, friend and three neighbors to my left.

Jim Schlappich was a lumberjack who hailed from Michigan's rural Upper Peninsula. He fought with the 29th Infantry Regiment and, fortunately, walked away from the railroad massacre with only a minor wound.

"In Korea," Jim continued, "I seen men slaughtered, their arms and legs blown off and intestines hanging out and their guts and brains splattered all over the place. Men bleeding and dying and screaming in pain! What are we doing in this da__," he caught himself and switched to, "darn war anyway?" and turned up the volume as he proceeded. "We just got out of a world war and finally had peace. Now here we are again, thanks to the almighty Harry S. Truman! Korea is not our problem! Why should we risk our lives for those darn gooks regardless of which side of the line they're on? Let them kill each other!"

You could've heard a pin drop were it not for the swishing and swashing of sheets in a huge washer. A tool of some sort must have made its way into the machine that banged against the side during each cyclical spin. I shifted position and brought my knees up to my chin and hugged them while waiting for a response.

"We have a few issues here," said the chaplain, his stool creaking as it returned to an upright position. He spoke gently but firmly, "I'll react to the first by saying that never did innocence suffer more than Christ on the cross, put there by you and me. You see, there's an adversary on the battlefield besides the Korean and Chinaman. His name is Satan. We're living on enemy territory, and no one gets out alive. We're only traveling through, my friend, and we desperately need the Lord for the journey.

"Second, we don't always know why God allows bad things to happen since His ways are not our ways. But we do know He doesn't cause the bad things. Death and suffering are a consequence of sin. Adam and Eve lived in a five-star resort with all the perks, and they messed up big time. You and I are paying for that."

"That's not fair!" said Dan, with a pained grimace.

I didn't think so either. *Why should we have to suffer for something gone wrong between God and Satan?*

"Of course, it's not," said Berman. "But, it's not the end of the story. Even though we came in on the group plan, God created each one of us individually with free choice to be who we want to be. For those who follow Him, our gracious and merciful Heavenly Father provides a loophole from this fallen world. 'I love you,' He says. 'I showed how much when I sacrificed my Son so you might have life eternal. Eye has not seen, nor ear heard, nor has entered into the heart of man the things which I have prepared for they who love Me.'"

Using God and love in the same sentence was entirely new to my ears. The preacher in my home church was heavy into fire and brimstone, constantly thrusting fear into the congregation caused by a far-away God, a harsh taskmaster who punished for the tiniest misdeed. Perhaps love was assumed, but no one ever expressed it. The only preaching I'd ever heard was formal and stereotyped, sprinkled with thee's and thou's. Our chaplain talked as though God were a personal friend, almost as though He were sitting amongst us.

"Now, Jim," spoke Berman, "getting back to your comment on our country's involvement in another war front, let me give you a little history lesson.

"Have you forgotten our Commander in Chief sought congressional support before using military force? Have you forgotten Truman's earlier decisiveness on the bomb attack in Japan? Have you forgotten that Abraham Lincoln was unpopular in both the North and the South for going to war? Have you forgotten that Churchill was unpopular with his own people when he wanted to stop the Germans from going into Poland? Have you forgotten that our nation became involved in war against the Axis powers in the name of freedom, not only to defend the Allies against an evil power, but also to protect the United States from being overtaken by evil?

"I love the famous quote from the God-fearing Sergeant York who served our country in WWI, 'We don't go to war to take lives, but to save lives.'

"World War II had its threat of world rule by crazed tyrants like Hitler, Hirohito, and Mussolini, and we need to throw Stalin into that sorry mix. Now Korea has its threat of communism with oppression and tyranny spreading from Russia and China straight down through the Korean peninsula. Washington feels it's in the best interest of the American people to stop communism in its tracks before it takes over.

"You see, that's the beauty of history. We can see today how decisions of the past have played out, and we can see the wisdom in dealing with communism at the initial stage. Anyway, that's the political answer to your question." Berman paused to let it all sink in, which was indeed much. "There's a spiritual one, too."

An audible sigh swept through the room, each of us probably wondering how God was involved in this devastating, debilitating police action.

"God looks at the big picture," Berman said. "He's blessed America with freedom and abundance. I believe it's so we can reach out and help people of other nations who are less fortunate, people who are oppressed, people who are deprived and weak and hungry. Jesus says in Matthew 25:40, '...Verily I say unto you, inasmuch as you have done it unto one of the least of these my brethren you have done it unto Me.'"

"Seems to me everyone here was oppressed when we did battle with the chinks," said Jim. "I fail to see how God figures THAT into His big picture!"

Oh, man, that was not a good thing to say, I thought, always respecting authority, especially God's. *He ought to fix that.*

He didn't, but Berman did.

"If you know your Bible, you'll know the answer," he rebuked. "In the Army, you study codes. You need to know how to take a rifle apart and reassemble it. Well, God wrote a book. It's called the Bible. It's our instruction manual for life. It tells us where the mines are in the minefield. Put on the armor of God by breaking the Book down, studying it, and then applying what you learned to your life."

His words were like dashing cold water in my face. Reading the Bible would go on my list of things to do when I got home, next to learning how to swim.

"I went to church from the time I was born and helped mom make up care packages for the needy until getting into this friggin' war," Dan said tersely. "You'd think that would count for something."

I was thinking, *I, too, went every Sunday to church growing up, but all I did was listen, and I didn't do that very well.*

"I hate to burst your bubble," Berman said, "but going to church and doing good works does not make you a Christian any more than going into a garage makes you a car."

Dan looked stunned, like a fighter hit with a solid upper cut.

"We need to take that message from the pulpit and change what we've been doing and commit ourselves to the Lord," continued the chaplain.

"For salvation?" I asked tentatively. A couple of days earlier, someone aboard ship whom the guys labeled a religious fanatic had asked if I was saved. I didn't know how to respond, so I simply looked at him, probably blinked a couple of times and then walked away, looking about to make certain no one I knew saw me talking with this creep.

"Let's be clear about this. We are not saved BY good works; rather, we're saved FOR good works. Salvation is not a given. We can never be good enough to deserve it. It's a gift from God, paid for by His Son's sacrifice on the cross."

"Then how do we get it?"

"By accepting Jesus Christ as your personal Lord and Saviour. We are saved by God's grace through faith in Him, not by our works." He paused for effect and repeated slowly, "We are saved by God's grace through faith, not works. Say it with me, I am saved by grace through faith, not works."

I did.

"Now everyone."

"I am saved by grace through faith, not works."

"Again."

"I am saved by grace through faith, not works."

Berman must have recognized the puzzled expression on our faces for he said this time,

"I don't want to get too heavy on you guys, so let's unpack all of this. You get to that commitment by prayer and studying and trusting God's Word and developing a personal relationship with His Son Jesus, that's how."

"Now, let's return to an earlier question. If you have a Bible, turn with me to Psalms in the Old Testament. If you don't have one, share with someone who does, or raise your hand."

A small red pocket version of the New Testament that Mom had sent along was back in my duffel bag, unopened to date. The chaplain had a few King James Bibles stacked on the floor by his feet that were provided to all servicemen by the military. He distributed to those without. Paul, whose right arm was in a sling, struggled with his left hand until he received assistance from a buddy.

"Psalms," reminded our custodian of the cloak after he noticed my flanked companions and me fidgeting over the Book's location. "Psalms is about half way through. If you get to Proverbs, retreat by one. If you see Job, keep marching."

"Okay, Psalm 89, Verse 1." He read, "'I will sing of the mercies of the Lord forever,' says the psalmist. 'With my mouth will I make known Your faithfulness to all generations.'" The Army chaplain leaned forward. His eyes scanned the room and settled on me. "Does that answer your earlier question?"

What? I thought you'd forgotten.

"God is always faithful," he continued without my answer. "There will never be a point in time when He is not faithful. We must learn to trust in His faithfulness. To be more direct, God was there when your buddy was killed, just like He was with you and you and you," he said, redirecting his attention to Jim, Paul, and Mike. "He was at the Holocaust. He was in Normandy. He was in Iwo Jima. In Korea. He was in exactly the same place He was when His Son was crucified."

"So what! So what if God was faithful and by my side when my body was blown to bits!" said Mike, the scar on his face turning a bright crimson.

We learned later that Mike was with the 25th Division Artillery and had been severely wounded by an exploding grenade. There was silence in the room. It seemed even the good chaplain was speechless.

"What good did that do me?" said Mike, breaking the silence. "I'll never walk again!" His words had choked to a close.

"I wouldn't be so sure," countered Berman, softly. "Don't put the God of the universe in a box. Remember, He's a God of miracles. He yearns to fix you, Mike, but he waits instead for you to come to Him for help.

"He made us from nothing, and He can put us back together from nothing. We don't know why we have to go through these trials. We don't understand them. We just need to know He is with us through it all. 'My grace is sufficient for you, for My strength is made perfect in weakness,' Jesus says in Second Corinthians 12. And St. Paul writes, 'For when I am weak, then I am strong.'"

Wow! He memorized Bible verses like we memorized poker cards.

"I guess God singled me out for an illustration then," said Mike with an edge.

"Sometime down the road," Berman said, "you'll have an ah-ha moment. Ah-ha, so that's what that was all about! You see, God always shines the brightest against the darkest backdrop. 'I will never leave you or forsake you,' He promises. Lean on Him. Ask for His help. Turn it all over to Him. Trust Him, and you'll see what He can do if you get yourself out of the way. Next question."

A guy sitting next to Paul raised his hand.

"I was in your session three days ago, and you said something then that the earth was created in only six days and that it's really only six thousand years old. Well, a million questions came to my mind since then about how it ties into with what scientists say."

"What do they say?"

"Well, they claim things can only be proven by tests and experiments."

"I think if you check it out, most scientists agree they cannot determine life beyond the atom, like in the atom bomb. Excuse me; they cannot determine origin beyond the split atom. Where did that come from? The controversial Charles Darwin claimed that all species of life evolved from a single cell and certainly not from the hand of God. But even he doubted his own theories before he died.

"If we took your DNA, which is your ID, Scott, and unraveled it, it would stretch from here to the moon. Where did your DNA come from?"

Scott shrugged.

Berman went on, adopting a less moderate tone.

"Albert Einstein said he does all his mathematical formulas to try to figure out how God did it. Isaac Newton, probably the greatest scientist of all time, was passionately devoted to God and credited science as an integral part of an Intelligent and Powerful Being. He published his findings in a three-volume book called Principia. It's the most significant contribution to the scientific community to date. If you are technically inclined, go to the Smithsonian Institute when you return to the States, and look it up."

You should have seen Scott's chin drop. His eyes widened with visions probably like mine of a document seven stories high filled with complicated formulas and mathematical calculations. He started to make a comment, but Berman beat him to the draw.

"Now, who's next?"

This chaplain of ours spoke in riddles, and it was easy to see he had answers for everything. But I thought of something that would surely baffle him like it had me. I said,

"When my buddy Baker and I were in Japan on R&R, we visited Buddhist temples. I understand the people were praying to some unseen god, but that it was not the God we Christians know."

"What is your question then?"

"How do we know which is the true God?"

My question brought a murmur of surprise from the floor. Berman, smooth fingers gently stroking his smooth chin, gazed at the wall behind me.

"Would each of you point to true north?" he said.

What? There he goes again, answering a question with a question. It was frustrating. Long before I entered the supply room, an off-shoot to the laundry, I lost my bearings as to what was where, not to mention the constant rock and roll of the floor beneath to confuse things even more. Now, this cleric asked us to point to true north. *This is nuts.*

Slowly, fifteen arms rose, and index fingers pointed in almost as many different directions. Berman surveyed the results and chuckled.

"Now that's very interesting! Surely you can't all be right, can you? There is only one true north, and, by the way, it's that way," he said, pointing toward the upper corner behind me. "We can go in many directions, but there is only one true way. Jesus says in John 14:6, 'I am the way, the truth and the life; no man comes to the Father but by Me.'"

"So why should I believe that?" someone asked.

"Faith, my lad. Faith. Let's go to Hebrews 11." He called on him to read the first and third verses.

"Now faith is the substance of things hoped for, the evidence of things not seen. Through faith, we understand that the worlds were framed by the Word of God so that things which are seen were not made of things which do appear."

So what does it all mean, I wondered.

As if he read my thoughts, Berman said,

"See that bulb?" He pointed to the light bulb hanging above and got up and reached back to the wall switch. With a blink of an eye, the light was off, then back on again.

"We have faith," he said, "that when I turn this switch that the light will either come on or go out, barring any problems with the generator, that is."

That brought a chuckle.

"It's by faith you know you get fed this evening when you go to the galley and that in the morning the sun will rise again. It's by faith and trust in God's Word that we know Jesus died on the cross that we might be saved."

"I'm not convinced about this business of being saved and heaven. Seems a bit farfetched to know we'll eventually go to a place up in the sky. I believe that when you're dead you're dead, and that's da end of it." Dan was from Brooklyn.

"Well, I'm not convinced you really believe that," said our chaplain. "Sounds to me like you pick and choose from the Bible only what you want to believe. If you don't want to be with God forever, you have an alternative, and it's not very attractive."

Our ears heard.

Our minds reacted.

Our laughs emerged.

"You'll have plenty of company, Bud," Dan's neighbor said, poking him in the ribs with the elbow.

"Okay, then," said Berman, going on. "It comes back to faith, my friend. Or if you want something tried and true, check out prophecy in the Bible. Biblical prophecy has been validated throughout history. That's enough for me to know that prophecies for our future will be fulfilled.

"Take, for example, the Second Coming. Jesus scored a spectacular victory that Good Friday two thousand years ago. After being resurrected from the grave and before ascending to Heaven, He promised He'd return for the dead and the living who accepted Him. I believe that promise with my whole heart."

Yeah, me, too, I said to myself with a conviction I never understood or even thought about before. Talking informally about God and Jesus in an informal setting was a new and refreshing experience.

"But how can we be sure Jesus was resurrected?" challenged another.

"How can we be sure George Washington lived?" challenged Berman.

"No, seriously, how do we know the man Jesus rose from the dead?"

"Seriously, how can we know the man George Washington lived?"

"I guess because people saw him?"

"Does that answer your question? Next."

"Okay, I get your point. But, now I have another one. How can we know this Book is for real? My pop told my mom the Bible's just a storybook. And, to tell you the truth, I myself have trouble believing stories about men being nine hundred years old and talking snakes and a sea parting and a man swallowed by a big fish who comes out again!"

Berman stared at his closed Bible.

"Hmmm, storybook," he repeated thoughtfully. "Your father was probably right to some extent, but it's not JUST a storybook. True, some things are allegorical, meaning they are not literal, but the events you mentioned were for real."

"That's a matter of individual interpretation!" was one student's scholarly comment.

"I hear what you're saying. But, we need to interpret scripture with scripture. Take for example…

"The Bible is full of contradictions," interrupted another.

"Name one." Berman waited. Hearing none, he moved on,

"The Bible does not contradict itself. Researching the Book and history prove that. It's actually a history of our planet. And, here's something else that's very interesting." He held up the Bible with his right hand like it was a pillar of strength. "The Old and New Testaments were written over a fifteen hundred year period. Sixty-six small books within here were authored by forty-four different people inspired by the Holy Spirit. Yet prophecies throughout are amazingly coherent."

There was silence for a moment or two while we groped for understanding. At one time or another, probably in Catechetical Class, I memorized the names of each of those sixty-six books and in the correct order. But like the chaplain said about going into the garage does not make you a car, my memorizing those books gave me absolutely no knowledge of the Bible itself or of the authors who wrote it. And it did seem a mystery how each could know what the other would say.

Really, how could that be?

"Now you might say, how can that be?" said Berman. "Well, let me tell you how. Scribes down through the ages painstakingly transcribed scripture word for word. If an error was made, they started all over again to assure the accuracy of God's Word for those of us yet to come.

"To add to that, archeologists continue to find artifacts that validate the Bible. Why just four years ago, an Arab shepherd boy found in a cave northwest of the Dead Sea documents that were two thousand years old. Among them was a complete scroll of Isaiah, exactly as we know it today. Other Hebrew manuscripts were..."

No doubt about it, our chaplain was on a roll. But again he was interrupted. I believe it was I.

"Then why do Buddhists believe one thing and American Indians believe something different and the Koreans something else? How can we all be right if there's only one book that says it all?"

"Yeah, and we Christians have hundreds of denominations!" chirped my neighbor. "How does that figure?"

"These are excellent questions. Shows you're thinking. The answer is rather simple albeit complex at the same time. It's called tradition.

"Remember, it hasn't been until recent centuries that the average person could read and, those who could, had no availability to Written Scripture. Prior to the Reformation, the Bible was kept under lock and key in both language and accessibility. And going back even further, to the early part of the fourth century if you will, the first of the Constantine's was crowned Emperor of Rome, and, thereafter, became a nominal Christian. He baptized the entire Roman army and married pagan Rome and the church, using the pagan temples for churches. That's actually how pagan customs and festive days came into play. You can see now how false doctrine mired in church bureaucracy invaded early Biblical teachings.

"Let's back up to other philosophies and belief systems you alluded to. Buddha didn't die for our sins. Krishna didn't die for us. Mohammed didn't die for us. Only Jesus Christ died on the cross for us so that we might live a life everlasting.

"Let me add, too, that in studying mythology in seminary, I was surprised to learn that most cultures and counterfeit religions trace their beginnings to a similar creation story, even motifs for death, resurrection, afterlife, and so on. It all comes back to tradition. Through eons of time, stories were handed down by word of mouth from generation to generation, and things naturally got lost in translation along the way.

"To demonstrate, I'd like to play a little game. I'll whisper in Mike's ear and, Mike, I want you to repeat in a hushed tone what you heard to the man next to you and so on and so on until we come to Paul here at the end."

Paul, whose face was partially disfigured from burns, was seated in a wheelchair next to Chaplain Berman. They appeared to know each other well.

"No cheating," Berman added, reacting to some joshing amongst his small audience, and then flashed one of his radiant smiles. "No cheating," he said again. "You may say it only once."

He stood up, and, leaning over, whispered into Mike's right ear.

The fellow on my right stood up and bent over to receive the message from Mike and then whispered to me. I cupped my hand and murmured what I heard to my neighbor on the left, and so the mysterious message circled the room.

"Paul," said Berman. "Please tell this group what your companion just told you."

Paul hesitated and looked for support from the group before speaking.

"The band played glory glory to three frogs in the works."

The room exploded with laughter.

"What I told Mike was, and, Mike, you can attest to this," said Chaplain Berman, grinning, "The Son of Man will come in the glory of God the Father and will reward each according to his works."

"Wow! Did that get screwed up!"

"My point precisely. That explains why there are many religions out there and why so many denominations and sects. Beware though, there's a little bit of truth in each that can be quite deceptive. It's only the whole truth of the inspired Word of God, this Holy Bible," he said, tapping the black leather cover respectfully, "and prayer, and a personal relationship with Jesus that will set you heaven-bound. No more, no less!" Our good chaplain checked his wristwatch. "Well, let's bring this in for a landing and close by kneeling together in prayer for those who can." He dropped to his knees, and we others shuffled about and repositioned ourselves, following suit.

"Paul, you can begin," Berman said this time.

I broke out in a cold sweat. I never prayed aloud with anyone in all of my twenty-one years. I wouldn't know what to say and much too self-conscious to try. I wanted to just push myself away from the wall and run out of the room. But pride kept me from showing how afraid I was. Instead, I joined hands and, in my own fumbling way, participated.

Home Sweet Home

...From the mountains, to the prairie,
To the oceans, white with foam,
God Bless America,
My Home Sweet Home.
                              - Irving Berlin

In the months following the attack on Pearl Harbor, the FBI maintained an active underground war against spy rings in our country and abroad. They checked leaks in the economic barrier the United States built up against the Axis powers and apprehended many alien agents who had landed on our coast by submarine. Had they not done this, had their vigilance not been managed carefully, there might have been a long series of explosions and war plants and similar disasters equal to Pearl Harbor taking place on our very own continental soil.

The reason I mention this is that the average American never realized how infiltrated the enemy was along our coasts. I myself didn't realize this until I recently checked out a map to locate Adak where, after two weeks at sea, we were expected to stop to pick up fresh water. My goodness, the Japanese, occupying the Aleutian chain of islands, home to Adak, had been literally camped on the

doorstep of the United States! Fortunately, American forces drove
them out in 1943, which I alluded to earlier, and the area became
Alaska's shortcut to Tokyo, supporting the illustration on the map of
how this irregular land mass points like a dagger toward Japan. (See
Addendum.)

We watched eagerly for signs of terra firma. Early one morning, we
saw pillars of rock protruding above the sea's surface. By noontime,
we headed down a narrow passageway with steep cliffs. The channel allowed only a one hundred yard clearance on either side of the
ship while we passed between two small islands, leaving little margin
for navigational error. Awesome as it was, it seemed a strange desolate hideaway. We finally came upon a half-dozen buildings and an
apron of lawn with a gray backdrop of storage tanks secured behind
a high chain link fence. I'm sure there was more. But not much else
was visible through the fog.

When they tied up the ship, I stood chatting with a couple of
fellows on deck. A rasping voice over the loudspeaker commanded:

NO ONE, I REPEAT, NO ONE
IS ALLOWED OFF THIS SHIP!

"How are we ever going to say we were in Adak if we don't set
foot on the island?" said the brilliant I.

My companions agreed, and a plan was made. The ramp was
only twenty feet away. We'd nonchalantly amble over to the ramp,
make a wild dash down, hang a U on a small patch of green, run back
up, and reboard. We'd employ the strategy I used as a child. If there
was something I wanted to do and the answer was no that was the
end of it. If I didn't ask and proceeded in accord with my own will, I
achieved the goal in spite of later consequences. Aboard ship? Well,
we'd test the waters. Three of us took off running like a bat out of you
know where when we heard a thunderous voice behind us, shouting,
"Hey, you! Come back here!"

Being the good guys we were, we listened, but only after we completed our sprint, accomplished in less time than it takes a thorough-
bred to clear the starting gate. We stopped breathless at the top of
the ramp before two scornful-looking naval officers. One wore what

appeared out of the side of my eye to be a gold oak leaf. He might have been a major or maybe a lieutenant commander, but I didn't want to give him a complex by staring at his collar to get it right. He's the dude who ended up dragging me by the ear to the bridge where several more unhappy naval officers, including a full colonel in charge of all Army personnel on board, confronted us.

None of us wore insignia or chevrons, by the way, and, since they hadn't bothered to ask name, rank, and serial number, we remained anonymous.

"You know, of course, you were in direct conflict with issued orders," said the marine with the military buzz cut. "What do you have to say for yourselves, young men?" Actually, he hadn't posed this as a question, rather, a challenge. His snarl in the process would have made a mongoose quiver.

Undaunted, my one partner-in-crime stood defense.

"What the (censored)! That's the kind of stuff privates do," he said in faked surprise.

"I'm sure down in the mess galley they can use a couple of privates to do some scrubbing and cleaning!" said the marine. He instructed a chief petty officer to take us below.

The deck was crowded as we shoved past the men waiting in chow line. They gave that familiar salute you get sometimes when people don't like what you do. You know the one, the one exhibiting half of a victory sign. You know the one, the one telling you you're number one—something very close to the truth...

"Hey! No bucking the line!"

"The line starts in the rear!"

"Where @#$% do you think you're going?"

All of a sudden, like the eruption of a spring storm, they ganged up, punching, scratching, and spitting big time! For once, I hoped to hear an MP's whistle. Okay, so I over-inflated their reaction. Seriously, were they better organized, they would have had the makings of a real riot. When we approached the serving area, the chief tried to make himself heard above the mountain of noise.

"I brought you some help!" he shouted to the head cook. The chief petty officer left us and returned to more important business than disciplining a couple of Army brats.

"What's up? Why are you here?" asked the tee-shirted head cook, squinting suspiciously beneath a top-heavy, dough-boy hat. His bare arms displayed so many tattoos he looked like an art gallery.

"The chief brought us down to get ahead of the chow line so we can get back on top to stand guard," one of us lied.

"Okay, then. Grab a tray." To the disgruntled, he hollered, "Make room! Let them through!"

That was the end of it.

No further consequence.

Every evening, I was out on the bow of the ship searching for a west coast radio station. The first several days I only picked up Japanese stations. This was supposed to be a trans-oceanic radio, but most of the time I got nothing at all. Around the eighteenth day at sea, the ship's loudspeaker announced we'd spot land by 2100. Eyes were glued to clocks and watches as in countdown New Year's Eve. After 2100, eyes shifted instead to search the dark coastline for signs. The P.A. system came on within the hour:

ATTENTION! ATTENTION! WE HAVE
JUST ENTERED THE PUGET SOUND!

The atmosphere was jubilant as you can well imagine! Soldiers and sailors alike were overwhelmingly happy to arrive on American soil and let out a roar so deafening it could have outdone today's ear-shattering heavy metal! At exactly 2200, the Swing and Sway with Sammy Kaye Band played "Harbor Lights" on my radio. Before the tune ended, we spotted lights on shore. We heard later someone from the ship's bridge called the radio station requesting the song. But we doubted since no welcome remarks preceded or followed the song. In any event, timing was perfect. WE WERE ALMOST HOME!

We spent the night aboard ship anchored in the bay at Seattle. Late the next morning, our ship moved. The layover had been a stall tactic to celebrate our arrival. As we approached the Seattle wharf, fire-fighting tugboats put on a showy display of fireworks and water sprays. A flight of F86 Sabres zoomed overhead, making a series of low flying passes with wispy jet streams trailing behind. A prop plane turned on the smoke and dipped its wings in salute. Ships' horns blew, and whistles shrieked around the harbor.

Tugboats arrived to nudge us toward a pier where a crowd cheered, and the U.S. Army Band played military march music below Old Glory, the stars and stripes snapping proudly in the morning breeze. They switched to the National Anthem when the actual debarkation began and continued until Yours Truly stepped on to the dock.

My throat tightened from the lump that was in it, and I bit my lip until it bled at the overwhelming joy of it all. I may have been last to arrive but not first to tear when placing foot on American soil. Some had even bent down and kissed the pier. America the Beautiful, our Home Sweet Home!

I believe they gathered every Army truck and bus in the state of Washington to move us to Fort Lawton. But by the time I came off the gangplank, they were full. I moved from truck to truck, but the answer was always the same, making me akin to Mary and Joseph.

"We have no room."

"We have no room."

When I reached the head of the convoy, the answer was still the same,

"We have no room."

Teacher read the Christmas Story to her second grade class. Afterward, she gave them a simple little quiz to determine if they had paid attention.

"What were Mary and Joseph told when they stopped at an inn for a place to sleep?"

"They were told there was no room for them," one learned little boy replied.

"That's right. So then where did they finally go if there was no room for them in the inn?"

A little girl seated in the rear of the room because her surname began with "Z" raised her hand, waving it eagerly for attention. Teacher called on the little girl.

"They went into the Nativity scene," the little girl squeaked.

(Sorry, I couldn't resist inserting that entertaining snippet.)

"Okay, I'll ride up front!" I boasted to no one in particular. I threw my bag up to a lucky recipient. As it turned out, the truck already had two men up front, so I jumped on the bumper, swung myself up on the hood and sat on the top of the cab with my legs dangling over the center of the windshield.

Only minutes before departure from the dock area, the following announcement broadcasted loudly through the beautiful morning air:

YOUR CONVOY IS THE FIRST GROUP OF KOREAN VETS RETURNING! WE'RE TREATING YOU TO A PARADE THROUGH DOWNTOWN SEATTLE BEFORE YOU RETURN TO FORT LAWTON!

Trucks with canvas tops were instructed to remove the canvas, fold, and place inside. On our truck, half a dozen guys jumped down, untied the ropes and pulled it to the ground. In less than a minute, the tarp was neatly folded and thrown on the back of the truck. There's no letter "I" in the word "team," I mused momentarily. When we left Seattle in '48, most of us were still moist behind the ears. Now we returned as mature men organized to win a war. United we stand, divided we fall. We were united.

Atypical for this misty, rainy city, the morning fog burned off and the day turned warm and sunny. The parade had not the hoopla and fanfare like when the boys came home from World War II. After all, the war in Korea still waged. Nonetheless, people paid honor, taking pause while shopping or at lunch breaks from work. Men on the streets doffed their hats, and time-worn soldiers from earlier wars saluted. Pretty girls waved or blew kisses from factory and office windows along the route, making the whole day even more exceptional.

Many families of returning vets were present, cheering and screaming when they sighted loved ones coming down the street. Mine were not there. I hadn't notified anyone. No more phone hassles for this kid. A letter? I'd probably beat a letter home anyway. Per military strategy, let there be an element of surprise!

First stop at Fort Lawton was the mess hall. The large juicy steaks were so tender it's a wonder the cows could walk. You could have two if you wanted, or, as much of anything for that matter. French fries, ice cream, cakes, pies, all manner of American fat fare. During lunch, they passed out an itinerary sheet that explained our route of processing. We'd be off base before sundown. Last stop was the paymaster. My back pay amounted to something like $1,500, a small fortune at the time (even today).

Just minutes before processing was complete, the newsboys were on base with papers and pictures of the parade.

READ ALL ABOUT IT! READ ALL ABOUT IT!

"Okay, kid. Let's see what you got there," I said, handing him two bits.

Who do you think was on the front page of the Seattle News? You got it. Sergeant Walter M. Zweizig, perched just as grand as he pleased on the cab of the lead truck as it crawled along the parade route! I bought three copies of the newspaper and stuffed them in my bag. Like so many things, they were inadvertently tossed out at one time or another. Otherwise, I'd have a picture in this book.

The quickest way home was flying. But this same newspaper informed us of an ongoing airline strike. Several of the guys rang Boeing Field and requested a charter. We learned this was possible if we filled up the plane and kept the cost down. Three of us cornered a cab and took off directly for the airfield. When we arrived, there were already more than one hundred ahead of us with the same idea. Several flights were arranged as a result. I was on the second one out that left Seattle at sundown.

First stop was Denver, then St. Paul; Chicago next, and Washington, D.C. by dawn's early light. By the time we left D.C. for La Guardia, only three of us remained. The next eight hours were spent going from cab to cab, waiting room to waiting room, and bus to bus. By the final leg of the journey, I was alone.

It was late afternoon by the time the bus rolled down the Pottsville Pike toward Hamburg. The countryside was alive and fresh, like a plush green carpet had been rolled out in honor of my return. Newly planted fields of corn were already sprouting row upon row of succulent shoots at least four inches tall. Trees were in full bloom, and the grass everywhere was lush from the apparent spring rains. At all the farms, black and white Holstein cows waited impatiently outside barnyard gates. Soon these gates would open and the feeding and milking would begin.

All so ordinary.

All so peaceful.

All so wonderful.

Although the landscape outside the bus window was inviting and refreshingly familiar, there were sure to be many changes since my departure over three years ago. Changes to myself, how I viewed the world I lived in. Changes to others. By people hardly aware we were at war.

There were some straight off the farm like me who were returning home from war. Some from the city and from the south and from the north and the midwest. Some celebrating their homecoming, others not so, coming home crippled or blinded (or in a box), returning from fighting a cause they didn't understand and wouldn't want to talk about it even if they did. What about Mike from the 25th Division Artillery whom I had met in the Bible study aboard ship?

Mike was in a wheelchair. I doubt he'd feel uplifted as was I at meeting the folks. Could he cope with all the challenges that lay ahead in his new lifestyle? Would he walk again, or, would he remain angry and bitter and defeated?

I didn't know it then, not at that point, but in my own experience, I've since reflected that it was during the down times in my life that Jesus was all I had and that Jesus was all I needed, just like Berman. Somehow we heal. And just like Berman, one carries on. We do carry on. Would Mike?

Would he heal? Would the trauma in his life bring him to the Lord? After all, isn't that what it's all about, accepting Jesus? Jesus, our ticket out of this cruel world? No more tears? No more death? No more pain and suffering?

Oh, my! Am I becoming one of those religious fanatics? Not really. Spiritual? Yes, maybe. Hopefully.

After the bus dropped me off south of Hamburg, I wanted to phone the farm from Werley's gas station to have someone come and pick me up. Unfortunately, one of the five parties on our five-party party line must have been gossiping, and I couldn't get through. In utter frustration, I picked up my duffel bag and walked the remaining three miles to the place of my rearing.

Sheppie, my uninformed welcoming committee, came bounding down the farm lane, scattering Rhode Island reds and white leghorns in every direction. Gratefully, I stooped to greet my four-footed friend and threw my arms around his soft and fluffy neck. He planted me in place with his front paws on my shoulders all the while smothering my face in huge sloppy kisses. *Thank you, God, for small favors.*

I was truly happy.

I was alive.

I was in one piece.

Korea grew me up, but I came home Mama's little boy.

The date was June 11, 1951.

EPILOGUE

There are two powers in the world,
the sword and the spirit.
In time the spirit will prevail.
- Napoleon Bonaparte

Korea, "The Forgotten War," is not forgotten by those who served and survived. But to say a man fights to preserve his flag, his country, or his way of life is really only hogwash. Agreed, it has a beautiful sound to it and makes you feel good. But take it from this aging warrior who has been around the block a time or two, I can tell you that, on the day of battle, the soldier fights only for his friends around him and for his unit to which he is assigned. He wants only for that day's encounter to end successfully. And, of course, to come out of the whole mess alive.

God is good. Not only was I alive but also in one piece when I returned home on furlough from my first tour of duty that began in Occupied Japan and ended up in Korea. In 1952, I became part of SCARWAF (Special Category Army with Air Force) that took me on a second tour of duty in Korea where I remained until the war's end in July 1953. Yet another overseas tour followed in 1954. This time to the Baffin Island and Frobisher Bay (Alaska), lengthening a runway and assisting in the establishment of a defense for the Northern Distant Early Warning (DEW) Line. I had spent a total of 58 months overseas at various military bases, retiring as a Sergeant Major in 1971, having served more than seven years in active duty and thirteen in the Pennsylvania Army National Guard.

As a Korean combat veteran, I received the Bronze Star and the Purple Heart and participated in seven campaigns. Additional awards received during my military career include: Combat Infantryman's Badge, the Good Conduct Medal with Cluster, U.S. Army Occupational Medal, United Nations Service Medal, Korean Service Medal with seven battle stars, National Service Defense Medal, a Presidential Unit Citation to our regiment from South Korea

President Snygman Rhee, Meritorious Unit Emblem and the Armed Forces Reserve Medal. I was also awarded the Pennsylvania Commendation Medal (the first Berks countian to receive this award), the General Stewart Medal, and the prestigious General Arthur D. Bertolet Award. In 1966, I had the great honor of being named Soldier of the Year by my battalion for "…efficiency in gunnery, overall advancement of our unit and leadership and soldierly qualities."

During my civilian life, I was employed as a supervisor by Dana Corporation located in Reading, PA and retired in 1988 after 34 years of service. During that employment and into my twilight years, I devoted much time to the Hamburg Lions Club as well as a private hunting lodge located upstate, and served for many years as a Republican committeeman within my local jurisdiction. In my spare time, I wrote a book.

The lovely Jean Hess, who married me on June 13, 1953, and I have "lived happily ever after" in a cozy rural home near Shoemakersville, PA, always with numerous collies, cats, and birds in our domain.

This is Walt. Over and Out.

ADDENDUM

*Historical, contemporary, and authorial trivia
that relate to the events of the story*

Chapter 1: Getting It Right

• Walt's first night at basic training had him dreaming of far-away places, specifically Germany where he hoped to be assigned. In Germany, he mused, they would have dairy barns similar to his family's Swiss German style bank barn with colorful hex signs. Most likely that would have been so, except that the word "hex" sign was an American creation for the popular geometric six-pointed star pattern painted on Pennsylvania Dutch barns. The German word for six is "sechs" which sounded like hex to their English-speaking neighbors and, in time, these patterns became commonly known as hex signs.

• Walt makes mention that most everyone in the service smoked back then. Today, most of the older population have kicked the habit. Still, it is estimated that 350,000 people a year die from smoke-related causes. (WHYY, Oct 18, 2006.)

Chapter 2: Making the Best of It.

• Losing one's personnel records in the military may become an obsolete problem. A surgically implanted chip on the soldier called RFID (radio frequency identification) that stores multiple data can eliminate the need for dog tags, medical records, and so on. Today, the RFID is the brain behind the GPS that sits on your car's dash and also tracks your kids on the cell phone. RFID chips are also used to tag animals and are embedded in key government employees who work on military installations and in other tight security situations. While surveillance technology collected on individuals for innocent purposes can be very useful, the flip side is it can ultimately lead to government control of our lives and remove our privacy. It's called,

"Big Brother is Watching You" syndrome. (<u>Shadow Government</u>, Grant R. Jeffrey.) The powerful Bilderbergers, who have been meeting secretly ever since the Second World War, hope to have every human being microchipped by the year 2017 as a major step toward New World Order. (JVI Ministries, Aug. 25, 2010.)

• Canned Spam was "invented" in 1937 and became the most popular meat of the World War II era on both the battlefield and home front.

Chapter 3: The Tour Begins

• The "Made in Japan" items Walt referred to that were abundant in Miller's Five & Dime back home were generally ceramic. After the war ended, MacArthur got the ceramic industry up and running soon after the occupation began because it was the easiest business to revive.

• While riding the train through Japan, Ziggy reflects on his youth on the farm, driving the new tractor and working the crops. Today, the law has gone back and forth on restricting farmers from allowing youngsters under eighteen to operate heavy equipment. After some battle, legislators have omitted tractors from targeted law enforcement, but it is illegal for youth to operate heavy equipment using a farm truck. Farmers today are also required to keep activity logs and take health maintenance exams, something unheard of in Walt's growing up days on the farm. (Reading Eagle, Feb. 26, Mar. 2, 3, 2010.)

• Back in Zweizig's youth, Pennsylvania German farmers had a variety of crops to sustain them in the event of failure of one crop or another. They also applied crop rotation for best soil conservation. For example, corn robs soil of nitrogen so it was planted in the same field only once in four years with other crops planted in between to replenish the nitrogen. Today, farming methods have changed considerably. Single crops are planted on a large scale, and cornfields, for one, are now heavily fortified with chemical fertilizers that allow planting in the same fields year after year. (Thanks to Nazi Chemist Dr. Heinz Howert's successful lab experiment, harnessing nitrogen from the air and converting it into fertilizer. Science Fantastic, WEEU, April 2010.)

Chapter 4: A New Life Begins

• In the 21st century, the laptop is the "street corner" for the prostitute.

• The military considers "Sleeping on Guard Duty" a serious offense. In fact, in wartime, an offender is sentenced to death. Walt read this for himself three years later in the Courts Martial Manual, Uniform Code of Military Justice.

Chapter 5: First Assignment as Corporal

• What school authorities didn't tell students during the Second World War was that: 1) the idea for sterilization of the feeble and the building of a master race was not only a Nazi invention but also a brainstorm of liberal justice of the U.S. Supreme Court, Oliver Wendell Holmes. This American connection was quickly swept under the rug when things went wrong on the European front. (Chuck Colson, Break Point, Oct. 2, 2003); 2) German American Fritz Kuhn spearheaded Nazi youth camps under the guise of "summer camps" on Long Island and in New Jersey in the thirties, subscribing to Hitler's statement, "It doesn't matter whether adults go with us or not, we have their children." Kuhn was later jailed in 1939. (Glenn Beck, Fox News, Mar. 13, 2010.)

• Still, something else going on behind the scenes before the war was Father Coughlin, a Catholic priest campaigning for social justice, boasting that when he'd get through with the Jews, German's condemnation techniques would be put to shame by comparison. (Glenn Beck, Fox News, Mar. 13, 2010.) Still another was the little-known Henry Ford connection. Ford personally disliked Jews and, prior to the U.S. entering the war, supported Germany's extermination efforts.

• Pre-WWII, the average German citizen knew what was going on with the Jews. "If the German church and Christian community had stood up to Hitler in the thirties (like the Polish church did against post-war communism), war on the European front could have been avoided and millions upon millions of lives spared.... Evil triumphs if good people do nothing," says Hillar Von Campe, former Hitler youth and German soldier and now born-again Christian and USA citizen, in his book entitled <u>Defeating the Totalitarian Lie</u>. His assessment that present day America is moving in the direction of Nazi Germany is terrifying!

• Relative to Ziggy's dialogue with Baker on bio-methane gas, it is interesting to note that in an attempt to solve the current day energy crisis, some 50,000 homes in Southern California are "paddy-powered" by bio-methane coming from dairy farms within the locale. (WEEU News, Oct. 13, 2006.)

Chapter 9: Mysteries of War

• On this the 65th anniversary of the dropping of the bomb on Hiroshima, President Obama sent an official delegation to Japan's memorial event. James Tibbetts, son of the late Colonel Tibbetts who piloted the Enola Gay on August 6, 1945, says that his father would turn over in his grave would he know of Obama's apology. "We need to leave it alone," says James. (Feedback, WEEU, Aug. 6, 2010.)

• Speaking of Far East earthquakes, a devastating earthquake occurring on May 12, 2008, in the central Sichuan Province of China, registering 8.1, shook the world and killed and wounded hundreds of thousands of people. The reason I bring this up is not only because of its geological impact, horrendous as that was, but also because of the scientific investigation afterward that determined the earthquake was triggered by a massive underground nuclear explosion. China denies this evidence and the press has suppressed it. So was it the earthquake that triggered the nuclear explosion or was it the other way around? (<u>Shadow Government</u>, Grant R. Jeffrey.)

Chapter 12: Back to School

• Just to relate how much technology has advanced since Ziggy attended typing class at the USAFI in Osaka, I'm re-creating here a recent dialogue that took place between a twelve-year old boy and the librarian at our local library. While the library is equipped with the latest in computers for both library and public use, an old-fashioned typewriter is kept around for simple functions. One day, Mary was typing an envelope she had rolled into the typewriter when the young boy asked what that thing was she was working at. It's called a typewriter, Mary answered and then showed him how it worked. Oh, that is so cool, the boy said. Can I try it? Sure, she said. Again, he said, this is so cool; can I show it to my Dad? (Today, the typewriter has gone the way of the rotary phone, the fold-up road map, and film cameras.)

• To further compare Archibald Nessling to other brains, remember that Thomas Edison's teacher said he was too stupid to learn anything, and Beethoven's teacher said he was hopeless as a composer. And then there was Albert Einstein who couldn't speak until he was four, couldn't read until he was seven. His teacher described him as mentally slow, unsociable, and forever lost in foolish dreams. Archibald Nessling?

• Zweizig talks of his Pennsylvania German heritage known as the Pennsylvania Dutch. There is some confusion out there as to who really are the Pennsylvania Dutch. I'll explain. There are the plain Dutch, such as the Amish and some Mennonite groups, and then there are the fancy or worldly Dutch. Both are of German or Swiss German descent, coming to this country early 1700's. For the plain Dutch, time has stood still since the day they settled neighboring Lancaster County. They travel by horse and buggy and avoid modern convenience and activity of a world gone crazy with turmoil and terror. Folk in the world but not of it. Major occupations are farming, carpentry, and handcrafts. They have strict religious codes and conduct worship services in the home, alternating bi-weekly within the farm community. On the other hand, the worldly Dutch, of which Sergeant Zweizig was one, are a people who continued with the times from day one, while still retaining the German culture and dialect. They are generally Lutheran or Reformed (UCC), and sacrifice their sons and daughters along with the rest of the populace in defending America against aggression and preserving its freedom. Amish are conscientious objectors.

• The earthquake that Mr. Maknihara experienced in 1923 had many devastating effects. One of these was pointed out by James Bradley in Flyboys. The Japanese government, in an effort to divert funds for rebuilding the country following the Great Kanto quake, cut back on army personnel, thereby, establishing a system of military training within the school system. Thousands of active duty army officers were placed in the schools to inculcate "right thinking." This right thinking philosophy eventually caused the death of hundreds of thousands of civilians and military on both sides of the line during WWII.

• Walter relates to an occasional visit to the principal's office for misconduct while growing up in the Perry Township school system. Back then, the infamous trip to the principal's office was made by the student, not the teacher. Now, it's the other way around. Case in point: A friend of mine, Ron Miller, a former teacher in the Schuylkill Valley Area School District (near Reading, PA), experienced first hand the result of legally absenting God from public schools. A student in his fourth grade classroom sneezed, and Mr. Miller verbally offered the traditional "God Bless You." The child reported the incident to a parent, and the parent complained to the school board. The school's principal called Mr. Miller into the office and admonished him for his divine blessing.

Chapter 15: Meanwhile, Back in Washington

• Interesting to note that our troops have been guarding the DMZ between North and South Korea ever since the Korean Conflict. Yet our own borders in the United States are not secured. In fact, our federal government has sued the state of Arizona as being unconstitutional in their attempt to try doing the job they claim the U.S. Government should be doing in protecting the state's southern border from illegal entries. (Feedback, WEEU, July 29, 2010.)

Chapter 16: We Have Arrived

• July 4, 2006, fifty six years from the day Ziggy and Baker arrived on the Korean Peninsula responding to a call to war, North Korea shot off its own fireworks to celebrate the United States' 230th birthday anniversary. The unpredictable totalitarian nuclear regime of Kim Jong Il (son of Korean War's Kim Il Sung) test launched seven missiles, including a long-range rocket designed to reach the U.S. that failed and fell into the Sea of Japan. It is said that North Korea is the most potential nuclear threat of any other nation in the world.

• When the 27th Infantry Regiment landed in Korea over a half century ago, they had with them only antiquated equipment left over from WWII. Little did they know that several decades later, the military would be using unheard of high technology such as Star-Trek type phase weapons, electric pulse weapons, photon-directed energy weapons, the "Voice of God" weapon (one that can project a verbal or even a visual message into the mind of an enemy combatant), particle-beam weapons, electronic guns, term baric rifles, and robotic technology, weather manipulation technology, suitcased nuclear bombs and on and on. There is more high technology in a little chip in a greeting card that sings Happy Birthday than was ever in World War II and the Korean War combined. (Shadow Government, Grant R. Jeffrey.)

• On wars: Fatalities from all participating nations during the war in Iraq's fourth year claimed 25 for every 100,000 people. By contrast, violence in Venezuela, Columbia, and South Africa has claimed more than double this number in supposedly peaceful times. Our city of New Orleans (before Katrina) claimed 53/100,000 due to violence. The city of Chicago has more murders a year than American fatalities during the same period of time in Iraq. And back to the big stats, Atlanta and Washington D.C. each exceeded 37/100,000. Moral of the story: It's safer to be in Iraq's war zone than in some of our country's larger cities, including the nation's capital. (Rush Limbaugh, May 2006.)

• More on wars: Over 150,000,000 people were killed in the 20th century, not in wars, but by their own governments. (The Patriot Express Newsletter, May 16, 2010.) "...millions more have died at the hands of their own government than in wars with other nations, all in order to preserve someone's power." (<u>Kingdoms in Conflict</u>, Charles Colson, p.270.)

• Zweizig's CO, Captain Bond, was a family man. Interestingly, in 269 AD, by the stroke of a pen, Rome's Emperor Claudius outlawed marriage amongst soldiers, stating they spent too much time with their families rather than serving the Empire. A priest by the name of Valentine continued to perform clandestine marriages in spite of the edict and was found out, captured, and imprisoned. When the people threatened revolt, Valentine was asked to renounce his faith in exchange for life. He refused and was executed by stoning. Claudius died a year later, and Rome revoked the marriage ban. Posthumously, the church canonized Valentine with sainthood and dedicated February 14 as St. Valentine's Day. (Adventures in Odyssey, WBYN. July 11, 2005.)

Chapter 17: On the Road Again

• Ziggy compares his experience with the brilliant night sky in the hills of Korea to his home in northeastern U.S. In today's arguments for a cleaner environment, little thought is given to the airplane's contribution to global warming. Yet millions of gallons of fuel and exhaust are dumped into the atmosphere daily by these marvelous great-winged birds. Not to mention heat from their monstrous engines. Not to mention spacecraft launches. Government regulates emissions into our air from land-based activity but does not control aviation fuel emissions. Air pollutants caused by: industry 61%, cars and trucks 25%, other road vehicles 11%, and 4 cycle gasoline engines 3% equaling 100%. Aviation? Spacecraft? (This data was posted in a small engine repair shop so it might possibly be biased information.)

• To add to the debate on global warming: Some city-reared member of the U.S. Congress proposes the farmer be taxed $125 a head for every cow in a herd of 25 or more and hogs at $60 a head, assessing on the theory that these barnyard animals contribute greatly to air pollution with their belching, flatulence, and poop. (Feedback, WEEU, 2009.)

• More trivia: The United States has 5% of the world's population, but to accommodate the American consumer's convenient lifestyle, it uses 25% of the world's resources. The small island of Tuvaloo in the South Pacific predicts its disappearance within twenty years because of rising ocean waters caused by glacial meltdown caused by global warming caused by pollution caused by the United States (it says). In fact, they threaten to sue the U.S. Government. (Turning Point, WBYN, 2005.)

• These environmental statements are just the tip of the iceberg. Are we on a collision course to self-destruct? In all due respect, though, for America and in major defense of its dairy and pig farmers, this author feels the finger should point toward China whose coal-burning, booming economy is much to blame for pollutants impacting America's glacial shores. But then again, one this author is most inclined to favor, there's the "cyclical" argument on climate change...

Chapter 25: China Intervenes

• The 25th Infantry Division's enemy was both the North Korean and the Chinese communists. Throughout the 20th century and into the 21st, communism has had a grossly negative impact on humanity. One example, Dictator and Premier Josef Stalin, during his reign of terror in the Soviet Union, murdered 20 million people (some stats claim 40 million). Once asked how he expected the people to follow him when he inflicted pain and oppression, he demanded that a chicken be brought to him. Stalin coddled the chicken and began pulling the feathers out one by one, and the chicken was in great pain. After it was denuded, he stepped away and put breadcrumbs on the floor. The chicken came over and pecked at them. Stalin said, "That's how you do it. That chicken will always follow me for food." This illustration equates to the modern day American government, creating a need in the people for more dependence upon government. (SW Radio Ministries, WBYN.)

• Re Ziggy's and Baker's observation on over-populated China, please note: After the Korean War, China began carrying out what was commonly known as the One-Child Policy. Officials resorted to such harsh measures as female infanticide, forced sterilization, and late term abortions to prevent the country's population of 1.2 billion from expanding even more. In 2002, the Chinese Parliament eased the deeply unpopular policy. Instead of forbidding extra children outright, the new law allowed couples multiple offspring if they paid big fines. In some of the rural provinces, there still exists a brutal campaign of forced abortions and sterilizations to maintain low population counts.

• The rest of the world is catching up on this matter of infanticide. In the Netherlands, doctors legitimately kill disabled infants. In the U.S., more and more unborn are aborted because of down syndrome or other presumed maladies detected through ultrasound. Not to mention the 40 million healthy babies legally aborted since Roe v Wade in 1973. Not to mention partial birth abortion when the baby is pulled through the birth canal and then immediately killed (Focus on the Family, 2006).

• An additional challenge to the pro-life stance: The U.S. Senate voted (vetoed by President George W. Bush in 2006) to use taxpayers' monies to fund embryonic stem cell research, knowing that adult stem cells which have no moral or ethical implications have been successfully proven to defeat illness in both horses and humans. (More than one hundred healthy "snowflake" children have been born from embryo storage as of the above date.) Since his inauguration, President Obama approved thirteen new human embryonic stem cell lines for experimentation. Science creating life to destroy it in the name of research? (Prophetic Observer, Aug. 2010.)

• It is politically rumored that the cap and trade bill proposed by the Obama administration in 2009 would provide carbon credits to couples who limit their family size to one child. The left wing's incentive is based on the theory that humans are destroying the planet.

Chapter 26: Withdrawal to a Point

• Relative to the chaplain's blessing on the Christmas meal, I need to point out that, today, public blessings, religious visual displays, celebrations and so forth are considered a violation of church and state. This, in spite of the fact that our Christian founding fathers based the U.S. Constitution upon Christian principles. Contemporary examples follow.

• Georgia Senior Citizen Center has been barred from prayer before meals because the Center receives, however minimal, government funding. (WEEU, May 11, 2010.)

• An author was denied the use of a room at the public library to assemble a group to discuss her book. The reason? The book's content was on Christian evangelism. (SRN News, Aug. 15, 2010).

• The ACLU ordered the removal of a huge cross on public display on City of Reading (Berks Co., PA) property. (Feedback, WEEU, 2009.)

• At this writing, a public school is in federal court for being involved in prayer during public assembly. (SRN News, WBYN, Mar. 16, 2010.)

• On the heels of the above, be it known that U.S. public schools are disallowed Bible studies or any mention of our Christian God, yet a particular public school in San Diego allows Muslim students to break out of the classroom routine for ritualistic Islamic prayers. (SRN News, WBYN.)

• Likewise, an article by Jen Shroder to the Berks County Patriots, local tea party organization, states that: "... Today's {public school} textbooks are indoctrinating our children into Islam and are backed by court rulings, allowing teachers to require our children to bow down and pray to Allah...'"

• The parents of a sixth grade student in a California public school were fined $50,000 for the boy's wearing of a PRO LIFE tee shirt. The reason? The message on the shirt was considered "Christian and disruptive." (SRN News, Aug. 14, 2010.)

• A liberal contingent within our political infrastructure proposes the elimination of AD and BC behind dates as well as the celebration of Christmas. (SRN News, Mar. 2010.)

• Did I mention that during his first one hundred days in office, President Barack Hussein Obama proclaimed to state heads in Turkey and Venezuela that "America is not a Christian nation?"

Chapter 27: Seoul Lost Again

• When Sgt. Zweizig assisted in the funerals and burials of four compatriots, he says that, "...Taps echoed only across the bleak plateau of our minds." Do you know the story behind this famous tune? Reportedly, it began in 1862 during the Civil War when Union Army Captain Robert Elicombe was with his men near Harris' Landing in Virginia. The Confederate Army was on the other side of the narrow strip of land. During the night, Capt. Elicombe heard moans. The captain risked his life and brought the stricken man back for medical attention, after which he discovered the wounded soldier was a confederate, and he was dead, and to his utmost disbelief and grief, his own son. The boy studied music in the South when the war broke out and enlisted in the Confederate Army without telling his folks. Bottom line, the father asked permission to give his son a full military burial. The request was denied since the soldier was confederate, yet they allowed him one musician. The captain chose a bugler and asked him to play a series of musical notes found on paper in the pocket of the dead youth's uniform. Taps. (Circulated via email, May 13, 2005.)

• Walt's observation of starving Koreans was worrisome. Still is. Five and a half decades later, Koreans, specifically those north of the DMZ, where the government controls who gets the food and who doesn't, still suffer from malnutrition. In fact, death by hunger claims daily the lives of 10,000 people worldwide. It is said Americans spend more on the family pet than the average third world family spends on food. Americans spend as much as $43 billion a year on their pets, per Crown Ministries, Mar. 18, 2006. But here are some more startling statistics. In the United States, under President Obama, 40 million people receive food stamps from the government, a 50% increase over two years ago. And 10 million people are drawing unemployment benefits, four times the number of 2007. Unemployment benefits have been extended eight times, giving recipients up to 99 weeks of benefits. (Talk Tuesday, WEEU, Aug. 31, 2010.)

• EarthSave, a nonprofit environmental organization, believes that producing animal foods is an inefficient use of planet earth's resources in order to feed the world's ever-growing population. This California group has compiled many stats to support its view. A few follow: It takes one square mile in Australia's Outback and some areas of the American West to sustain one good beef cow. (One "bad" cow can contaminate 16 tons of hamburger). In contrast, pounds of food that can be produced on one acre of prime land are: carrots 30,000; celery 60,000; beef 250. It takes 16 pounds of grain/soy to produce one pound of beef. It takes 23 gallons of water to produce one pound of tomatoes and 1,630 gallons to produce one pound of pork or 5,214 gallons for one pound of beef. According to EarthSave, if Americans reduced their meat intake by ten percent, the number who could be fed using the land, water, and energy resources that would be freed from the growing of livestock would be upwards to 60,000,000 people. Food for thought?

• Chaplains during the Korean War were not handcuffed like today. U.S. Navy Chaplain Gordon J. Klingenschmidt at this writing faces court martial for praying "in Jesus' name." (Janet Folger, Commentator, WBYN, May 3, 2006.)

• Chaplains attending a veteran ward in a Virginia hospital became involved in lawsuits on the grounds that they were too invasive with patients, like asking such questions as: Do you believe in God? Do you pray? How often do you pray? (Janet Folger, Commentator, WBYN, Oct. 11, 2006.) Islam is protected in the U.S. military but Christian views are stamped out. (Faith and Action in the Nation's Capital, Aug. 2010.)

• The Obama administration's repeal of Don't Ask Don't Tell in the military puts tight constraints on today's chaplain as to how he/she can administer to and counsel military men and women and their families with biblical truths. The military's Commander in Chief is stepping off the field of battle into social engineering. (Focus on the Family, Aug. 13, 2010.)

• There is a campaign on to remove official government chaplains in the Senate and House of Representatives. (Faith and Action in the Nation's Capital, Aug. 2010.)

• An employee at a Home Depot store wore a pin in his lapel in honor of his brother going off to the war in Iraq. The pin said, "...one nation under God, indivisible, with liberty and justice for all...." The young employee was suspended for violating the company's dress code. (WEEU, Oct. 31, 2009.)

• The ACLU ordered the national monument in the form of a cross in the Mojave Desert to be removed. Following up, a judge ordered it to be torn down. An appeal to maintain the cross then went all the way to the Supreme Court who reversed the action to local jurisdiction. In the meantime, vandals desecrated the Christian symbol, and, at this date, the battle still goes back and forth between those who care and those in government/courts as to whether the cross can be restored in both shape and location or whether it be eradicated permanently. Two months ago, an appeal to restore this memorial, by the way, the only one in our country dedicated to World War I veterans, has gone to President Obama for a decision with no response to date. Time is truly running out on religious liberty. (Focus on the Family, July 29, 2010.)

Chapter 28: R&R

• Both Baker and Ziggy were in awe of the shrines in Nara and later compared what they had seen to what they knew of Christianity. In truth, followers of Christ, Moses, Mohammed, Hindu's Krishna and the Buddhist's Dalai Lama are all judged by the same Creator God who wrote on everyone's heart the "Law" known as the Ten Commandments, the rules and regulations for life in any culture. So even pagans know the difference between right and wrong.

Chapter 29: The Supreme Sacrifice

• Did you know there is a meaning for each one of those folds in the flag that the families back home would receive following the burials Zweizig and Baker assisted in? (The following was circulated via email from the Air Force Academy's website.) First fold: Symbol of life. Second: Symbol of eternal life; Third: Honor/ remembrance of veteran who gave life or a portion for country; Fourth: Man's weakness; we turn to God in times of peace and war; Fifth: To country in dealing with other countries; Sixth: With hearts, we pledge allegiance to flag of USA and to republic for which it stands, one nation under God, indivisible, with liberty and justice for all; Seventh: To Armed Forces, protecting country and flag against enemies; Eighth: Tribute to mother; Ninth: Tribute to womanhood that molded men and women through faith, love, loyalty, devotion; Tenth: Tribute to father; Eleventh: For Hebrews, lower portion of seal of Kings David and Solomon and glorifies God of Abraham, Isaac, Jacob; Twelfth: For Christians, an emblem of eternity, glorifying God the Father, Son, and Holy Spirit. When flag is completely folded, stars are uppermost, reminding us of national motto, "In God we Trust." The triangular form, a reminder of the cocked hat of first commander of Military Armed Forces, General George Washington.

• It's sad to note that today's youth do not always respect the Stars and Stripes. In a weekly radio talk show, a panel of students from local school districts were interviewed and asked how they felt about the fact that at that time presidential hopeful, Barack Hussein Obama, did not salute the American flag. A senior from Hamburg Area High said she thought it mattered not, that "the flag is just a piece of fabric." (Voice of Berks County, WEEU, Mar. 2008.)

• Used in the Korean War, napalm had been invented during WWII by Harvard President James Conant, and scientists at MIT, DuPont and Standard Oil. They found that mixing napththenic and palmitic acids with gasoline produced a sticky yellow paste that stuck to materials and burned slowly. This jellied gasoline stuck to anything—roofs, walls, humans. A perfect incendiary, it could not be extinguished. Water only splattered it. If a glob landed on the back of a hand, it burned until it consumed itself. If the victim patted the burning napalm, the result was scorched fingers and a badly burnt hand. (Flyboys, p.307.)

• It was Dow Chemical that actually produced napalm that burnt at 2,000 degrees. "Dow Produces Napalm!" was the rally on college campuses during the Viet Nam anti-war protests. (American Experience, PBS, May 29, 2006.)

• The white phosphorus that Walt and Baker used when they encountered the Chinese in the Korean village burnt at 2,000 degrees. Today, a phosphorus grenade burns at 5,000 degrees.

Chapter 30: The Good News

• The good news was: "...Uncle Sam's nephew is coming home." Did you know that there really was an Uncle Sam? Samuel Wilson, born on September 13, 1766 in Arlington, Mass, operated a meat-packing business, supplying provisions for American soldiers fighting in the War of 1812. Barrels of prime meat were stamped with a large "U.S.," indicating provisions were government-owned. On the day that a government inspector came to the plant, an Irish watchman guarded a large shipment of wooden barrels. The inspector asked what the "U.S." meant. The Irishman didn't know, but guessed Uncle Sam. Uncle Sam who, asked the inspector. Uncle Sam Wilson, of course, responded the watchman. He's the one who's been hired to feed the United States Army. In short order, U.S. came to mean Uncle Sam, and Uncle Sam in turn became the nickname of the United States Government. Much later, Artist James Montgomery Flagg memorialized Sam Wilson in a recruitment poster for both World Wars I and II. Old posters were still seen around at the time Walt enlisted in the Army.

Chapter 32: Tell it to the Chaplain

• Chaplain Berman told the Bible study group that those in his Jewish family who stayed behind when he left Poland were never heard from again. This makes me think of the words written by a Holocaust victim scratched on a camp wall: "...I believe in the sun, even though it doesn't shine; I believe in God even though He is silent." She, too, was never heard from again.

• What Chaplain Berman didn't mention to the Bible study participants is that the Roman Emperor Constantine, converted from paganism to Christianity, changed the worship day from the Sabbath to Sunday to entice fellow pagans into the Christian church. Too, he made Sunday a public holiday while still emphasizing its sacredness to the female sun god. (Hence the name Sunday.) In fact, he made it a civil crime for Christians not to switch over to Sunday-keeping worship. The Sunday-keeping tradition has carried on down through the ages.

• Chaplain Berman made mention of the ills of the spread of communism and that this was the reason for the war in Korea. Similarly, Sergeant York's words that "we go to war to save lives" supports America going to war in Iraq and removing Saddam Hussein under whose reign millions of people had suffered and died. Here's additional wisdom from Paul Harvey (2008) who said, "...If we get out of Iraq like the terrorists demand, then next we'll be getting out of Afghanistan, then getting our presence out of the Middle East entirely, leaving them {Islamic Fascists} free to control the Muslim world from Spain to the Phillipines."

• More on Muslim infiltration. A Muslim center/mosque is proposed next to Ground Zero where, on September 11, 2001, radical Muslims murdered 3,000 innocent Americans during an unprovoked act of war in the name of Islam. In spite of the public's sensitivity and outcries against the proposed building's location, President Obama, speaking at Ramadan, a religious Islam event held at the White House in August, staunchly defended the Muslim's site choice. (SRN News, Aug. 2010.) Conversely, a Christian Greek Orthodox church demolished during the 9/11 Attack on America has met one government obstacle after another in its request to rebuild at the same site. Where is wisdom?

• The American people's freedom of religion, speech, press, and right of assembly in the home or public square is threatened. Case in point: Fifteen people assembled for a Bible study/prayer meeting in a private home and were "found out" by a San Diego authority who stated they were in violation of county regulations. The group was warned they would be fined if they met again without a special permit costing $10,000. (Feedback, WEEU, May 28, 2009.) How soon until Christians are required to have a permit for worship in churches? How soon until the Fairness Doctrine is reinstated and conservative talk shows and Christian radio/TV ministries are once again strangled out of the public arena. How soon until patriots in the Tea Party movement are no longer free to march on Washington to restore honor to God and country? Under the risk of losing tax exemption, how soon until Christian pastors are forced to marry same-sex couples when requested even though it's against biblical truths? (It's already happening in some states.) How soon until medics are forced to abort babies even if their conscience disagrees to such murderous acts? (It's already in the courts.) How soon until the elderly, through the government's new socialized health care program, are dropped from health care services that could prolong their lives? How soon?

Chapter 33: Home Sweet Home

• As mentioned in the final chapter, little did we realize how infiltrated the Axis enemy was within America. On our east coast, a German U-boat hit the Port of Bayonne, thinking they'd hit the U.S. Naval Yard. Our Army caught them, of course, and managed to cover it up as a dock fire.

• Shirley Aldenderfer, one of the critiquers of this book, said a one-time neighbor related an experience she had as an Army wife living in New Jersey during WWII. She was sitting on her porch one day that overlooked the Hudson Bay when suddenly up popped a periscope. She immediately called the authorities, and the German U-boat was apprehended.

Shirley Zweizig Nestler

BIBLIOGRAPHY

Air Force Academy website (circulated via email).

American Wildlife Illustrated. W.M.H. Wise and Co. New York. 1949.

Army, U.S. *Map Reading and Land Navigation (Field Manual)*. Wash., D.C. 1993. (Letter of Permission dated Oct. 2, 2006.)

Army, U.S. *Chaplaincy Facts*. WWII Event. June 3, 2005.

Backus, William. The Paranoid Prophet. New York. Bethany Publishing House. 1986. (Letter of Permission dated Oct. 24, 2006.)

Barr, Janet. *Wartime Work*. "In our Neck of the Woods." Hamburg Item. Jan. 9, 2002.

Bender, Edwin. Contributor to The Patriot Express. May 16, 2010. *2005 Berks County Data Book*. Berks County Planning Commission. April 2005.

Bradley, James. Flyboys. New York. Little, Brown and Company. 2003.

Brandt, Emily. *Unlikely Brothers*. Visitor. Nov. 1999.

Campbell, Joseph. The Power of Myth. New York. Doubleday (Batham). 1988.

Caretti, Matthew. Letter on Buddhism. April 25, 2004.

DeMarco, Mario. *Looking Hollywood Way*. Good Old Days. Sept. 2001.

Encyclopedia Britannica. Vol. 13 (pp.467-468). University of Chicago. 1966.

Reading Eagle, *WWII Internment Camps*, Aug. 25, 2001.

Reading Eagle, *Change in Spelling Unites Koreas*. Sept. 21, 2003.

Reading Eagle, *Unraveling the Confusion about PA Germans*. Oct. 13, 2002.

Reading Eagle, *Farmers Up in Arms over new Tractor Rules*. Feb. 26, 2010; *New Rules Would Not Apply to Tractors*. March 2, 2010; *No Police Focus on Farm-truck Operators*. March 3, 2010.

Federer, William J. What Every American Needs to Know About the Qur'an. St. Louis. Amerisearch. 2007.

Footprints. Almar. 1992.

Faith and Action in the Nation's Capital. Aug. 2010.

Folger, Janet. Radio Commentator, WBYN. May 3, 2006 and Oct. 11, 2006.

Golden, Arthur. Memoirs of a Geisha. New York. Random House. 1997.

Goulden, Joseph C. Korea, The Untold Story of the War. New York. McGraw Hill, Inc. 1982.

Griffin, John Howard. Black Like Me. New York. Penquin Putnam. 1960.

Harvey, Paul. WEEU Radio. Aug. 3, 2006.

Hersey, John. Hiroshima. New York. Random House. 1989.

Jeffrey, Grant R. Shadow Government. New York. Random House. 2009.

Jeremiah, David. Escape the Coming Night. W Publishing Company. 1990.

Jones, Forrest. *China Snapping Up U.S. Assets Like Never Before.* NEWSMAX. July 2010.

Kellog, Grace. The Bible Today on Whale Stories. *(heard on radio.)*

Kennedy, David M. *Crossing the Moral Threshold.* TIME. Aug. 1, 2005.

New King James Version, Holy Bible. New York. Thomas Nelson. 1979.

Kroll, Woodrow. An Interview with God. Chicago. Moody Publishers. 2004.

Nestler, Shirley L. *Reading Teamwork in Action.* Solid Stater. May 1985.

Newark, Tim. Turning the Tide of War. London. Hamlyn. 2001.

North, Oliver L. *War Stories: Heroism in the Pacific.* Regnery Publishing, Inc. 2004.

O'Donnell, Richard W. *Uncle Sam, a Real Yankee Doodle Dandy.* Good Old Days. May 2002.

Osho. Buddha, His Life and Teachings. UK. Bridgewater Book Co. 2004.

Roberts, Monty. The Man Who Listens to Horses. New York. Random House. 1997. (Letter of Permission dated Nov. 10, 2006.)

Robbins, John. EarthSave, a nonprofit California organization.

Roth, Ariel. *Isaac Newton's Greatest Discovery.* Signs of the Times. Jan. 2005.

Ryaang, Sonia. *The Great Kanto Earthquake.* Anthropological

Quarterly. Fall 2003.

Shandong, Hannah Beech. *Enemies of the State?* TIME. Sept. 19, 2005.

Shroder, Jen. *Islam Indoctrination in U.S. Textbooks*. Berks County Patriots. June 6, 2010.

Smither, John. From Here to There and Back Again. Bloomington, IN. 1stBooks. 2003.

Tregaskis, Richard. Guadalcanal Diary. New York. Random House. 1955.

Vandeman, George E. *Born to Fly*. Signs of the Times. Sept. 2004. (Letter of Permission dated Jan. 30, 2007.)

Walters, Barbara. *In Search of Heaven*. Reader's Digest. Dec. 2005.

WBYN Radio. Adventures in Odyssey (St. Valentine's). July 11, 2005

WBYN Radio. Focus on the Family (abortion). Jan. 2006.

WBYN Radio. SRN News. Mar. 16, 2010.

WBYN Radio. SW Ministries on Stalin. 2007.

WEEU Radio re bio-Methane, Oct. 13, 2006; ACLU on cross display, 2009; prayer before meals, May 11, 2010. (Mighty Mike Faust's Feedback.)

WEEU Radio. Jo Painter's Talk Tuesday. Aug. 31, 2010.

Wheeler, Keith. *The Railroaders*. New York. Time, Inc. 1973.

WHYY TV. American Experience. Alcan Highway – 2005; Buffalo Soldiers – May 2, 2006; Million Man March – May 29, 2006.

Yamazaki, Masakazu. *Reading Japan's Moods*. Parade. Jan. 12, 2003.

Zweizig, Walter M. Act Now, Think Later. Circa 1997.

CONTACT INFORMATION

If you would like to contact the author, please feel free to do so
by sending an email to the following address:
rivermeadows@juno.com.

CPSIA information can be obtained at www.ICGtesting.com
Printed in the USA
BVOW070618150413

318156BV00001B/5/P